THE ROOT OF CHINESE CHI KUNG

The Secrets of Chi Kung Training

YMAA Chi Kung Series

#1

"...The Heart (Upper Burner, Fire) and the Kidney (Lower Burner, Water) keep each other in check and are dependent upon one another. The Spirit of the Heart and the essence of the Kidneys cooperate in establishing and maintaining human consciousness..."

By DR. YANG JWING-MING

DISCLAIMER

The author(s) and publisher of this material are not responsible in any manner whatsoever for any injury which may occur through reading or following the instructions in this material.

The activities, physical or otherwise, described in this material may be too strenuous or dangerous for some people, and the reader(s) should consult a physician before engaging in them.

Publisher's Cataloging in Publication
(Prepared by Quality Books Inc.)

Yang, Jwing-Ming, 1946-
    The root of Chinese Chi Kung : the secrets of Chi Kung training / Yang Jwing-Ming.
    p. cm.
    Includes index.
    ISBN 0-940871-07-6

    1. Ch'i kung. 2. Martial arts 3. Health. I. Title.

RA781.8.Y36 1994   613.7'14'8
                                   QBI94-85

First Printing 1989
10,10,3,3,5

ISBN: 0-940871-07-6

Library of Congress No: 88-051189

Printed in the USA

YMAA Publication Center
Yang's Martial Arts Association (YMAA)

38 Hyde Park Avenue • Jamaica Plain, Massachusetts 02130

To My Brother Dr. Tim Chun-Chieh Yang

ACKNOWLEDGEMENT

Thanks to A. Reza Farman-Farmaian for the photography, David Ripianzi, David Sollars, John Hughes, Jr. and James O'Leary, Jr. for proofing the manuscript and for contributing many valuable suggestions and discussions, to Wen-Ching Wu for drawings and general help, and to Sierra for drawings and the cover design. Special thanks to Alan Dougall and Eric Hoffman for their editing.

ABOUT THE AUTHOR

DR. YANG JWING-MING, Ph.D.

Dr. Yang Jwing-Ming was born in Taiwan, Republic of China, in 1946. He started his Wushu (Kung Fu) training at the age of fifteen under the Shaolin White Crane (Pai Huo) Master Cheng Gin-Gsao. In thirteen years of study (1961-1974) under Master Cheng, Dr. Yang became an expert in White Crane defense and attack, which includes both the use of barehands and of various weapons such as saber, staff, spear, trident, and two short rods. With the same master he also studied White Crane Chin Na, massage, and herbal treatment. At the age of sixteen Dr. Yang began the study of Tai Chi Chuan (Yang Style) under Master Kao Tao. After learning from Master Kao, Dr. Yang continued his study and research of Tai Chi Chuan with several masters in Taipei. In Taipei he became qualified to teach Tai Chi. He has mastered the Tai Chi barehand sequence, pushing hands, the two-man fighting sequence, Tai Chi sword, Tai Chi saber, and internal power development.

When Dr. Yang was eighteen years old he entered Tamkang College in Taipei Hsien to study Physics. In college he began the study of traditional Shaolin Long Fist (Chang Chuan) with Master Li Mao-Ching at the Tamkang College Kuoshu Club (1964-1968), and eventually became an assistant instructor under Master Li. In 1971 he completed his M.S. degree in Physics at the National Taiwan University, and then served in the Chinese Air Force from 1971 to 1972. In the service, Dr. Yang taught Physics at the Junior Academy of the Chinese Air Force while also teaching Wushu. After being honorably discharged in 1972, he returned to Tamkang College to teach Physics and resume study under Master Li Mao-Ching. From Master Li, Dr. Yang learned Northern style Wushu, which includes both barehand (especially kicking) techniques and numerous weapons.

In 1974, Dr. Yang came to the United States to study Mechanical Engineering at Purdue University. At the request of a few students Dr. Yang began to teach Kung Fu, which resulted in the foundation of the Purdue University Chinese Kung Fu Research Club in the spring of 1975. While at Purdue, Dr. Yang also taught college-credited courses in Tai Chi Chuan. In May of 1978 he was awarded a Ph.D. in Mechanical Engineering by Purdue.

Currently, Dr. Yang and his family reside in Massachusetts. In January of 1984 he gave up his engineering career to devote more time to research, writing, and teaching at Yang's Martial Arts Association (YMAA) in Boston.

In summary, Dr. Yang has been involved in Chinese Wushu for more than twenty-five years. During this time, he has spent thirteen years learning Shaolin White Crane, Shaolin Long Fist, and Tai Chi Chuan. Dr. Yang has twenty years of instructional experience: seven years in Taiwan, five years at Purdue University, two years in Houston, Texas, and six years in Boston, Massachusetts.

Dr. Yang has published ten other volumes on the martial arts and Chi Kung:

1. *Shaolin Chin Na*, Unique Publications, Inc., 1980.
2. *Shaolin Long Fist Kung Fu,* Unique Publications, Inc., 1981.
3. *Yang Style Tai Chi Chuan*, Unique Publications, Inc., 1981.
4. *Introduction to Ancient Chinese Weapons*, Unique Publications, Inc., 1985.
5. *Chi Kung - Health and Martial Arts*, Yang's Martial Arts Association (YMAA), 1985.
6. *Northern Shaolin Sword*, Yang's Martial Arts Association (YMAA), 1985.
7. *Advanced Yang Style Tai Chi Chuan, Vol.1, Tai Chi Theory and Tai Chi Jing*, Yang's Martial Arts Association (YMAA), 1986.
8. *Advanced Yang Style Tai Chi Chuan, Vol.2, Martial Applications*, Yang's Martial Arts Association (YMAA), 1986.
9. *Analysis of Shaolin Chin Na*, Yang's Martial Arts Association (YMAA), 1987.
10. *The Eight Pieces of Brocade*, Yang's Martial Arts Association (YMAA), 1988.

Dr. Yang has also published the following videotapes:

1. *Yang Style Tai Chi Chuan and Its Applications*, Yang's Martial Arts Association (YMAA), 1984.
2. *Shaolin Long Fist Kung Fu - Lien Bu Chuan and Its Applications*, Yang's Martial Arts Association (YMAA), 1985.
3. *Shaolin Long Fist Kung Fu - Gung Li Chuan and Its Applications*, Yang's Martial Arts Association (YMAA), 1986.
4. *Shaolin Chin Na*, Yang's Martial Arts Association (YMAA), 1987.
5. *Wai Dan Chi Kung, Vol. 1 -- The Eight Pieces of Brocade*, Yang's Martial Arts Association (YMAA), 1988.

Dr. Yang Jwing-Ming

FOREWORD

Dr. Yang Jwing-Ming, Ph.D.

Chi Kung is the science of cultivating the body's internal energy, which is called Chi in Chinese. The Chinese have been researching Chi for the last four thousand years, and have found Chi Kung to be an effective way to improve health and to cure many illnesses. Most important of all, however, they have found that it can help them to achieve both mental and spiritual peace.

Until recently, Chi Kung training was usually kept secret, especially within martial arts systems or religions such as Buddhism and Taoism. Only acupuncture and some health-related Chi Kung exercises were available to the general public. During the last twenty years these secrets have become available to the general public through publications and open teaching. Medical people have finally been able to test Chi Kung more widely and scientifically, and they have found that it can help or cure a number of diseases which Western medicine has difficulty treating, including some forms of cancer. Many of my students and readers report that after practicing Chi Kung, they have changed from being weak to strong, from depressed to happy, and from sick to healthy.

Since Chi Kung can bring so many benefits, I feel that it is my responsibility to collect the available published documents and compile them, filter them, understand them, and introduce them to those who cannot read them in their original Chinese. It is, however, impossible for one person alone to experience and understand the fruit of four thousand years of Chi Kung research. I hope that other Chi Kung experts will share this responsibility and publish the information that they have been taught, as well as what they have learned through research and experimentation.

Even though Chi Kung has been researched in China for four thousand years, there are still many questions which can only be answered through recourse to today's technology and interdisciplinary knowledge. Contemporary, enthusiastic minds will have plenty of opportunity to research and promote the art. This is not a job which can be done through one individual's effort. It requires a group of experts including Western-style doctors, Chi Kung experts, acupuncturists, and equipment design specialists to sit down and work together and exchange their research results. A formal organization with adequate financial support will be needed. If this research is properly conducted, it should succeed not only in providing validation of Chi Kung for the Western mind, but it may also come up with the most efficient methods of practice. I feel certain that Chi Kung will become very popular in a short time, and bring many people a healthier and happier life. This is a new field for Western science, and it will need a lot of support to catch up to the research which has already been done in China. I hope sincerely that Chi Kung science will soon become one of the major research fields in colleges and universities in this country.

Dr. Yang Jwing-Ming, Ph.D

FOREWORD

Dr. Thomas G. Gutheil, M.D.
Associate Professor of Psychiatry
Harvard Medical School

When Nixon opened China to the West in the 1970's, great interest was kindled into the possibilities of Americans learning many previously-hidden secrets of the "inscrutable" Orient. One of the realms of exploration most eagerly awaited, particularly by western physicians, was the science of Oriental healing: exotic practices such as acupuncture, shiatsu massage, Tai Chi Chuan, and the curious and puzzling notion of Chi, or vital energy. Popular magazines at the time featured arresting photographs of men and women lying calmly on operating tables, nearly disemboweled during major surgery, yet apparently requiring no more anesthesia than a few gleaming needles thrust into the skin of their foreheads.

Since these earliest dramatic harbingers, serious investigation of phenomena based on Chinese conceptualizations have both waxed and waned. Interest in Tai Chi, for example -- a form of exercise, health maintenance, and combat -- has risen steadily, especially in the western United States, stimulated in part by the fact that a large part of the Chinese citizenry practice this exercise daily to apparently good effect, and in part by the fact that Tai Chi masters, who regularly win mixed martial arts tournaments, seem to become better with age, rather than slower and weaker as do aging practitioners of other martial forms such as Kung Fu.

In contrast, after a spate of studies and articles attempting to define the physiologic bases for the generally unchallenged efficacy of acupuncture, interest in this area has waned markedly. Most early investigators tended toward the beliefs either that some form of suggestibility was involved, like that of hypnosis, another time-honored and effective anesthetic; or else that some known neural mechanism was being employed, such as "gating," where stimulation of some nerves with acupuncture needles functionally blocked impulses (presumably pain impulses) in others.

At the present time in the public mind a mixed feeling, an ambivalence, seems to hold sway, between forces of acceptance and of resistance toward these oriental concepts. To place the value of the present book in some perspective, therefore, it will be useful to understand these opposing forces.

The current forces tending toward acceptance of Chinese healing theory and practice draw from multiple origins. The first is the upsurge of interest in physical fitness. A few years ago the "high energy, high effort" fitness wave swept over the country; thousands of formerly sedentary individuals ran, jogged, danced, pumped and stretched in search of greater health and strength or, at least, an improved silhouette. Then, as many would-be athletes nursed injured or over strained muscles, bones and joints, interest in "low-impact" exercise surfaced. Ironically, Chi Kung practices were already providing this valuable type of conditioning centuries ago. Thus, the Westerner familiar with low-impact aerobics can readily understand the value of Chi Kung forms.

A second force tending toward acceptance is the average person's awareness of the link between mind and body; the concept of psychosomatic illness -- mental conditions causing physical illnesses -- is familiar from the popular press, from the revelations of celebrities and from everyone's personal experience of tension headaches, stress ulcers and the like. In a comparable fashion, some recent investigations by Herbert Benson, M.D. and others on the beneficial physical effects of mental calmness (as in the "relaxation response") have given solid support to the power of mental states to heal or harm. Thus the emphasis in Chi Kung practice on mental conditioning as a prerequisite and companion to physical improvement is not so foreign a notion at all.

On the other side of the ledger, certain factors tend to elicit resistance to these Eastern teachings and disbelief in both their relevance to modern persons and their scientific validity. One such factor is the radical interweaving in Chi Kung of what purports to be an essentially physiologic theory with philosophy and even religion or cosmology. Westerners used to partaking of their philosophy and science at separate tables may be alienated by their frank combination in Chi Kung principles.

A second factor is the absence at the present time of a "hard-science" physiology for Chi, its vessels and its actions. Some provocative preliminary findings have emerged correlating alterations in electric impedance in the skin at those points thought to be significant as acupuncture meridians and points; yet, alas, careful and replicable research with impeccable methodology has largely been lacking in this area. Instead, dubiously convincing, largely anecdotal material dominates the written works on the subject.

Another factor causing resistance is the tendency of writers in this field, following very ancient traditions and philosophical themes, to use the names of familiar body organs to describe conditions of the body related to Chi for which no other terminology exists. The western reader becomes lost in the question of whether such phrases as "weakness of the liver" are meant to be metaphoric (that is, meaning, more literally, "a certain condition of bodily energy, otherwise indescribable, which affects those body sites which historical tradition has identified with the liver"); or whether the reader should, indeed, look to the condition of the actual liver to find some form of pathology, for which no clear picture comes to mind, since the liver performs so many different functions that "weakness" conveys nothing meaningful.

Finally, many Westerners appear to be put off by the inherently poetic and metaphoric terminology common in Chinese nomenclature for, say, types of Chi and physical exercise techniques. To pick one example, a particular stance in Shaolin style Kung Fu is called "Golden Rooster Stands on One Leg"; such flowery language can have a jarring effect on the Westerner who is more accustomed to such more mundane descriptions as "side deltoid stretch."

For the Westerner who can bridge the gap between western and oriental conceptualizations, this book (and, indeed, the planned series) offers an exceptionally valuable resource in summarizing in a clear and straightforward way the historical development of this ancient field of learning. Through his exhaustive efforts to bring together ancient and more recent Chinese texts in this book, Dr. Yang has performed essential services in two ways. First, by tracing the history and evolution of these concepts, the reader can gain a sense of the development of ideas whose roots reach back over the centuries -- ideas which are desperately in need of just such cross-cultural illumination as this book provides. Second, Dr. Yang is issuing a challenge to others to bring the focus of careful research to this area to provide a durable empirical basis for both theory and practice of these sciences and arts. For both of these important steps, clearly, the time has come.

Dr. Thomas G. Gutheil, M.D.

PREFACE

Since my first Chi Kung book "Chi Kung -- Health and Martial Arts" appeared, I have received many compliments and thank-you's, as well as numerous questions, and many valuable suggestions from doctors, readers with medical problems, and the general public. This has led me to believe that my introductory book has opened the door to Chi Kung for many people, and has brought health benefits to more than a few. This response has encouraged me to continue my research and publishing in this subject. However, most of my Chi Kung experience and knowledge was obtained through my Tai Chi and Shaolin practice, and was therefore limited to a few Taoist and Buddhist Chi Kung exercises, as well as some of the common Chi Kung exercises which are popular in China. Because of this limitation in my Chi Kung knowledge, I have spent a lot of time analyzing, researching, pondering, and experimenting with many other Chi Kung styles about which I have read in my collection of Chi Kung documents. This research has greatly increased my knowledge.

In August of 1986 I had a chance to go back to Taiwan to visit my family. This visit also gave me the opportunity to see what Chi Kung documents had been published since I left Taiwan in 1974. To my surprise, there are a great many new publications available. I was so happy to learn that many documents had been published which described training techniques heretofore kept secret. With my brother's encouragement and financial support, I was able to purchase all of the expensive documents which I found worthwhile. Once I returned to the United States, I started to read and study them, and to experiment with some of the methods. These documents made me realize how limited my knowledge was, and opened up a whole new field of Chi Kung study for me.

In my excitement and enthusiasm I decided to compile them, filter out the parts which seemed questionable, and introduce the results to my readers. An unfortunate problem arose in that most of the documents explain **WHAT** to do, but do not explain **WHY**, and some will even just tell the process without explaining how to do it. Despite the obstacles, I decided to try my best, through research and contemplation, to determine the secrets of the techniques.

After two years of research and experimentation, I feel that it will take at least five years and eight volumes of introductory books to initiate the reader into the broad field of Chinese Chi Kung. Although these eight volumes will be based on the documents available to me, they will not be direct translations of these documents, except for the ancient poetry or songs which are the root of the training. This approach is necessary simply because these documents do not have any systematic introduction or way of tying everything together. What I can do is read them and study them carefully. Then I can compile and organize the information, and discuss it carefully in the light of my own Chi Kung knowledge and experience.

This approach will allow me to cautiously bring long-concealed Chi Kung knowledge to the reader. The only thing lacking is the experience. Many of the methods require more than twenty years of training to complete, and I would have to spend more than three lifetimes studying the various methods before I could discuss them with authority. I realize that it is impossible for me alone to introduce the results of four thousand years of Chi Kung research with these eight books, but I would still like to share the knowledge which I have gained from these documents, and the conclusions which I have drawn from my training. Please take these books in the tentative spirit in which they are written, and not as a final authority or bible. I sincerely hope that many other Chi Kung experts will step forward and share the traditional teachings which were passed down to them, as well as the fruits of their experience.

At present, the following books are planned:

1. *THE ROOT OF CHINESE CHI KUNG* -- The Secrets of Chi Kung Training

2. *MUSCLE/TENDON CHANGING AND MARROW WASHING CHI KUNG* -- The Secret of Youth (Yi Gin Ching and Shii Soei Ching)

3. *CHI KUNG MASSAGE* -- Chi Kung Tuei Na and Cavity Press for Healing (Chi Kung Ann Mo and Chi Kung Dien Shiuh)

4. *CHI KUNG AND HEALTH* -- For Healing and Maintaining Health

5. *CHI KUNG AND MARTIAL ARTS* -- The Key to Advanced Martial Arts Skill (Shaolin, Wuudang, Ermei, and others)

6. *BUDDHIST CHI KUNG* -- Charn, The Root of Zen

7. *TAOIST CHI KUNG* (Dan Diing Tao Kung)

8. *TIBETAN CHI KUNG* (Mih Tzong Shen Kung)

In this first volume we will discuss the roots of Chinese Chi Kung by dividing it into four parts. The first part will introduce the history of Chi Kung, the basic concepts and terminology commonly used in Chi Kung society and documents, the different Chi Kung categories, and will discuss Chi and the human body, and fundamental Chi Kung training theory and principles. This first part will give you a general concept of what Chi Kung is, and the various subjects that it includes. The second part will discuss the general keys to Chi Kung training, and give you the foundation of knowledge which is necessary for successful practice. This part serves as a map of the What and the How of Chi Kung training, so that you can choose your goal and the best way to get there. The third part will review the Chi circulatory system in your body, which includes the twelve primary Chi channels and the eight extraordinary Chi vessels. This part will give you a better understanding of how Chi circulates in your body. Finally, the fourth part of the book will list some of the many questions about Chi Kung which still remain unanswered.

The second volume in this series will cover Yi Gin and Shii Soei Chi Kung, which are translated as "Muscle/Tendon Changing and Marrow Washing Chi Kung." Marrow Washing is deep, and difficult to understand. It has been found in documents detailing both Buddhist and Taoist Chi Kung and meditation training, and it has been known in China since the Liang dynasty, more than fourteen hundred years ago. Because, however, the training usually involves stimulation of the sexual organs, it has traditionally been passed down only to a few trusted students.

In addition to the eight in-depth books, YMAA is also introducing a series of instructional books and videotapes on specific Chi Kung exercise sets. This series is designed for people who want to learn exercises that they can do on their own to improve or maintain their health. These books and tapes will be easy to understand both in theory and in practice. The first book and tape are on "The Eight Pieces of Brocade," one of China's most popular Chi Kung sets.

CONTENTS

ACKNOWLEDGMENTS
ABOUT THE AUTHOR
FOREWORD BY DR. YANG JWING-MING, Ph.D.
FOREWORD BY DR. THOMAS G. GUTHEIL, M.D.
PREFACE

PART ONE. GENERAL INTRODUCTION................................. 1

Chapter 1. Introduction.. 3
1-1. Prelude.. 3
1-2. General Definition of Chi and Chi Kung............................ 6
1-3. About This Book.. 10
Chapter 2. History of Chi Kung...................................... 13
2-1. Before the Han Dynasty (Before 206 B.C.)......................... 13
2-2. From the Han Dynasty to the Beginning of the Liang
     Dynasty (206 B.C.-502 A.D.) 15
2-3. From the Liang Dynasty to the End of Ching Dynasty (502-
     1911 A.D.) 16
2-4. From the End of Ching Dynasty to the Present (1911 A.D.-)... 18
Chapter 3. Basic Concepts of Chi Kung............................ 20
3-1. The Three Treasures - Jieng, Chi, and Shen...................... 20
3-2. Yi and Hsin.. 30
3-3. Dan Tien... 31
3-4. Three Flowers Reach the Top (San Huea Jiuh Diing).............. 34
3-5. Five Chi's Toward Their Origins (Wuu Chi Chaur Yuan)......... 34
Chapter 4. Chi and the Human Body................................ 36
4-1. About Chi.. 36
4-2. Chi and Bio-Electromagnetic Energy............................... 40
4-3. Some Hypotheses.. 42
4-4. Opening the Chi Gates.. 55
Chapter 5. Categories of Chi Kung................................. 57
5-1. Chi Kung and Religion.. 57
5-2. Categories of Chi Kung,.. 59
    1. Scholar Chi Kung - for Maintaining Health.................... 60
    2. Medical Chi Kung - for Healing................................ 62
    3. Martial Chi Kung - for Fighting............................... 64
    4. Religious Chi Kung - for Enlightenment or Buddhahood... 66
Chapter 6. Chi Kung Theory... 73
6-1. Introduction... 73
6-2. Wai Dan (External Elixir).. 74
6-3. Nei Dan (Internal Elixir).. 75

PART TWO. GENERAL KEYS TO CHI KUNG TRAINING....... 85

Chapter 7. General Concepts... 87
7-1. Introduction... 87
7-2. Building Chi... 88
7-3. Kan and Lii.. 94

Chapter 8. Regulating the Body (Tyau Shenn)...................... 97
   8-1. Introduction... 97
   8-2. Relaxation Theory... 98
   8-3. Relaxation Practice.. 99
   8-4. Rooting, Centering, and Balancing............................. 104
Chapter 9. Regulating the Breath (Tyau Shyi).................... 112
   9-1. Breathing and Health.. 112
   9-2. Regulating the Breath.. 113
   9-3. The Different Methods of Chi Kung Breathing...................... 114
   9-4. General Keys to Regulating Normal Breathing.................. 131
   9-5. Six Stages of Regulating the Breath.......................... 133
Chapter 10. Regulating the Emotional Mind (Tyau Hsin)...... 137
   10-1. Introduction.. 137
   10-2. Hsin, Yi, and Niann.. 139
   10-3. Methods of Stopping Thought (Niann)......................... 141
   10-4. Yi and Chi... 144
   10-5. Yi and the Five Organs... 145
   10-6. Hsin, Yi, and Shen.. 146
Chapter 11. Regulating the Essence (Tyau Jieng)............... 148
   11-1. Introduction.. 148
   11-2. Strengthening Your Kidneys..................................... 149
   11-3. Regulating the Essence (Tyau Jieng)......................... 154
Chapter 12. Regulating the Chi (Tyau Chi)....................... 157
   12-1. Introduction.. 157
   12-2. What Chi Should be Regulated?................................. 158
   12-3. Regulating the Chi (Tyau Chi)................................... 159
Chapter 13. Regulating the Spirit (Tyau Shen).................. 165
   13-1. Introduction.. 165
   13-2. Regulating the Spirit (Tyau Shen)............................. 166
Chapter 14. Important Points in Chi Kung Practice............ 169
   14-1. Introduction.. 169
   14-2. Common Experiences for Chi Kung Beginners.............. 170
   14-3. Sensations Commonly Experienced in Still Meditation........ 175
   14-4. Deviations and Corrections....................................... 178
   14-5. Twenty-Four Rules for Chi Kung Practice.................. 187

PART THREE. THE CHI CHANNELS AND VESSELS............ 193

Chapter 15. General Concepts.. 195
Chapter 16. The Twelve Primary Chi Channels.................. 200
   16-1. Introduction.. 200
   16-2. The Twelve Primary Channels.................................. 201
   16-3. Important Points.. 225
Chapter 17. The Eight Extraordinary Chi Vessels.............. 227
   17-1. Introduction.. 227
   17-2. The Eight Extraordinary Vessels............................... 229

PART FOUR. CONCLUSION... 243

Chapter 18. One Hundred and One Questions.................... 245
Chapter 19. Conclusion.. 254
Appendix A. Glossary.. 258
Appendix B. Translations of Chinese Terms....................... 268

PART ONE

GENERAL INTRODUCTION

Chapter 1

Introduction

1-1. Prelude

In their seven thousand years of history, the Chinese people have experienced all possible human suffering and pain. Chinese culture is like a very old man who has seen and experienced all of the painful side of human life. Yet through his experience, he has also accumulated a great store of knowledge. Chinese culture, as reflected in its literature and painting, ranks among the greatest achievements of the human spirit. It reflects mankind's joy and grief, pleasure and suffering, peace and strife, vitality, sickness, and death.

Within this complex cultural and historical background, the Chinese people have long sought ways of living healthy and happy lives. However, as they looked for ways to better themselves and seek spiritual upliftment, they have also tended to believe that everything that happens is due to destiny, and that it is prearranged by heaven. Despite this fatalistic belief, they have still looked for ways to resist the apparent inevitability of sickness and death.

The Chinese have devoted a large part of their intellectual effort to self-study and self-cultivation in the hope of understanding the meaning of their lives. This inward-feeling and looking, this spiritual searching, has become one of the major roots of Chinese religion and medical science. Chi, the energy within the human body, was studied very carefully. As people perceived the link between the Chi in the human body and the Chi in nature, they began to hope that this Chi was the means whereby man could escape from the trap of sickness and death. Over the years, many different sectors of Chinese society have studied and researched Chi.

Of all the researchers, the scholars and the doctors have had the longest history, and they have brought the understanding of Chi to a very deep level. It was they who learned the methods of maintaining health and curing sickness. Chinese medical science has developed out of the Chi research of the physicians.

When Indian Buddhism was imported into China, it profoundly influenced Chinese culture. Naturally, Chinese Chi Kung was also affected by the Buddhist meditative practices. The Taoist religion was created out of a mixture of traditional scholarly Taoism and Buddhism. Since that time, Buddhist and Taoist Chi Kung have been considered among the greatest achievements of Chinese culture.

Taoism and Buddhism have not only brought the Chinese people a peaceful, spiritual mind which may untie the mystery of human life and destiny, they have also created a hope that the development of Chi Kung may give people a healthy and happy life while they are alive, and an eternal spiritual life after death. When viewed from this historical background, it is not hard to understand why a major part of Chinese culture in the last two thousand years, other than warfare and possibly medical science, were based on the religions of Taoism and Buddhism, and spiritual science.

The emphasis on the spiritual life, rather than the material, is one of the major differences between Eastern and the Western cultures. An example of this is in the maintenance of health, where the West emphasizes the physical body more, while the East tends to also treat the person's spiritual and mental health.

Most Westerners believe that if you strengthen your physical body, you also improve your health. They emphasize the exercising and training of the physical body, but they ignore the balancing of the body's internal energy (Chi), which is also related to the emotions and the cultivation of spiritual calmness. Taoists call this "Tsorng Wai Jiann Kung" (building the strength externally) or "Yeuan Hsin Jy Wai Kung Yunn Dong" (distant mind's external exercises, meaning "external exercises without mental concentration or attention").

People who exercise a lot and whose bodies are externally strong are not necessarily healthier or happier than the average person. In order to have true good health you must have a healthy body, a healthy mind, and also smooth and balanced Chi circulation. According to Chinese medicine, many illnesses are caused by imbalances in your mind. For example, worry and nervousness can upset your stomach or harm your spleen (*1). Fear or fright can hinder the normal functioning of your kidneys and bladder. This is because your internal energy (Chi circulation) is closely related to your mind. In order to be truly healthy, you must have both a healthy physical body and a calm and healthy mind. True good health is both external and internal.

When someone gets involved in body building, he will emphasize building strong muscles. According to acupuncture and Chi Kung theory, he will also energize his body, stimulate his mind, and increase the level of the Chi circulation. If he trains properly, he will naturally gain physical health. However, if he exercises too much, he will over-energize his body and over-excite his mind and Chi. This will make his physical body too Yang (positive). According to Chinese philosophy, too much of something is excessive Yang and too little is excessive Yin, and neither extreme is desirable. When your body is too Yang or too Yin, your internal organs will tend to weaken and to degenerate sooner than they ordinarily would. A person who seems to be externally strong and healthy may be weak internally.

(*1). When Chinese medicine refers to an organ, such as the spleen, kidney, or bladder, they are not necessarily referring to the physical organ, but rather to a system of functions which are related to the organ.

In addition, when a body builder gets older, his over-stressed muscle fibers may lose their elasticity and degenerate faster than those of the average person. This causes the Chi to stagnate in the Chi channels. This phenomenon is well known among older practitioners of external martial arts, where it is called "Sann Kung," meaning "energy dispersion." The proper amount of exercise will generate only enough Chi to stimulate the organs and help them function normally and healthily. Overdoing exercise is like getting too much sunshine, which we now know will cause your skin cells to degenerate faster than the lack of sun.

Chi Kung practitioners believe that in order to gain real health you must not only do external exercises, but must also "Tsorng Nei Jwu Ji" (build the foundation internally), or do "Shiang Hsin Jy Nei Kung Yunn Dong" (literally "toward the mind's internal exercise," meaning internal exercise with mental concentration). Strengthening yourself internally and externally at the same time is called "Shing Ming Shuang Shiou." Shing means natural characteristics, personality, temperament, or disposition. It is shown internally. Ming is life, and refers to the life or death of the physical body. Shuang Shiou means double cultivation. The expression therefore means that if you desire to gain real health, you must cultivate your character internally and strengthen your body both internally and externally. The internal side is approached through meditation and Chi Kung exercises.

Many people believe that Chi Kung is a product only of China, India, or other Oriental countries. As a matter of fact, internal energy cultivation has also been common in the Western world, usually within the context of religion. Many people have been able to find their internal foundation and strength through meditation or praying in their church, temple, or mosque. Through their devotions and the practice of prayer, they are able to build up their concentration, confidence, and will, all of which are prerequisites to internal strength. The practice of such disciplines allows the energy in the body to become balanced, bringing health and strength to some, and even, in some cases, seemingly supernatural powers. Jesus is credited with many miracles, but he told his disciples "He that believeth on me, the works that I do, shall he do also, and greater works than these shall he do" (John 14:12). All of the major Western religions have had branches or sects which used practices similar to the Oriental Chi Kung disciplines.

However, there have also been people without any particular religious belief who have meditated by themselves and, through the buildup and circulation of Chi, developed psychic or healing abilities. Unfortunately, in earlier times such people were often killed as witches or heretics, so people who found they had such powers tended to view themselves as freaks or worse, and hid their powers. These negative attitudes only kept people from researching and understanding such abilities.

Many people in China and India have developed amazing powers through their meditation training. Fortunately, these powers were understood as being a result of Chi Kung, and so people were encouraged to train and research the subject. Although Chi Kung is becoming a more acceptable subject in the West, the Chinese and Indians are still way ahead in this internal mental and physical science.

Since 1973, acupuncture has been widely accepted by the American people, and even by many in the medical establishment. More and more people are becoming familiar with the concept of Chi. Chi-related arts such as Tai Chi Chuan and Chi Kung exercises are getting much more attention than ever before. Many people are learning that the study of Chi can be very beneficial, and I feel certain that in the next twenty years Chi Kung will become one of the hottest fields of research.

1-2. General Definition of Chi and Chi Kung

Before we define Chi and Chi Kung, you should understand that so far, there is no one scientific definition of Chi which is accepted generally by Chi Kung practitioners and Chinese medical society. The way people define Chi varies, depending upon their individual background and experience. Some people think Chi is an electric energy, others believe that it is a magnetic energy, and many others believe that Chi is heat or some other type of energy. However, anyone who has carefully researched the historical background of Chi would not define it by any one of these narrow definitions.

It is the same with Chi Kung. Chi Kung is often narrowly thought of as only exercises or meditations which can be used to improve one's health or to cure sickness. In fact, however, the range of Chi Kung and the scope of its research is much wider. You should understand this point so you will be able to view Chi and Chi Kung in an accurate and open way.

In this section we will discuss the general definition of Chi and Chi Kung. Specific terms concerning Chi and Chi Kung which are directly related to the human body will be discussed later in a separate section.

General Definition of Chi:

Chi is the energy or natural force which fills the universe. Heaven (the sky or universe) has Heaven Chi (Tian Chi), which is made up of the forces which the heavenly bodies exert on the earth, such as sunshine, moonlight, and the moon's affect on the tides. In ancient times, the Chinese believed that it was Heaven Chi which controlled the weather, climate, and natural disasters. In China, the weather is still referred to as Tian Chi (Heaven Chi). Every energy field strives to stay in balance, so whenever the Heaven Chi loses its balance, it tries to rebalance itself. Then the wind must blow, rain must fall, even tornados or hurricanes must happen in order for the Heaven Chi to reach a new energy balance.

Under Heaven Chi, which is the most important of the three, is Earth Chi. It is influenced and controlled by Heaven Chi. For example, too much rain will force a river to flood or change its path. Without rain, the plants will die. The Chinese believe that Earth Chi is made up of lines and patterns of energy, as well as the earth's magnetic field and the heat concealed underground. These energies must also balance, otherwise disasters such as earthquakes will occur. When the Chi of the earth is balanced, plants will grow and animals thrive.

Finally, within the Earth Chi, each individual person, animal, and plant has its own Chi field, which always seeks to be balanced. When any individual thing loses its Chi balance, it will sicken, die, and decompose. All natural things, including man, grow within and are influenced by the natural cycles of Heaven Chi and Earth Chi. Human Chi is usually considered a separate type of Chi, different from the Chi of the earth, and of plants and animals. The reason for this is simply that because we are human, we are particularly concerned with Human Chi, and have devoted a great deal of study to it.

Chi can be generally defined as any type of energy which is able to demonstrate power and strength. This energy can be electricity, magnetism, heat, or light. In China, electric power is called "Diann Chi" (electric Chi), and heat is called "Reh Chi" (heat Chi). When a person is alive, his body's energy is called "Ren Chi" (human Chi).

Chi is also commonly used to express the energy state of something, especially living things. As mentioned before, the weather is called "Tian Chi" (heaven Chi) because it indicates the energy state of the heavens. When a thing is alive it has "Hwo Chi" (vital Chi), and when it is dead it has "Syy Chi" (dead Chi) or "Goe Chi" (ghost Chi). When a person is righteous and has the spiritual strength to do good, he is said to have "Jeng Chi" (Normal Chi or Righteous Chi). The spiritual state or morale of an army is called "Chi Shyh" (energy state).

You can see that the word Chi has a wider and more general definition than most people think. It does not refer only to the energy circulating in the human body. Furthermore, the word "Chi" can represent the energy itself, and it can also be used to express the manner or state of the energy. It is important to understand this when you practice Chi Kung, so that your mind is not channeled into a narrow understanding of Chi, which would limit your future understanding and development.

General Definition of Chi Kung:

We have explained that Chi is energy, and that it is found in the heavens, in the earth, and in every living thing. In China, the word "Kung" is often used instead of "Kung Fu," which means energy and time. Any study or training which requires a lot of energy and time to learn or to accomplish is called Kung Fu. The term can be applied to any special skill or study as long as it requires time, energy, and patience. Therefore, **THE CORRECT DEFINITION OF CHI KUNG IS ANY TRAINING OR STUDY DEALING WITH CHI WHICH TAKES A LONG TIME AND A LOT OF EFFORT.**

The Chinese have studied Chi for thousands of years. Some of the information on the patterns and cycles of nature has been recorded in books, one of which is the "I Ching" (Book of Changes; 1122 B.C.). When the I Ching was introduced to the Chinese people, they believed that natural power included Tian (Heaven), Dih (Earth), and Ren (Man). These are called "San Tsair" (The Three Natural Powers) and are manifested by the three Chi's: Heaven Chi, Earth Chi, and Human Chi (Figure 1-1). These three facets of nature have their definite rules and cycles. The rules never change, and the cycles repeat periodically. The Chinese people used an understanding of these natural principles and the I Ching to calculate the changes of natural Chi. This calculation is called "Ba Kua" (The Eight Trigrams). From the Eight Trigrams are derived the 64 hexagrams. Therefore, the I Ching was probably the first book which taught the Chinese people about Chi and its variations in nature and man. The relationship of the Three Natural Powers and their Chi variations were later discussed extensively in the book "Chi Huah Luenn" (Theory of Chi's Variation).

Understanding Heaven Chi is very difficult, however, and it was especially so in ancient times when the science was just developing.

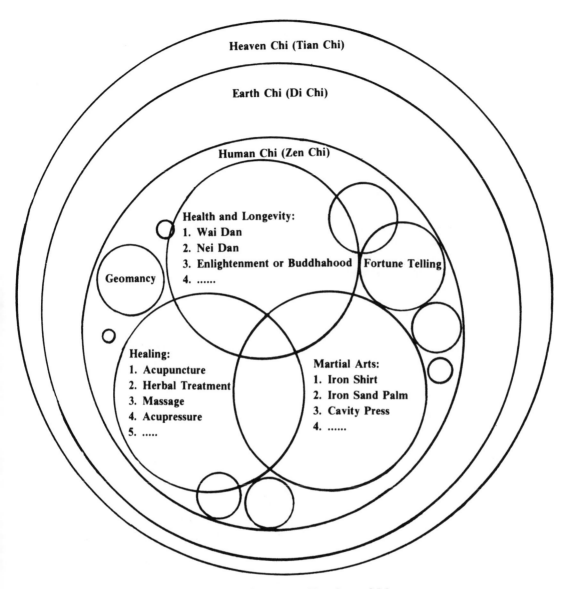

Figure 1-1. The three Chi's of Heaven, Earth, and Man

But since nature is always repeating itself, the experience accumulated over the years has made it possible to trace the natural patterns. Understanding the rules and cycles of "Tian Shyr" (heavenly timing) will help you to understand natural changes of the seasons, climate, weather, rain, snow, drought, and all other natural occurrences. If you observe carefully, you will be able to see many of these routine patterns and cycles caused by the rebalancing of the Chi fields. Among the natural cycles are those of the day, the month, and the year, as well as cycles of twelve years and sixty years.

Earth Chi is a part of Heaven Chi. If you can understand the rules and the structure of the earth, you will be able to understand how mountains and rivers are formed, how plants grow, how rivers move, what part of the country is best for someone, where to build a house and which direction it should face so that it is a healthy place to live, and many other things related to the earth. In China today there are people, called "Dih Lii Shy" (geomancy teachers) or "Feng Shoei Shy" (wind water teachers), who make their living this way. The term Feng Shoei is commonly used because the location and character of the wind and water in a landscape are the most important factors in evaluating a location. These experts use the accumulated body of geomantic knowledge and the I Ching to help people make important decisions such as where and how to build a house, where to bury their dead, and how to rearrange or redecorate homes and offices so that they are better places to live and work in. Many people even believe that setting up a store or business according to the guidance of Feng Shoei can make it more prosperous.

Among the three Chi's, Human Chi is probably the one studied most thoroughly. The study of Human Chi covers a large number of different subjects. The Chinese people believe that Human Chi is affected and controlled by Heaven Chi and Earth Chi, and that they in fact determine your destiny. Therefore, if you understand the relationship between nature and people, in addition to understanding human relations (Ren Shyh), you will be able to predict wars, the destiny of a country, or a person's desires and temperament and even his future. The people who practice this profession are called "Suann Ming Shy" (calculate life teachers).

However, the greatest achievement in the study of Human Chi is in regard to health and longevity. Since Chi is the source of life, if you understand how Chi functions and know how to regulate it correctly, you should be able to live a long and healthy life. Remember that you are part of nature, and you are channeled into the cycles of nature. If you go against this natural cycle, you may become sick, so it is in your best interests to follow the way of nature. This is the meaning of "Tao," which can be translated as "The Natural Way."

Many different aspects of Human Chi have been researched, including acupuncture, acupressure, herbal treatment, meditation, and Chi Kung exercises. The use of acupuncture, acupressure, and herbal treatment to adjust Human Chi flow has become the root of Chinese medical science. Meditation and moving Chi Kung exercises are used widely by the Chinese people to improve their health or even to cure certain illnesses. Meditation and Chi Kung exercises serve an additional role in that Taoists and Buddhists use them in their spiritual pursuit of enlightenment.

You can see that the study of any of the aspects of Chi including Heaven Chi, Earth Chi, and Human Chi should be called Chi Kung. However, since the term is usually used today only in reference to the cultivation of Human Chi through meditation and exercises, we will only use it in this narrower sense to avoid confusion.

Before we finish this section, we would like to discuss one more thing. The word Nei Kung is often used, especially in Chinese martial society. "Nei" means "internal" and "Kung" means "Kung Fu." Nei Kung means "internal Kung Fu," as opposed to Wai Kung which means "external Kung Fu." Nei Kung is martial arts training which specializes in internal Kung Fu, which builds up the Chi internally first and then coordinates the Chi with martial techniques. Typical Chinese Nei Kung martial styles are Tai Chi Chuan, Liu Ho Ba Fa, Ba Kua, and Hsing Yi. In contrast to Nei Kung, Wai Kung emphasizes developing the muscles, with some build up of Chi in the limbs. Typical Wai Kung martial styles are: Praying Mantis, Tiger, Eagle, White Crane, Dragon, and so on. Many of the external styles originated in the Shaolin Temple.

1-3. About This Book

I hope this book will lay down a theoretical foundation which interested Chi Kung practitioners can use in their training. Hopefully this book can explain to you the How, Why, and What of Chi Kung, and help you to avoid being confused and misled.

It is extremely difficult to write a book which covers more than four thousand years of study and research, especially since a large portion of the knowledge was kept secret until the last twenty years. Even though the study of Chi Kung has reached very high, there are still many questions which must be answered through recourse to today's technology and interdisciplinary knowledge. Contemporary, enthusiastic minds will have plenty of opportunity to research and promote the art.

One of the major purposes of this book is to stimulate Western scholars and medical society to get involved with and study this newly-revealed science. Hopefully other Chi Kung experts will be encouraged to share their knowledge with the public. I believe that in a short time Chi Kung will reach new and exciting heights in the Western world. This would be one of the greatest cross-cultural achievements since East and West opened their doors to each other.

Most available documents are not systematically organized and do not explain the subject very well. As I compile them and try to explain them in a logical and scientific way, I must use my own judgement, and I must explain them based on my personal Chi Kung background and my understanding of the documents. It is impossible for one person alone to do justice to this enormous field. You are encouraged to question everything stated in this text, and to always remember that many conclusions come from my own judgement. The main purpose of this book is to lead you to the path of study -- it is not meant to be the final authority.

When you read this book, it is important that you keep your mind open, and let go of your habitual ways of thinking. When we find ourselves in a new environment or start studying something new, it is human nature to view the new from the standpoint of what we have already learned. Unfortunately, this tends to make us conservative and narrow minded. This is commonly seen in tourists who visit another country, but judge the local customs and behavior according to their own country's standards. This usually leads to a lot of confusion and misunderstanding. If, however, you try to understand other people according to their own culture and historical background, you will have a much better chance of understanding their behavior. Please do this when you start studying this science of Chi Kung. If you keep your mind open and try to understand it according to its historical background, you will find it a fascinating and challenging subject.

It is true that it is very hard to break from tradition. In many old cultures, tradition must be obeyed absolutely. If anyone is against the tradition, he is considered a traitor to the culture. However, the correct approach to research and study involves questioning tradition and proving its inaccuracies through the use of modern thought and technology. This is especially necessary in regard to ancient sciences which were developed before this century. New study will allow us to prove and establish their accuracy. You should understand that this is not a form of betrayal. It is our responsibility to prove the truth and bring facts to light.

Many of the theories which have been passed down were based upon many years of experience. Regardless of how you modify a theory, the fact is, it is still the root of the entire science. Therefore, the correct approach to study and research involves respect and study of the past. From this respect and study, you will be able to find the root of the entire science. If you forget this root, which has been growing for thousands of years, you are studying only the branches and flowers.

You should judge this inner science of Chi Kung in a logical and scientific manner. Of course, the words "logic" and "scientific" are not absolute terms. They are relative to the science and understanding which we possess. Remember, though, that although science has been developing for thousands of years, it was only in the last hundred years or so that it suddenly began to swell in the width and depth of its understanding. We can be sure, therefore, that our understanding today is still in its infancy. There are many facts and phenomena which cannot be explained by today's science. Therefore, when you read this new inner science, be logical and scientific, yet don't reject explanations which lie outside of what you presently accept as true. What is accepted as true in a few years may be quite different from what we now accept.

All sciences were developed from daring assumptions which were then proven by careful experimentation. The results which we get from our experiments allow us to modify our assumptions and to create new experiments which explore our new hypotheses. This process enables us to develop a complete theory, and determine what next needs to be studied.

It is the same with Chi Kung practice. If you look and study carefully, you will see that, although many of the Chi-related theories were proven accurate and have been widely used in China, there are still many questions which still need to be answered.

During the course of study you must be patient and persevering. Strong will, patience, and perseverance are the three main components of success. This is especially true in Chi Kung training. Your will and wisdom must be able to dominate and conquer your emotional laziness. I believe that a person's success depends on his attitude toward life and his moral character, rather than his wisdom and intelligence. We've all known people who were wise, but yet ended up losers. They may be smart, and they pick things up more quickly than other people, but they soon lose interest. If they don't persevere, they stop learning and growing, and they never achieve their goals. They never realize that success demands moral virtues, and not just wisdom. A person who is truly wise knows that he must develop the other requirements for success.

In addition, a person who is truly wise will know when to start and when to stop. Many opportunities to succeed are lost by people who are too proud of their intelligence. There is a Chinese story about a group of people who competed in a snake-drawing contest. One man completed his drawing of a snake faster than anybody else. He was very proud of himself, and he thought "I'm so fast I could even draw four legs on the snake and still win!" So he drew the legs on, but when the judge chose the winner, it was somebody else. The man was very upset, and asked the judge why he didn't win; after all, he had finished before everyone else. The judge said: "You were supposed to draw a snake. Since snakes don't have legs, what you drew was not a snake." So, as smart as the man was, he didn't have the sense to know when to stop.

A person who is really wise understands that real success depends not only his wisdom but also on his moral character. Therefore, he will also cultivate his moral character and develop his good personality. Confucius said: "A man who is really wise knows what he knows and also knows what he does not know."(*2) Too often people who are smart become satisfied with their accomplishments and lose their humility. They feel that they know enough, and so they stop learning and growing. In the long run they will only lose. Remember the story of the tortoise and the hare. If the rabbit had not been so proud and satisfied, he would not have lost the race.

Once you understand what has been passed down to you, you should be creative. Naturally, this creativity must be under one condition: that you must understand the old way clearly and thoroughly. Only after you understand the old knowledge to a deep level will your mind be qualified to think "what if....." Then you will be able to come up with good ideas for further study and research. If all Chi Kung practitioners only practice the old ways and never search for new ones, the science of Chi Kung will stagnate at its current level. In that case, we will have lost the real meaning of and attitude toward learning.

This book is the most fundamental of the YMAA Chi Kung book series. It offers you the foundation of knowledge and training practices which is required to understand subsequent YMAA Chi Kung books. This book consists of four major parts. The first part will briefly summarize Chi Kung history, explain the necessary Chi Kung terminologies, and discuss the major Chi Kung categories. The second part will discuss the theory and major keys to Chi Kung training. This will enable the Chi Kung beginner to enter the door to the Chi Kung garden, and will offer the experienced practitioner a directory to the various types of Chi Kung. The third part will review the Chi channels and vessels to help you understand the Chi circulatory system in the human body. Finally, the fourth part will conclude the discussion in this book, and list some of the many questions I have about Chi Kung.

(*2). 孔子曰："知之為知之，不知為不知，是智也。"

Chapter 2

History of Chi Kung

The history of Chinese Chi Kung can be roughly divided into four periods. We know little about the first period, which is considered to have started when the "I Ching" (Book of Changes) was introduced sometime before 1122 B.C., and to have extended until the Han dynasty (206 B.C.) when Buddhism and its meditation methods were imported from India. This infusion brought Chi Kung practice and meditation into the second period, the religious Chi Kung era. This period lasted until the Liang dynasty (502-557 A.D.), when it was discovered that Chi Kung could be used for martial purposes. This was the beginning of the third period, that of martial Chi Kung. Many different martial Chi Kung styles were created based on the theories and principles of Buddhist and Taoist Chi Kung. This period lasted until the overthrow of the Ching dynasty in 1911, when the new era started in which Chinese Chi Kung training is being mixed with Chi Kung practices from India, Japan, and many other countries.

2-1. Before the Han Dynasty (Before 206 B.C.)

The "I Ching" (Book of Changes; 1122 B.C.) was probably the first Chinese book related to Chi. It introduced the concept of the three natural energies or powers (San Tsair): Tian (Heaven), Dih (Earth), and Ren (Man). Studying the relationship of these three natural powers was the first step in the development of Chi Kung.

In 1766-1154 B.C. (the Shang dynasty), the Chinese capital was in today's An Yang in Henan province. An archeological dig there at a late Shang dynasty burial ground called Yin Shiu discovered more than 160,000 pieces of turtle shell and animal bone which were covered with written characters. This writing, called "Jea Guu Wen" (Oracle-Bone Scripture), was the earliest evidence of the Chinese use of the written word. Most of the information recorded was of a religious nature. There was no mention of acupuncture or other medical knowledge, even though it was recorded in the Nei Ching that during the reign of the Yellow emperor (2690-2590 B.C.) Bian Shyr (stone probes) were already being used to adjust people's Chi circulation. The archeologists did, however, discover stones at the dig which they believed were Bian Shyr (Figure 2-1).

（土出陽安墟殷南河）石砭

Figure 2-1. Acupuncture stone probes (Bian Shyr)

During the Jou dynasty (1122-934 B.C.), Lao Tzyy (Li Erh) mentioned certain breathing techniques in his classic "Tao Te Ching" (Classic on the Virtue of the Tao). He stressed that the way to obtain health was to "concentrate on Chi and achieve softness" (Juan Chi Jyh Rou). Later, "Shyy Gi" (Historical Record) in the Spring and Autumn and Warring States Periods (770-221 B.C.) also described more complete methods of breath training. About 300 B.C. the Taoist philosopher Juang Tzyy described the relationship between health and the breath in his book "Nan Hwa Ching." It states: "The men of old breathed clear down to their heels..." This was not a figure of speech, and confirms that a breathing method for Chi circulation was being used by some Taoists at that time.

During the Chin and Han dynasties (221 B.C.-220 A.D.), there are several medical references to Chi Kung in the literature, such as the "Nan Ching" (Classic on Disorders) by the famous doctor Bian Chiueh, which describes the use of breathing to increase Chi circulation. "Gin Guey Yao Liueh" (Prescriptions from the Golden Chamber) by Chang Jong-Jiing discusses the use of breathing and acupuncture to maintain good Chi flow. "Jou I Tsan Torng Chih" (A Comparative Study of the Jou (dynasty) Book of Changes) by Wey Bor-Yang explains the relationship of human beings to nature's forces and Chi. It can be seen from this list that up to this time, almost all of the Chi Kung publications were written by scholars such as Lao Tzyy and Juang Tzyy, or medical doctors such as Bian Chiueh and Wey Bor-Yang.

Let us conclude with a few important points about the Chi Kung in this period:

1. Historical documents for this period are scarce today, and it is difficult to obtain detailed information, especially about Chi Kung training.
2. There were two major types of Chi Kung training. One type was used by the Confucian and Taoist scholars, who used it primarily to maintain their health. The other type of Chi Kung was for medical purposes, using needles or exercises to adjust the Chi or to cure illness.
3. There was almost no religious color to the training.
4. All of the training focused on following the natural way and improving and maintaining health. Actively countering the effects of nature was considered impossible.

2-2. From the Han Dynasty to the Beginning of the Liang Dynasty (206 B.C.-502 A.D.)

Because many Han emperors were intelligent and wise, the Han dynasty was a glorious and peaceful period. It was during the Eastern Han dynasty (c. 58 A.D.) that Buddhism was imported to China from India. The Han emperor became a sincere Buddhist, and Buddhism soon spread and became very popular. Many Buddhist meditation and Chi Kung practices, which had been practiced in India for thousands of years, were absorbed into the Chinese culture. The Buddhist temples taught many Chi Kung practices, especially the still meditation of Charn (Zen), which marked a new era of Chinese Chi Kung. Much of the deeper Chi Kung theory and practices which had been developed in India were brought to China. Unfortunately, since the training was directed at attaining Buddhahood, the training practices and theory were recorded in the Buddhist bibles and kept secret. For hundreds of years the religious Chi Kung training was never taught to laymen. Only in this century has it been available to the general populace.

Not long after Buddhism was imported into China, a Taoist by the name of Chang Tao-Ling combined the traditional Taoist principles with Buddhism and created a religion called Tao Jiaw. Many of the meditation methods were a combination of the principles and training methods of both sources.

Since Tibet had its own branch of Buddhism with its own training system and methods of attaining Buddhahood, Tibetan Buddhists were also invited to China to preach. In time, their practices were also absorbed.

It was in this period that the traditional Chinese Chi Kung practitioners finally had a chance to compare their arts with the religious Chi Kung practices imported mainly from India. While the scholarly and medical Chi Kung had been concerned with maintaining and improving health, the newly imported religious Chi Kung was concerned with far more. Contemporary documents and Chi Kung styles show clearly that the religious practitioners trained their Chi to a much deeper level, working with many internal functions of the body, and strove to have control of their bodies, minds, and spirits with the goal of escaping from the cycle of reincarnation.

While the Chi Kung practices and meditations were being passed down secretly within the monasteries, traditional scholars and physicians continued their Chi Kung research. During the Gin dynasty in the 3rd century A.D., a famous physician named Hwa Tor used acupuncture for anesthesia in surgery. The Taoist Jiun Chiam used the movements of animals to create the Wuu Chyn Shih (Five Animal Sports), which taught people how to increase their Chi circulation through specific movements. Also, in this period a physician named Ger Horng mentioned using the mind to lead and increase Chi in his book Baw Poh Tzyy. Sometimes in the period of 420 to 581 A.D. Taur Horng-Jiing compiled the "Yeang Shenn Yan Ming Luh" (Records of Nourishing the Body and Extending Life), which showed many Chi Kung techniques.

Characteristics of Chi Kung during this period were:

1. There were three schools of religious Chi Kung which influenced and dominated the Chi Kung practice in this period. These are Indian Buddhism, Tibetan Buddhism, and Taoism.
2. Almost all of the religious Chi Kung practices were kept secret within the monasteries.
3. Religious Chi Kung training worked to escape from the cycle of reincarnation.
4. Relatively speaking, religious Chi Kung theory is deeper than the theory of the non-religious Chi Kung, and the training is harder.
5. Chi circulation theory was better understood by
   this time, so the Chi Kung sets created in this period seem to be more efficient than the older sets.

2-3. From the Liang Dynasty to the End of Ching Dynasty (502-1911 A.D.)

During the Liang dynasty (502-557 A.D.) the emperor invited a Buddhist monk named Da Mo, who was once an Indian prince, to preach Buddhism in China. When the emperor decided he did not like Da Mo's Buddhist theory, the monk withdrew to the Shaolin Temple. When Da Mo arrived, he saw that the priests were weak and sickly, so he shut himself away to ponder the problem. When he emerged after nine years of seclusion, he wrote two classics: "Yi Gin Ching" (Muscle/Tendon Changing Classic) and "Shii Soei Ching" (Marrow Washing Classic). The Muscle/Tendon Changing Classic taught the priests how to gain health and change their physical bodies from weak to strong. The Marrow Washing Classic taught the priests how to use Chi to clean the bone marrow and strengthen the blood and immune system, as well as how to energize the brain and attain enlightenment. Because the Marrow Washing Classic was harder to understand and practice, the training methods were passed down secretly to only a very few disciples in each generation.

After the priests practiced the Muscle/Tendon Changing exercises, they found that not only did they improve their health, but they also greatly increased their strength. When this training was integrated into the martial arts forms, it increased the effectiveness of their techniques. In addition to this martial Chi Kung training, the Shaolin priests also created five animal styles of Kung Fu which imitated the way different animals fight. The animals imitated were the tiger, leopard, dragon, snake, and crane.

Outside of the monastery, the development of Chi Kung continued during the Swei and Tarng dynasties (581-907 A.D.). Chaur Yuan-Fang compiled the "Ju Bing Yuan Hou Luenn" (Thesis on the Origins and Symptoms of Various Diseases), which is a veritable encyclopedia of Chi Kung methods listing 260 different ways of increasing the Chi flow. The "Chian Gin Fang" (Thousand Gold Prescriptions) by Suen Sy-Meau described the method of leading Chi, and also described the use of the Six Sounds. The use of the Six Sounds to regulate Chi in the internal organs had already been used by the Buddhists and Taoists for some time. Suen Sy-Meau also introduced a massage system called Lao Tzyy's 49 Massage Techniques. "Wai Tai Mih Yao" (The Extra Important Secret) by Wang Tour discussed the use of breathing and herbal therapies for disorders of Chi circulation.

During the Song, Gin, and Yuan dynasties (960-1368 A.D.), "Yeang Sheng Jyue" (Life Nourishing Secrets) by Chang An-Tao discussed several Chi Kung practices. "Ru Men Shyh Shyh" (The Confucian Point of View) by Chang Tzyy-Her describes the use of Chi Kung to cure external injuries such as cuts and sprains. "Lan Shyh Mih Tsarng" (Secret Library of the Orchid Room) by Li Guoo describes using Chi Kung and herbal remedies for internal disorders. "Ger Jyh Yu Luenn" (A Further Thesis of Complete Study) by Ju Dan-Shi provided a theoretical explanation for the use of Chi Kung in curing disease.

During the Song dynasty (960-1279 A.D.), not long after the Shaolin Temple started using Chi Kung in their martial training, Chang San-Feng is believed to have created Tai Chi Chuan. Tai Chi followed a different approach in its use of Chi Kung than did Shaolin. While Shaolin emphasized Wai Dan (External Elixir) Chi Kung exercises, Tai Chi emphasized Nei Dan (Internal Elixir) Chi Kung training. (Wai Dan and Nei Dan are described in Chapter 6).

In 1026 A.D. the famous brass man of acupuncture was designed and built by Dr. Wang Wei-Yi. Before this time, although there were many publications which discussed acupuncture theory, principles, and treatment techniques, there were many disagreements among them, and many points which were unclear. When Dr. Wang built his brass man, he also wrote a book called "Torng Ren Yu Shiuh Jen Jeou Twu" (Illustration of the Brass Man Acupuncture and Moxibustion). He explained the relationship of the 12 organs and the 12 Chi channels, clarified many of the points of confusion, and, for the first time, systematically organized acupuncture theory and principles.

In 1034 A.D. Dr. Wang used acupuncture to cure the emperor Ren Tzong. With the support of the emperor, acupuncture flourished. In order to encourage acupuncture medical research, the emperor built a temple to Bian Chiueh, who wrote the Nan Ching, and worshiped him as the ancestor of acupuncture. Acupuncture technology developed so much that even the Gin race in the North requested the brass man and other acupuncture technology as a condition for peace. Between 1102 to 1106 A.D. Dr. Wang dissected the bodies of prisoners and added more information to the Nan Ching. His work contributed greatly to the advancement of Chi Kung and Chinese medicine by giving a clear and systematic idea of the circulation of Chi in the human body.

Later, in the Southern Song dynasty (1127-1279 A.D.), Marshal Yeuh Fei was credited with creating several internal Chi Kung exercises and martial arts. It is said that he created the Eight Pieces of Brocade to improve his soldiers' health. He is also known as the creator of the internal martial style Hsing Yi. In addition to that, Eagle style martial artists also claim that Yeuh Fei was the creator of their style.

From then until the end of the Ching dynasty (1911 A.D.), many other Chi Kung styles were founded. The well known ones include Fwu Buh Kung (Tiger Step Kung), Shyr Er Juang (Twelve Postures) and Jiaw Huah Kung (Beggar Kung). Also in this period, many documents related to Chi Kung were published, such as "Bao Shenn Mih Yao" (The Secret Important Document of Body Protection) by Tsaur Yuan-Bair, which described moving and stationary Chi Kung practices; and "Yeang Sheng Fu Yeu" (Brief Introduction to Nourishing the Body) by Chen Jih-Ru, about the three treasures: Jieng (essence), Chi (internal energy), and Shen (spirit). Also, "Yi Fang Jyi Jieh" (The Total Introduction to Medical Prescriptions) by Uang Fann-An reviewed and summarized the previously published materials; and "Nei Kung Twu Shwo" (Illustrated Explanation of Nei Kung) by Wang Tzuu-Yuan presented the Twelve Pieces of Brocade and explained the idea of combining both moving and stationary Chi Kung.

In the late Ming dynasty (around 1640 A.D.), a martial Chi Kung style, Huoo Long Kung (Fire Dragon Kung) was created by the Tai Yang martial stylists. The well known internal martial art style Ba Kua Chang (Eight Trigrams Palm) is believed to have been created by Doong Hae-Chuan late in the Ching dynasty (1644-1911 A.D.). This style is now gaining in popularity throughout the world.

During the Ching dynasty, Tibetan meditation and martial techniques became widespread in China for the first time. This was due to the encouragement and interest of the Manchurian Emperors in the royal palace, as well as others of high rank in society.

Characteristics of Chi Kung during this period were:

1. Chi Kung was adapted into the martial arts, and martial Chi Kung styles were created.
2. Chi circulation theory and acupuncture reached a peak. More documents were published about medical Chi Kung than the other categories of Chi Kung exercises.
3. Religious Chi Kung practice remained secret.
4. Chi Kung exercises had become more popular in Chinese society.

2-4. From the End of Ching Dynasty to the Present

Before 1911 A.D., Chinese society was still very conservative and old fashioned. Even though China had been expanding its contact with the outside world for the previous hundred years, the outside world had little influence beyond the coastal regions. With the overthrow of the Ching dynasty in 1911 and the founding of the Chinese Republic, the nation started changing as never before. Since this time Chi Kung practice has entered a new era. Because of the ease of communication in the modern world, Western culture is having a great influence on the Orient. Many Chinese have opened their minds and changed their traditional ideas, especially in Taiwan and Hong Kong. Various Chi Kung styles are now being taught openly, and many formerly secret documents have been published. Modern methods of communication have opened up Chi Kung to a much wider audience than ever before, and people now have the chance to study and understand many different styles. In addition to that, people are now able to compare Chinese Chi Kung to similar arts from other countries such as India, Japan, Korea, and the Middle East.

I believe that in the near future Chi Kung will be considered the most exciting and challenging field of research. It is an ancient science just waiting to be investigated with the help of the new technologies now being developed at an almost explosive rate. Anything we can do to speed up this research will greatly help humanity to understand and improve itself.

Chapter 3

Basic Concepts
of Chi Kung

There are a number of special terms that are commonly used by Chi Kung practitioners, and are found in the documents which have been passed down from generation to generation. Since most of these terms are key words which will help you to grasp the basic concepts of Chi Kung practice, it is important that you understand their real meaning. In this chapter we will discuss the major terms which are directly related to Chi Kung training. Other terms will be discussed in Appendix B.

3-1. The Three Treasures - Jieng, Chi, and Shen

Understanding Jieng (Essence), Chi (internal energy), and Shen (spirit) is one of the most important requirements for effective Chi Kung training. They are the root of your life and therefore also the root of Chi Kung practice. Jieng, Chi, and Shen are called "San Bao," which means "The Three Treasures," "San Yuan," which means "The Three Origins," or "San Been," which means "The Three Foundations." In Chi Kung training, a practitioner learns how to "firm his Jieng" (Guh Jieng; Guh means to firm, solidify, retain, and conserve) and how to convert it into Chi. This is called "Liann Jieng Huah Chi," which means "to refine the Jieng and convert it into Chi." Then he learns how to lead the Chi to the head to convert it into Shen (also called nourishing Shen). This is called "Liann Chi Huah Shen," which means "to refine the Chi and convert it into (nourish) the Shen." Finally, the practitioner learns to use his energized Shen to govern the emotional part of his personality. This is called "Liann Shen Leau Shing," or "to refine the Shen to end human (emotional) nature."

These conversion processes are what enable you to gain health and longevity. As a Chi Kung practitioner, you must pay a great deal of attention to these three elements during the course of your training. If you keep these three elements strong and healthy, you will live a long and healthy life. If you neglect or abuse them, you will be sick frequently and will age fast. Each one of these three elements or treasures has its own root. You must know the roots so that you can strengthen and protect your three treasures.

Jieng:

The Chinese word Jieng means a number of things depending on where, when, and how it is used. Jieng can be used as a verb, an adjective, or a noun. When it is used as a verb, it means "to refine." For example, to refine or purify a liquid to a high quality is called "Jieng Liann." When it is used as an adjective, it is used to describe or signify something which is "refined," "polished" and "pure without mixture." For example, when a piece of art work is well done, people say "Jieng Shih" which means "delicate and painstaking" (literally, "pure and fine"), or "Jieng Liang" which means "excellent quality" (literally "pure and good"). When Jieng is used to apply to personal wisdom or personality, it means "keen" and "sharp." For example, when someone is smart or wise, they are called "Jieng Ming," which means "keen and clever." When Jieng is applied to a thought, it means "profound" or "astute," and indicates that the idea or plan was well and carefully considered. When used as a noun for an object, Jieng means "the essence" or "the essentials." When it is used for the energy side of a being, it means "spirit" or "ghost." Since Chinese people believe that the male sperm or semen is the refined and the most essential product of a man, Jieng also means sperm or semen.

When Jieng is used as "essence," it exists in everything. Jieng may be considered the primal substance or original source from which a thing is made, and which exhibits the true nature of that thing. When Jieng is used in reference to animals or humans, it means the very original and essential source of life and growth. This Jieng is the origin of the Shen (spirit) which makes an animal different from a tree. In humans, Jieng is passed down from the parents. Sperm is called "Jieng Tzyy," which means "the essence of sons." When this essence is mixed with the mother's Jieng (egg), a new life is generated which is, in certain fundamental respects, an intertwinement of the Jiengs of both parents. The child is formed, the Chi circulates, and the Shen grows. The Jieng which has been carried over from the parents is called "Yuan Jieng," which means "Original Essence."

Once you are born, Original Jieng is the fountainhead and root of your life. It is what enables you to grow stronger and bigger. After your birth you start to absorb the Jieng of food and air, converting these Jiengs into the Chi which supplies your body's needs. You should understand that when Jieng is mentioned in Chi Kung society, it refers usually to Yuan Jieng (Original Jieng). Chi Kung practitioners believe that Original Jieng is the most important part of you, because it is the root of your body's Chi and Shen. The amount and quality of Original Jieng is different from person to person, and it is affected significantly by your parents' health and living habits while they were creating you. Generally speaking, it does not matter how much Original Jieng you have carried over from your parents. If you know how to conserve it, you will have more than enough for your lifetime. Although you probably cannot increase the amount of Jieng you have, Chi Kung training can improve its quality.

In Chi Kung training, knowing how to conserve and firm your Original Jieng is of primary importance. To conserve means to refrain from abusing your Original Jieng through overuse. For example, if you overindulge in sexual activity, you will lose Original Jieng faster than other people and your body will degenerate faster. To firm your Jieng means to keep and protect it. For example, you should know how to keep your kidneys strong. Kidneys are thought of as the residence of Original Jieng. When your kidneys are strong, the Original Jieng will be kept firm and will not be lost without reason. The firming of your Original Jieng is called "Guh Jieng," which is translated "to make solid, to firm the essence." Only after you know how to retain (meaning to conserve and firm) your Original Jieng can you start seeking ways to improve its quality. Therefore, conserving and firming your Jieng is the first step in training. In order to know how to conserve and firm your Jieng, you must first know: the root of your Jieng, where the Original Jieng resides, and how Original Jieng is converted into Chi.

The root of your Original Jieng before your birth is in your parents. After birth, this Original Jieng stays in its residence, the kidneys, which are now also its root. When you keep this root strong, you will have plenty of Original Jieng to supply to your body.

If you look carefully at how you were formed, you can gain interesting insights into life. You started as one sperm which, because it managed to reach and penetrate the egg before any of the other millions of sperm could, was one of the strongest and luckiest sperm alive. Once this sperm entered the egg, one human cell formed and then started to divide, from one to two, and from two to four. Finally, the baby formed. All of the baby's health depended on the sperm and egg which were generated from the Jieng of the parents. As the baby was being formed it was immersed in liquid, and it received all of its nutrition and oxygen from the mother through the umbilical cord. Notice that the umbilical cord connects at the navel, which is very close to both the Dan Tien and your body's center of gravity. The umbilical cord is very long, and because it is hard for the mother alone to push the necessary supplies to the baby, the baby needs to help. The baby must draw the nutrients to itself with an in and out pumping motion of its abdomen.

Once you are born, you start taking in oxygen through your nose and food through your mouth. Since you no longer need the abdominal motion to pump in nutrients, it gradually stops, and, finally, you forget how to use it. In Chi Kung, the Lower Dan Tien or abdomen is still considered the original Chi source because it is here that Chi is made from the Original Jieng which you inherited from your parents.

According to Chinese medical and Chi Kung society, the Original Jieng which you obtained from your parents stays in your kidneys after your birth. This Original Jieng is the source of your life and growth. This Original Jieng is converted continuously into Chi which moves into the Lower Dan Tien, and stays stored there in its residence for future use. The Dan Tien is located on the Conception Vessel -- one of the eight Chi "reservoirs" in the body which regulate the Chi flow in the other Chi channels (this will be discussed further in Part Three). Dan Tien Chi is considered "Water Chi," and is able to cool down the "Fire Chi" which is generated from the Jieng of food and air and which resides at the Middle Dan Tien.

As you may realize from the above discussion, if you wish to stay strong and healthy, you must first conserve your Original Jieng. Remember that Original Jieng is like the principal in your savings account in that it is an original investment which will continue to return interest as long as it is conserved. Jieng can produce Chi, so if you handle this Jieng carefully, you will continue to have Jieng and Chi. However, if you abuse yourself with an unhealthy lifestyle, you may damage and reduce your original Jieng.

In order to conserve your Jieng, you must first control your sexual activity. The gonads are called the "external kidneys" in Chinese medical society. This is because Chinese doctors believe that sperm is a product of Original Jieng and the Jieng from food and air. The more ejaculations you have, the faster you will exhaust your Original Jieng, and the shorter your life will be.

Please understand that the Chinese doctors and Chi Kung practitioners are not saying that in order to conserve your Jieng, you must stop your sexual activity completely. As a matter of fact, they encourage the proper amount of sexual activity, believing that it will energize and activate the Jieng, which makes the Jieng-Chi conversion more efficient. Remember, Jieng is like fuel, and Chi is like the energy generated from this fuel. The more efficiently you can convert your fuel into energy, the less you will waste.

In addition, the proper amount of sexual activity will energize the Chi so that it nourishes the Shen (spirit). This will help you stay mentally balanced, and raise your Shen. It is very important to keep your Shen raised, otherwise you will tend to get depressed and will be afraid to face life. It is very hard to define how much sex is the proper amount. It depends on the individual's age and state of health. According to Chi Kung, the Jieng which resides in the external kidneys (gonads) is the main source of the Chi which fills up the four major Chi vessels in the legs. These four Chi reservoirs (vessels) keep the legs strong and healthy. Therefore, if you feel that your legs are weak due to the amount of sexual activity, you have lost too much of your Jieng.

The second thing you must do in order to conserve your Original Jieng is to prevent your Original Chi from leaking out of your body. There are two acupuncture cavities called "Shenshu" or "Jiengmen" (Essence Doors). These two cavities are the doors through which the kidneys communicate with the outside, and they are used to regulate the Chi production in the kidneys. When Chi is converted from Original Jieng, most of it moves forward to the Dan Tien. However, some Chi is lost backward through the Kidney Doors. If you lose too much Chi, your Jieng will be depleted as you try to make up for the loss. In Chi Kung practice, one of the major trainings is learning how to lead the converted Chi from the kidneys to the Dan Tien more efficiently.

Chi:
Since we have already discussed Chi at the beginning of this chapter in general terms, we will now discuss Chi in the human body and in Chi Kung training. Before we start, we would like to point out one important thing. At this time, there is no clear explanation of the relationship between all of the circulatory systems and the Chi circulatory system. The Western world knows of the blood system, nervous system, and lymphatic system. Now, there is the Chi circulation system from China. How are, for example, the Chi and the nervous system related? If the nervous system does not match the Chi system, where does the sensing energy in the nervous system come from? How is the lymphatic system related to the Chi system? All of these questions are still waiting for study by modern scientific

methods and technology. Here, we can only offer you some theoretical assumptions based on the research conducted up to now.

Chinese medical society believes that the Chi and blood are closely related. Where Chi goes, blood follows. That is why "Chi Shiee" (Chi-Blood) is commonly used in Chinese medical texts. It is believed that Chi provides the energy for the blood cells to keep them alive. As a matter of fact, it is believed that blood is able to store Chi, and that it helps to transport air Chi especially to every cell of the body.

If you look carefully, you can see that the elements of your physical body such as the organs, nerves, blood, and even every tiny cell are all like separate machines, each with their own unique function. Just like electric motors, if there is no current in them, they are dead. If you compare the routes of the blood circulatory system, the nervous system, and the lymphatic system with the course of the Chi channels, you will see that there is a great deal of correspondence. This is simply because Chi is the energy needed to keep them all alive and functioning.

Now, let us look at your entire body. Your body is composed of two major parts. The first part is your physical body, and the second is the energy supply which your body needs to function. Your body is like a factory. Inside your body are many organs, which correspond to the machines required to process the raw materials into the finished product. Some of the raw materials brought into a factory are used to create the energy with which other raw materials will be converted into finished goods. The raw materials for your body are food and air, and the finished product is life.

The Chi in your body is analogous to the electric current which the factory power plant obtains from coal or oil. The factory has many wires connecting the power plant to the machines, and other wires connecting telephones, intercoms, and computers. There are also many conveyer belts, elevators, wagons, and trucks to move material from one place to another. It is no different in your body, where there are systems of intestines, blood vessels, complex networks of nerves and Chi channels to facilitate the supply of blood, sensory information and energy to the entire body. However, unlike the digestive, circulatory, and central nervous systems -- all of whose supportive vessels can be observed as material structures in the body -- Chi channels are non-material and cannot be observed as physical objects. The circulatory, nervous, and Chi systems all possess similar configurations within the body, and are distributed rather equally throughout the body.

In a factory, different machines require different levels of current. It is the same for your organs, which require different levels of Chi. If a machine is supplied with an improper level of power, it will not function normally and may even be damaged. In the same way, your organs, when the Chi level running to them is either too positive or too negative, will be damaged and will degenerate more rapidly. The ancient Chinese character for Chi was formed of two words (*1). On the top is the word "nothing" and at the bottom is the word "fire." This implies that Chi is "no fire." That means that when the organs are supplied with the proper amount of Chi, they will not be overheated and "on fire."

(*1). " 炁 "

In order for a factory to function smoothly and productively, it will not only need high quality machines, but also a reliable power supply. The same goes for your body. The quality of your organs is largely dependent upon what you inherited from your parents. To maintain your organs in a healthy state and to insure that they function well for a long time, you must have an appropriate Chi supply. If you don't have it, you will become sick.

Chi is affected by the quality of air you inhale, the kind of food you eat, your lifestyle, and even your emotional make-up and personality. The food and air are like the fuel or power supply, and their quality affects you. Your lifestyle is like the way you run the machine, and your personality is like the management of the factory.

The above discussion clarifies the role that Chi plays in your body. However, it should be noted that the above metaphor is an oversimplification, and that the behavior and function of Chi is much more complex and difficult to handle than the power supply in a factory. You are neither a factory nor a robot, you are a human being with feelings and emotions. Unfortunately, your feelings have a major influence on your Chi circulation. For example, when you pinch yourself, the Chi in that area will be disturbed. This Chi disturbance will be sensed through the nervous system and interpreted by your brain as pain. No machine can do this. Moreover, after you have felt the pain, unlike a machine, you will react either as a result of instinct or conscious thought. Human feelings and thought affect Chi circulation in the body, whereas a machine cannot influence its power supply. In order to understand your Chi, you must use your feelings, rather than just the intellect, to sense its flow and make judgements about it.

Now a few words as to the source of human Chi. As mentioned, Chinese doctors and Chi Kung practitioners believe that the body contains two general types of Chi. The first type is called Pre-birth Chi or Original Chi (Yuan Chi). Original Chi is also called "Shian Tian Chi," which, translated literally, means "Pre-heavenly Chi." Heaven here means the sky, so pre-heaven means before the baby sees the sky. In other words, before birth. Original Chi comes from converted Original Jieng which you received before your birth. This is why Original Chi is also called Pre-birth Chi.

The second type is called Post-birth Chi or "Hou Tian Chi," which means "Post-heaven Chi." This Chi is drawn from the Jieng of the food and air we take in. As mentioned, the residence of the Post-birth Chi is the Middle Dan Tien (solar plexus). This Chi then circulates down and mixes with the Pre-birth or Dan Tien Chi (Original Chi). Together, they circulate down, passing into the Governing vessel, from where they are distributed to the entire body.

Pre-birth Chi is commonly called "Water Chi" (Shoei Chi) because it is able to cool down the Post-birth Chi, which is called "Fire Chi" (Huoo Chi). Fire Chi usually brings the body to a positive (Yang) state, which stimulates the emotions and scatters and confuses the mind. When the Water Chi cools your body down, the mind will become clear, neutral and centered. It is believed in Chi Kung society that Fire Chi supports the emotional part of the body, while Water Chi supports the wisdom part.

After the Fire Chi and Water Chi mix, this Chi will not only circulate to the Governing vessel, but will also supply the "Thrusting vessel" (Chong Mei) which will lead the Chi directly up through the bone marrow in the spine to nourish the brain and energize the Shen and soul. As will be discussed later, energizing the brain and raising the Shen are very important in Chi Kung practice.

According to its function, Chi can be divided into two major categories. The first is called "Ying Chi" (Managing Chi), because it manages or controls the functioning of the body. This includes the functioning of the brain and the organs, and even body movement. Ying Chi is again divided into two major types. The first type circulates in the channels and is responsible for the functioning of the organs. The circulation of Chi to the organs and the extremities continues automatically as long as you have enough Chi in your reservoirs and you maintain your body in good condition. The second type of Ying Chi is linked to your Yi (mind, intention). When your Yi decides to do something, for example to lift a box, this type of Ying Chi will automatically flow to the muscles needed to do the job. This type of Chi is directed by your thoughts, and therefore is related closely to your feelings and emotions.

The second major category of Chi is "Wey Chi" (Guardian Chi). Wey Chi forms a shield on the surface of the body to protect you from negative outside influences. Wey Chi is also involved in the growth of hair, the repair of skin injuries, and many other functions on the surface of the skin. Wey Chi comes from the Chi channels, and is led through the millions of tiny channels to the surface of the skin. This Chi can even reach beyond the body. When your body is positive (Yang), this Chi is strong, and your pores will be open. When your body is negative (Yin), this Chi is weak, and your pores will close up more to prevent Chi from being lost.

In the summertime, your body is Yang and your Chi is strong, so your Chi shield will be bigger and extend beyond your physical body, and the pores will be wide open. In the wintertime, your body is relatively Yin (negative), and you must conserve your Chi in order to stay warm and keep pathogens out. The Chi shield is smaller and doesn't extend out much beyond your skin.

Wey Chi functions automatically in response to changes in the environment, but it is also influenced significantly by your feelings and emotions. For example, when you feel happy or angry, the Chi shield will be more open than when you are sad.

In order to keep your body healthy and functioning properly, you must keep the Ying Chi functioning smoothly and, at the same time, keep the Wey Chi strong to protect you from negative outside influences such as the cold. Chinese doctors and Chi Kung practitioners believe that the key to doing this is through Shen (spirit). Shen is considered to be the headquarters which directs and controls the Chi. Therefore, when you practice Chi Kung you must understand what your Shen is and know how to raise it. When people are ill and facing death, very often the ones with a strong Shen, which is indicative of a strong will to live, will survive. The people who are apathetic or depressed will generally not last long. A strong will to live raises the Shen, which energizes the body's Chi and keeps you alive and healthy.

In order to raise your Shen, you must first nourish your brain with Chi. This Chi energizes the brain so that you can concentrate more effectively. Your mind will then be steady, your will strong, and your Shen raised. Shen will be more thoroughly discussed in a later section.

There is another way to categorize the body's Chi: Fire Chi and Water Chi. As we discussed previously, the Chi generated from the food and air you take in warms the body, and so it is called Fire Chi. This Chi is associated with the emotions. The second type of Chi is called Water Chi. It is also called Original Chi because it is generated from Original Jieng. It has its root in the kidneys, and it has a cooling effect on the body. It is associated with Yi and wisdom. As a Chi Kung practitioner you want Water Chi and Fire Chi to be balanced, so that your body and mind are centered and balanced. It is also said that your Yi should be in the center of your emotions. This way wisdom rules and the emotions are controlled, not suppressed.

As a Chi Kung practitioner, in addition to paying attention to the food and air you take in, it is important for you to learn how to generate Water Chi and how to use it more effectively. Water Chi can cool down the Fire Chi and, therefore, slow down the degeneration of the body. Water Chi also helps to calm your mind and keep it centered. This allows you to judge things objectively. During Chi Kung practice, you will be able to sense your Chi and direct it effectively.

In order to generate Water Chi and use it efficiently, you must know how and where it is generated. Since Water Chi comes from the conversion of Original Jieng, they both have the kidneys for their root. Once Water Chi is generated, it resides in the Lower Dan Tien below your navel. In order to conserve your Water Chi, you must keep your kidneys firm and strong.

Shen:

It is very difficult to find an English word to exactly express Shen. As in so many other cases, the context determines the translation. Shen can be translated as spirit, god, immortal, soul, mind, divine, and supernatural.

When you are alive, Shen is the spirit which is directed by your mind. When your mind is not steady it is said "Hsin Shen Buh Ning," which means "the (emotional) mind and spirit are not peaceful." The average person can use his emotional mind to energize and stimulate his Shen to a higher state, but at the same time he must restrain his emotional mind with his wisdom mind (Yi). If his Yi can control the Hsin, the mind as a whole will be concentrated and the Yi will be able to govern the Shen. When someone's Shen is excited, however, it is not being controlled by his Yi, so we say, "Shen Jyh Buh Ching," which means "the spirit and the will (generated from Yi) are not clear." In Chi Kung it is very important for you to train your wisdom Yi to control your emotional Hsin effectively. In order to reach this goal, Buddhists and Taoists train themselves to be free of emotions. Only in this way are they able to build a strong Shen which is completely under their control.

When you are healthy you are able to use your Yi to protect your Shen and keep it at its residence: the Upper Dan Tien. Even when your Shen is energized, it is still controlled. However, when you are very sick or near death, your Yi becomes weak and your Shen will leave its residence and wander around. When you are dead, your Shen separates completely from the physical body. It is then called a "Hwen" or "soul." Often the term "Shen Hwen" is used, since the Hwen originated with the Shen. Sometimes "Shen Hwen" is also used to refer to the spirit of a dying person since his spirit is between "Shen" and "Hwen."

Chinese believe that when your Shen reaches a higher and stronger state, you are able to sense and feel more sharply, and your mind is more clever and inspired. The world of living human beings is usually considered a Yang world, and the spiritual world after death is considered a Yin world. It is believed that when your Shen has reached this higher, sensitive state you can transcend your mind's normal capacity. Ideas beyond your usual grasp can be understood and controlled, and you may develop the ability to sense or even communicate with the Yin world. This supernatural Shen is called "Ling." "Ling" is commonly used by the Chinese to describe someone who is sharp, clever, nimble, and able to quickly empathize with people and things. It is believed that when you die this supernatural Shen will not die with your body right away. It is this supernatural Shen (Ling) which still holds your energy together as a "ghost" or "Goe." Therefore, a ghost is also called "Ling Goe" meaning "spiritual ghost" or "Ling Hwen" meaning "spiritual soul."

You can see from the above discussion that Ling is the supernatural part of the spirit. It is believed that if this supernatural spiritual soul is strong enough, it will live for a long time after the physical body is dead and have plenty of opportunity to reincarnate. Chinese people believe that if a person has reached the stage of enlightenment or Buddhahood when he is alive, after he dies this supernatural spirit will leave the cycle of reincarnation and live forever. These spirits are called "Shen Ming," which means "spiritually enlightened beings," or simply "Shen," which here implies that this spirit has become divine. Normally, if you die and your supernatural spiritual soul is not strong, your spirit has only a short time to search for a new residence in which to be reborn before its energy disperses. In this case, the spirit is called "Goe," which means "ghost."

Buddhists and Taoists believe that when you are alive you may use your Jieng and Chi to nourish the Shen (Yeang Shen) and make your Ling strong. When this "Ling Shen" is built up to a high level, your will is able to lead it to separate from the physical body even while you are alive. When you have reached this stage, your physical body is able to live for many hundreds of years. People who can do this are called "Shian," which means "god," "immortal," or "fairy." Since "Shian" originated with the Shen, the "Shian" is sometimes called "Shen Shian," which means "immortal spirit." The "Shian" is a living person whose Shen has reached the stage of enlightenment or Buddhahood. After his death, his spirit will be called "Shen Ming."

The foundation of Buddhist and Taoist Chi Kung training is to firm your Shen, nourish it, and grow it until it is mature enough to separate from your physical body. In order to do this, Chi Kung practitioner must know where the Shen resides, and how to keep, protect, nourish, and train it. It is also essential for you to know the root or origin of your Shen.

Your Shen resides in the Upper Dan Tien (forehead), in the place often known as the third eye. When you concentrate on the Upper Dan Tien, the Shen can be firmed. Firm here means to keep and to protect. When someone's mind is scattered and confused, his Shen wanders. This is called "Shen Buh Shoou Sheh," which means "the spirit is not kept at its residence."

According to Chi Kung theory, though your Hsin (emotional mind) is able to raise up your spirit, this mind can also make your Shen confused, so that it leaves its residence. You must use your Yi (wisdom mind) constantly to restrain and control your Shen at the residence.

In Chi Kung, when your Chi can reach and nourish your Shen efficiently, your Shen will be energized to a higher level and, in turn, conduct the Chi in its circulation. Shen is the force which keeps you alive, and it is also the control tower for the Chi. When your Shen is strong, your Chi is strong and you can lead it efficiently. When your Shen is weak, your Chi is weak and the body will degenerate rapidly. Likewise, Chi supports the Shen, energizing them and keeping them sharp, clear, and strong. If the Chi in your body is weak, your Shen will also be weak.

Once you know the residence of your Shen, you must understand the root of your Shen, and learn how to nourish it and make it grow. We have already discussed Original Essence (Yuan Jieng), which is the essential life inherited from your parents. After your birth, this Original Essence is your most important energy source. Your Original Chi (Yuan Chi) is created from this Original Essence, and it mixes with the Chi generated from the food you eat and the air you breathe to supply the energy for your growth and activity. Naturally, this mixed Chi is nourishing your Shen as well. While the Fire Chi will energize your Shen, Water Chi will strengthen the wisdom mind to control the energized Shen. The Shen which is kept in its residence by the Yi, which is nourished by the Original Chi, is called Original Shen (Yuan Shen). Therefore, the root of your Original Shen is traced back to your Original Essence. When your Shen is energized but restrained by your Yi it is called "Jieng Shen," literally "Essence Shen," which is commonly translated "spirit of vitality."

Original Shen is thought of as the center of your being. It is able to make you calm, clear your mind, and firm your will. When you concentrate your mind on doing something, it is called "Jiuh Jieng Huey Shen," which means "gathering your Jieng to meet your Shen." This implies that when you concentrate, you must use your Original Essence to meet and lift up your Original Shen, so that your mind will be calm, steady, and concentrated. Since this Shen is nourished by your Original Chi, which is considered Water Chi, Original Shen is considered Water Shen.

For those who have reached a higher level of Chi Kung practice, cultivating the Shen becomes the most important subject. For Buddhists and Taoists the final goal of cultivating the Shen is to form or generate a Holy Embryo (Shian Tai) from their Shen, and nourish it until the spiritual baby is born and can be independent. For the average Chi Kung practitioner however, the final goal of cultivating Shen is to raise up the Shen through Chi nourishment while maintaining control with the Yi. This raised-up Shen can direct and govern the Chi efficiently to achieve health and longevity.

In conclusion, we would like to point out that your Shen and brain cannot be separated. Shen is the spiritual part of your being and is generated and controlled by your mind. The mind generates the will, which keeps the Shen firm. The Chinese commonly use Shen (spirit) and Jyh (will) together as "Shen Jyh" because they are so related. In addition, you should understand that when your Shen is raised and firm, this raised spirit will firm your will. They are mutually related, and assist each other. From this you can see that the material foundation of the spirit is your brain. When it is said "nourish your Shen," it means "nourish your brain." As we discussed previously, the original nourishing source is your Jieng.

This Jieng is then converted into Chi, which is led to the brain to nourish and energize it. In Chi Kung practice, this process is called "Faan Jieng Buu Nao," which means "to return the Jieng to nourish the brain."

3-2. Yi and Hsin

Chinese people will frequently use both "Yi" and "Hsin" at different times to mean "mind," often confusing people who are not familiar with the Chinese language. Before advancing any further, you should first be sure that you have a clear understanding of the subtle differences between these two words.

Yi is the mind which is related to wisdom and judgement. When Yi has an idea, it strives to bring it to actualization in the physical world as either an event you will seek to bring about, or as an object you will create. The Yi is focused and firmed by the will.

Chinese people also use the word "Hsin" to mean "mind," although the word literally means "heart." While Hsin also denotes the presence of an idea, this idea is much weaker than that expressed in Yi. Hsin is generated from and affected by the emotions. This mind is passive instead of active like the Yi. When someone says he has Yi to do something, this means he intends to do it. If he says he has Hsin to do it, this means his emotions intend to do it, he has within him the desire to do it, but he may lack the strength of resolve to actually commit himself. For example, your wisdom mind (Yi) knows you must do something before a certain deadline, but your emotional mind (Hsin) tries to convince you that it is not a big deal, and you needn't worry too much about it. In most people, the emotional mind is stronger than the wisdom mind. They act according to how they feel, instead of what they think. We've all heard the comment at one time or another: "You're your own worst enemy." Your emotional mind is your wisdom mind's enemy. The emotional mind is the source of laziness, bad temper, emotional upset, and so on. If your wisdom mind is able to dominate your emotional mind, you will surely be a success in whatever you attempt.

Sometimes people will put both words together and say "Hsin Yi" to denote the mind which is generated from both emotion and thought. Since most of the thought was generated and given its primal nature by the emotions first, before being refined by the will, the word Hsin is placed before Yi. This is a good example of how Hsin is used to denote the emotional mind, and Yi is used for the mind of wisdom, intention, and will. In meditation society it is said: "Yii Hsin Huey Yi," which means "modulate the Hsin (emotional mind) to match the Yi (wisdom mind)." This means that the emotional aspect and the wisdom aspect of your mind must work together in harmony during meditation. Only then will you be able to use your Yi to regulate your body, for it is also said: "Yii Yi Huey Shenn" which means "use your Yi to meet the body."

Hsin and Shen are commonly used together as "Hsin Shen." This refers to the emotional mind which affects or is affected by Shen. When a person is absent-minded or confused, people say "Hsin Shen Buh Ning," which means "mind and spirit are not stable." Spirit is also related to Yi, or the wisdom mind. However, the Yi aspect of the mind is still the strongest, being generated from thought and will. This mind can firm the scattered emotional mind and the spirit, thereby raising up the spirit. When the spirit is raised and firmed, the emotional mind (Hsin) will be steady. "Yi" is commonly used together with will--"Yi Jyh." This implies that the wisdom mind and the will are working together. The wisdom mind is firmed by the will, and the will firms the wisdom mind.

In Chinese Chi Kung society it is believed that the emotional mind (Hsin) is mainly generated from the Post-birth Chi or Food Chi (Shyr Chi), which is converted from the food Essence, while the wisdom mind (Yi) comes from the Pre-birth Chi (Yuan Chi) which is converted from the Original Essence you inherited from your parents. The Post-birth Chi is considered to be "Fire" Chi, while the Pre-birth Chi is considered "Water" Chi. It is believed that your emotions and temper are closely related to the food you eat. It can be seen that the animals who eat plants are more tame and non-violent than the animals which eat meat. Generally speaking, food which generates excessive Chi in the Middle Dan Tien usually makes the body more positive and makes the person more emotional. This effect can also be caused by dirty air, dirty thoughts, or the surrounding Chi (for example, in the summer when it is too hot). Certain foods and drugs can also directly interfere with clear thinking. For example, alcohol and drugs can stimulate your emotional mind and suppress your wisdom mind. The Chi generated from food is normally classified as Fire Chi, and it can reside in the Middle Dan Tien (solar plexus).

One part of Chi Kung training is learning how to regulate your Fire Chi and Water Chi so that they are balanced. This involves learning to use your wisdom mind to dominate and direct your emotional mind. One of the more common methods of strengthening the Water Chi (and wisdom mind) and weakening the Fire Chi (and emotional mind) is to greatly reduce or eliminate meat from the diet, and live mainly on vegetables. Taoists and Buddhists periodically fast in order to weaken the Fire Chi as much as possible, which allows them to strengthen their Water Chi and wisdom mind. This process of "cleaning" their bodies and minds is important in ridding the monks of emotional disturbance.

3-3. Dan Tien

Dan Tien is translated literally as "Elixir Field." In Chinese Chi Kung society, three spots are considered Dan Tien. The first one is called "Shiah Dan Tien" (Lower Dan Tien). In Chinese medicine it is called Qihai, which means "Chi Ocean." It is located about one to one and a half inches below your navel and about one to two inches deep, depending of course on the individual. In both Chinese medicine and Chi Kung society, the Lower Dan Tien is considered the well-spring of human energy. It is the residence of Original Chi (Yuan Chi), which has been converted from Original Essence (Yuan Jieng).

The human body has twelve Chi channels which are like rivers of Chi. They circulate Chi throughout the body, and connect the organs to the extremities. In addition to these twelve Chi rivers, there are eight "extraordinary Chi vessels." These are like reservoirs of Chi, and they regulate the flow of Chi in the rivers (the twelve channels). In order to be healthy, the Chi reservoirs must be full and the Chi must flow smoothly without stagnation in the rivers (see the detailed explanation of human Chi circulation in Part 3).

Among the eight vessels is the Conception vessel, which is Yin, and the Governing vessel, which is Yang. They are located on the center line of the front and the back of the torso and head, respectively, and run into one another, creating a closed loop about the body (Figure 3-1). The Chi in these two vessels must be full and circulate smoothly in order to regulate all of the Chi in the twelve rivers properly. At any particular time, there is a section of this circle where the Chi flow is stronger than in the other sections. This section is called "Tzyy Wuu Liou Juh," which means "mid-night and noon major flow," and it keeps the Chi flowing in these two vessels. Chi behaves like water. If there is no difference in potential the Chi will stay still and become stagnant, and you are likely to become ill. Normally, this area of stronger Chi moves around the circle of these two vessels once every day.

Chinese Chi Kung practitioners believe that the Chi must be full and circulate strongly in these two vessels, for then the Governing vessel will be able to govern the entire body's Chi effectively. They also believe that as a child you continually move the abdomen while breathing, which keeps the path of these two vessels clear. However, as you get older and gradually lose the habit of this abdominal movement, the path becomes obstructed and the Chi circulation weakens. The most significant blockage can occur in the Huiyin cavity (Figure 3-2). Try an experiment. Use one finger to press firmly at your Huiyin cavity while your abdomen is moving in and out. You will discover that the Huiyin cavity moves up and down in sync with the in and out motion of the abdomen. It is this up and down motion of the perineum which keeps the Huiyin cavity clear for

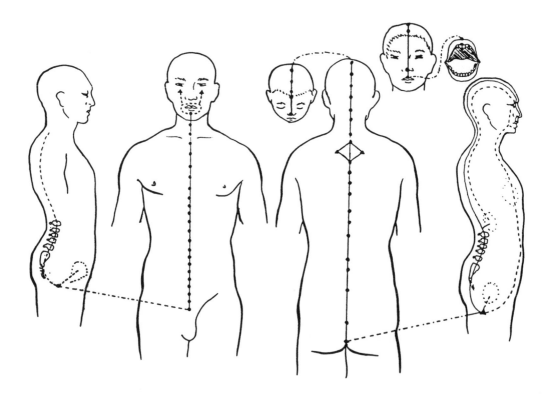

Conception Vessel   Governing Vessel

Figure 3-1. Conception and Governing Vessels

Chi circulation. For this reason, exercises which move the abdomen in and out are called "Faan Torng" (back to childhood) exercises.

Abdominal exercises not only open the Chi channels, they can also draw Original Chi from its residence in the Lower Dan Tien to join the Post-birth Chi in its circulation. Original Chi is considered the original vital source of human energy. Therefore, in and out abdominal exercise is also called "Chii Huoo," which means "start the fire." This hints at the way the Taoists build up Chi energy. The Taoists consider the Dan Tien to be the furnace in which they can purify and distill the elixir (Chi) for longevity.

The second of the three Dan Tiens is called the Middle Dan Tien (Jong Dan Tien), and it is located at the solar plexus. The Middle Dan Tien is considered the center where the Post-birth Chi is produced and gathered. Post-birth Chi is the energy which is converted from the Jieng (essence) of air and food. Post-birth Chi is affected therefore by the type of food you eat and the quality of the air you breathe. The level of your Post-birth Chi is also influenced by such things as whether you are getting enough sleep, whether you are tired, irritable, nervous, sad, and so on.

It is believed in Chinese medical society that the lungs and the heart are the places where the air Jieng is converted into Chi. The stomach and the digestive system are the center where the food Jieng is absorbed and then converted into Chi. This Chi then resides at the Middle Dan Tien, and follows the Conception and Governing vessels to disperse throughout the entire body. The conversion of air and food to Chi is similar to the burning up of wood to give heat. Therefore, the lung area is called the Upper Burner (Shang Jiao), the stomach is called the Middle Burner (Jong Jiao), and the lower abdomen is called the Lower Burner (Shiah Jiao). The three are referred to collectively as the "Triple Burner" (Sanjiao).

You can deduce from the above description that the Upper Burner is the burner which handles air Chi, while the Middle and Lower

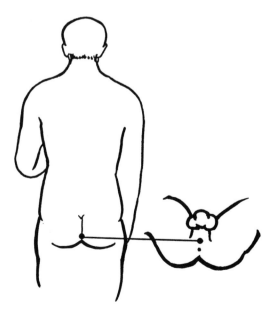

Figure 3-2. Huiyin cavity

Burners handle food Chi. The Lower Burner, in addition to separating the pure from the impure and eliminating waste, also processes the Lower Dan Tien Chi. When someone has eaten too much positive food such as peanuts or sesame seeds, the excess Chi will cause heat. This is called "Shang Huoo," which means simply that the body is "on fire." When you don't get enough sleep, the body can also pass into the "on fire" state. When the Post-birth Chi is too positive, it is called "Huoo Chi," which means "fire Chi."

When the Post-birth Chi is too positive and is directed to the organs, the organs will become positive and degenerate faster. When the Post-birth Chi is too weak, for example because of starvation, there is not enough Chi to supply the organs and the body, and you will gradually become more unbalanced until you become ill. Most people get more than enough food, so their Post-birth Chi is too positive. For this reason, Post-birth Chi is usually called Fire Chi. There is a Chi Kung practice which leads the Water Chi (Pre-birth Chi) at the Lower Dan Tien up to mix with the Fire Chi (Post-birth Chi) at the Middle Dan Tien in order to cool the Fire Chi.

The third Dan Tien is located on the forehead and is called the Upper Dan Tien (Shang Dan Tien). Your brain uses a lot of energy (Chi) for thinking. This Chi is supplied by one of the vessels called Chong Mei (Thrusting Vessel), which flows through the marrow in the spine up to the brain. Your spirit resides in your Upper Dan Tien, and when it is amply supplied with Chi, it is "raised," or energized. If the Chi stopped nourishing your brain and spirit, you would lose your mental center, your judgement would become faulty, and you would become depressed and mentally unbalanced.

You can see from this discussion that all three Dan Tiens are located on the Conception Vessel. The Conception Vessel and the Governing Vessel together form the most important Chi reservoir in the body, and it is important for it to be full.

3-4. Three Flowers Reach the Top (San Huea Jiuh Diing)
Taoists commonly call the three treasures (Jieng, Chi, and Shen) the three flowers. One of the final goals of Taoist Chi Kung training is to gather the three flowers at the top of the head (San Huea Jiuh Diing).

The normal Taoist Chi Kung training process is 1. to convert the Jieng (essence) into Chi (Yii Jieng Huah Chi); 2. to nourish the Shen (spirit) with Chi (Yii Chi Huah Shen); 3. to refine the Shen into emptiness (Liann Shen Huan Shiu); and 4. Crush the Emptiness (Feen Suory Shiu Kong). The first step is to firm and strengthen the Jieng, then convert this Jieng into Chi through meditation or other methods. This Chi is then led to the top of the head to nourish the brain and raise up the Shen. When a Taoist has reached this stage, it is called "the three flowers meet on the top." This stage is necessary to gain health and longevity. Now the Taoist can start training to reach the goal of enlightenment.

3-5. Five Chi's Toward Their Origins (Wuu Chi Chaur Yuan)
According to Chinese medical science, among the twelve main organs are five Yin organs which have a great effect on the health. These five organs are: heart, lungs, liver, kidneys, and spleen. If any internal organ does not have the appropriate level of Chi, it is either too Yang (positive) or too Yin (negative). When this happens, it is like running the wrong level of electric current into a machine. If the condition remains uncorrected, the organs will run less efficiently. This will

affect the body's metabolism, and eventually even damage the organs. Therefore, one of the most important practices in Chi Kung training is learning to keep the Chi in these five organs at the proper level. When the Chi of these organs has reached the appropriate levels it is called "Wuu Chi Chaur Yuan," which means "the five Chi's toward their origins." Your organs can now function optimally, and your health will be maintained at a high level.

There are twelve Chi channels and eight extraordinary Chi vessels. The Chi in the twelve channels should be at the levels appropriate for the corresponding organs. The Chi in these twelve channels changes with the time of day, the seasons, and the year. This Chi is affected by the food you eat, the air you breathe, and your emotions. Therefore, in order to keep your five Chi's at their right levels, you must know how Chi is affected by time, food, and air, and you must learn how to regulate your emotions.

Chapter 4

Chi and the Human Body

In order to understand human Chi Kung, you must understand the nature of the Chi in the human body, and how it functions. This includes understanding what kinds of Chi are in the body, what functions they perform, and how they carry out these functions.

In the first three chapters we have offered a general definition of Chi, discussed how human Chi is included in and affected by Heaven Chi and Earth Chi, and shown how Chi relates to other aspects of our bodies, such as spirit and Essence. In Part Three of this book we will review how Chi circulates in the human body.

In this chapter we will first focus on the general characteristics of Chi in our bodies. This will provide a foundation to help you understand the rest of the chapter. We will then concentrate on a number of subjects which will lead you to a deeper understanding of human Chi, such as Chi's Yin and Yang, and the quality of Chi. Once you understand the traditional concept of Chi, we will discuss the modern concept of bioelectromagnetic energy. Following this, we will offer some hypotheses based upon this energy which Western science has recently discovered. Finally, we will discuss the theory of how Chi gates can be opened through Chi Kung practice.

4-1. About Chi

In this section, we will first discuss the natural characteristics of Chi and the relationship between Chi and the human body. Then we will explain how Chi's Yin and Yang are defined, and how the quality of Chi is determined.

The Nature of Chi:

To understand the nature of Chi, you should first know where Chi originates. Something cannot come from nothing, so Chi (any type of energy) must come from matter, usually through some kind of chemical reaction. Matter is a physical form of energy, and energy is an unlocked potential (or an insubstantial form) of matter. For example, you may burn a piece of wood or gas and obtain Chi in the form of heat and light. Similarly, food and air are taken into your body, and through biochemical reaction are converted into Chi, which is commonly in the form of heat and bioelectromagnetic energy. Whenever you take in more food than your body requires, the unexcreted excess is stored in your body as fat.

Next you should understand that Chi generally manifests as heat, light, electromagnetic force. Strictly speaking, light is an alternative form of electromagnetic wave, so, in effect, there are only two types of energy which we deal with in our daily lives. As a matter of fact, very often light and heat exist at the same time.

Finally, you should recognize that Chi moves from the area of higher potential to the area of lower potential, and this acts to naturally and automatically bring your system into balance.

Chi in the Human Body:

Although, according to the general definition, heat is considered a type of human Chi, heat is not the type of Chi which is circulating in your body. Oftentimes you will feel heat when Chi is circulating strongly, but the heat is not the circulating Chi itself. There is another type of Chi which circulates throughout your body to nourish the cells and keep them functioning, and even to repair damage.

Since electricity has become more familiar to people in China over the last fifty years, many Chi Kung practitioners have come to believe that the Chi which circulates in the body is actually electromagnetic energy. If you run an electric current through a wire, the wire will heat up because of the resistance of the wire. The heat is an effect caused by the current, but it is not the current itself. According to this theory, as Chi circulates through your body, the resistance of your body causes part of the Chi to be converted into heat.

Chi Kung practitioners believe that the light which is sometimes perceived during meditation is also Chi. Light is a form of electromagnetic energy. Since all types of energy are convertible, heat can generate electromagnetic power and vice versa, and light can also generate heat, and vice versa. Once you have reached the higher levels of meditation, you will sense light in your eyes and mind. At an even higher level, your head will generate a glow like a halo. All of these can be considered transformations that the electric Chi undergoes when your training has reached a higher level.

The Behavior of Human Chi:

Chinese doctors and Chi Kung practitioners have traditionally described the behavior of Chi as being similar to water. This is seen in a number of ways. First, just as water flows from higher areas to lower areas, Chi flows from areas of higher potential to areas of lower potential. In this way, Chi balances itself naturally. Second, if muddy water is left undisturbed, the sand will settle to the bottom, leaving the water above it calm and clear. However, if you stir up the water, the sand will rise up and dirty the water again. This is similar to how, when the mind is steady, the Chi will be calm and clear, but when the mind is scattered, the Chi will be disturbed and excited. Third, the Chi channels which supply Chi to the entire body are usually compared to rivers, and the vessels which store the Chi are compared to reservoirs. Water and Chi should both flow smoothly and continuously. When a river or channel is obstructed, the water/Chi flow will be agitated and uneven. In an obstructed channel, the water/Chi flow will be higher, and may overflow the banks.

Chi's Yin and Yang:

When it is said that Chi can be either Yin or Yang, it does not mean that there are two different kinds of Chi like male and female, fire and water, or positive and negative charges. Chi is energy, and energy itself does not have Yin and Yang. It is like the energy which is generated from the sparking of negative and positive charges. Charges have the potential of generating energy but are not the energy itself.

When it is said that Chi is Yin or Yang, it means that the Chi is too strong or too weak for a particular circumstance. It is relative and not absolute. Naturally, this implies that the potential which generates the Chi is strong or weak. For example, the Chi from the sun is Yang Chi and Chi from the moon is Yin Chi. This is because the sun's energy is Yang in comparison to Human Chi, while to moon's is Yin. In any discussion of energy where people are involved, Human Chi is used as the standard. People are always especially interested in what concerns them directly, so it is natural that we are interested primarily in Human Chi and tend to view all Chi from the perspective of human Chi. This is not unlike looking at the universe from the perspective of the Earth.

When we look at the Yin and Yang of Chi within and in regard to the human body, however, we must redefine our point of reference. For example, when a person is dead, his residual Human Chi (Goe Chi or ghost Chi) is weak compared to a living person's. Therefore, the ghost's Chi is Yin while the living person's is Yang. When discussing Chi within the body, in the Lung channel for example, the reference point is the normal, healthy status of the Chi there. If the Chi is stronger than it is in the normal state, it is Yang, and, naturally, if it is weaker than this, it is Yin. There are twelve parts of the human body that are considered organs in Chinese medicine, six of them are Yin and six are Yang. The Yin organs are the Heart, Lungs, Kidneys, Liver, Spleen, and Pericardium, and the Yang organs are Large Intestine, Small Intestine, Stomach, Gall Bladder, Urinary Bladder, and Triple Burner. Generally speaking, the Chi level of the Yin organs is lower than that of the Yang organs. The Yin organs store Original Essence and process the Essence obtained from food and air, while the Yang organs handle the digestion and excretion. We will discuss this subject in more detail in the Part 3 of this book.

When the Chi in any of your organs is not in its normal state, you feel uncomfortable. If it is very much off from the normal state, the organ will start to malfunction, and you may become sick. When this happens, the Chi in your entire body will also be affected and you will feel too Yang, perhaps feverish, or too Yin, such as the weakness after diarrhea.

Your body's Chi level is also affected by natural circumstances such as the weather, climate, and seasonal changes. Therefore, when the body's Chi level is classified, the reference point is the level which feels most comfortable for those particular circumstances. Naturally, each of us is a little bit different, and what feels best and most natural for one person may be a bit different from what is right for another person. That is why the doctor will usually ask "how do you feel?" It is according to your own standard that you are judged.

Breath is closely related to the state of your Chi, and therefore also considered Yin or Yang. When you exhale you expel air from your Lungs, your mind moves outward, and the Chi around the body expands. In the Chinese martial arts, the exhale is generally used to expand the Chi to energize the muscles during an attack. Therefore, you can see that the exhale is Yang--it is expanding, offensive, and strong. Naturally, based on the same theory, the inhale is considered Yin.

Your breathing is closely related to your emotions. When you lose your temper, your breathing is short and fast, i.e. Yang. When you are sad, your body is more Yin, and you inhale more than you exhale in order to absorb the Chi from the air to balance the body's Yin to bring the body back into balance. When you are excited and happy, your body is Yang. Your exhale is longer than your inhale in order to get rid of the excess Yang which is caused by the excitement.

As mentioned before, your mind is also closely related to your Chi. Therefore, when your Chi is Yang, your mind is usually also Yang (excited) and vice versa. In addition, as we discussed in the previous section, the mind can also be classified according to the Chi which generates it. The mind (Yi) which is generated from the calm and peaceful Chi obtained from Original Essence is considered Yin. The mind (Hsin) which originates with the food and air Essence is emotional, scattered, and excited, and it is considered Yang. Finally, the Shen, which is related to the Chi, can also be classified as Yang or Yin based on its origin.

Do not confuse Yin Chi and Yang Chi with Fire Chi and Water Chi. When the Yin and Yang of Chi are mentioned, it refers to the level of Chi according to some reference point. However, when Water and Fire Chi are mentioned, it refers to the quality of the Chi. This will be discussed in the next section.

The Quality of Human Chi:
Some people think that Chi is of good quality when it is neither too Yin nor too Yang. However, they are wrong. When Chi is neither too Yin nor too Yang, this means that the **level** of the Chi is right. It is a quantitative statement rather than a qualitative one. The quality of Chi refers to its purity, as well as its contents. This quality depends on where and how the Chi originated. Usually, the quality of the Chi determines how it behaves and how it affects the body's Yin and Yang when it is circulating in your body.

Within the human body, Chi Kung practitioners have generally categorized Chi into "Fire Chi" and "Water Chi" to express the qualitative purity of the Chi. The terms "Fire" and "Water" indicate the effects that the Chi has on our body. For example, when Chi that is impure or of poor quality circulates in the human body, it may cause heat in the body and organs, and make the body too Yang. It is therefore called "Fire Chi." If, however, the Chi is pure, clean, and circulating smoothly, it will enable the body to remain calm, keep the mind clear and steady, and allow the body to function properly. This Chi is called "Water Chi" because it is the Chi which enables the body to remain calm and cool, like water.

In the thousands of years that Chi Kung has been studied, practitioners have found that the Chi which comes from "Original Jieng" (and is therefore called Original Chi) is "Water Chi." It is pure and smooth, like sunshine in the winter, like crystal-pure water flowing smoothly in a stream, very comfortable and natural. This Chi makes it possible for the wisdom mind (Yi) to remain calm and grow stronger. When this Chi is circulating in the human body, it is smooth and will keep the physical body functioning in a steady, calm, and Yin state.

Conversely, the Chi which comes from food and air is not of as high a quality as Original Chi. Because the body cannot discriminate between good and bad raw materials, many undesirable ingredients in the food and air are also converted into Chi. The quality of this Chi is dirty, and nonuniform, like water which has been polluted. When this Chi goes to your brain, it can excite your emotions and upset your emotional balance. When this Chi is circulating in your body, the undesirable ingredients can change the body into Yang and cause problems. For example, the Chi which was converted from fat can convert back into fat, and plug up the Chi paths. Plugged up Chi channels can have undesirable effects, such as high blood pressure, which speeds up the degeneration of the internal organs. For this the reason, diet is a part of Chi Kung practice. Generally speaking, the Chi generated from food which comes from animal sources has more contaminants than the Chi generated from food obtained from plants.

You can see from this discussion that it is very important to distinguish both the level of Chi and its quality. The level of Chi (Yin or Yang) depends on the circumstances, and must have a reference point. The quality of Chi depends upon the Essence from which it comes.

4-2. Chi and Bio-Electromagnetic Energy

In ancient China, people had very little knowledge of electricity. They only knew from acupuncture that when a needle was inserted into the acupuncture cavities, some kind of energy other than heat was produced which often caused a shock or a tickling sensation. It was not until the last few decades, when the Chinese people were more acquainted with electromagnetic science, that they began to recognize that this energy circulating in the body, which they called Chi, might be the same thing as what today's science calls "bioelectricity."

It is understood now that the human body is constructed of many different electrically conductive materials, and it forms a living electromagnetic field and circuit. Electromagnetic energy is continuously being generated in the human body through the biochemical reaction of food and air, and circulated by the electromagnetic forces (EMF) generated within the body by, for example, thinking or movement.

In addition, you are also constantly being affected by external electromagnetic fields such as that of the earth, or the electrical fields generated by clouds. When you practice Chinese medicine or Chi Kung, you need to be aware of these outside factors and take them into account.

Countless experiments have been conducted in China, Japan, and other countries to study how external magnetic or electrical fields can affect and adjust the body's Chi field. Many acupuncturists use magnets and electricity in their treatments. They attach a magnet to the skin over a cavity and leave it there for a period of time. The magnetic field gradually affects the Chi circulation in that channel. Alternatively, they insert needles into cavities and then run an electric current through the needle to reach the Chi channels directly. Although many experimenters have claimed a degree of success in their experiments, none has been able to publish any detailed and convincing proof of his results, or give a good explanation of the theory behind his experiment. As with many other attempts to explain the How and Why of acupuncture, conclusive proof is elusive, and many unanswered questions remain. Of course, this theory is quite new, and it will probably take a lot more study and research before it is verified and completely understood. At present, there are many conservative acupuncturists who are skeptical.

To untie this knot, we must look at what modern Western science has discovered about bioelectromagnetic energy. Many bioelectric related reports have been published, and frequently the results are closely related to what is experienced in Chinese Chi Kung training and medical science. For example, during the electrophysiological research of the 1960's, several investigators discovered that bones are piezoelectric; that is, when they are stressed, mechanical energy is converted to electrical energy in the form of electric current (*1). This might explain one of the practices of Marrow Washing Chi Kung in which the stress on the bones and muscles is increased in certain ways to increase the Chi circulation (electric circulation).

Dr. Robert O. Becker has done important work in this field. His book "The Body Electric"(*2) reports on much of the research concerning the body's electric field. It is presently believed that food and air are the fuel which generates the electricity in the body through biochemical reaction. This electricity, which is circulated throughout the entire body through electrically conductive tissue, is one of the main energy sources which keep the cells of the physical body alive.

Whenever you have an injury or are sick, your body's electrical circulation is affected. If this circulation of electricity stops, you die. But bioelectric energy not only maintains life, it is also responsible for repairing physical damage. Many researchers have sought ways of using external electrical or magnetic fields to speed up the body's recovery from physical injury. Richard Leviton reports that "Researchers at Loma Linda University's School of Medicine in California have found, following studies in sixteen countries with over 1,000 patients, that low-frequency, low intensity magnetic energy has been successful in treating chronic pain related to tissue ischemia, and also worked in clearing up slow-healing ulcers, and in 90 percent of patients tested, raised blood flow significantly."(*3)

Mr. Leviton also reports that every cell of the body functions like an electric battery and is able to store electric charges. He reports that: "Other biomagnetic investigators take an even closer look to find out what is happening, right down to the level of the blood, the organs, and the individual cell, which they regard as 'a small electric battery'."(*3) This has convinced me that our entire body is just like a big battery which is assembled from millions of small batteries. All of these batteries together form the human electromagnetic field.

Furthermore, much of the research on the body's electrical field relates to acupuncture. For example, Dr. Becker reports that the conductivity of the skin is much higher at acupuncture cavities, and that it is now possible to locate them precisely by measuring the skin's conductivity. Many of these reports prove that the acupuncture which has been done in China for thousands of years is reasonable and scientific.

(*1)."Life's Invisible Current" by Albert L. Huebner, East West Journal, June 1986.
(*2)."The Body Electric" by Robert O. Becker, M.D. and Gary Selden, Quill, William Morrow, New York, 1985.
(*3)."Healing with Nature's Energy" by Richard Leviton, East West Journal, June 1986.

Some researchers use the theory of the body's electricity to explain many of the ancient "miracles" which have been attributed to the practice of Chi Kung. A report by Albert L. Huebner states: "These demonstrations of body electricity in human beings may also offer a new explanation of an ancient healing practice. If weak external fields can produce powerful physiological effects, it may be that fields from human tissues in one person are capable of producing clinical improvements in another. In short, the method of healing known as the laying on of hands could be an especially subtle form of electrical stimulation."(*1)

Another frequently reported phenomenon is that when a Chi Kung practitioner has reached a high level of development, a halo would appear behind and/or around his head during meditation. This is commonly seen in painting of Jesus Christ, the Buddha, and other Oriental gods. Frequently the light is pictured as surrounding the whole body. This phenomenon may again be explained by body electric theory. When a person has cultivated his Chi (electricity) to a high level, the Chi may be led to accumulate in the head. This Chi may then interact with the oxygen molecules in the air, and ionize them, causing them to glow.

Although the link between the theory of the body electric and the Chinese theory of Chi is becoming more accepted and better proven, there are still many questions still to be answered. For example, how can the mind lead Chi (electricity)? How actually does the mind generate an EMF (electromagnetic force) to circulate the electricity in the body? How is the human electromagnetic field affected by the multitude of other electric fields which surround us, such as radio and television waves, or the fields generated by household electrical wiring or electrical appliances? How can we readjust our electromagnetic fields and survive in outer space or on other planets where the magnetic field is completely different from earth's? You can see that the future of Chi Kung and bioelectric science is a challenging and exciting one. It is about time that we started to use the modern technologies to understand the inner energy world which has been ignored by Western society.

4-3. Some Hypotheses

There are a number of questions which have puzzled Chi Kung practitioners and acupuncturists for many years. If Chi is the same thing as what is now being called bioelectricity, which Western medical science is just discovering, then certain deductions or hypotheses can be made which might offer convincing explanations for many of these puzzles. In this section I will try to link together these aspects of Eastern and Western sciences, based on my understanding. In this section, I would like to raise up some questions and draw some hypotheses concerning, as an example, how a human body may react to and be influenced by external electromagnetic fields such as that of the Earth. I hope this section will stimulate your thinking and help the more conservative Chi Kung practitioners to accept this new science and participate in future analysis and discussion.

1. The Electromagnetic Field in the Human Body:

A. How Is the Human Electromagnetic Field Formed?

Since we and all other living things are formed and live in the Earth's magnetic field, our bodies also have a magnetic field of their own. The magnetic field of our body always corresponds with and is affected by the Earth's field. Modern science has shown that magnetic fields and electrical fields cannot be separated, and indeed are aspects of the same force. Where there is one, there is also the other. This type of field is commonly called an electromagnetic field.

When a piece of steel is placed inside a magnetic field, it becomes a magnet (Figure 4-1). Since our bodies are made up of conductive material, and we are in the magnetic field of the Earth, it is reasonable to assume that our bodies are like magnets. Since a magnet has two poles which must be located on the centerline of the magnet, we can easily guess that the poles of our bodies must be somewhere on the head and the bottom of the abdomen. Thus, our first task is to locate the poles of the human magnet.

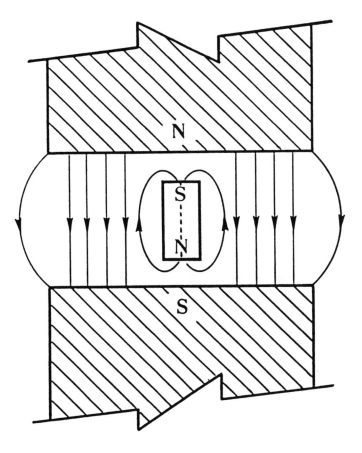

Figure 4-1. A piece of steel becomes a magnet when placed in a magnetic field

Before we continue, let us review some of the concepts concerning the Earth's magnetic field. You need to understand the difference between four terms which are often confused: 1. The north and south poles of a magnet; 2. The North and the South Magnetic Poles of the Earth; 3. The geographic North and the South Poles of the Earth; and 4. The actual north and south poles of the Earth-magnet.

Everybody knows that there is a magnetic field in the Earth. If we place a bar magnet in the Earth's magnetic field, the magnet will align itself with the Earth's field. The "north" pole of this bar magnet is the 'north-seeking pole,' which points toward North of the Earth's magnetic field, which is called the "North Pole" (Figure 4-2). Naturally, the pole which points to the South is defined as the "south pole." Therefore, the poles on a magnet are defined according to the directions in which they point **within** the Earth's magnetic field.

Furthermore, we have defined the pole of the Earth toward which a magnet's north pole points as the Earth's "Magnetic North Pole" while the other end is the Earth's "Magnetic South Pole." Essentially, this means that, for ease of navigation and through convention, the Earth's Magnetic North Pole is for all intents and purposes considered to lie in

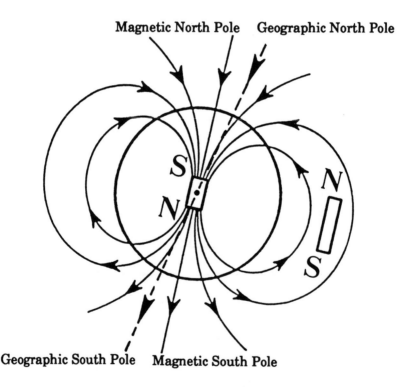

Figure 4-2. The Earth's magnetic field

the same direction as the Earth's Geographic North Pole. (In fact, however, the geographic poles do not actually coincide with the magnetic poles.) (Figure 4-2).

We still do not know how the Earth's magnetic field was formed. The most acceptable explanation is that there is a circulating current deep within the Earth, or in the upper atmosphere, or both. We also do not know exactly how the magnetic poles came to be so close to the geographic poles.

We know that the Earth's magnetic field has started at the geographic South Pole and ended at the geographic North Pole for at least the last million years (although evidence suggests that during the last several million years the magnetic poles of the Earth have reversed several times)(*4 and 5). This conflicts with how we understand the magnetic field of a bar magnet to be, because the lines of force outside the magnet start at the north pole and end at the south pole, and the lines of force inside the magnet go from the south pole to the north pole (Figure 4-3). Therefore, what we usually call the Earth's North Magnetic Pole is actually the south pole of the Earth's magnetic field. In other words, the actual magnetic poles of the earth are the reverse of how they are shown on navigation maps (Figure 4-2).

Once you have assimilated these concepts, consider your body's magnetic field. Since your body's magnetic field is formed under the influence of the Earth's magnetic field, the north and south poles of your body will be determined by whether you are in the Northern or Southern Hemisphere. For example, if you are standing in the

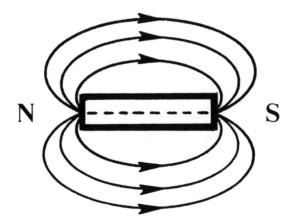

Figure 4-3. Magnetic field of a magnet

(*4)."What Flips Earth's Field," by Arthur Fisher, Popular Science, January 1988.
(*5)."College Physics," by Franklin Miller, Jr., Harcourt Brace Jovanovich, Inc., 1972.

Northern Hemisphere, for example in the United States, then the lines of force of the Earth's magnetic field will enter your body through your head and emerge out from the bottom of your body. Naturally, if you are in the Southern Hemisphere, say in Brazil, then the lines of force of the Earth's magnetic field will enter the bottom of your body and exit from your head (Figure 4-4). This means that if you are in the Northern Hemisphere your head will be a south pole while your abdomen will be a north pole. Naturally, the situation will be reversed if you are in the Southern Hemisphere.

When you are lying down or on the equator, the poles are on the side of your body, and they change every time you move. This probably means that under these circumstances the Earth's magnetic field has only minimal effect on your body.

Now let us discuss how this is related to Chi Kung. Assuming that you are in the Northern Hemisphere, your head should be a south pole while your abdomen is a north pole (Figure 4-5). Excluding all other factors such as location, weather, etc, the strength of your magnetic field depends on the natural qualities of your body. This may be what the Chinese mean by "Original Essence." It is analogous to the fact

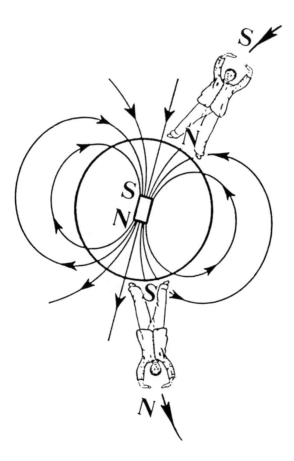

Figure 4-4. Human magnets in the Northern Hemisphere and the Southern Hemisphere

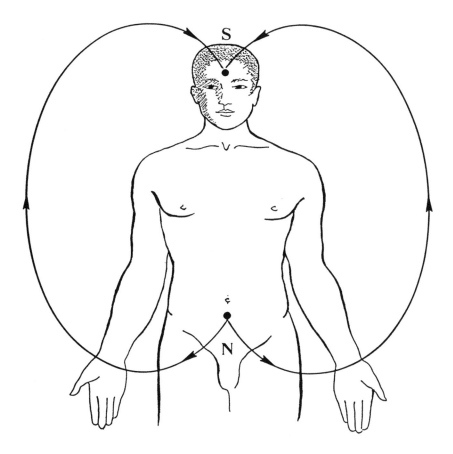

Figure 4-5. A human magnet in the Northern Hemisphere

that when you place high quality refined steel in a magnetic field, the magnet formed will have a stronger magnetic field than if you had used poorly refined steel. Since this magnet is stronger, the magnetic energy will last longer. Similarly, if you received high quality Original Essence from your parents, your body's magnetic field will be strong, and the Chi or electrical energy circulating in your body will be strong and smooth. This means that your vitality will be great, and you will probably have a long and healthy life.

If this line of reasoning is valid, then we are able to explain something which has been confusing Chi Kung meditators. According to past experience (mostly from meditators in the Northern Hemisphere), when a person meditates facing south he is be able to obtain a stronger Chi flow and is able to balance his Chi more quickly than if he were facing another direction. Facing south lines up the incoming energy with the "Small Circulation" of energy down the center of the front of the body and up the spine. Since the front of the body is Yin, it absorbs energy more easily than the back or sides. Another possible explanation is related to the fact that we tend to turn and look at people who are talking to us as if this let us hear them better. Since your mind has a considerable influence on your body's energy, facing into the incoming energy may also help you to absorb and "digest" it. We can also explain why many Chi Kung practitioners claim that if they sleep with their head pointing north they sleep better, and feel more rested and balanced the next morning. (However, if you sleep sitting up, you should again face south.) These two claims become reasonable and understandable if we accept the concept of a bipolar human magnetic field.

Next we must consider other phenomena which have the power to influence the Earth's and human magnetic fields. It is believed that there is a type of sudden and short-lived change in the Earth's magnetic field. These "magnetic storms" are correlated with sunspot outbreaks or moving clouds and are a result of temporary currents of ions in the upper atmosphere.

It is clear that the energy patterns in the human body are affected by natural forces. It is also clear that the energy from the sun has a more significant affect than the energy from the earth. This leads me to believe that when you are meditating during the day you should face the East simply because the influence of the sun's energy is more significant than that of the Earth's magnetic field. During the night, when the influence of the sun has waned, it is probably best to face south if you are in the Northern Hemisphere.

Within the human magnet, we may again assume that there are millions of smaller magnets which correspond to the cells. (Figure 4-6). Just as every cell has its own minute electrical field, so too does each cell have its own magnetic field. Indeed, the two are merely different aspects of the same force. When all of these small magnetic fields are combined together, they form a complete human magnetic field. All of these magnetic fields remain steady as long as there is no other energy source to disturb them. However, whenever any extra energy is generated either inside or outside of this field, the field will no longer be steady, and an electrical current will be generated. Each time this happens, the body's field must rebalance itself, and a new pattern of energy must be formed.

This means that if there is no energy source for the human magnet, the magnetic field will not be disturbed and naturally there will be no energy circulating in this field. In this case the body is dead. However, when you are alive, food and air Essence generates energy inside your magnetic field through biochemical reaction. This energy builds up in your solar plexus, and then circulates throughout your body by way of the Chi channels, which are highly conductive paths through the facial tissue. As the energy circulates in your body, it is important that every part, especially the organs, receives the right amount in order to function properly.

Let us take an even closer look. According to Chinese medical science, the electricity (Chi) circulates throughout your body from one channel to the next in a specific order. One end of each channel is therefore positive, and the other end negative. If an acupuncturist wishes to use a magnet to correct the Chi level of a channel, he must know how the magnetic field will influence the internal Chi circulation. He must know how Chi circulates and and in what direction it circulates. He must also know how to orient the poles of the magnet. Wrong orientation will only worsen the situation. According to reports I have read about the use of magnets in acupuncture, sometimes it works and sometimes it doesn't. Possibly the failures are due to the acupuncturist's not taking orientation of the magnets into account.

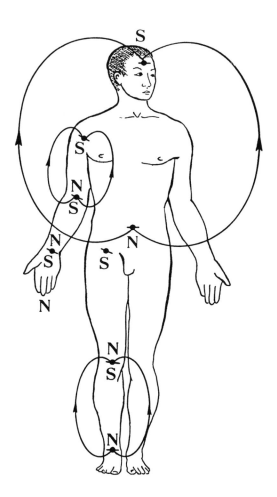

Figure 4-6. Human magnets in the Northern Hemisphere

B. Time and the Human Magnetic Field

Since we are part of the Earth's electromagnetic field, our own fields are affected by variations in the Earth's energy field. These variations can be caused by such sources as the moon, the sun, or even the stars. The most obvious cycle that we are exposed to is that of the day. Every twenty-four hours our bodies should go through a cycle as the earth rotates once and goes through a cycle of light and day. The rotation of the Earth is in turn affected by the sun's energy. It has been proposed that there is another cycle generated by the moon's influence on the Earth's energy pattern which repeats every twenty-eight days. Since the sun moves higher and lower above the southern horizon throughout the year, our bodies also go through a yearly cycle as well. The Chinese believe that the Earth and human beings go through other cycles every twelve and sixty years because of the influence of the stars. If you wish to study the human electromagnetic field, you must also take all of these cycles into your consideration.

C. A Human Magnetic Model

Based on the above information, I would like to offer a magnetic model for a human being in the Northern Hemisphere on Earth. In Chi Kung society it is common knowledge that there are three energy storage areas from which energy can be taken and used without limit. These three places are called Dan Tien, or the Fields of Elixir. The Lower Dan Tien is thought of as the furnace of Original Chi. Let us consider it the north pole of the human magnetic field since the energy originates there. Let us consider the Upper Dan Tien (the third eye) to be the south pole because it receives energy (Figure 4-5). Science tells us that the lines of force in a magnetic field start from the north pole and end up at the south pole. In Chi Kung practice, the Chi originates at the Lower Dan Tien and ends up at the Upper Dan Tien to nourish the brain. The north pole is higher in energy and is in a relatively excited state while the south pole is lower in energy and is in a calm and steady state.

In his report on biomagnetics, Richard Leviton states: "One magnet practitioner, both a physician and a researcher, is Dr. Richard Broeringmeyer, a chiropractor, nutritionist, and publisher of the 'Bio-Energy Health Newsletter' in Murray, Kentucky. 'Life is not possible without electromagnetic fields,' he said, 'and optimum health is not possible if the electromagnetic fields are out of balance for long periods of time. Magnetic energy is nature's energy in perfect balance.' Each of a magnet's two poles has a different energy and influence, says Broeringmeyer. The bipolar function is near the heart of biomagnetism."(*3)

In regards to the two poles, I believe that it is the magnetic north pole at the Lower Dan Tien which offers energy or Chi. It is able to increase the overall vital life force, strength, and development of a living system. In contrast, the south pole or the Upper Dan Tien accepts energy or Chi. It acts to slow down, to calm, and to control the development of a living system.

You may understand now why I have located the poles of our magnetic field on either side of the Middle Dan Tien (solar plexus). The Middle Dan Tien can be considered the furnace where the Essences of food and air are converted into electricity and generate an EMF for circulation.

The above assumptions are based on Chinese Chi Kung systems which were developed in the Northern Hemisphere of the Earth over the last several thousand years. I do not know if this theory is accurate, or how the poles affect living things in the Southern Hemisphere. The implication, however, is that people in the Southern Hemisphere have their magnetic poles reversed from how they are in the Northern Hemisphere. In other words, their Upper Dan Tien will offer energy while the Lower Dan Tien will receive it. Can this mean that, while the brains of people in the Northern Hemisphere are constantly being nourished, the brains of people in the Southern Hemisphere are being depleted? Does this explain why most technology was developed in the Northern Hemisphere? Do people in the Southern Hemisphere live longer because their Lower Dan Tien is their south pole and it absorbs and retains Chi better than the Dan Tien of a person in the Northern Hemisphere? I have heard of several doctors who recommend that patients who have lost their energy balance spend time on the equator, where the earth's magnetic field has a minimal affect, and their bodies will be able to rebalance themselves. These are exciting and challenging ideas. It is time for a wide-scale study of human energy or Chi Kung in every corner of this world.

2. Channels:

If Chi channels are areas where the electrical conductivity of the body tissue is higher than elsewhere, then we have answered one of the big questions of Chi Kung. In addition to explaining how Chi circulates, this can also enable us to learn what the ancients were never able to discover: what is the shape of the channels, and where exactly are they located? In the past we have only been able to do Chi research on living people, but now we should be able to use cadavers and measure electrical conductivity throughout the body, and thereby determine the precise location and shape of the channels.

3. Vessels:

We may assume that what is called the Chi vessels are tissues which are able to store electrical charges like a capacitor. The body has eight of these capacitors (called the eight extraordinary vessels) which are responsible for regulating the current circulating in the twelve channels. If this assumption is true, we should be able to determine the exact location and characteristics of these vessels with today's technology.

4. Cavities:

Acupuncture cavities are small spots where the electrical conductivity is higher than the surrounding areas (*2). Electricity is conducted between the main electrical channels (Chi channels) and the surface of the skin more easily at these locations than elsewhere. These cavities are the gates where needles, magnets, electricity, and other means such as lasers can be used to affect the flow of electricity in the Chi channels. The "Five Centers" or "Five Gates" (two Laogong cavities, two Bubbling Well cavities, and the Baihui cavity) are probably larger openings where either the electric conductivity is higher or the conductive channels are larger.

5. Electromagnetic Force (EMF):

In order to have electric circulation, there must be an electromagnetic force (EMF). Without the EMF, the electric potential in the circuit will be the same throughout, and an electric current will not occur. The same principle applies to your body's electrical circuit. Generally, I can think of four possible causes for the generation of EMF in the human circuit: 1. Through the influence of natural energy. That means the EMF generated in the human body circuit can be affected by external energy interference, for example from the sun and the moon. Alternatively, you may expose your body to radioactive area or even an electromagnetic field which can influence the electrical circulation in your body. 2. From the conversion of food and air essence. Whenever food and air are taken in, they are converted into bioelectric energy. This increase of the electricity will generate EMF for circulation. 3. From exercise. Whenever you move your muscles, part of the stored essence in your body is converted into electricity and generates an EMF in the exercised area. 4. From the mind and Shen (spirit). Your mind plays an important role in the generation of EMF. It might not be easy for the average person to understand this concept, however, if you understand that your thinking is able to affect the body's Chi circulation, you may be able to understand that the mind can generate an EMF. For example, your mind leads electricity to the limbs to energize the muscle tissues. Exactly how this happens is a question still waiting for a complete answer.

In Chi Kung training, you are training to increase your EMF through proper intake of food and air, Chi Kung exercises, and focused thought.

6. Stagnation:

The flow of electricity can be reduced when the muscles are tightened or the structure of the channels (the conductive tissue) is changed. In Chinese medicine this would be called Chi stagnation. Tightening the muscles increases resistance to the flow of electricity and causes thereby an increase in temperature. It is still hard to say just how the resistance is increased. It may be due to a biochemical reaction generated by the mind, or possibly a change in the conductive tissue. The electric circulation can also be significantly affected when the conductive tissue is contaminated with low-conductivity material such as fat.

Obviously, relaxation is able to increase electrical circulation. In acupuncture, when a cavity is affected by a needle or magnet, the electrical field in that area is stimulated or sedated. It may possibly also convert the fat into heat and therefore open the path.

7. The Sensation of Heat:

If Chi is electromagnetic energy circulating in the body, then the heat which it produces is caused by the body's resistance to the electrical flow. If you run an electric current through a wire, when the current encounters resistance, electric energy is converted into heat. Therefore, the heat which is felt during acupuncture treatments and Chi Kung practice is not Chi, but rather a symptom of the presence of Chi. If this is true, then when practicing Chi Kung it is desirable to circulate the Chi so smoothly that it does not generate any sensation of heat. This is like running your current through a copper wire with low resistance instead of an iron one with high resistance. Whenever you generate too much heat in your body, especially in the organs, the tissue will begin to degenerate faster. Remember that the original Chinese symbol for Chi was constructed of two words "no fire." Therefore, as a Chi Kung practitioner, you should not try to feel your Chi as heat. It is better to feel it as an electrical sensation. If you keep this in mind, you will be able to avoid making your body too Yang during practice.

When we practice Chi Kung or Tai Chi, it is common to experience warmth on the skin, especially in the center of the palms (Laogong cavities), the bottom of feet (Bubbling Well cavities), and on the face. We know that warmth is an indication of increased Chi circulation, but exactly how is this heat caused?

Before we continue, I would like to quote a report by Albert L. Huebner: "In England, doctors have discovered that children can regrow lost fingertips, perfect in every detail, when a procedure is followed that bears an interesting resemblance to limb regeneration in amphibians. A salamander won't regenerate its limb if the stump has become covered with skin, presumably because this blocks the 'current of injury' known to form there. Dr. Cynthia Illingworth of Sheffield found that if a child's fingertip is to grow back, the stump must also be left uncovered."(*1)

This seems to indicate that the conductivity of muscle tissue is much higher than that of skin tissue. When skin has covered the injured area, it prevents the electric energy from extending beyond the stump and effecting the multiplication of cells and finally the regeneration of the finger.

I now believe that skin tissue is less conductive than muscle tissue, and both are less conductive than bone. When we have an injury deep in the muscle, the pain is more significant than when the injury is superficial. Likewise, the pain from an injury deep enough to reach the bone is even worse. The bone marrow and the brain are probably the two places where electric conductivity is the highest in the human body. However, it must be stressed that this is, in large measure, speculation. Experimentation and empirical evidence will be the only way to actually prove the correctness of the theory.

If you can accept these ideas, then it should be very easy for you to accept the explanation of how heat is generated in the skin during internal martial arts and Chi Kung. In these practices you often learn to relax and lead Chi to the ends of the limbs. The Chi or electricity will pass easily through the muscle and connective tissue, but when it reaches the skin the conductivity is suddenly lower. This means that resistance to the flow is increased. In combination with the fat (also of low electric conductivity) which normally accumulates between the skin and the muscle, the electricity is stopped and converted into heat (Figure 4-7).

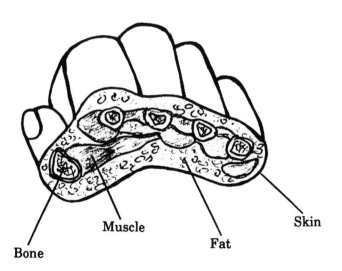

Figure 4-7. Cross section of a hand

You can see from this discussion why one of the purposes of Chi Kung is to reduce the heat and to open up the electrical blockages between the muscles and the skin and therefore increase the Chi flow to the surface of the skin. This insures that the skin, hair, and nails receive an abundance of electricity to maintain health and increase growth.

8. Healing:

The ideas we have discussed can also explain how some people can heal another person by touching him with his hands. The average person can move only a limited amount of Chi through his body, and can bring only a very small amount to the surface of the skin. However, some people, including Chi Kung practitioners, can move Chi easily to the surface of the skin and beyond, and can even affect another person's Chi. If they can determine the status of the Chi throughout a person's body, they can supply energy to the areas that are low, and withdraw excess energy from areas which are oversupplied. Once they do this, it is important to rid their own bodies of the excess Chi through various Chi regulating methods.

9. Opening the Gates:

One of the major goals of Chi Kung is "opening the gates" (Tong Guan). This means to remove any cause of electric (Chi) stagnation. Stagnation is when the flow of current is hindered in the Chi channels, usually around cavities. This is caused by improper food, low quality air, and aging of the body tissues. Various Chi Kung styles, which are based upon different theories, have various methods of opening the gates (this is discussed in Chapter 6). However, regardless of the style, the key to opening the gates is increasing the flow of current. This clears away obstructions and widens constricted areas ("gates" or "cavities"), smoothing the circulation. In order to increase the current flow, the EMF must be increased. This can be done by Chi Kung exercises and meditation in which the concentrated mind plays the main role.

10. The Measurement of Chi:

If the theories discussed above can be proven to be valid, then we have finally answered the big question of just what Chi is. We have also solved another big problem, namely what unit of measurement to use. If Chi is bioelectricity, then we can simply use the same units of measurements we use with electricity. This is a great step forward, because with a standard unit of measurement we can now scientifically compare and evaluate results of tests and experiments.

Before we conclude this section, I would like to remind you of several things. Although we have used modern science's concepts of the magnetic field to draw comparisons with the magnetic fields which surround all living things, you should understand that the field around your body is much more complicated than the field around a simple magnet. Perhaps the main cause of this is due to your mind, which can affect your magnetic field. Exactly how the mind generates EMF is another one of the many mysteries of the brain. We also do not know exactly how food and air Essences are converted into electric power.

Please remember also that many of the ideas discussed above are not proven facts. Although experimental evidence and scientific proof are accumulating, there are still many areas which are not understood. I have offered explanations for many of the big questions of Chi Kung, but they are personal theories and conclusions only. You should not take them as fact, because they still need more experimental proof. I hope that this section will stimulate people to think, and encourage a synthesis of the theories of Chi and bioelectricity.

4-4. Opening the Chi Gates

The proceeding discussion should give you an idea of some of the problems that need to be overcome in order to practice Chi Kung. To maintain your health, you must keep your Chi flowing smoothly in the proper pathways. Reducing the amount of bad food you eat, which is the main source of contaminated Chi, will help to maintain a smooth Chi flow. Then you must learn how to open all of the gates (cavities) which are obstructed and are causing Chi stagnation. This is a major part of the Chi Kung which is practiced for health.

In Chi Kung, opening the gates is called "Tong Guan" (literally "to get through the gates"). The theory of opening these gates is very simple. First think of what you would do if the drainpipe in your sink were partially blocked. You probably would run a lot of water through it to increase the pressure on the obstruction and wash it away. You would know when the pipe was clear because the water would pass through it quickly and strongly. You can use the same method with your Chi channels by running more Chi through them. But in order to move more Chi, you must first generate it. In Wai Dan Chi Kung, when Chi is built up in the limbs it flows back into the body more strongly than before. As you continue to practice, the Chi will gradually widen the channels. Now, you might think that since increasing the Chi flow opens the gates, the more you increase the Chi, the more quickly you will open up the gates. However, you must remember one important thing. Your internal organs are designed to operate at certain levels of Chi, and if they receive too much Chi, they will become too Yang and will degenerate more quickly.

It is very important in Chi Kung to do only enough to raise your Chi level just slightly above its normal level. As you continue to practice, the Chi channels will gradually widen so that the Chi level comes back down to normal, and the obstructed gates will slowly open. Then you can again increase the Chi level a little, the channels will become cleaner, and they will gradually become wider. Regular practice of the right exercises will smooth out the circulation, and keep the organs running properly. The proper amount of practice will maintain your health, while too little practice will allow the channels to become plugged up, and too much practice will make your body too Yang, and will shorten your life. This is the key theory of Wai Dan.

There is no difference in the theory of Nei Dan. However, in Nei Dan training you normally open the gates in the Conception and Governing vessels first. These two vessels are considered the major Chi reservoirs which govern the Chi, and so your must open them first if you want to regulate the Chi. Once this is done, you have completed Small Circulation (Sheau Jou Tian). There are three gates in this path which are considered the most difficult and dangerous when you practice. When you open these three gates up, it is called "Tong San Guan" ("to get through the three gates").

After you have completed the Small Circulation, you then lead the Chi to the limbs to open up all of the gates located on the Chi channels. Once you have completed this, you have accomplished Grand Circulation (Dah Jou Tian). For further information, please refer the author's books "Chi Kung - Health and Martial Arts" and "Muscle/Tendon Changing and Marrow Washing Chi Kung."

Chapter 5

Categories of Chi Kung

Chi Kung is the study of your body's energy field, and it is directly related to your physical, emotional, mental, and even spiritual health. Both Eastern and Western religions influence the body's Chi, either indirectly through emotional or mental means, or directly through conscious manipulation. In the East, religion has been responsible for some of the greatest developments in Chi Kung. The Oriental religions have been more aware than the Occidental religions of the role Chi plays in our spiritual and emotional lives. Chi Kung starts with physical science (strengthening the body), then moves on to energy science (Chi), then with mental science (neutralizing the mind), and finally reaches spiritual science (enlightenment). When you study Chinese Chi Kung, you should be aware of the large role that religion has played in its development. As you learn more about Chi Kung, you will become more aware of the ways in which the Western religions have also practiced this science.

In this chapter we will first discuss the relationship between Chi Kung and the Chinese religions, and then we will discuss the different categories of Chi Kung.

5-1. Chi Kung and Religion

It is part of the human condition that we frequently experience conflict between out hearts and our minds. So often we want to do things that we know we shouldn't. A part of us knows where our duties and moral obligations lie, but at the same time, our desires are pulling us in the opposite direction. All too often we find that wisdom and desire are in direct conflict. Desires which we feel we cannot control drive us into acts of foolishness or even violence. When we do things we know we shouldn't, we feel an inner pain caused by the spiritual/moral conflict.

The Buddhists and Taoists say that there are seven human emotions: joy, anger, sorrow, fear, love, hate, and lust; and six desires which originate in the six roots: the eyes, ears, nose, tongue, body, and mind. These seven emotions and six desires are products of the emotional mind. Although some of the emotions, like love, can act to uplift us, most of the emotions and desires lead us to the evil and ugly side of life, the side of human disaster. If we learn to strengthen the wisdom mind we can gain calmness and peace, and this can help us to develop patience, perseverance, strong will, and a sense of justice and harmony. These virtues enable us to overcome the disasters created from the emotional mind. People need to be taught how to strengthen the good side and overcome the negative side of their nature. A proper education cultivates and matures the wisdom mind -- the ability to judge which can control the seven emotions and six desires.

Part of our nature is greedy and selfish, and causes us to struggle for money and power. When the moral part of our natures is suppressed, our minds seem to become evil -- murder, theft, rape, anything becomes possible. Throughout history, many people have worshiped as heroes those who could kill, conquer, and enslave others. Today's movies and TV programs are filled with stories of killing and violence. The younger generations are continually being educated into this mindset when they watch these programs, and even in history classrooms. In this way the seed of the ugly side of human nature is planted and continually nourished. This seed will grow, and the next generation will perpetuate the violence, hatred, and greed.

These violent emotions can often suppress or distort the love and peace in people, but there is a cost. Since the longing for love and peace is an inborn part of human nature, the violent and hateful emotions constantly cause an inner conflict. It is this conflict which has generated the different religions of mankind. Religion brings a hope for peace, and encourages people to strengthen the good side of their natures. Many people gain peace and confidence, and overcome the sometimes crushing fear and uncertainty which surround us in this life.

All of the different religions seem to have one point of similarity -- the believers must learn to meditate in order to gain peace of mind. Meditation (and prayer, which is a form of meditation) is able to bring spiritual consolation and calmness, and build self-confidence. Meditation regulates the mind, and balances the Chi which had been disturbed by emotional distress. Many people have found that prayer brings them an inner peace which has helped them recover from illness. With the increase of self-confidence, the spirit is raised and firmed. This raised spirit has become a major force in the fight to lessen the suffering in this world.

Buddhism and Taoism teach, like Christianity, that there is a heavenly kingdom and there is a hell. If you are good and have done good deeds while you were alive, you will be reborn as a human being, or you may even go to heaven as a Buddha or saint and leave the cycle of reincarnation behind. If you have been evil, you may end up in the hell of suffering and punishment, and/or be reborn as an animal. Almost everyone in ancient times was uneducated. They were worried and confused about their lives, and they were afraid of what might happen after death. Religions teach about heaven and hell to encourage people to be good instead of bad. Once people were trying to behave morally, religion taught them how to gain peace of mind through meditation.

Not surprisingly, a great number of meditation techniques were developed by religious practitioners, and the Chinese Buddhists and Taoists deeply researched the related field of Chi Kung. In fact, it was the religious Chi Kung practitioners who made the greatest achievements in the development of Chi Kung. This is especially true in the highest level of Chi Kung, which is enlightenment. At this level the study of human energy is spiritual science, and it becomes independent of religion.

From this discussion you can see that religion and Chi Kung are deeply intertwined. A thorough research of Chinese Chi Kung should also include the study of the historical background and theory of those religions which have influenced Chinese culture. It could also involve a comparison of Chinese Chi Kung with Western religious meditation techniques. I believe that this would help you to understand more clearly the relationship between human nature and Chi Kung.

5-2.Categories of Chi Kung

In the several thousand years since Chi and its relationship to health were discovered, every level of the Chinese population has practiced Chi Kung at some time. There are four major schools or categories which were created by the different classes of people. The scholars, medical doctors, martial artists, and religious monks all had their distinctive categories of Chi Kung. The martial Chi Kung was again divided into external and internal styles, and the religious Chi Kung was divided into Buddhist, Taoist, and Tibetan styles.

In order to obtain a healthy body, you must cultivate both Shing (Human Nature) and Ming (Physical Life). A major part of Chinese philosophy has focused on the study of human nature, feelings, and spirit, as can be seen especially in Chinese scholarly and Buddhist (also Tibetan) religious society. Of all the different categories of Chi Kung, the scholarly and religious Chi Kung categories originated from and focused on the cultivation of human nature and spirit.

Human nature and spirit, as a matter of fact, were the most basic root of scholarly and religious philosophy in China. Physical life was considered to be not as important as the spiritual life. For this reason, most of the still meditation, which specializes in the cultivation of the spirit, was developed and studied by the scholars and Buddhist monks.

However, these two groups were striving for different goals. The scholars believed that the major illnesses were caused by emotional and spiritual imbalance. They used meditation to regulate the mind and spirit, and thereby gain good health. The Buddhist monks were aiming for spiritual independence and ultimately the stage of enlightenment or Buddhahood. Of these two groups, the Buddhist (including Tibetan) monks were able to reach the highest levels of meditation, which almost no other style in China was able to do. However, even though these two schools of Chi Kung emphasized spiritual meditation, they also used a limited number of Chi Kung exercises which trained the physical body, such as Da Mo's Muscle/Tendon Changing exercises.

The Chinese medical doctors, on the other hand, thought that although spiritual meditation was important, physical cultivation was even more critical for health and healing. Furthermore, it was difficult to teach laymen still meditation, which was very hard to understand and practice. Therefore, the Chi Kung exercises created by the medical doctors focused on physical health and healing, and used mostly physical Chi Kung exercises. The physicians also relied heavily on acupuncture and herbs to adjust irregular Chi caused by sickness.

However, according to the available documents, many Chi Kung practitioners of different categories feel that the Taoist Chi Kung was probably the most complete both in theory and training because it emphasized the spiritual and physical equally. The Taoists also researched how different herbs affect the Chi circulation, and used these herbs to speed and smooth their progress. They even studied how one Chi Kung practitioner could share his Chi with his partners, or through mutual assistance help each other to speed up the cultivation. The effect of diet on the Chi circulation was also deeply studied. Their research was extensive and practical. Their training methods therefore spread widely in Chinese Chi Kung society.

According to the available documents, we can roughly classify Chi Kung into five major categories, according to their purpose or final goal: 1. maintaining health; 2. curing sickness; 3. prolonging life; 4. martial skill; and 5. enlightenment or Buddhahood. Even though we show a different training purpose or aim for each category, you should understand that it is not possible to define all of the categories strictly according to their training purpose. This is simply because almost every style of Chi Kung serves more than one of the above purposes. For example, although martial Chi Kung focuses on increasing fighting effectiveness, it can also improve your health. The Taoist Chi Kung aims for longevity and enlightenment, but to reach this goal you need to be in good health and know how to cure sickness. Because of this multi-purpose aspect of the categories, it will be simpler to discuss their backgrounds rather than the goals of their training. Knowing the history and basic principles of each category will help you to understand their Chi Kung more clearly. In this section we will discuss each category in more detail.

1. Scholar Chi Kung - for Maintaining Health:

In China before the Han dynasty, there were two major schools of scholarship. One of them was created by Confucius (551-479 B.C.) during the Spring and Autumn Period, and the scholars who practice his philosophy are commonly called Confucians. Later his philosophy was popularized and enlarged by Mencius (372-289 B.C.) in the Warring States Period. The people who practiced this were called Ru Jia (Confucianists). The key words to their basic philosophy are Loyalty, Filial Piety, Humanity, Kindness, Trust, Justice, Harmony, and Peace. Humanity and the human feelings are the main subjects of study. Ru Jia philosophy has become the center of much of Chinese culture.

The second major school of scholarship was called Tao Jia (Taoism) and was created by Lao Tzyy in the 6th century B.C. Lao Tzyy is considered to be the author of a book called the "Tao Te Ching" (Morality Classic) which described human morality. Later, in the Warring States Period, his follower Juang Jou wrote a book called "Juang Tzyy," which led to the forming of another strong branch of scholarship. Before the Han dynasty, Taoism was not considered a religion, but rather another branch of scholarship. It was not until the Han dynasty that traditional Taoism was combined with the Buddhism imported from India, and it began gradually to be treated as a religion. Therefore, the Taoism before the Han dynasty should be considered scholarly Taoism rather than religious.

In regards to their contribution to Chi Kung, both schools of scholarship emphasized maintaining health and preventing disease. They believed that many illnesses are caused by mental and emotional excesses. When a person's mind is not calm, balanced, and peaceful, the organs will not function normally. For example, depression can cause stomach ulcers and indigestion. Anger will cause the liver to malfunction. Sadness will cause stagnation and tightness in the lungs, and fear can disturb the normal functioning of the kidneys and bladder. They realized that if you want to avoid illness, you must learn to balance and relax your thoughts and emotions. This is called "regulating the mind."

Therefore, the scholars emphasized gaining a peaceful mind through meditation. In their still meditation, the main part of the training is getting rid of thoughts so that the mind is clear and calm. When you become calm, the flow of thoughts and emotions slows down, and you feel mentally and emotionally neutral. This kind of meditation can be thought of as practicing emotional self-control. When you are in this "no thought" state, you become very relaxed, and can even relax deep down into your internal organs. When your body is this relaxed, your Chi will flow smoothly and strongly naturally. This kind of still meditation was very common in ancient Chinese scholarly society.

In order to reach the goal of a calm and peaceful mind, their training focused on regulating the mind, body, and breath. They believed that as long as these three things were regulated, the Chi flow would be smooth and sickness would not occur. This is why the Chi training of the scholars is called "Shiou Chi," which means "cultivating Chi." Shiou in Chinese means to regulate, to cultivate, or to repair. It means to maintain in good condition. This is very different from the Taoist Chi training after the Han dynasty which was called "Liann Chi," which is translated "train Chi." Liann means to drill or to practice to make stronger. Taoist Chi Kung after the Han dynasty will be discussed later.

Many of the Chi Kung documents written by the Confucians and Taoists were limited to the maintenance of health. The scholar's attitude in Chi Kung was to follow his natural destiny and maintain his health. This philosophy is quite different from that of the Taoists after the Han dynasty, who denied that one's destiny could not be changed. They believed that it is possible to train your Chi to make it stronger, and to reach the goal of longevity. It is said in scholarly society: "Ren Sheng Chii Shyr Guu Lai Shi,"(*1) which means "in human life seventy is rare." You should understand that few of the common people in ancient times lived past seventy because of the lack of good food and modern medical technology. It is also said: "An Tian Leh Ming," which means "peace with heaven and delight in your destiny"; and "Shiou Shenn Ai Ming," which means "cultivate the body and await destiny." Compare this with the philosophy of the later

---

(*1). " 人生七十古來稀."

Taoists, who said: "Yi Bae Er Shyr Wey Jy Yeau,"(*2) which means "one hundred and twenty means dying young." They believed and have proven that human life can be lengthened and destiny can be resisted and overcome.

Confucianism and Taoism were the two major schools of scholarship in China, but there were many other schools which were also more or less involved in Chi Kung exercises. We will not discuss them here because there is only a limited number of Chi Kung documents from these schools.

To conclude, the basic characteristics of scholarly Chi Kung training include:

A. Spiritual and mental Chi Kung was emphasized more than physical Chi Kung.

B. The published documents which are related to Chi Kung discuss it in a random, unorganized, and unsystematic fashion.

C. Maintaining health was the goal of Chi cultivation. Overcoming death and destiny was considered impossible.

D. Before the Han dynasty, Taoism was considered a branch of scholarship, whereas after the Han dynasty it became involved in religion and became the Taoist religion. Therefore, the Chi Kung developed by the Taoists before the Han dynasty was considered scholarly Taoist Chi Kung.

2. Medical Chi Kung - for Healing:

In ancient Chinese society, most emperors respected the scholars and were affected by their philosophy. Doctors were not regarded highly because they made their diagnosis by touching the patient's body, which was considered characteristic of the lower classes in society. Although the doctors developed a profound and successful medical science, they were commonly looked down on. However, they continued to work hard and study, and quietly passed down the results of their research to following generations.

Of all the groups studying Chi Kung in China, the doctors have been at it the longest. Since the discovery of Chi circulation in the human body about four thousand years ago, the Chinese doctors have devoted a major portion of their efforts to the study of the behavior of Chi. Their efforts resulted in acupuncture, acupressure or Cavity Press massage, and herbal treatment.

In addition, many Chinese doctors used their medical knowledge to create different sets of Chi Kung exercises either for maintaining health or for curing specific illnesses. Chinese medical doctors believed that doing only sitting or still meditation to regulate the body, mind, and breathing as the scholars did was not enough to cure sickness. They believed that in order to increase the Chi circulation, you must move. Although a calm and peaceful mind was important for health, exercising the body was more important. They learned through their medical practice that people who exercised properly got sick less often, and their bodies degenerated less quickly than was the case with people who just sat around. They also realized that specific body movements could increase the Chi circulation in specific organs. They reasoned from this that these exercises could also be used to treat specific illnesses and to restore the normal functioning of these organs.

(*2). " 一百二十謂之夭 . "

Some of these movements are similar to the way in which certain animals move. It is clear that in order for an animal to survive in the wild, it must have an instinct for how to protect its body. Part of this instinct is concerned with how to build up its Chi, and how to keep its Chi from being lost. We humans have lost many of these instincts over the years that we have been separating ourselves from nature.

Many doctors developed Chi Kung exercises which were modeled after animal movements to maintain health and cure sickness. A typical, well known set of such exercises is "Wuu Chyn Shih" (Five Animal Sports) created by Dr. Jiun Chiam. Another famous set based on similar principles is called "Ba Duann Gin" (The Eight Pieces of Brocade). It was created by Marshal Yeuh Fei who, interestingly enough, was a soldier rather than a doctor.

In addition, using their medical knowledge of Chi circulation, Chinese doctors researched until they found which movements could help cure particular illnesses and health problems. Not surprisingly, many of these movements were not unlike the ones used to maintain health, since many illnesses are caused by unbalanced Chi. When this imbalance continues for a long period of time, the organs will be affected, and may be physically damaged. It is just like running a machine without supplying the proper electrical current -- over time, the machine will be damaged. Chinese doctors believe that before physical damage to an organ shows up in a patient's body, there is first an abnormality in the Chi balance and circulation. **ABNORMAL CHI CIRCULATION IS THE VERY BEGINNING OF ILLNESS AND PHYSICAL ORGAN DAMAGE.** When Chi is too positive (Yang) or too negative (Yin) in a specific organ Chi channel, your physical organ is beginning to suffer damage. If you do not correct the Chi circulation, that organ will malfunction or degenerate. The best way to heal someone is to adjust and balance the Chi even before there is any physical problem. Therefore, correcting or increasing the normal Chi circulation is the major goal of acupuncture or acupressure treatments. Herbs and special diets are also considered important treatments in regulating the Chi in the body.

As long as the illness is limited to the level of Chi stagnation and there is no physical organ damage, the Chi Kung exercises used for maintaining health can be used to readjust the Chi circulation and treat the problem. However, if the sickness is already so serious that the physical organs have started to fail, then the situation has become critical and a specific treatment is necessary. The treatment can be acupuncture, herbs, or even an operation, as well as specific Chi Kung exercises designed to speed up the healing or even to cure the sickness. For example, ulcers and asthma can often be cured or helped by some simple exercises. Recently in both mainland China and Taiwan, certain Chi Kung exercises have been shown to be effective in treating certain kinds of cancer.(*3)

Over the thousands of years of observing nature and themselves, some Chi Kung practitioners went even deeper. They realized that

---

(*3).There are many reports in popular and professional literature of using Chi Kung to help or even cure many illnesses, including cancer. Many cases have been discussed in the Chinese Chi Kung journals. One book which describes the use of Chi Kung to cure cancer is **New Chi Kung for Preventing and Curing Cancer** (新氣功防治癌症), by Yeh Ming, Chinese Yoga Publications, Taiwan, 1986.

the body's Chi circulation changes with the seasons, and that it is a good idea to help the body out during these periodic adjustments. They noticed also that in each season different organs had characteristic problems. For example, in the beginning of Fall the lungs have to adapt to the colder air that you are breathing. While this adjusting is going on, the lungs are susceptible to disturbance, so your lungs may feel uncomfortable and you may catch colds easily. Your digestive system is also affected during seasonal changes. Your appetite may increase, or you may have diarrhea. When the temperature goes down, your kidneys and bladder will start to give you trouble. For example, because the kidneys are stressed, you may feel pain in the back. Focusing on these seasonal Chi disorders, the meditators created a set of movements which can be used to speed up the body's adjustment. These Chi Kung exercises will be introduced in a later volume.

In addition to Marshal Yeuh Fei, many people who were not doctors also created sets of medical Chi Kung. These sets were probably originally created to maintain health, and later were also used for curing sickness.

The characteristics of medical Chi Kung are:

A. Medical Chi Kung emphasizes moving meditative exercises more than sitting still meditation.

B. The major goals of medical Chi Kung are maintaining health and curing sickness.

C. Chi Kung exercises were only a small part of Chinese medical science. Herbal treatment, acupuncture, and acupressure remained the major methods of healing.

3. Martial Chi Kung - for Fighting:

Chinese martial Chi Kung was probably not developed until Da Mo's Muscle/Tendon Changing Classic was developed in the Shaolin Temple during the Liang dynasty (502-557 A.D.). When Shaolin monks trained Da Mo's Muscle/Tendon Changing Chi Kung, they found that they could not only improve their health but also greatly increase the power of their martial techniques. Since then, many martial styles have developed Chi Kung sets to increase their effectiveness. In addition, many martial styles have been created based on Chi Kung theory. Martial artists have played a major role in Chinese Chi Kung society.

When Chi Kung theory was first applied to the martial arts, it was used to increase the power and efficiency of the muscles. The theory is very simple--the mind (Yi) is used to lead Chi to the muscles to energize them so that they function more efficiently. The average person generally uses his muscles at under 40% maximum efficiency. If one can train his concentration and use his strong Yi to lead Chi to the muscles effectively, he will be able to energize the muscles to a higher level and, therefore, increase his fighting effectiveness.

As acupuncture theory became better understood, fighting techniques were able to reach even more advanced levels. Martial artists learned to attack specific areas, such as vital acupuncture cavities, to disturb the enemy's Chi flow and create imbalances which caused injury or even death. In order to do this, the practitioner must understand the route and timing of the Chi circulation in the human body. He also has to train so that he can strike the cavities accurately and to the correct depth. These cavity strike techniques are called "Dien Shiuh" (Pointing Cavities) or "Dim Mak" (Pointing Vessels).

Most of the martial Chi Kung practices help to improve the practitioner's health. However, there are other martial Chi Kung practices which, although they build up some special skill which is useful for fighting, also damage the practitioner's health. An example of this is Iron Sand Palm. Although this training can build up amazing destructive power, it can also harm your hands and affect the Chi circulation in the hands and the internal organs.

Since the 6th century, many martial styles have been created which were based on Chi Kung theory. They can be roughly divided into external and internal styles.

The external styles emphasize building Chi in the limbs to coordinate with the physical martial techniques. They follow the theory of Wai Dan (external elixir) Chi Kung. In Wai Dan Chi Kung, Chi is usually generated in the limbs through special exercises. The concentrated mind is used during the exercises to energize the Chi. This increases muscular strength significantly, and therefore increases the effectiveness of the martial techniques. Chi Kung can also be used to train the body to resist punches and kicks. In this training, Chi is led to energize the skin and the muscles, enabling them to resist a blow without injury. This training is commonly called "Iron Shirt" (Tiee Buh Shan) or "Golden Bell Cover" (Gin Jong Jaw). The martial styles which use Wai Dan Chi Kung training are normally called external styles (Wai Kung) or hard styles (Ying Kung). Shaolin Kung Fu is a typical example of a style which uses Wai Dan martial Chi Kung.

Although Wai Dan Chi Kung can help the martial artist increase his power, there is a disadvantage. Because Wai Dan Chi Kung emphasizes training the external muscles, it can cause over-development. This can cause a problem called "energy dispersion" (Sann Kung) when the practitioner gets older. In order to remedy this, when an external martial artist reaches a high level of external Chi Kung training he will start training internal Chi Kung, which specializes in curing the energy dispersion problem. That is why it is said "Shaolin Kung Fu from external to internal."

Internal Martial Chi Kung is based on the theory of Nei Dan (internal elixir). In this method, Chi is generated in the body instead of the limbs, and this Chi is then led to the limbs to increase power. In order to lead Chi to the limbs, the techniques must be soft and muscle usage must be kept to a minimum. The training and theory of Nei Dan martial Chi Kung is much harder than those of the Wai Dan martial Chi Kung. The interested reader should refer to the author's book: "Advanced Yang Style Tai Chi Chuan--Tai Chi Theory and Tai Chi Jing." Several internal martial styles were created in the Wuudang and Ermei Mountains. Popular styles are Tai Chi Chuan, Ba Kua, Liu Ho Ba Fa, and Hsing Yi. However, you should understand that even the internal martial styles, which are commonly called soft styles, must on some occasions use muscular strength while fighting. Therefore, once an internal martial artist has achieved a degree of competence in internal Chi Kung, he should also learn how to use harder, more external techniques. That is why it is said: "the internal styles are from soft to hard."

In the last fifty years, some of the Tai Chi Chi Kung or Tai Chi Chuan practitioners have developed training which is mainly for health, and is called "Wu Chi Chi Kung," which means "no extremities Chi Kung." Wu Chi is the state of neutrality which precedes Tai Chi, which is the state of complimentary opposites. When there are thoughts and feelings in your mind, there is Yin and Yang, but if you can still your mind you can return to the emptiness of Wu Chi. When you achieve this state your mind is centered and clear and your body relaxed, and your Chi is able to flow naturally and smoothly and reach the proper balance by itself. Wu Chi Chi Kung has become very popular in many parts of China, especially Shanghai and Canton.

You can see that, although Chi Kung is widely studied in Chinese martial society, the main focus of training was originally on increasing fighting ability instead of health. Good health was considered a by-product of the training. It was not until this century that the health aspect of martial Chi Kung started receiving greater attention. This is especially true in the internal martial arts. Please refer to the future YMAA in-depth Chi Kung book series: "Chi Kung and Martial Arts."

4. Religious Chi Kung - for Enlightenment or Buddhahood:

Religious Chi Kung, though not as popular as other categories in China, is recognized as having achieved the highest accomplishments of all the Chi Kung categories. It used to be kept secret, and it is only in this century that it has been revealed to laymen.

In China, religious Chi Kung includes mainly Taoist and Buddhist Chi Kung. The main purpose of their training is striving for enlightenment, or what the Buddhists refer to as Buddhahood. They are looking for a way to lift themselves above normal human suffering, and to escape from the cycle of continual reincarnation. They believe that all human suffering is caused by the seven emotions and six desires. If you are still bound to these emotions and desires, you will reincarnate after your death. To avoid reincarnation, you must train your spirit to reach a very high stage where it is strong enough to be independent after your death. This spirit will enter the heavenly kingdom and gain eternal peace. This is hard to do in the everyday world, so they frequently flee society and move into the solitude of the mountains, where they can concentrate all of their energies on self-cultivation.

Religious Chi Kung practitioners train to strengthen their internal Chi to nourish their spirit (Shen) until this spirit is able to survive the death of the physical body. Marrow Washing Chi Kung training is necessary to reach this stage. It enables them to lead Chi to the forehead, where the spirit resides, and raise the brain to a higher energy state. This training used to be restricted to only a few priests who had reached an advanced level. Tibetan Buddhists were also involved heavily in this training. Over the last two thousand years the Tibetan Buddhists, the Chinese Buddhists, and the Taoist have followed the same principles to become the three major religious schools of Chi Kung training.

This religious striving toward enlightenment or Buddhahood is recognized as the highest and most difficult level of Chi Kung. Many Chi Kung practitioners rejected the rigors of this religious striving, and practiced Marrow Washing Chi Kung solely for the purpose of longevity. It was these people who eventually revealed the secrets of Marrow Washing to the outside world. Marrow Washing Chi Kung will be discussed in the second volume of YMAA's in-depth Chi Kung book series.

Buddhist Chi Kung - for Buddhahood:

Buddhism was created by an Indian prince named Sakyamuni (558-478 B.C.). When he was 29 years old, he became dissatisfied with his comfortable and sheltered life and left his country. He went out into the world among the common people to experience the pain and suffering in their lives. Six years later, he suddenly apprehended the "Truth," and started to travel around and spread his philosophy.

Buddhism was imported into China during the Eastern Han dynasty (58 A.D.). The Han emperors became sincere Buddhists, and Buddhism became the main religion in China. Naturally, the Buddhist meditation methods were also learned by the Chinese Buddhist monks.

Buddhist Chi Kung training is very similar to Chinese scholarly Chi Kung. The main difference is that while scholarly Chi Kung aims at maintaining health, Buddhist Chi Kung aims at becoming a Buddha. Meditation is a necessary process in training the priest to stay emotionally neutral. Buddhism believes that all human suffering is caused by the seven passions and six desires (Chii Ching Liow Yuh). The seven passions are joy, anger, sorrow, fear, love, hate, and lust. The desires are generated from the six roots which are the eyes, ears, nose, tongue, body, and mind (Hsin). Buddhists also cultivate within themselves a neutral state separated from the four emptinesses of earth, water, fire, and wind. They believe that this training enables them to keep their spirits independent so they can escape from the cycle of repeated reincarnation.

The early priests were not so concerned with their physical health, and meditated in order to train themselves to stay emotionally neutral. Naturally, most of the priests did not have long physical lives.

This situation lasted until the Liang dynasty (502-557 A.D.), when physical Chi Kung exercises began to be emphasized in a limited number of Buddhist temples. There is a famous story about Da Mo. Da Mo was an Indian Buddhist prince who was invited to China to preach by emperor Liang. When the emperor did not favor his philosophy, Da Mo went to the Shaolin Temple. He discovered that all of the priests were weak and sickly, so he decided to help them. He shut himself away to ponder the problem, and stayed in seclusion for nine years. When he emerged he had written two books, the Yi Gin Ching (Muscle/Tendon Changing Classic), and the Shii Soei Ching (Marrow Washing Classic). The techniques taught in the Muscle/Tendon Changing Classic were practiced by many Buddhist priests. They believed that they needed strong and healthy bodies to complete their training.

The Shaolin priests learned that when they practiced these exercises, not only did their health increase, but their physical power also increased significantly. They naturally used this power in coordination with their fighting techniques when they had to defend themselves. This change marked one more step in the growth of Chinese martial arts: Martial Chi Kung. This was discussed earlier. Many sets of physical Chi Kung exercise have been developed over the years based on the principles expounded in Da Mo's book on Muscle/Tendon Changing.

Although it was often necessary to defend oneself during that violent period, there were many priests who were against the martial training. They believed that as Buddhist priests they should avoid all violence. For this reason, most of the temples practiced only the still meditation for cultivating their Buddhahood.

Da Mo's Marrow Washing Classic describes how a priest can strengthen his health and increase his longevity. Once he has finished this training he can go on to more advanced training which has the goal of attaining Buddhahood. Before a priest started his Marrow Washing training he had to first complete the Muscle/Tendon Changing, which was considered the foundation. Unfortunately, the theory of Marrow Washing is very difficult to understand, and the whole process was kept secret by the monks, so for many centuries it was thought to be lost. It was only in the last twenty years that some of the documents have been revealed to the public.

Da Mo is considered the ancestor of the Chinese Charn Tzong, or the Zen sect of Buddhism. The traditional teaching philosophy which has been attributed to him is: "Jiaw Wai Bye Chwan, Buh Lih Wen Tzyh, Jyr Jyy Ren Hsin, Jiann Shing Cherng For"(*4) (Do not pass on to people outside of our religion, words should not be written down, point directly to the person's mind, to see and cultivate the personality, humanity, and becoming a Buddha).

When Da Mo died, it was said that he passed his Charn Buddhist philosophy and his Marrow Washing Classic techniques to his best and trusted disciple, Huoy Kee. Huoy Kee's name as a layman was Jih Guang. He was a scholar who gave up his normal life and became a priest in order to conquer himself. Huoy Kee passed the Buddhist philosophy on to Seng Tsann. It then went to Tao Shinn, Horng Zen, and Huoy Neng. Including Da Mo, these six are called the Six Ancestors of Charn (Charn Tzong Liow Tzuu). Later, Chinese Buddhist society honored another monk, Shen Huey of the Tarng dynasty of Kai Yuan (713-742 A.D.), and subsequently referred to the Seven Ancestors of Charn (Charn Tzong Chii Tzuu).

Since Da Mo came from India, part of the Chi Kung training theory developed by him was identical to Indian Yoga (such as the still meditation), which had existed for some time in India. Later, Charn theory and training was brought to Japan by Chinese Buddhist monks, and became the Zen meditation of Japan.

You can see that before the Liang dynasty, the Buddhists used only still meditation. Since the Liang dynasty, many priests learned Da Mo's exercises, and then adopted the movements of various animals to use in Chi Kung sets, or even for martial purposes.

To summarize:

A. Before Da Mo (527 A.D.), still meditation was the major part of Chinese Buddhist training. After Da Mo, moving Chi Kung exercises--The Muscle/Tendon Changing Classic--was introduced.

B. Muscle/Tendon Changing was the foundation of Marrow Washing. Muscle/Tendon Changing can change a person's physical body from weak to strong, and Marrow Washing is able to train a monk to use his Chi to keep his marrow clean, and reach the goal of Buddhahood.

C. Because the Muscle/Tendon Changing training is able to increase the strength of the body, it has been used by Buddhists and non-

---

(*4). "教外別傳，不立文字，直指人心，見性成佛。"

Buddhists in their martial training. Since then, many martial Chi Kung styles have been created.

D. The Marrow Washing Classic is hard to understand and train, and has been kept secret for a long time.

E. Da Mo was the ancestor of Charn or Zen meditation.

Tibetan Chi Kung - for Buddhahood:

Tibet was significantly influenced by both Indian and Chinese cultures. Buddhism had a great effect, so the root of Tibetan Chi Kung is similar to that of Indian Buddhism. However, over thousands of years of study and research, the Tibetans established their own unique style of Chi Kung meditation. The Tibetan priests are called Lamas (Laa Ma), and many of them also learned martial arts. Because of the different cultural background, not only are the Lamas' meditation techniques different from those of the Chinese or Indian Buddhists, but their martial techniques are also different. Tibetan Chi Kung meditation and martial arts were kept secret from the outside world, and were therefore called "Mih Tzong," which means "secret style." Because of this, and because of the different language, there are very few documents available in Chinese. Generally speaking, Tibetan Chi Kung and martial arts were not spread into Chinese society almost until the Ching dynasty (1644-1911 A.D.). Since then, however, they have become more popular.

However, even though Tibetan Chi Kung training techniques are sometimes different from those of the Chinese and Indian Buddhists, they still have the same goal of all Buddhists -- Buddhahood. According to the available documents, Tibetan Chi Kung training emphasizes spiritual cultivation through still meditation like the Buddhist meditation, although they use many physical Chi Kung exercises which are similar to Indian Yoga.

To summarize:

A. Tibetan Chi Kung is part of Buddhist Chi Kung, although it has developed its own unique system of cultivation.

B. Tibetan still meditation theory and training is similar to that of the Buddhists. However, they also have some physical Chi Kung training similar to Indian Yoga.

C. Documents on Tibetan Chi Kung are scarce. Hopefully someone who is specializing in researching Tibetan culture can fill this void.

Taoist Chi Kung - for Enlightenment:

Taoism was created by Lao Tzyy (Li Erh) in the 6th century B.C. He wrote a book titled Tao Te Ching (Classic on Morality) which discusses natural human morality. Later, his follower Juang Jou in the Warring States Period wrote a book called Juang Tzyy. Soon, another branch of Scholarship developed, which was separate from Confucianism. Before the Han dynasty, Taoism was purely a form of Scholarship. It studied the human spirit and nature but, according to the available documents, it was not considered a religion.

In the Eastern Han dynasty (25-168 A.D.), Chang Tao-Ling created the Taoist religion (Tao Jiaw). Taoism worshiped primarily the "Yuan Shyy Tian Tzuen" (The Primal Celestial Excellency - a Taoist Deity. After the Song dynasty it was called Yuh Hwang Dah Dih - The Supreme Deity) and Lao Tzyy (popularly titled Tai Shang Lao Jiun, or Old Lord of the Ultimate). In Tao Jiaw philosophy, they believed there was a heavenly kingdom ruled by "The Primal Celestial Excellency." Only the immortals and the gods lived in this kingdom, which controlled everything on the earth. You can see that the original concept of Heaven Chi has been modified, and a religious color added. These religious Taoists also believed that when a person died, if he had done something very good, he would become a saint. Heaven would offer him a position which allowed him to rule the living. If a person did not do anything especially good while alive, when he died he would reincarnate as a human being. However, if a person had been bad, his soul would be sent to one of the 18 levels of hell for punishment. There, the King of Hell (Yan Luo Wang) would decide what kind of animal he should reincarnate as. If someone had been very bad, he would not reincarnate, but would stay in hell for an eternity of torture.

The religious philosophy and views on reincarnation of the Taoists were very similar to those of the Buddhists. This may be related to the fact that the Taoist religion was created only about one hundred years after Buddhism was imported into China. It is said that religious Taoism is a blend of Buddhism and traditional Taoism.

Like the Buddhists, the Taoists believe that if they can build up their spirit (Shen) so that it is independent and strong, they will be able to escape from the cycle of repeated reincarnation. When a Taoist or Buddhist has reached this stage, he has reached the goal of enlightenment or Buddhahood. It is said that he has attained eternal life. However, if he cannot build his spirit strong enough before he dies, his soul or spirit will not go to hell, and he will be able to control his own destiny and either stay a spirit or be reborn as a human. They believed that it is only possible to develop the human spirit while in a body, so that the continual cycle of rebirth is necessary to attain enlightenment.

The monks found that in order to enhance their spirit, they had to cultivate the Chi which was converted from their Jieng (Essence). The normal Taoist Chi Kung training process is 1. to convert the Jieng (essence) into Chi (Yii Jieng Huah Chi); 2. to nourish the Shen (spirit) with Chi (Yii Chi Huah Shen); 3. to refine the Shen into emptiness (Liann Shen Huan Shiu); and 4. to crush the emptiness (Feen Suory Shiu Kong). The first step is to firm and strengthen the Jieng, then convert this Jieng into Chi through meditation or other methods. This Chi is then led to the top of the head to nourish the brain and raise up the Shen. When a Taoist has reached this stage, it is called "the three flowers meet on the top." This stage is necessary to gain health and longevity. Finally, the Taoist can start training to reach the goal of enlightenment. However, the biggest obstacle to achieving this goal is the emotions, which affect the thinking and upset the balance of the spirit. This is the reason they hid themselves away in the mountains, away from other people and their distractions. They also abstained from eating meat, feeling that it muddied thinking and increased the emotions, leading the spirit away from self-cultivation.

While striving for enlightenment or Buddhahood, most Buddhist monks concentrate all their attention on the cultivation of the spirit. The Taoists, however, feel that in order to reach the final goal, you have to first be in good physical health. This may be the reason why more Taoists than Buddhists have lived very long lives. In their nineteen hundred years of research, they found many more ways to strengthen the body and to slow down the degeneration of the organs, which is the key to obtaining a long life. There have been many Taoists who have lived more than 150 years. In Taoist society it is said: "one hundred and twenty means dying young." Unfortunately, all of this Chi Kung training has been passed down secretly in the monasteries. It was not until the last twenty years that these secret theories and training methods were revealed to the outside world.

An important part of this training to prolong life is Marrow Washing Chi Kung. The basic idea of Marrow Washing Chi Kung is to keep the Chi circulating in your marrow so that the marrow stays clean and healthy. Your bone marrow manufactures your blood cells. The blood cells bring nourishment to the organs and all the other cells of the body, and also take waste products away. When your blood is healthy and functions properly, your whole body is well-nourished and healthy, and can resist disease effectively. When the marrow is clean and fresh, it manufactures an enormous number of healthy blood cells which will do their job properly. Your whole body will stay healthy, and the degeneration of your internal organs will be significantly slowed. Your body is not unlike an expensive car. It will run a long time if you use a high quality fuel; but if you use a low quality fuel, the car engine will deteriorate a lot faster than it needs to.

Although the theory is simple, the training is very difficult. You must first learn how to build up your Chi and fill up your eight Chi vessels (the 12 major Chi channels and 8 Chi vessels will be discussed in Part Three), and then you must know how to lead this Chi into the bone marrow to "wash" the marrow. Except for some Taoist monks, there are very few people who have lived more than 150 years. The reason for this is that the training process is long and hard. You must have a pure mind and a simple lifestyle so that you can concentrate entirely on the training. Without a peaceful life, your training will not be effective. This is why the Taoist monks hide themselves in the mountains. Unfortunately, this is simply not possible for the average person. Marrow Washing Chi Kung training will be discussed in the second volume of the YMAA in-depth Chi Kung book series.

Do not be misled into thinking that the Buddhist Charn (Zen) meditation is inferior to the Taoist approach. In fact, the Buddhists often had much greater success in reaching enlightenment than the Taoists through their use of still meditation. Additionally, many of the Taoist Chi Kung practices originated with the Buddhists. The Taoists then modified them to suit their own circumstances and purposes, and some of the practices, like Marrow Washing, were practiced much more widely by the Taoists than the Buddhists.

Many Taoist Chi Kung styles are based on the theory of cultivating both the spirit and the physical body. In Taoism, there are generally three ways of training: Gin Dan Dah Tao (Golden Elixir Large Way), Shuang Shiou (Double Training), and Tao Wai Tsae Yaw (Herb Picking outside of the Tao). Gin Dan Dah Tao teaches the ways of Chi Kung training within yourself. This approach believes that you can find the elixir of longevity or even enlightenment within your own body.

In the second approach, Shuang Shiou (double training), a partner is used to balance one's Chi more quickly. Most people's Chi is not entirely balanced. Some people are a bit too positive, others too negative, and individual channels also are positive or negative. If you know how to exchange Chi with your partner, you can help each other out and speed your training. Your partner can be either the same sex or opposite.

The third way, which is called Tao Wai Tsae Yao, uses herbs to speed and control the cultivation. Herbs can be plants such as ginseng, or animal products such as musk from the musk-deer.

According to the training methods used, Taoist Chi Kung can again be divided into two major schools: Ching Shiou Pay (Peaceful Cultivation Division) and Tzai Jie Pay (Plant and Graft Division). This division was especially clear after the Sung and Yuan dynasties (960-1367 A.D.). The meditation and the training theory and methods of the Ching Shiou Division are close to those of the Buddhists. They believed that the only way to reach enlightenment is Gin Dan Dah Tao (Golden Elixir Large Way), according to which you build up the elixir within your body. Using a partner for the cultivation is immoral and will cause emotional problems which may significantly affect the cultivation.

However, the Tzai Jie Pay claims that in addition to Gin Dan Dah Tao, their methods of Shuang Shiou (Double Training) and Tao Wai Tsae Yaw (Herb Picking outside of the Tao) make the cultivation faster and more practical. For this reason, Taoist Chi Kung training is also commonly called "Dan Diing Tao Kung," which means "the Tao Training in the Elixir Crucible." The Taoists originally believed that they would be able to find and purify the elixir from herbs. Later, they realized that the only real elixir was in your body.

According to my understanding, the major difference between the two Taoist schools is that the Ching Shiou Pay aims for enlightenment in a way similar to the Buddhists' striving for Buddhahood, while the Tzai Jie Pay uses the training to achieve a normal, healthy, long life. We will discuss these two major Taoist schools more extensively in a later volume.

You can see that Taoism has already been a religion and a scholarly study of Chi Kung methods. As a modern and scientific Chi Kung practitioner, you should only adopt the Chi Kung training methods which can benefit you. Superstition should be filtered out. However, you need to know the historical background so that you will understand the root and the motivation of the training.

To conclude, the characteristics of Taoist Chi Kung are:

A. Taoist Chi Kung and enlightenment theories were based on those of the Buddhists. It later developed into its own unique style.
B. Taoist religion was a mixture of Buddhism with traditional Taoism.
C. Original Taoist Chi Kung training aimed for enlightenment, and later was used for improving health and longevity.
D. There are two major schools of Taoist Chi Kung training, one of which is similar to Buddhist training.

Chapter 6

Chi Kung Theory

6-1. Introduction

Many people think that Chi Kung is a difficult subject to understand. In some ways, this is true. However, regardless of how difficult the theory and practice of a particular style of Chi Kung might be, the basic Chi theory and principles are very simple and remain the same for all of the Chi Kung styles. Basic Chi theory and Chi Kung principles are the roots of all Chi Kung practice, and it is from these roots that the different styles of training blossomed. Naturally, the results and the depth achieved are different from style to style. If, however, you understand the root of what you are doing, it does not matter which style you are practicing, because you will be able to grasp the key to the practice and grow.

As discussed in the last chapter, there are three major purposes of Chi Kung other than martial: health, longevity, and spiritual enlightenment. Although all three groups use the same basic Chi theory in their training, they use different training theories and methods to reach their goals. For example, people who are training for longevity use deeper, more advanced training methods than people who are practicing to improve their health, while the people who are striving for enlightenment use training theories and methods which are deeper still.

If you wish to understand the science of Chi Kung, you must understand the different categories and their respective training theories. This will be like a map of the terrain making it easier for you to select your goal and plan your route. Without this map, you will wander around confused, uncertain of your goal.

Previous sections have discussed general Chi theory, and some of the ways in which Chi affects human beings. Chi circulation theory will be discussed in greater detail later. Now, we will discuss general training theory and methods, and what each approach has to offer you.

Generally speaking, all Chi Kung practices, according to the training theory and methods, can be divided into two general categories: Wai Dan (External Elixir) and Nei Dan (Internal Elixir).

Understanding the difference between them will give you an overview of most Chinese Chi Kung practices.

6-2. Wai Dan (External Elixir)

"Wai" means "external or outside," and "Dan" means "elixir." External here means the limbs, as opposed to the torso, which includes all of the vital organs. Elixir is a hypothetical, life prolonging substance for which Chinese Taoists have been searching for millennia. They originally thought that the elixir was something physical which could be prepared with herbs or chemicals purified in a furnace. After thousands of years of study and experimentation, they found that the elixir is in the body. In other words, if you want to prolong your life, you must find the elixir in your body, and then learn to protect it and nourish it.

Sometimes Wai Dan also refers to herbal pills which can be used to adjust or increase the Chi circulation in the body. In this book we will only discuss the Chi Kung Wai Dan training theory and methods, and leave the discussion of herbal Wai Dan theory to qualified herbal masters.

The human body has twelve major Chi channels (Gin) (actually pairs of channels, one on either side of the body), which are comparable to rivers. Six of these are connected to the fingers, and the other six are connected to the toes. All of these twelve are connected to internal organs. The body also has eight Chi vessels which serve as reservoirs, and also regulate the Chi in the twelve channels. Millions of tiny channels (Lou) carry Chi from the major channels to every part of the body, from the skin to the bone marrow. Whenever the Chi is stagnant in any of the twelve major channels, the related organ will receive an incorrect amount of Chi. This will cause the organ to malfunction, or at least to degenerate sooner than normal, and this in turn will cause illness and premature aging if left uncorrected. Just as a machine needs the correct amount of current to run properly, your organs must have the right amount of Chi to function well. Therefore, the most basic way to maintain the health of the organs is to keep the Chi flow balanced and smooth. This is the idea upon which Wai Dan (External Elixir) Chi Kung is based.

The theory is very simple. When you do Wai Dan exercises you concentrate your attention on your limbs. As you exercise, the Chi builds up in your arms and legs. When the Chi potential in your limbs builds to a high enough level, the Chi will flow through the channels, clearing any obstructions and nourishing the organs. This is the main reason that a person who works out, or has a physical job, is generally healthier than someone who sits around all day.

There are many available Wai Dan Chi Kung sets. A typical one is Da Mo's Muscle/Tendon Changing Classic (Wai Dan Yi Gin Ching). In this set, the practitioner slightly tenses up the local limb muscles in specific postures, such as tensing up the wrist while holding both arms in front of the chest, and then relaxing completely. This repeated tensing and relaxing builds up a greater concentration of Chi in the area being exercised. When the practitioner finishes the exercise and relaxes, the accumulated Chi flows to the organs. In this category of Wai Dan training, the specific stationary postures and the tensing and relaxing of the muscles are the two ways in which the Chi circulation is increased.

There are other Wai Dan sets which, in addition to tensing and relaxing the muscles, also move the arms and legs in specific ways so that the muscles around certain organs are stretched and then relaxed. In addition to building up Chi in the limbs, these exercises increase the Chi circulation around and in the organs more directly than the Muscle/Tendon Changing Classic does. For example, you may raise your arms over your head and then lower them repeatedly, exercising the muscles around the lungs, extending and releasing them gently to massage the lungs and stimulate the flow of Chi and blood. A typical set of Wai Dan which uses moving exercises is the Eight Pieces of Brocade.

Many Chi Kung beginners believe mistakenly that since Wai Dan Chi Kung theory and training are simple, these sets are only for beginners. In fact, most people who train Nei Dan Chi Kung later come back to Wai Dan, and combine the two to increase their control over their Chi.

These two categories of Wai Dan training methods, in addition to improving martial arts performance, also give you a healthy body, and can even cure some illnesses. Improved health may increase the length of your life, but not to the 150 years that was achieved by some of the Taoists and Buddhists. These results require deeper theory and training, under the supervision of a qualified master. Longevity Chi Kung exercises will be discussed in the section on Nei Dan Chi Kung. I would like to conclude with three points about Wai Dan Chi Kung:

1. Wai Dan Chi Kung aims at maintaining health, and has only a limited effect on longevity. Many Wai Dan Chi Kung exercises were created to increase martial ability.
2. Wai Dan Muscle/Tendon tension and relaxation practice focuses on training the Chi in the limbs. The main purpose of increasing the Chi in the limbs is to energize the muscles to their highest efficiency. The specific postures also train the coordination of the muscles in the torso with those in the limbs. If you understand that one of the major purposes of Da Mo's Wai Dan exercises is to increase martial power, then you will see why the limbs are emphasized in the training. After Da Mo, many sets were created from the same theory, mostly by martial artists. Naturally, these exercises will also improve health. However, many martial artists who trained the Da Mo Wai Dan exercises heavily for a long time found that they over-developed their muscles the way weight lifters often do. Although they were healthy as long as they were able to practice, once they got old their muscles degenerated much faster than normal. This is called "San Kung" (energy dispersion). Because of this, Da Mo created a set of Nei Dan exercises which is also included in the Muscle/Tendon Changing Classic. This set builds up and circulates the Chi internally, preventing the Chi channels from plugging up when the practitioner gets older.
3. The moving Wai Dan practices focus on increasing the Chi circulation around the organs through specific movements. This category of Wai Dan practice will not build the muscles like the last category. Wai Dan exercises like this are used mainly for health.

6-3. Nei Dan (Internal Elixir)

Nei means internal and Dan means elixir. Thus, Nei Dan means to build the elixir internally. Here, internally means in the body instead of in the limbs. Whereas in Wai Dan the Chi is built up in the limbs and then moved into the body, Nei Dan exercises build up Chi in the body and lead it out to the limbs.

Generally speaking, Nei Dan theory is deeper than Wai Dan theory, and its training theory and methods are more difficult to understand and practice. Traditionally, most of the Nei Dan Chi Kung practices have been passed down more secretly than those of the Wai Dan. This is especially true of the highest levels of Nei Dan, such as Marrow Washing, which were passed down to only a few trusted disciples. There are a number of reasons for this:

1. Nei Dan is hard to understand, so only the disciples who were intelligent and wise enough to understand it were taught.
2. Nei Dan practice can be dangerous. Inaccurate practice may cause crippling, paralysis, or even death. This can happen especially to the disciple who does not understand the what, why, and how of his practice.
3. In much of Nei Dan Chi Kung you are working with and guided by very subtle feelings and sensations. Under the guidance of a master you should be able to grasp the key to the training in a short time. However, if you try to figure it out by yourself, you may get confused, or injure yourself seriously.
4. In order to reach the higher levels of Nei Dan Chi Kung, you must conserve your Jieng and restrain your sex life. Also, you must spend a lot of time in practice, which makes normal married life impossible. Furthermore, in order to reach a spiritual balance, you must train yourself to be emotionally neutral and independent. In order to preserve your Jieng and have a peaceful environment for your training, you almost have to go away to the mountains and become a hermit, or become a monk in a monastery. Still, though Nei Dan is difficult to understand and practice, it is practiced by many laymen. They, however, can only reach a certain level of achievement, such as health and longevity, but not enlightenment.

Before we discuss the training categories of Nei Dan, you should understand how Nei Dan Chi Kung practice relates to the Chi circulation in the human body. As we have mentioned, the human body has twelve Chi channels which are considered Chi rivers. Each of these channels is connected to a finger or toe, and is also associated with an internal organ. In order to keep the twelve organs healthy, the Chi flowing in the Chi rivers must be smooth and continuous, and the Chi level running in each channel must be appropriate for that channel. Whenever the Chi flow is stagnant or the Chi level abnormal, the organs will not function properly and may eventually be damaged. Therefore, the first goal of this Chi Kung practice is to keep the Chi running smoothly and at the appropriate levels in the channels.

In addition to these twelve channels, there are eight vessels which are considered Chi reservoirs and which regulate the Chi running in the Chi rivers. In order to have the potential to supply and regulate the Chi, the vessels must be full. When there is enough Chi in the reservoirs to supply and regulate the Chi in the rivers, you will be healthy. Therefore, the second goal of Chi Kung practice is to learn to fill up the Chi reservoirs with Chi.

When you have attained these two goals, you have built a good foundation for a healthy body. The training methods you must practice to reach these two goals are explained clearly in Da Mo's

Muscle/Tendon Changing Classic. However, if you desire longevity, you must enter a deeper level of Nei Dan Chi Kung exercises. This level is described in Da Mo's Marrow Washing Classic.

In order to have a long life, you need to have not only a healthy physical body and smooth Chi circulation, but also training in two more disciplines. The first concerns your blood, the second your spirit. Your blood runs through your entire body. If your blood cells are not healthy, it does not matter how healthy and strong your physical body and organs appear to be, because your physical body will degenerate quickly. The marrow is the factory which makes your blood cells. If you know how to keep your marrow healthy and fresh, the quality of the blood cells will be high. When these healthy and fresh blood cells are running in your physical body, the degeneration process will slow down and your lifespan will increase.

When you train Marrow Washing Chi Kung, you must also learn how to lead Chi to your brain and raise up your Shen. When the Shen is raised, you will have a center or headquarters which will be able to effectively control your Chi and strengthen your body's Guardian Chi so that it is better able to repel negative outside influences. The raised Shen will also direct the Chi so that the organs function properly. However, the most important benefit of Marrow Washing training is the fresh, nourishing Chi brought to your brain, which insures its health. Marrow Washing training will keep your brain strong, calm, and peaceful.

Before we discuss Nei Dan practice further, you should understand that there are many different methods of Nei Dan practice. We will discuss the two major ones: Da Mo's Muscle/Tendon Changing Classic (Yi Gin Ching), and his Marrow Washing Classic (Shii Soei Ching).

A. Da Mo's Muscle/Tendon Changing Classic (Da Mo Yi Gin Ching):

As mentioned before, Da Mo's Muscle/Tendon Changing Classic includes two parts. The first part is the Wai Dan external Chi Kung exercises, and the second part is the Nei Dan internal Chi Kung training. The Wai Dan external Chi Kung has already been discussed, so we will discuss the Nei Dan internal training here. Da Mo's Nei Dan training includes two major practices:

I. Small Circulation (Sheau Jou Tian):

One of the major purposes of Nei Dan training is to fill up the Chi reservoirs, i.e. the eight vessels. When the Chi there is abundant, you will be able to supply enough Chi to the rest of your body. Small Circulation has two major purposes. The first purpose is to build up Chi at the Lower Dan Tien, and the second purpose is to store and circulate Chi in the two major reservoirs: the Conception and Governing vessels.

You must learn abdominal breathing in order to build up Chi at your Lower Dan Tien. Then you must lead this Chi to circulate in the vessels and open up the cavities which are plugged up or where the Chi flow is sluggish. For example, when you were a child, the Huiyin cavity (Figure 6-1) in the perineum was wide open. However, as you got older and abandoned abdominal breathing, it gradually plugged up so that the Chi circulation through it became sluggish. There are a number of other cavities where the Chi path narrows and the circulation slows down. Wherever the circulation is sluggish and unsmooth, the Chi supply to the organs and the entire body will lose its balance and you may become sick.

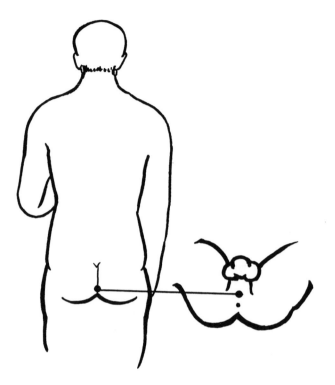

Figure 6-1. Huiyin cavity

There are a number of ways in which Chi can be circulated in the body through the Small Circulation. However, there are two major ones which are commonly practiced: the "Fire Path" and the "Wind Path."

a. The Fire Path:

The Fire Path is the way Chi naturally circulates in the human body. The Chi moves down the Conception Vessel (Ren Mei) and up the Governing Vessel (Du Mei)(Figure 6-2). The Conception vessel is considered Yin (negative), and runs down the center of the front of the body. The Governing vessel is considered Yang (positive). It runs from the Huiyin, where it connects to the Conception vessel, up along the outside of the spine to the back of the neck, passes over the head to the top of the inside of the mouth where it connects with the Yin vessel on the tongue.

Normally, Post-birth Chi (Fire Chi), which was converted from the Jieng of food and air in the "Sanjiou" (triple burner). After this Chi is converted, it is stored in the Middle Dan Tien. This Chi moves down to the Lower Dan Tien and mixes with Water Chi. The mixed Chi moves down to the Huiyin, and at the Huiyin it divides into two Chi flows. One of them enters the Thrusting Vessel (Chong Mei) in

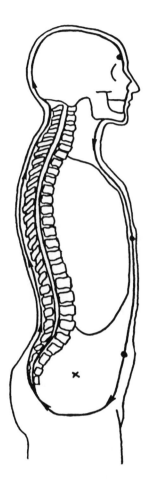

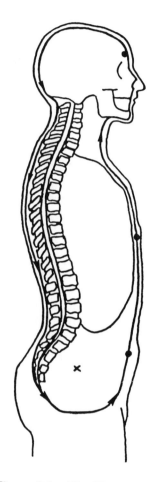

Figure 6-2. The Fire Path of Chi circulation

Figure 6-3. The Wind Path of Chi circulation

the marrow of the spine and moves up to nourish the brain. This path is considered the "Water Path" and is the path trained in Marrow Washing Chi Kung. The Water Path will be discussed later. The second flow passes the Huiyin and moves up the back following the Governing vessel (along the outside of the spine), passes over the crown and finally connects to the Conception vessel to complete the cycle. This second path is the "Fire Path."

As Chi circulates through the Fire Path, there is always one part of the path where the Chi level is higher than elsewhere, and this area circulates around the path regularly twenty four hours. It is this area of higher Chi potential which keeps the Chi flowing. (I believe that this potential is created by the earth's spinning inside the sun's electromagnetic field.) Just as water will only flow from a higher to a lower level, Chi will only move from a place of higher potential to one of lower potential. In Chinese medicine, this place of higher potential is called "Tzyy Wuu Liou Juh." Tzyy refers to the two hours between 11 PM and 1 AM, and Wuu refers to the time between 11 AM to 1 PM. Liou means "flow," and Juh means "tendency." Tzyy Wuu Liou Juh therefore means "the major Chi flow tendency which follows the time change." In the Fire path, the place of higher potential normally starts at noon at the Middle Dan Tien (solar plexus) and moves down to reach the Lower Dan Tien and mix with the Dan Tien Chi between 2-4 PM. Next, it goes down to the Huiyin at sunset and moves to the back in the evening, reaching the top of the head at midnight At sunrise the Chi is in the face, and by noon it has reached the Middle Dan Tien to complete the cycle.

One of the major purposes of Small Circulation practice is to build up Original Chi at the Lower Dan Tien. Original Chi is created from the Original Essence drawn from the kidneys, which mixes with and dilutes the Post-birth Chi which comes from food and air. Post-birth Chi, which contains undesirable products from the food and air, is considered Fire Chi because it has a heating effect on the body. Original Chi is considered Water Chi, and it is pure and cools down the Fire Chi. Diluting and cooling down the contaminated Chi is the first step in cooling down the fire in your physical body. This process will slow your body's degeneration. In the Fire Path, a practitioner usually learns to build or strengthen his Water Chi in the Lower Dan Tien (Field of Elixir) through abdominal breathing or mental concentration. When the Chi is built up to a certain level, the mind leads the Chi to circulate through the Conception and Governing Vessels.

Another task in Small Circulation is the opening of cavities where the Chi flow is sluggish. In Fire Path Chi Kung training, there are three cavities which must be opened and are considered dangerous. If you do not understand this and do not proceed cautiously, you might cause yourself serious injury. The Fire Path will be discussed in greater detail in a later volume on Taoist meditation. You may also refer to the chapter on Nei Dan in the author's Chi Kung book: "Chi Kung - Health and Martial Arts."

b. The Wind Path:

Generally speaking, the Wind Path of Chi circulation is not as popular as the Fire Path. Because it circulates Chi in the direction opposite to the normal flow, many Chi Kung practitioners believe that it will disturb the natural Chi circulation and cause problems. There are very few documents which discuss this path. However, some discuss a portion of the complete cycle, usually from the Lower Dan Tien up to the Middle Dan Tien, and many Chi Kung practitioners have trained it.

In this portion of the Wind Path Chi circulation, once the Original Chi is built up in the Dan Tien, the practitioner leads it up to circulate in the direction opposite to the one trained in the Fire Path (Figure 6-3). Normally, this is trained when you have completed your Fire Path Small Circulation. There are two reasons for circulating the Wind Path:

1. To slow down the natural Chi circulation in the Conception and Governing Vessels by circulating Chi against the flow. If the Chi flow in your Fire path is too Yang because of excitement, injury, sickness, or even eating poor food, your whole body will become too Yang when this Chi is distributed through the twelve Chi channels. This Yang Chi will damage your organs, and make your mind excited and scattered. The Wind Path can regulate the Chi circulating in your Fire Path, and rebalance the Chi in your body.

2. An important Chi Kung practice is raising up the Pre-birth Chi (Essence Chi or Water Chi) generated in the Lower Dan Tien to cool down the Post-birth Chi (food and air Chi, or Fire Chi) which is generated in the Middle Dan Tien at the solar plexus. When this is done, the clean Water Chi will be able to dilute the contaminated Fire Chi before it starts to circulate. This raising of the Water Chi is done through the Wind Path.

Wind Path circulation will be discussed in more detail in a later volume on Taoist meditation.

II. Large Circulation (Dah Jou Tian):

After you have opened up the path of the Conception and Governing vessels, you have completed what is called "Sheau Jou Tian," or "Small Circulation." This was the first step in the Nei Dan part of Da Mo's Muscle/Tendon Changing Classic. The second step is opening the twelve channels to keep the Chi flowing in the organs and limbs. As we mentioned before, Nei Dan differs from Wai Dan Chi Kung in that it builds up Chi in the body and then circulates it outward to the limbs.

Only after you have opened up all of the twelve channels and the Chi is able to flow to the extremities are you protected from the Chi blockages which are associated with the Wai Dan Muscle/Tendon exercises. Once you have completed your Large Circulation, you have completed Da Mo's Nei Dan Muscle/Tendon Chi Kung training. This training must be completed before a Chi Kung practitioner begins Da Mo's Marrow Washing Chi Kung training.

B. Da Mo's Marrow Washing Classic (Da Mo Shii Soei Ching):

Da Mo's Marrow Washing Classic was kept secret until only the last ten years. It explains the secret of longevity and of reaching the goal of enlightenment and Buddhahood. Both the theory and the training are deep. Normally, only those who thoroughly understood Chi Kung training theory and had long years of Chi Kung experience, especially of Da Mo's Muscle/Tendon Changing Classic, were taught the Marrow Washing Classic.

The Chinese name of the work is "Shii Soei Ching." Shii means "to wash, to keep clean and fresh." Soei means two things, the marrow which is called "Guu Soei" and the brain which is called "Nao Soei." Ching is a treatise or classic. You can see from this that the main goal of Shii Soei Ching is to wash the bone marrow and the brain and keep them clean and fresh.

Generally speaking, Marrow Washing has two major purposes: longevity, and enlightenment or Buddhahood. Laymen usually strive for longevity, while monks sought enlightenment or Buddhahood as the culmination of their Taoist or Buddhist training. We will discuss these two purposes briefly here. The interested reader should refer to the YMAA book "Muscle/Tendon Changing and Marrow Washing Chi Kung."

1. Longevity:

According to Chinese medicine, your body deteriorates as you age mainly because your blood loses its ability to feed and protect your body. Your bone marrow produces the red blood cells and one type of the white blood cells, but as you grow older, the marrow becomes "dirty," and produces fewer and fewer useful blood cells. However, if you know how to "wash" the marrow, it will start once again to produce fresh, healthy blood. Your body will begin to rejuvenate itself, and restore itself to the glowing health of youth.

You should understand that in order to produce healthy blood cells, the marrow must be alive, fresh (clean), and active. To keep the marrow fresh and alive and functioning properly, Chi must be plentiful and continuously supplied. Whenever there is a shortage of Chi, the marrow will not function normally. In Marrow Washing Chi Kung, you must first learn how fill up the "eight extraordinary Chi vessels" with Chi. These vessels are your reservoirs of Chi. With plenty of Chi stored in them, you will have enough Chi to supply your muscles, organs, and marrow. In order to fill up the reservoirs, you must learn how to efficiently convert your Essence into Chi. You must also learn how to increase your Essence so that you will have enough material to convert into Chi. Essence is like the fuel, Chi is like the energy generated, and bone marrow is the factory. With plenty of energy supplied, the production line of the blood cells will be healthy. When the fresh and healthy blood cells are circulated throughout your body, they will carry out their mission efficiently. This will slow down the degeneration of your physical body so that it lasts a lot longer. It is just like running an expensive car with good quality fuel - the car will run more efficiently and last a lot longer.

2. Enlightenment:

For the Chinese monks, Marrow Washing is only a step necessary for reaching the final goal of enlightenment or Buddhahood. In order to reach this purpose, the Chi must be led up through the marrow in the spine to nourish the brain. When the brain is nourished, the Shen is also nourished, and it will grow stronger and stronger until it is able to reach the final goal of spiritual independence.

According to Chinese medical science, the Chong Mei (Thrusting Vessel) is the major Chi reservoir which supplies Chi to the brain. Chong Mei is located in the marrow of the spine. Therefore, in order to have plenty of Chi to continuously nourish the brain and Shen, the Chong Mei reservoir must be kept full.

You can see that religious Marrow Washing concentrates on the spine marrow. However, for good health and longevity you must wash the marrow in all of the bones so that all of the blood cell factories function properly. Many techniques have been developed by Chi Kung practitioners to achieve this purpose. However, the most complete and profound study both in theory and training is credited to the Taoists. Since ancient times, Taoists have practiced Chi Kung for both longevity and enlightenment.

Do not think that there is no health and longevity benefit when the Chi is led to nourish the brain and raise up the Shen. As a matter of fact, your brain and spirit are the center and headquarters of your whole being. When your brain is healthy, you will be able to think clearly. You need to have a healthy brain if you want a healthy body. In the same way, your Shen is your Chi control center. When your spirit is high the Chi can be led efficiently to every part of the body, but when your spirit is low your energy level will be low and the Chi will not circulate smoothly.

Generally, there are three steps to Marrow Washing Chi Kung training:

1. To increase the Essence:

The Essence which is converted into Chi in Marrow Washing is not primarily from the kidneys, but rather from the sexual organs (testicles in men and ovaries in women). Essence here means the hormones. Many ways have been developed to increase this Essence. This will be discussed more fully in the YMAA book "Muscle/Tendon Changing and Marrow Washing Chi Kung."

2. To convert the Essence into Chi:

There are two vessels or Chi reservoirs in your legs which are called "Yinchaio Mei." Their main Chi source is the Essence which comes from your sexual organs. When the Chi that is in these vessels is withdrawn, more Chi will automatically be converted. Therefore, you must know how to draw Chi from these reservoirs. This is done in the next step.

3. To sublimate the Chi upward:

This means to lead your Chi upward into the Chong Mei (Thrusting vessel) to wash the spine marrow, and then into the brain to nourish the brain and raise up the Shen.

You can see that the processes discussed above include "converting the Essence into Chi" (Liann Jieng Huah Chi) and "nourishing the Shen with the Chi" (Liann Chi Huah Shen). There are two more steps to reach the final goal of enlightenment. These two steps are: "to refine the Shen and enter emptiness" (Liann Shen Huan Shiu) and "to crush the emptiness" (Feen Suory Shiu Kong). This will be discussed in the YMAA book on Marrow Washing Chi Kung.

The Water Path:

Now that you have some idea of Marrow Washing Chi Kung training, it is time to discuss the water path of Chi Kung circulation. Water path Chi Kung, which passes through the marrow of the spine, is one of the higher levels of Chi Kung practice. Once you have built your Pre-birth Chi in the Dan Tien, you use your mind and special training to lead the Chi into the branch of the Thrusting Vessel (Chong Mei) which is located in the marrow of the spine (Figure 6-4). The water path, which is used in Marrow Washing, uses the Water Chi generated from the Lower Dan Tien, but it also generates Chi through a different method, for example, by using the sexual organs as mentioned above.

The average person already has some circulation in the water path to nourish the brain. In the evening, when the Chi circulation is strongest in the Huiyin, it divides into two flows. One flow circulates in the fire path outside of the spine, and the other passes through the marrow of the spine and moves up to nourish the brain and Shen. This usually happens at midnight while you are sleeping. Between midnight and early morning, the Chi also flows to the groin to energize the area and stimulate the generation of hormones and semen (Jieng or Essence). A major part of Marrow Washing Chi Kung is increasing the efficiency of the conversion of semen into Chi and leading it to nourish the brain and energize the Shen (spirit). The energized mind is then able to adjust the Chi level in the organs and other parts of the body. This Chi Kung practice is difficult to do, but, once competence has been achieved, the practice is the most efficient. It is reported that priests who reach this level are able to slow down the aging process to a minimum, and some are able to live over two hundred years.

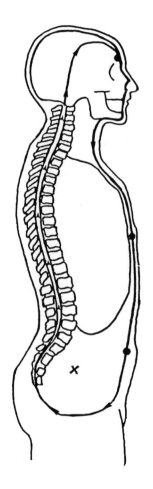

Figure 6-4. The Water Path of Chi circulation

PART TWO

GENERAL KEYS TO
CHI KUNG TRAINING

Chapter 7

General Concepts

7-1. Introduction

When the average person goes to an apple orchard, he will usually pay attention only to the fruit. If he goes to a nursery, he will notice only the beauty and fragrance of the flowers. Few people consider that the fruit and flowers are only the result of a great deal of planning, preparation, and hard work. In the same way, when most people see another person's success, few will stop to think about how that person could be so successful. Chinese people say: "When there is a result, there must be a cause," and "If you want to harvest rice, you must first plant rice." You have to know what you want and plan how to get it. Without this, there is no beginning. Next your project must be patiently nourished, watered, and protected. If the root is not nourished and protected, the tree will not grow strong, and the harvest will not be bountiful.

Chi Kung training is not much different from growing a tree. In order for the Chi Kung tree to grow well and give an abundant harvest, you must plant a healthy seed. This means you must first do some research about the different kinds of trees so that you will know how to pick a seed which will grow into the kind of tree you want. In Part One we spread out all the seeds in front of you so that you could understand the background of the various Chi Kung training categories. Next you must learn how to plant the seed, water it, protect it, and make it grow. If you nourish and protect it, the root of the plant will grow strong, and you can expect a good harvest. If the root is weak, your Chi Kung tree will wither and die.

The purpose of Part Two is to show you how to plant the seed, nourish it, and protect it. You should understand that it does not matter which type of tree you are growing, the general theory and methods for making the tree grow healthily remain the same. You always need sunshine, water, good soil, fertilizer, and protection from insects, and you always need to know where and when to plant your seed.

There are five things which you must know in order to make your Chi Kung tree grow well. These are: regulating the body (Tyau Shenn), regulating the breathing (Tyau Shyi), regulating the mind (Tyau Hsin), regulating the Chi (Tyau Chi), and regulating the Shen (Tyau Shen). You also need to know how they are interrelated. These are the foundation of successful Chi Kung practice. Without this foundation, your understanding of Chi Kung and your practice will remain superficial.

This gives you an idea of the "How" in Chi Kung training. However, knowing "How" is not enough. It only offers you the theory and principles of training which have been developed by previous Chi Kung practitioners. Following the past may lead you to great success in your Chi Kung training, but it will not help you to develop Chi Kung training any further. For this you must not only know "How," you must also know "Why." A farmer may know the "How" of growing apple trees well, but only someone who understands the "Why" of it all will be able to improve the growing techniques or develop new variety of apples. It is the same in Chi Kung training, you want to be a Chi Kung botanist instead of just a Chi Kung farmer. "Why" and "How" are the roots of understanding. They are the theory and principle of study.

Having an understanding of the "Why" of the training is especially important when you are just beginning. It lets you make an informed choice of a style which is best for you, and since you have a clear idea of where you are going, you can be confident, patient, and strong willed enough to complete the training.

The rest of this chapter will discuss the key parts of Chi Kung training, such as how to build up Chi and the importance of Kan and Lii. Chapters 8 to 13 will discuss the general keys to Chi Kung training, such as how to regulate your body, breath, emotional mind, Essence, Chi, and Shen (spirit). Finally, Chapter 14 will review some important points in Chi Kung practice.

7-2. Building Chi

Before we go any further in our discussion of the keys to Chi Kung training, you should first understand how Chi is generated in your body. Generally, the Chi is generated or converted naturally and automatically from the Essences within your body. These Essences include the inherited Original Essence which goes to make Water Chi, and the Essence from food and air which is transformed into Fire Chi. This natural Chi generation is the major source of your lifeforce. If you eat more than you need, and don't excrete the surplus, the extra food Essence will be stored in your body as fat. If you do not eat enough to provide for your daily energy needs, the food Essence stored as fat will be converted into Chi.

When you practice Chi Kung you are looking to build up the Chi in your body, to increase the efficiency of the conversion of Essence into Chi, and to increase the smoothness of the Chi circulation. In order to increase the smoothness of the circulation you must build up the level of Chi and create Chi potential. When there is a difference in potential, the Chi will flow from the area of higher potential to the area of lower potential, thereby increasing the circulation. This will also clear up blockages that hinder the flow of Chi.

There are many ways to build up Chi in the body. Analysis of the Chi Kung practices known to the author shows that the methods of building up Chi can be divided into four categories: 1. physical stimulation, 2. mental stimulation, 3. energizing the Shen, and 4. others.

1. Physical Stimulation:

Physical stimulation is probably the easiest and most basic method of building up Chi. The theory is very simple. Whenever you move you need Chi to energize the muscles. If you keep moving for an extended period of time, Chi will have to be continuously supplied to the muscles. In order to keep supplying Chi, your body has to be continuously converting the Essence stored in your body into Chi. The more you exercise, the more Chi will be converted, and the more Chi will be built up in the area you are exercising. Once you stop your exercises, part of this accumulated Chi will be dissipated into the air from your skin, and the remainder will flow into the body to increase the Chi circulation in the Chi channels.

We would like to remind you that if you over-exercise a particular area, your Chi may become too positive. As this Chi overflows into the channels, it may make your internal organs too positive, and speed up their degeneration. This is sometimes seen in people who do a lot of weightlifting. However, if you exercise properly, the Chi will circulate smoothly and your organs will receive only the proper amount of Chi. People who exercise correctly and regularly are usually healthier than people who do not exercise.

As discussed in the sixth chapter, exercises which build up Chi in the limbs are called Wai Dan. Wai Dan Chi Kung exercises are simple. They are almost like any of the exercises which are common in the Western world. The only two differences are that when you practice you must concentrate your mind at the area being trained, and that the movements are designed for special purposes such as regulating specific organs. You should understand that it is your mind which leads the Chi to the area being trained. When you concentrate, you can build up and circulate the Chi more efficiently than when you don't concentrate. This is especially true right after exercising, when you are relaxed. When your muscles are relaxed and loose, the Chi channels are wide open. If you concentrate and use your Yi to lead the Chi you have built up to your body, in coordination with your inhalations, you will be able to reduce the amount of Chi dissipated into the air, and the Chi can more efficiently nourish your body.

Try the following experiment. It will help you to understand the key to building up and circulating Chi. It is a very simple Wai Dan exercise called "Goong Shoou," which means "Arcing the Arms." This exercise originated in Tai Chi, where it is very widely practiced. It provides the Chi Kung beginner with a simple way to experience Chi flow.

For this exercise, stand with one leg rooted on the ground and the other in front of it, with only the toes touching the ground. Both arms are held in front of the chest, forming a horizontal circle, with the fingertips almost touching (Figure 7-1). The tongue should touch the roof of the mouth to connect the Yin and Yang Chi Vessels (Conception and Governing Vessels respectively). The mind should be calm and relaxed and concentrated on the shoulders; breathing should be deep and regular.

When you stand in this posture for about three minutes, your arms and one side of your back should feel sore and warm. Because the arms are held extended, the muscles and nerves are stressed. Chi will build up in this area and heat will be generated. Also, because one leg carries all the weight, the muscles and nerves in that leg and in one side of the back will be tense and will thereby build up Chi. Because this Chi is built up in the shoulders and legs rather than in the Dan Tien, it is considered "local Chi" or "Wai Dan Chi." In order to keep the Chi build-up and the flow in the back balanced, after three minutes change your legs without moving the arms and stand this way for another three minutes. After the six minutes, put both feet flat on the floor, shoulder-width apart, and slowly

Figure 7-1. Posture of "Arcing
the Arms"

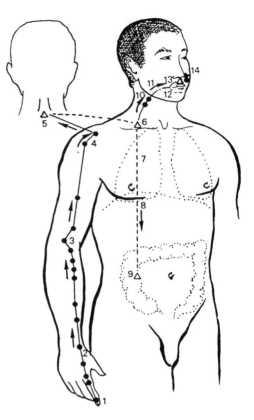

Figure 7-2. The Large Intestine
Channel of Hand-
Yang Brightness

lower your arms. The accumulated Chi will then flow into your arms
naturally and strongly. It is just like a dam which, after accumulating a
large amount of water, releases it and lets it flow out. At this time,
concentrate and calm the mind and look for the feeling of Chi flowing from
the shoulders to the palms and fingertips. Beginners can usually sense
this Chi flow, which is typically felt as warmth or a slight numbness.

Naturally, when you hold your arms out, you are also slowing the blood
circulation, and when you lower your hands the blood will rush down into
them. This may confuse you as to whether what you feel is due to Chi or
the blood. You need to understand several things. First, wherever there is
a living blood cell, there has to be Chi to keep it alive. Thus, when you
relax after the arcing hands practice, both blood and Chi will come down
to the hands. Second, since blood is material and Chi is energy, Chi can
flow beyond your body but your blood cannot. Therefore, it is possible for
you to test whether the exercise has brought extra Chi to your hands.
Place your hands right in front of your face. You should be able to feel a
slight sensation, which has to come from the Chi. You can also hold your
palms close to each other, or move one hand near the other arm. In
addition to a slight feeling of warmth, you may also sense a kind of electric
charge which may make the hairs on your arm move. Blood cannot cause
these feelings, so they have to be symptoms of Chi.

Sometimes Chi is felt on the upper lip. This is because there is a
channel (Hand Yangming Large Intestine) which runs over the top of the

shoulder to the upper lip (Figure 7-2). However, the feeling is usually stronger in the palms and fingers than in the lip, because there are six Chi channels which pass through the shoulder to end in the hand, but there is only one channel connecting the lip and shoulder. Once you experience Chi flowing in your arms and shoulders during this exercise, you may also find that you can sense it in your back.

This exercise is one of the most common practices for leading the beginner to experience the flow of Chi, and some Tai Chi styles place great emphasis on it. A similar type of Chi Kung exercise is also practiced by other styles, such as Ermei Dah Perng Kung.

2. Mental Stimulation:

In the third chapter we discussed how it is possible for your body to move. We said that in order to move, you must first generate an idea. This idea will lead the Chi to the muscles to energize them so that they execute the order from your brain. You can see that your mind plays a most important role in your Chi Kung practice. It is said: "Yii Yi Yin Chi"(*1), which means "Use your Yi (wisdom mind) to lead your Chi." Notice the word "**LEAD**." Chi must be led. The word "lead" means that your mind must go first, and your Chi will naturally follow. If your mind is not ahead of your Chi, the Chi will not be led and your muscles will not be energized.

For example, if you want to walk from one spot to another, you must first generate the idea of going to the second spot. This idea leads the Chi to the leg muscles and energizes them. If your mind stays at the first spot instead of going to the second one, you will not be able to move. You can see that it is your mind which you must activate first. Because of this, calming down and concentrating your mind is a very important part of Chi Kung training. **THE MORE YOU CAN CONCENTRATE, THE STRONGER YOUR YI WILL BE, AND, NATURALLY, THE STRONGER YOUR CHI WILL FLOW.**

Generally speaking, building up Chi by using the mind alone without physical movement is much harder than using the mind and movement together. However, since the mind is so important in Chi Kung training, learning how to regulate your mind has become one of the major trainings.

The mental buildup of Chi is divided into Wai Dan and Nei Dan. In Wai Dan, the mind focuses on the limbs. You must imagine that you are making an appropriate motion in order to generate the proper idea, because this idea will lead the Chi to the area. After you practice for a few minutes, the Chi will be built up in the area. The stronger you can concentrate, the more you will be able to feel the Chi.

Try this experiment. It will give you a feel for how Chi can be built up by your thinking. Hold your hands in front of you, where you feel that you can push downward most strongly (Figure 7-3). Your entire body must remain relaxed, especially your shoulders and arms. Inhale deeply, and as you exhale, image that you are pushing your hands down against a table. Do not actually move your body or arms, simply stand still with all of your muscles relaxed. If you are concentrating fully on what you are doing, after a few pushes your hands should start getting warm, and you may notice a sensation like air coming out of the center of your palms. This feeling will disappear when you inhale.

It is harder to feel the Chi in this exercise because there is no physical stimulation. However, if you concentrate and relax enough, you will soon

(*1). "以意引氣。"

Figure 7-3. Feeling Chi on the palms by imaging pushing downward

be able to feel something happening in your palms. This is a typical experiment in which you use your Yi (the idea that you are pushing) to lead the Chi to the palms. The more you practice, the stronger you will be able to lead the Chi to your palms. Naturally, this is only an experiment. An experienced Chi Kung practitioner is able to lead Chi to any part of his body simply by thinking. This particular exercise is of course a Wai Dan Chi Kung since the Chi is accumulated in the limbs.

In Nei Dan mental Chi generation, the theory remains the same. The differences are first, you must concentrate your mind at the Lower Dan Tien and build up the Chi there, and second, you do not imagine that you are moving. You can, however, use a different idea, such as that your Dan Tien area is on fire. Your mind must stay at your Dan Tien until you have built up the Chi. This training is called "Yi Shoou Dan Tien"(*2)(keeping your Yi on your Dan Tien). The more you can concentrate, the faster and stronger the Chi will be built up. This Dan Tien Chi generation without physical stimulation is the source of Chi for Buddhist still meditation. Naturally, this exercise is much harder than the Wai Dan one.

3. Energizing Shen:
When you are excited because of happiness or joy, you will often feel that your body is hot. This is because you have energized your spirit to a higher state, making your body too Yang, and your mind has directed the excess Chi to the skin to dissipate it so that the body can regain its energy balance. In the same way, when you are scared or nervous your body becomes too Yin and you may start

---

(*2)." 意守丹田。"

trembling. Your body will then automatically tense up to keep from losing Chi through the skin. Tensing the body narrows the Chi channels and cuts down the circulation. This tensing phenomenon is also common in the winter when you feel cold and are shivering. If, at such times, you relax and exhale as you lead Chi to your skin, you will be able to expand your Guardian Chi and stop feeling cold. Naturally, you will lose more Chi this way and will need to eat more to replenish the supply.

You may have guessed that your Chi is closely related to your feelings. But you should also know that your feelings are generated from your mind and directed by your spirit. In Chi Kung training, one of the most important practices is stabilizing and firming your spirit. This enables you to keep your emotions under control, and avoid extremes of excitation or depression. You are also able to build up or calm down your Chi by raising or calming your spirit. One of the final stages of Chi Kung training involves using your spirit to efficiently govern the Chi in your body.

Remember the times when you were tired both physically and mentally, and how easy it was to fall asleep then? When your mind is tired, your spirit gets weak, and loses control over your body. Your body seeks to recover from its fatigue, and let the Chi rebalance itself -- i.e. you fall asleep so that your Yi gets out of the way and doesn't interfere with the rebalancing. However, if you are excited over something, or worried, your mind won't relax, and the Chi in your brain will keep your spirit high.

For example, suppose at work you are assigned an important project which must be completed by a certain deadline. Furthermore, your boss promises that you will have a two week vacation once the assignment is finished. While working on the project you cannot sleep well, you are thinking about it all the time, and you are worried and excited. Your mind is always busy and your spirit is continually in a highly excited state. You may find that even though everyone else in your office catches the flu, you don't. Finally, the project is completed and you have a two week vacation. All of the pressure is gone and at last you can relax. However, you find that when you start your vacation, you suddenly become ill.

This is a common phenomenon which is very easy to explain according to Chi Kung principles. When you are in an excited and nervous state, your spirit is high. The spirit governs the Managing and Guardian Chi, and when the spirit is high it allows the Managing Chi to run your body very efficiently, and it builds up a strong shield of Guardian Chi around your body which effectively protects you from illness. However, once you have completed your project, the pressure is gone and your mind is relaxed, and so your spirit weakens. This allows the shield of Guardian Chi to weaken, and you get sick easily. Perhaps you've heard people say: "I don't get sick because I'm too busy to get sick." As a matter of fact, this is true. When you are busy, your excited mind raises your spirit and increase its efficiency in governing the Chi.

Perhaps you have heard of someone who was desperately ill, and the doctors gave up all hope. However, because the patient had great faith and a strong will to live, he miraculously recovered. Again, his spirit played a role. His faith and strong will to live raised his spirit, which caused his Chi to repair the damage.

In the first example, the spirit was raised mainly by the emotional mind, and in the second example it was raised by the calm and firm wisdom mind. Raising the spirit with a calm mind and strong will is closer to the idea of how Chi Kung trains the spirit.

In Chi Kung training, you balance your Chi with your spirit, which is different from how your Chi balances during rest or sleep. In Chi Kung training you first train to regulate your mind, which makes your spirit steady, firm, and regulated. Then you use your mind and spirit to regulate the Chi in your body while you are meditating. When your emotional mind is regulated, you will be able to raise your spirit with your Yi without getting excited. This raised spirit will be able to govern the flow of Chi and regulate it efficiently.

4. Others:

There are many other ways to build up the Chi or to increase its circulation in the body. Chinese medical society uses three: massage or acupressure, acupuncture, and herbal treatment. Massage and acupuncture use physical stimulation from outside of the body. Herbal treatment uses herbs either applied to the skin or taken internally. Controlling the diet is also considered an herbal internal regulating process. Chi Kung massage will be discussed in another YMAA Chi Kung book. Acupuncture and herbal treatment are discussed in many books available today.

7-3. Kan and Lii

The terms "Kan and Lii" occur frequently in Chi Kung documents. In the Eight Trigrams "Kan" represents "Water" while "Lii" represents "Fire." However, the everyday terms for water and fire are also often used. Kan and Lii training has long been of major importance to Chi Kung practitioners. In order to understand why, you must understand these two words, and the theory behind them.

Kan is water and represents Yin in relationship to Lii, which represents fire and Yang. Chi Kung practitioners believe theoretically that your body is always too Yang unless you are sick or have not eaten for a long time, in which case your body may be more Yin. When your body is always Yang, it is degenerating and burning out. It is believed that this is the cause of aging. If you are able to use "Water" to cool down your body, you will be able to slow down the degeneration process and thereby lengthen your life. This is the main reason why Chinese Chi Kung practitioners have been studying ways of improving the quality of the Water in their bodies, and of reducing the quantity of the Fire. I believe that as a Chi Kung practitioner, you should always keep this subject at the top of your list for study and research. If your earnestly ponder and experiment, you will be able to grasp the trick of adjusting "Fire" and "Water" in your body.

The Origins of "Fire" and "Water":

First you must understand that Fire and Water mean many things in your body. The first concerns your Chi. Chi is classified as "Fire" or "Water," which we have discussed earlier. When your Chi is not pure and causes your physical body to heat up and your mental/spiritual body to become unstable, it is classified as Fire Chi. The Chi which is pure and is able to cool both your physical and spiritual bodies is considered Water Chi. However, your body can never be purely water. Water can cool down the fire, but it must never totally quench it. If the fire in your body were put out, you would be dead. It is also said that Fire Chi is able to agitate and stimulate the emotions, and from these emotions generate a "mind." This mind is called "Hsin," and is considered the "Fire mind" or "emotional mind." On the other hand, when "Water" Chi generates a mind, it is calm, steady, and wise. This mind is called "Yi," and is considered the "Water mind" or "wisdom mind." If your spirit is nourished by the Fire Chi, although your spirit may be high, it will be scattered and confused. Naturally, if the spirit is nourished and raised up by the Water Chi, it will be firm and steady. This will allow your mind to also be firm, calm, and steady. When your Yi is able to govern your emotional Hsin effectively, your will (firm emotional intention) can be firm.

You can see from this discussion that your Chi is the cause of the "Fire" and "Water" of your physical body, and of your mind and spirit. Therefore, adjusting the Water and Fire Chi to a healthy level has become a major study in Chi Kung society.

How to Adjust "Water" and "Fire"

There are many ways to adjust your Water and Fire. Among the more common ways are the following.

1. Proper Food and Fresh Air:

Since Fire Chi comes from the food and air you take in, you are able to control it from its source. Generally speaking, meat products are worse than vegetables and fruit, and add more impurities to your body. But you should be aware that eating vegetables alone does not mean that you are improving your health. As a matter of fact, if you do not know what you are doing, you might end up with a severe protein deficiency. For most people, meat is the main source of protein. Among the vegetables, nuts and beans have the most protein. Soybeans have become one of the major foods for Buddhist and Taoist priests as well as laymen Chi Kung practitioners because of its high protein content. However, although some nuts and beans are high in protein, if you eat too much, or if you cook them the wrong way, they can also significantly increase your Fire Chi. For example, roasting peanuts is worse than boiling them in water.

Taoists and Buddhists have studied this subject extensively. Not only have they studied vegetables, they have also investigated the use of herbs to improve the quality of the Chi in the body. They have even found that living in the mountains is better because the quality of the air is better. You can see that food, air, and herbs are of major importance in adjusting your Kan and Lii.

2. Regulating the Mind and Breathing:

Regulating the mind and breathing are two of the basic techniques for controlling your Fire Chi. It is very important to remember that Fire Chi generates the emotional mind, and the emotional mind can increase your Fire Chi. Therefore, the first thing you must do is to learn how to regulate your mind. Once you can do this, your spirit will be firm and your emotions will be steady, and your Fire Chi will not be agitated to a high level. For example, if you have had too much alcohol, you will find that if you are able to keep your mind clear, and calm down your emotions, the Chi generated from the alcohol will not cause too much Fire in your body. However, if your wisdom mind is confused, your emotional mind will be agitated to a higher state and put your body on fire.

In addition, in order to keep your mind calm and steady, you must also regulate your breathing. Remember the trick is to use the "Metal" lungs to cool down the "Fire" Heart. When breathing is regulated, the Fire Chi residing at the Middle Dan Tien (solar plexus) will be led to the lungs, which will dissipate the heat and cool down the body. Next time you have heartburn, before you reach for the antacids, first try deep breathing.

Regulating the mind and the breathing cannot be separated. When the mind is regulated, the breathing can be regulated. When the breathing is regulated, the mind is able to enter a deeper level of calmness. They help each other mutually. We will discuss regulating the mind and the breath in more detail later.

3. Steadying the Spirit:

Fire Chi agitates and excites your emotional mind, which energizes your body and spirit. When you energize your spirit with your fiery emotional mind, the emotional mind will be scattered. On the other hand, when you raise your spirit with your watery wisdom mind, the wisdom mind becomes clearer. The emotional mind energizes and excites your spirit, while the wisdom mind raises and clears it.

In Chi Kung practice, once you have reached the higher levels, a large part of your efforts will be devoted to training your spirit. You want to raise your spirit, but you also want it to be firm. In Chi Kung training, it is said "Yi Shoou I Tien Gin Gang Chi"(*3), which means literally "Your mind keeps steady at one point metal steel Chi." The idea expressed here is that when you refine your Chi into one tiny point at the Upper Dan Tien, it can be as strong as steel. The Upper Dan Tien, which is the residence of your Shen, is the point where you train yourself to keep your mind. When your mind stays there, it is calm and your will is firm. Your spirit is the headquarters for controlling the Chi in your body. When your spirit is firm and steady, the Chi will be controlled efficiently, and you will be able to regulate the Fire Chi and prevent it from energizing your body.

4. Circulating the Wind Path:

It was mentioned in the sixth chapter that one of the Chi circulation methods trained in Chi Kung is the wind path, in which you circulate the Chi in the reverse direction. This is done to slow down or cool down the Fire Chi. Normally, this exercise focuses on the front of the body, bringing Water Chi from the Lower Dan Tien up the Conception vessel to cool the Fire Chi in the Middle Dan Tien. This cools down the Chi even before it starts to circulate. This will be discussed more extensively in a future publication.

5. Leading the Chi to the Water Path:

The major training of Marrow Washing Chi Kung is leading the Chi to the Water path beginning at the Huiyin cavity. When a portion of your Chi is led to the water path, it will weaken the Fire Chi and keep it from over-heating the body. This subject has been discussed briefly in the sixth chapter, and will be covered more thoroughly in a subsequent volume, "Muscle/Tendon Changing and Marrow Washing Chi Kung."

(*3). " 意守一點金鋼氣。"

Chapter 8

Regulating the Body
(Tyau Shenn)

8-1. Introduction

In Chi Kung training, you need to know how to regulate five things: your body, breath, Hsin (emotional mind), Chi, and Shen (spirit). In addition, in order to keep up a steady, adequate supply of Water Chi, you must also learn how to regulate the Essence from which it is converted. We will discuss them separately, but you must remember that in practice they are all closely linked together.

Before we continue with this chapter, you should first understand the word "regulating." Regulating means to adjust and tune constantly until the goal is reached. However, you should also understand that **THE REAL REGULATING HAPPENS ONLY WHEN YOU DON'T NEED TO CONSCIOUSLY REGULATE.** This means that if your mind has to pay attention to the regulating, you have not reached the final goal. The real regulating happens naturally, when you do not have to regulate it at all. It is just like when you are driving. Before you can drive, you must first learn how. While you are involved in the learning process, your mind will be on regulating your new skills. Once you have mastered the skill of driving, it isn't necessary for your conscious mind to actually be on the act of driving, and you will be able to drive without driving. It is the same with Chi Kung training. When you start regulating the above five elements of your training, you may have to place all of your attention on it. After you have practiced and mastered the skills, regulating will no longer be necessary. Then, you have reached the real regulating without regulating.

Regulating the Body is called "Tyau Shenn" in Chinese. It means to adjust your body until it is in the most comfortable and relaxed state. This implies that your body must be centered and balanced posturally. If it is not, you will be tense and uneasy, which will affect the judgement of your Yi and the circulation of your Chi. In Chinese medical society it is said: "(When) shape (i.e. body's posture) is not correct, then the Chi will not be smooth. (When) the Chi is not smooth, the Yi (mind) will not be at peace. (When) the Yi is not at peace, then the Chi is disordered."(*1) The relaxation of your body originates with your Yi. Therefore, before you can relax your body, you must first relax or regulate your mind (Yi).

However, before you can do this, you must first regulate your Hsin (emotional mind). It is the main reason that your Yi has difficulty being calm and peaceful. When you have regulated both the emotional and the wisdom minds as well as the body it is called "Shenn Hsin Pyng Herng"(*2), which means "Body and heart (mind) balanced." The body and the mind are mutually related. A relaxed and balanced body doesn't distract your attention, and lets your Yi relax and concentrate. When your Yi is at peace and can judge things accurately, your body will be centered, balanced, and relaxed.

8-2. Relaxation Theory

Relaxation is one of the major keys to success in Chi Kung. You should remember that **ONLY WHEN YOU ARE RELAXED WILL ALL YOUR CHI CHANNELS BE OPEN**. Relaxation includes two major parts: the mind (Yi and Hsin) and the physical body. Generally, mind relaxation must come first before the physical body is able to relax. We discussed before the two kinds of mind: Hsin (emotional mind) and Yi (wisdom mind). The emotional mind affects your feelings and the condition of your physical body. The wisdom mind is able to lead you to a calm and peaceful state, which allows you to exercise good judgement. Therefore, in order to be relaxed, your Yi must first be relaxed and calm. Then, Yi is able to control the emotional mind and let it relax too. Finally, when the peaceful Yi and Hsin coordinate with your breathing, the physical body will relax.

In Chi Kung practice, there are three levels of relaxation. The first level is external, physical relaxation, or postural relaxation. This is a very superficial level, and almost anyone can reach it. It consists of adopting a comfortable stance and avoiding unnecessary strain in posture and movement. When you reach this level of relaxation, although you **look** relaxed to the viewer, you are still tense internally. Of course, in order to reach this level of relaxation, the mind must first relax. Normally, your mind does not have to reach a very deep level to achieve this "looking relaxed" stage. Once you start to relax your mind, your body will follow naturally.

The second level involves relaxing the muscles and tendons. To do this, your meditative mind must be calm and peaceful enough to **feel** deep into the muscles and tendons. From this "feeling," your mind will know how to gauge the level of your relaxation. Only when you have reached this level will your mind be able to feel the Chi flow in the muscles and tendons. This level of relaxation will help open your Chi channels, and will allow the Chi to sink and accumulate in the Dan Tien.

(*1). "形不正，則氣不順。氣不順，則意不寧。意不寧，則氣散亂。"

(*2). "身心平衡。"

The final stage is the relaxation which reaches the internal organs and the bone marrow, and every pore in your skin. In order to be relaxed in your internal organs, your Yi must first have reached a very deep level of calmness and peace. Only then will you be able to **sense** the organs and marrow. Remember, **ONLY IF YOU CAN RELAX DEEP INTO YOUR BODY WILL YOUR MIND BE ABLE TO LEAD THE CHI THERE.**

Before we continue, you should understand the difference between feeling and sensing. The Chinese expression "Gaan Jywe" means "to feel" in the sense of touching and feeling something. The expression "Yi Shyh," which is translated "to sense," literally means "Yi recognition" or "to recognize with your Yi." When you feel something, it happens physically. Feeling is direct and active, while sensing is more indirect. In feeling, your emotional mind is able to touch the object. When sensing, however, you must use your Yi to perceive the situation. To sense, therefore, you must collect the information generated by the object, and process it so that you can understand and realize what is happening. Sensing involves a deeper level of spiritual intuition, beyond feeling, in which the object and the mind can communicate directly.

In Chi Kung relaxation training, the deeper levels of relaxation include sensing the marrow and the organs. When you have reached this stage the Chi will be able to reach any point in your body. Then you will feel light and transparent -- as if your whole body had disappeared. If you can reach this level of relaxation you will also be able to lead the Chi to your skin and strengthen your Guardian Chi. This will keep you from getting sick from outside causes. At this level of relaxation your Yi will also be able to adjust the Chi in your organs to cure Chi disorders. You will be able to protect your organs more effectively, and slow down their degeneration.

An important part of the training in Chi Kung involves "leading the five Chi's toward their origins." This involves adjusting the Chi in the five Yin organs (lungs, heart, kidneys, liver, and spleen) to the appropriate levels. Generally speaking, you are able to sense or even to feel the lungs much more easily than the other four organs. This is because your lungs move when you inhale and exhale. This obvious movement makes it very easy to be aware of them. The second organ that you can sense, once you have relaxed your lungs, is your heart. When you relax the heart, you can clearly sense and even feel it beating. The third organ is the kidneys. The kidneys can be sensed more easily than the liver and the spleen because there is liquid flowing constantly through them. The liver will be next, and then the spleen. Because the liver is much bigger than the spleen, it is easier to sense any movement, such as blood, inside it. We will discuss this idea further when we cover the regulation of organ Chi.

8-3. Relaxation Practice:

Relaxation practice can be done anytime and anywhere. It can also be done in any posture. The first key to relaxation is your mind, and the second key is your breathing. Remember: **WHEN YOU RELAX, YOU MUST FIRST RELAX YOUR MIND**. Only when your mind is relaxed will your body start to relax and your lungs loosen. When your lungs are loose, you will be able to regulate your breathing and slow down your heartbeat. When this happens, your mind will reach to a deeper level of calmness and peace. This deeper mind will relax your lungs again, slowing down your heartbeat a further step. These processes will lead you to a deeply calm state which allows you to feel and sense every cell of your body and every function of the internal organs. Only then may you say that you have relaxed your body completely.

1. Relaxing the mind:

The regulation of your mind and breathing will be discussed in detail later. At this point, in order to practice relaxation you must start to practice mind regulation. In practice, there are two steps in regulating your mind. The first step is to bring all of your thoughts from the outside world to your body. This is usually done by concentrating on your "third eye" or Upper Dan Tien. Then regulate your concentrated mind until it is relaxed, easy, and natural.

First, let your thoughts be calm and peaceful, so that you can concentrate your mind on relaxing. Your wisdom Yi must be able to control the thoughts or ideas generated from the emotional Hsin. Only then will your mind be clear. Then you will be able to disregard surrounding distractions and focus on your body. When you have reached this stage, although your mind is clear, it may still be tense from concentrating. Therefore, you must learn to concentrate without mental tension. Remember: **WHEN YOUR MIND IS TENSE, YOUR PHYSICAL BODY WILL ALSO BE TENSE**. Therefore, the second step of practice it to relax your concentrated mind. Sometimes when people cannot sleep they concentrate all their attention on falling asleep. This only makes things worse. The trick is to concentrate on something else. Normally in Chi Kung you concentrate your mind on your breathing and on the sensation of your lungs expanding and contracting. Every time you exhale, feel your physical body relax to a deeper level.

2. Relaxing your breathing:

Once you have relaxed your mind, you will be able to relax your breathing. Your breathing is closely related to your thoughts, and especially to emotional feelings. Once the mind is calm and peaceful, breathing can be independent of thought. The first step toward relaxing your breathing involves neutralizing the effect your emotions have on the breathing process. Normally, once you have relaxed your mind, you have reached this stage. Next, you must understand that breathing is caused by the physical motion of the body. For the average, untrained person, this means moving the chest. Since it is the muscles of the chest and the diaphragm which draw the air into your body and push it out, you must learn to relax all of the muscles which relate to your breathing.

Bring your calm and concentrated mind to your chest. Take in air and push it out slowly without holding your breath. While you are doing this, pay attention to how the muscles of the diaphragm move. The more you can feel them, the more your Yi is able to lead the relaxation to a deeper level.

When you do this breathing training, you will notice that the area around your solar plexus starts loosening up. When your chest is loose, you have reached the fundamental stage of relaxation.

3. Relaxing the body:

Relaxing the body is the first step in regulating your body. Only when your body is relaxed are you able to sense your physical body's center, root, and balance, and reach the goal of body regulation.

Relaxing the body includes relaxing the muscles, skin, marrow, and organs. Remember: only when you are able to relax all of these will the Chi flow smoothly and freely. Then you will be able to lead the Chi and feel that your body is transparent.

Because you use your mind to control your muscles whenever you move, relaxing your muscles is easiest. Your mind is able to feel them. Once your mind is calm, the mind will be able to effectively lead the muscles into a state of relaxation.

Relaxing the skin is the next easiest. Your skin is the interface between your body and your surroundings. Every time your skin feels something, the message is sent to your brain for evaluation. Because communication between the skin and the brain is happening all the time, it is easy for your Yi to reach the skin and lead it to a relaxed state.

Relaxing the organs is the next step. In order to reach this stage, your mind must have reached a deeper level of calmness and peace. There are five Yin organs which are most important in Chi Kung relaxation training. These organs are: lungs, heart, kidneys, liver, and spleen. Except for the lungs, which can be controlled by the mind directly, all the other organs must be reached or sensed indirectly. In order to sense the last four organs, you must first be able to feel the muscles surrounding them for clues about their condition. Once your mind is able to reach all of these muscles, your mind will be led to the organs and sense them clearly.

There is an important point to be aware of. When you practice communication between your mind and organs, the Chi will be led to those organs in order for your brain to sense them. If you are not careful, excess Chi will be led to them and make them too Yang, which will cause problems. This is especially true of the heart. Your heart is very sensitive to Chi, so the Chi level must be correct. When you place your mind on your heart, the heart will become Yang, and the heart beat will increase. Therefore, when you relax an organ, you must be very careful to avoid leading your mind directly to it. Instead, notice the area around the organ, as well as the organ itself. Do not zero in too intensely on an organ, or you will upset its natural balance. **ORGANS MUST FUNCTION NORMALLY WHILE YOU ARE RELAXING THEM**. Organs are not like your skin or muscles. They are vital and more sensitive to Chi. You should be able to see from this why leading the five Chi's to their origins is considered one of the hardest and highest stages of Chi Kung practice.

Relaxing the bone marrow is the hardest relaxation exercise. Your mind does not communicate directly with it as it does with the skin and muscle. Also, since there are no muscles connected to the marrow, you cannot use motion to sense it. The hardest discipline in Chinese Chi Kung is Marrow Washing, because your mind has such great difficulty communicating with the marrow. This will be discussed in a later book.

4. Postures for Practicing Relaxation:

There is no specific posture which you must use for relaxation training. In fact, no matter which posture you use, part of your body will be tensed to support your body. For example, your legs will be tensed when you stand, your thighs are pressed when you sit down, your back is pushed down by your body's weight when you lie down. Obviously, there is no relaxation posture which is absolutely good for the entire body.

The prerequisite to relaxing your mind and body is feeling comfortable and natural. Your body should be centered and balanced. You also need to consider how the environment might affect you. Is it too noisy, or is the surface you are lying or sitting on too hard? For the beginner, we suggest that you lie on your back. When you are lying down, you don't have to pay attention to your root, center, and balance, so it is easier for you to regulate your mind. Lying down for relaxation practice also has a disadvantage. When you lie down, your back muscles are pressed down by your weight, which restricts their ability to loosen up.

Once you are familiar with the relaxation exercises, you should also learn to relax while you are sitting. This is harder than lying down because part of your mind must be kept in your body's center to prevent your falling over. Sitting relaxation, however, is better for your trunk and upper limbs. You can see that the different postures have their advantages and disadvantages. Remember, it does not matter which posture you are using, as long as you feel **COMFORTABLE** and **NATURAL**.

5. Suggested Procedures for Relaxation Exercises:

There are many methods of relaxing. Once you have some experience with one method, you may find another exercise or set of exercises which are easier and better for you. Here, we will only suggest some procedures which will help you start out. We recommend that the beginner start lying down.

a. Bring your mind to your Shen:

Relax your body with a few comfortably deep breaths. Normally, most people can do this easily. Next, bring your mind from outside of your body to your Upper Dan Tien, where your Shen resides. When your mind is on the Shen, your spirit will be centered, and thoughts generated by outside distractions will start to disappear. Your mind will now be able to concentrate on feeling your body.

b. Relax your mind:

When you concentrate your attention on relaxing your mind, you will find that your mind stays tense. You have to relax it by moving the focus of your consciousness away from your mind. One of the best ways is to pay attention to your breathing.

c. Feel and sense your Middle Dan Tien:

Move your mind to the Middle Dan Tien (Solar Plexus), which is the center and residence of your Fire Chi. Feel the physical location of your solar plexus, and sense the Chi there. Remember, Fire Chi stimulates the emotional mind and emotional feelings, and increases tension. When you move your mind to the Middle Dan Tien, you will be able to feel what is happening with your Fire Chi.

d. Use breathing to cool down the Fire Chi:

In Chi Kung, the lungs are considered "Metal" and the heart is considered "Fire." Metal is able to absorb heat and cool down Fire. Whenever you have heartburn or an uneasy feeling in your chest, use deep breathing to cool down the Fire and release the pressure. Similarly, when you want to relax, you must first cool down your chest Fire and relax the chest area. Smooth, relaxed deep breathing will enable you to extend your relaxation from your chest to your entire body. When you reach this stage, you have completed the first step of relaxation.

e. Use your mind to direct the body:

Once you have relaxed your body at the surface level, you must enter a deeper level of relaxation. At this level, use your concentrated mind to feel and relax deep into the muscles and tendons. This stage allows you to open the Chi channels by relaxing any muscular tension which is constricting the channels and restricting Chi circulation.

When you do this, your breathing is deeper, your pulse is slower, and your meditating mind reaches a deeper level.

When you relax your whole body, start at the toes. Concentrate your mind on each of your toes and relax them. Next, move your mind up to your feet, ankles, calves, thighs, and hips. You may feel your lower body disappear, and feel as if you were floating. Keeping your lower body relaxed, move your mind to your fingers and repeat the same procedure -- from your fingers to the hands, wrists, forearms, elbows, and shoulders. Then concentrate your mind on your stomach, and move up to the chest and neck. Finally, focus on your head. After your head is relaxed, keep your mind relaxed while concentrating on feeling your whole body. When you have reached this level, you will be able to feel your muscles, tendons, and skin. The more you practice, the better your mind will be able to concentrate on the local areas and relax them. When you relax your body starting from the extremities, you are also relaxing and clearing the Chi channels. To relax the channels, you have to relax the ends first, then work your way down their length. If you start in the middle, you will relax in one direction, but the other side will be tense.

If you are able to practice twice a day, the Chi in your body will be able to rebalance itself easily and naturally. Your mind will be peaceful and you will be able to maintain your health. The best time to practice is two hours after lunch, when the Fire Chi is strongest at your Middle Dan Tien. If you can practice your relaxation at this time, you will be able to cool down and help your body. The second best time is right before you sleep. After a long day of physical and mental exercise, you will be able to relax your mind as well as your body. This will enable you to have a more relaxing sleep, with fewer dreams, and you will be able to effectively recover from fatigue.

f. Relaxing your organs:

If you are a Chi Kung practitioner, you will want to relax all the way into your organs in order to regulate the Chi in them. Generally, this stage is much harder for the person who does not know the theory and does not have the above relaxation training. In order for your mind to reach your organs, you will need to reach a much deeper level of meditation. The five Yin organs are considered the most vital. Generally speaking, to feel or sense the lungs is the easiest, followed by the heart, kidneys, liver, and spleen. When you are able to feel and sense these organs, you will be able to evaluate their status, and use your mind to regulate their Chi.

g. After you have reached the level of organ relaxation, you have come to the third level of relaxation:

The final stage involves relaxing your body deep into the marrow. Your marrow manufactures your blood cells. The marrow is alive, and must have a constant supply of Chi to keep functioning. Your conscious mind does not normally sense the Chi in the marrow and control it. In Marrow Washing Chi Kung training, however, you want Chi to be supplied to the marrow with maximum efficiency so that the blood will be kept fresh and healthy. In order to do this, your mind must be able to reach the marrow. This will be discussed in the next YMAA Chi Kung book: "Muscle/Tendon Changing and Marrow Washing Chi Kung."

You can see that relaxation is not as simple as many people think. Your final goal is to relax until you feel transparent. Only when you are at this stage will your Chi be able to flow smoothly and fluidly to every cell of your body.

8-4. Rooting, Centering, and Balancing

When you regulate your body, in addition to relaxing it you are also seeking its root, center, and balance. In order for you to feel natural, comfortable, and stable you must first have a firm root. The way of rooting for standing and sitting are different. When you stand, you build your root from your feet into the ground, while when you are sitting on a chair you build your root from your hips down to the ground. In every posture or movement, there is a root for that form or movement. Rooting includes rooting not just the body, but also the form and movement. Every posture or form has its unique way of rooting which is determined by its purpose or principle.

For example, in certain Chi Kung exercises you want to lead the Chi to your palms. In order to do this, you must image (*3) that you are pushing an object forward while keeping your muscles relaxed. In this exercise, your elbows must be down to build the sense of root for the push. If you raise the elbows, you lose the sense of "intention" of the movement because the push would be ineffective if you were pushing something for real. Since the intention or purpose of the movement is its reason for being, you now have a purposeless movement, and you have no reason to lead Chi in any particular way. In this case, the elbow is the first root of the movement. This root must be connected to the root of your body which is in the ground in order to be firm and complete. Therefore, the root of the arms is built upon the body's root. In order to connect these two roots strongly, your chest must be arched in to form the support (Figure 8-1). Furthermore, your stance cannot be straight up. When you push a heavy object, you have to lean slightly forward. When you are standing up, you will not have a pushing root. You must have a bow-and-arrow stance in order to push backward and generate forward pushing power. When you have all of these, you can say that you have a firm root for pushing. In order to push with maximum power, you must also seek your center and balance. When you have your root, center, and balance, your posture will be natural and comfortable, and your Yi will be strong enough to direct the pushing.

You can see that in order for a posture to have a root, you must first understand the purpose of the posture. When you understand the "Why"

_____

(*3). The verb "image" as used here means to mentally create something that you treat as if it were real. If you image that you are pushing something heavy, you have to adjust your posture exactly as if you were in fact pushing something heavy. You must "feel" its weight and resistance as you exert force against it, and realize the force and counterforce in your legs. If you mentally treat your actions as real, your body will too, and the Chi will automatically move appropriately for those actions. If you only "pretend" or "imagine" that you are pushing something heavy, your mind and body will not treat your actions as real, and the Chi will not move strongly or clearly.

Figure 8-1. Feeling Chi on the palms by imaging pushing forward

of the posture, your mind will not wander and you will know what you are looking for. Understanding the purpose and the theory is the root of everything. It firms your mind so that it can lead your body to a posture which offers you the best root, center, and balance. Naturally, in order to reach this stage, you must first have a relaxed mind and body.

Before you can develop your root, you must first relax and let your body "settle." As you relax, the tension in the various parts of your body will dissolve, and you will find a comfortable way to stand. You will stop fighting the ground to keep your body up, and will learn to rely on your body's structure for support. This lets the muscles relax even more. Since your body isn't struggling to stand up, your Yi won't be pushing upward, and your body, mind, and Chi will all be able to sink. If you let dirty water sit quietly, the impurities will gradually settle down to the bottom, leaving the water above it clear. In the same way, if you relax your body and let it settle, your Chi will sink to your Dan Tien and the Bubbling Wells in your feet, clearing your mind. Then you can begin to develop your root.

After you have gained your root, you must learn how to keep your center. The center includes the mind's center and the physical body's center. You must have your mind centered first in order to lead your body to its center. Naturally, in order to have your mind centered, you must first relax your body, which allows your mind to feel and sense every part of it. Although root is important to the process of locating your center, many times you are able to find your center without even having a root. For example, when you ski you do not have a root but you must have your center in order to balance. In stationary Chi Kung practice, however, having a root will help you to locate your center more easily; and when you have the center, the root will be even firmer. Both of them are related and cannot really be separated.

A stable center will make your Chi develop evenly and uniformly. If you lose this center, your Chi will not be led evenly. In order to keep your body centered, you must first center your Yi, and then match your body to it. It is very important for you to understand that very often your mind's center and your body's center do not match each other. For example, while standing in a bow and arrow stance you may lean slightly forward so that the center of your body is over your front foot. If you keep your mental center back further, you can still keep you body centered, even though someone looking at you would think that you are off balance to your front. If, however, your mental center is also off and moves forward, you will lose your center and balance. Naturally, if your physical center is off too much, you will not be able to use your mental center to balance it. The closer together your mental and physical centers stay, the more stable you will be. In Chi Kung practice, your mental and physical centers are keys which enable you to lead your Chi beyond your body.

Finally, after you have a relaxed body, firm root, and center, you will be able to balance your Yi, Chi, and physical body. Balance is the product of rooting and centering. Regardless of which aspect of balance you are dealing with, you must balance your Yi first. Only then can you balance your Chi and your physical body. If your Yi is balanced, it can help you to make accurate judgements, and to correct the path of the Chi flow. When your Yi is balanced, your Chi will be led evenly. Remember **THE TRICK TO EXPANDING YOUR CHI IS TO EXPAND IT EVENLY**. It is like when you push a car, you need a backward force in order to generate forward power.

Normally, a person's Chi is not balanced in both sides of the body simply because he uses one hand more than the other. For example, if you are right handed, your mind can lead the Chi to the right hand much more easily than it can to the left hand. You will find sometimes that one side of your shoe soles is flatter than the other. As a Chi Kung practitioner, you are looking for your mental center in this unbalanced situation. In order to do this, your mind must be very clear and able to judge the environment and your body's condition. For example, if you place your right arm into warm water and your left arm into cold water for three minutes, and then place both hands immediately into another container of water, one hand will feel warmer than the other. This kind of outside influence scatters your Yi and causes it to lose its center. In Chi Kung practice, therefore, you are looking for the practice which develops the Yi and body evenly. For example, practice the same form with both hands the same number of times.

In order to help you analyze rooting, centering, and balancing, we will discuss two of the most common stances. Once you understand these two, you should be able to use the same method to analyze any other stance.

Horse Stance (Maa Bu):

The horse stance is the most common stance used by Chi Kung practitioners and martial artists. The horse stance is used by martial artists to develop their root, center, and balance, as well as to strengthen the legs. For the non-martial Chi Kung practitioner, however, although rooting is important, it is not as critical as it is for marital artists who need a strong root for fighting. In Chi Kung, rooting is helpful in finding your center and balance, which in turn lets you feel relaxed, natural, and comfortable. Since the martial arts horse stance is harder and is the basis for the non-martial horse stance, we

Figure 8-2. Horse Stance of the
southern martial styles

Figure 8-3.Horse Stance of the
northern martial styles

will discuss it here. Once you understand it thoroughly, you may adjust it to fit your situation.

There are many ways to stand in the horse stance. For example, the width of the feet in the horse stance used by southern Chinese martial styles is narrower than the one used in Northern styles (Figure 8-2). This is because the Southern styles emphasize short range fighting, and the wider stance is more open and dangerous in short range techniques. The situation is different for the Northern styles. Because they emphasize long range techniques, a larger posture is more advantageous, so they use a much wider horse stance (Figure 8-3). You should understand that regardless of which style of horse stance is trained, the purpose, training principles, and theory remain the same.

In the horse stance, both legs share your weight equally. In Chi Kung training, the width of the stance depends on your feeling. If you are standing too narrow or too wide, you will have a uncomfortable feeling. You should try different widths to see which one is most comfortable and natural for you. Remember, when you feel comfortable and natural you will be able to relax and find your center and balance more easily.

If you are training a martial arts horse stance, how high you stand depends upon the style. For Chi Kung practice, how high you stand depends on your feeling. For example, if you stand lower, your leg muscles will be more tensed and it will be harder for the Chi to flow to the bottom of your feet. If you stand too high, your center of gravity is higher and your root will be shallower and less stable. However, since the leg muscles are more relaxed, you can lead the Chi to the bottom of your feet more easily. In Chinese internal martial styles such as Tai Chi Chuan, when a beginner's Chi cannot be efficiently directed to the bottom of the feet, the stance is lower. In this case, the beginner is able to lower his physical center of gravity to increase his root. When, however, a Tai Chi practitioner has reached a high level, he will stand higher and keep the leg muscles relaxed, allowing his Chi to reach the bottom of his feet.

In Chi Kung horse stance training, the best way to build a firm root is to begin with a height at which you get the strongest feeling of pushing upward. In other words, try out different heights, and at each one pretend you are pushing a heavy object upward. At one particular height you will feel that you can push upward most strongly. At this height your Yi can exert the strongest push upward, and it can therefore also exert the strongest push downward. It is this downward pushing of your Yi that builds your root. If you keep practicing, you will eventually start to feel that your Yi is leading your Chi into the ground, and that your root is starting to grow.

To root your body, you must imitate a tree and grow an invisible root beneath your feet. Naturally, your Yi must grow first, because it is the Yi which leads the Chi. Your Yi must be able to communicate with the ground in order to lead your Chi beyond your feet and build the root. This means your Yi must feel or sense the ground, noticing whether it is soft or hard, how flat the ground is, how slippery it is. Try different ways of standing, shift your weight on your feet, and notice the ground. With practice your Yi will be able to sink further into the ground, and you will develop a strong root. The more you practice, the deeper the root will grow (Figure 8-4). After practicing for a period of time, you will start to stand higher in order to relax the leg muscles more. In turn, this will help you to lead the Chi to the bottom more effectively.

Figure 8-4. Horse Stance with the root growing like a tree's

Figure 8-5. In a low stance, your body is stable within this area

Figure 8-6. In a high stance, your body is stable within this area

The Bubbling Well cavity is the gate which enables your Chi to communicate with the ground.

There is one more thing to remember when you build your root. A tree's root is very strong because it has many branches and spreads out far to the sides. You must do the same thing, and spread your roots to the sides as well as downward.

Once you have built your root, you can consider being centered and balanced. You can be centered physically and you can be centered mentally. When you are centered physically, a vertical line from your center of mass falls between your feet, so your root comfortably supports your weight. Being centered mentally is a matter of feeling. If you are mentally centered, you can be physically **balanced** even when you are not physically **centered**. An example of this is the person who cannot be pushed over even when he is standing in a very awkward position. When you start practicing, stand so that you are physically centered and have a good root, and be centered mentally in the same way. After a while, change your stance slightly so that you physical stance becomes less centered and less stable, and practice maintaining your balance and stability mentally. Remember, if you are not centered physically or mentally, you will not be able to maintain your balance.

The degree to which your physical body's center can be separated from the mind's center without losing balance depends on how you stand. Generally speaking, it depends on how wide you build your root. For example, if you stand low with a firm root, your body's center can be moved in the space between the two roots built by your feet (Figure 8-5). If you stand higher, the width is narrower, and the circle of movement you can allow your body will be smaller (Figure 8-6).

A highly skilled martial artist can defend himself even in a high, narrow stance. His range of movement is limited, but if he has strong Chi he will be able to build a strong root, and if his technique is good enough, he will be able to fight effectively. Remember, in order to reach this stage, you must start with a low, wide stance, and gradually narrow and raise it. The Chinese have a proverb: "Yean Gau Shoou Di"(*4), which means "Eyes are high and the hands are low." This scoffs at those people who keep dreaming of high levels of mastery while they are still at a very low level.

The final goal in developing your root is to make your stance like a mountain. Your stance must be wide and firm, and you must also train your Chi to cover your body and spread out as it goes down to the ground. Your mental image of yourself and your Chi should be shaped like a mountain or cone -- narrow on top and wide on the bottom (Figure 8-7). Once you can do this, it will be extremely difficult for anyone to push you over or make you lose your balance.

Bow and Arrow Stance or Mountain Climbing Stance:
The bow and arrow stance is another common stance used by both martial artists and non-martial artists. Generally speaking, this stance is harder than the horse stance. Because the weight of the body is not divided evenly and, therefore, the mind is also uneven. The bow and arrow stance is commonly used in moving and in exerting force forward. Normally, the front leg is used to stabilize the body and the rear leg is used to generate the forward power.

In this stance, as your rear leg pushes your body forward, you must keep your body straight up in order to keep your center and balance. Sometimes the body can lean forward slightly; in which case, however, you must keep your mind at the original center or you will easily lose your balance.

Figure 8-7. In the horse stance, stand like a mountain

(*4). "眼高手低。"

Figure 8-8. In the bow and arrow stance, stand like a mountain

Figure 8-9. Rooting and balance competition

In this stance, the trick to building the root lies in keeping the center and balance just as you did in the horse stance. Your root must be firm, deep, and wide. Again, your body must be low so you can build a foundation like a mountain (Figure 8-8). Finally, your mental and physical centers must actively adjust with each other to keep the body steady.

Once you have built your root and stability, there is a very common exercise you can do to test and strengthen them. You and your partner face each other in a bow and arrow stance. Then clasp your leading arms, and try to unbalance each other (Figure 8-9). This practice will help you to build your root, to coordinate your mental and physical centers, to build your own mountain, and finally to destroy the root of your partner. If you continue this practice you will find that, in order to win, you must stand low. Your body must be very soft to keep your partner from finding your center and root. When your body is tense, he can locate your center easily and destroy your balance. In addition, you must also learn how to feel and sense your partner's center. Once your mind and power are able to reach his center, you will be able to dislodge his root.

Chapter 9

Regulating the Breath
(Tyau Shyi)

9-1. Breathing and Health

Right after your birth, you started to rely on the two major sources of Essence to supply your body's needs. Once these two Essences, of food and air, are absorbed into your body, they are converted into Chi. The Chi obtained from food is called "Shyr Chi" (food Chi), while the Chi obtained from air is called "Kong Chi." (The Chinese call air "Kong Chi.") The Chi from these two sources is called Post-birth Chi or Fire Chi. Although your body needs Fire Chi, if it is of a poor quality it will cause your body to degenerate. In order to have good health and a long life, you must be serious about the quality of these two sources. The search for the right kinds of food and the correct quality of air has been an important part of Chi Kung practice. In this chapter we will discuss air Chi and how we benefit from practicing methods of regulating the breath.

In order to know how to regulate your breath, you must first know how you take in and expel air during inhalation and exhalation. You must understand that your lungs themselves cannot bring in and push out air. In order for the air to reach the lungs and then be pushed out, the muscles around the lungs and the diaphragm must expand and contract, sucking the air into and pushing it out of the chest cavity. When this process is going on, the oxygen will mix with the blood in the lung cells, and the blood will release the carbon dioxide it carries. When the diaphragm moves up and down during respiration, it massages the internal organs and increases the Chi circulation.

Once the oxygen is mixed with the blood, it is carried to every cell of the body to keep them functioning. Normally, when there is a shortage of oxygen, your brain will sense it first. According to experiments, the oxygen required for your brain cells is many times more than that which is required for muscle cells. Whenever the oxygen is insufficient, you feel dizzy, heavy, and cannot think clearly.

Normally after a baby is born, it retains the habit of breathing from the lower abdomen. The inhale is usually longer than the exhale. Since a child takes in plenty of oxygen, its mind is usually clearer than an adult's. When a person reaches 30, his breathing becomes shallower and generally takes place around the stomach rather than the lower abdomen. The inhale and exhale are almost equal. At this age, a person still has enough oxygen to supply body, and the diaphragm still moves up and down actively. This movement maintains health. When he is older, the breath becomes progressively shallower as the person relies on moving his chest to breath. The exhale is longer than the inhale and the oxygen supply is insufficient. Now the person starts losing his memory, his thinking ability, and his mental clarity. Because of the shallowness of the breathing, the diaphragm does not move up and down actively any more, and it does not massage the internal organs. The Chi becomes stagnant, and the organs degenerate. Also, the degeneration of the cells of the body is speeded by the shortage of oxygen.

You can see how important breathing is to your health. In Chi Kung practice, regulating the breathing is the most important training. The first step toward maintaining your health involves increasing your oxygen supply. You must resume breathing deep down in your abdomen like a baby does. This exercise is called "Fan Ton," which means "Back to Childhood." Once you have a sufficient supply of oxygen, you are able to relax, clear your mind, and circulate the Chi.

9-2. Regulating the Breath

It is important to learn how to regulate your breath so that you can obtain enough Essence from the air, and so that you can learn how to prevent the air Chi from overstimulating your body and making it too Yang. You need to be concerned with the quality of the air you breathe, and you need to learn the different methods of breathing which are used to achieve different goals. In the first stage of regulating your breath, it becomes calm, smooth, and peaceful. Once you have reached this point, the next step is to make your breathing deep, slender, long, and soft. This is the prerequisite for successful Chi Kung practice.

In order to make your breathing calm, smooth, and peaceful, you must first regulate your mind. Remember, your mind is the headquarters of your whole being. When your mind is not steady and calm, your emotions will be agitated. Your emotions are closely related to your breath. For example, when you are angry, you exhale more strongly than you inhale. When you are sad, you inhale more strongly than you exhale. When your mind is peaceful and calm, your inhalation and exhalation are relatively equal.

Therefore, in Chi Kung breathing training, you first have to regulate your emotional mind. This, in turn, will allow you to regulate your breathing, which in turn will allow you to regulate your mind more deeply. Again, the calmer and deeper your mind is, the calmer and deeper your breathing will be. After you have trained for a long time, your breathing will be full and slender, and your mind will be very clear. It is said: "Hsin Shyi Shiang Yi"(*1), which means "Heart (mind) and breathing (are) mutually dependent." When you reach this meditative state, your heartbeat slows down, and your mind is very clear: you have entered the sphere of real meditation.

(*1). " 心息相依 · "

Normally, when your emotional mind is agitated, not only is your breath affected, but your Chi circulation as well. Understand that your emotions are related to your internal organs. For example, anger can make your liver Chi supply lose its balance. Happiness can make your heart too Yang. Fear can make the Chi supply to your bladder deficient. Obviously, in order to regulate the Chi in your body, you must first regulate your emotional mind. Regulating your breathing will help you to do this.

The other side of the coin is that you can also use your breathing to control your Yi. When your breathing is uniform, it is like you are hypnotizing your Yi, which helps to calm it. But there is another way in which you can use breathing to control your Yi. Whenever you take in poor food or air you tend to get heartburn from the over-accumulation of Fire Chi, which normally resides in the Middle Dan Tien (solar plexus), stirring up your emotions and disturbing your wisdom mind (Yi). As you regulate your breath to dissipate the heart fire and calm your emotional mind (Hsin), you will also be calming your Yi.

We have established that Yi and breathing are interdependent. Deep and calm breathing relaxes you, keeps your mind clear, and fills your lungs with plenty of air so that your brain and entire body have an adequate supply of oxygen. In addition, deep and complete breathing enables the diaphragm to move up and down, which massages and stimulates the internal organs. For this reason, deep breathing exercises are also called "internal organ exercises."

Finally, one additional point: regulating the breath is not only the key to leading the mind into a deeper and calmer stage of meditation, it is also the key to leading the Chi to the extremities and the skin. When the Chi is led to the limbs, it can open up the channels in the limbs and complete the Grand Circulation, as well as increase the efficiency of the muscles to the higher power state needed by a martial artist. When the Chi is effectively led to the skin, you are able to strengthen and enlarge your Guardian Chi shield, which can keep you from sickness caused by outside negative influences.

Next we will discuss the thirteen methods of regulating the breath used in Chi Kung, starting with the most basic and ending with the most advanced. However, since the more advanced methods are difficult, both in understanding and practice, it is impossible to discuss them thoroughly here. A more detailed discussion of these advanced techniques will be presented in later volumes.

9-3. The Different Methods of Chi Kung Breathing
In the last four thousand years of study and experimentation, many ways have been developed to regulate the breath. Each technique has its unique theory and goal. These techniques are called "Tyau Shyi," which means "to regulate the breathing." It is also often called "Tuu Na" which means "To utter and to take in." The latter name is used especially when the nose is used to inhale and the mouth is used to exhale. Since there are many levels of Chi Kung practice, the methods of regulating the breath are classified according to their difficulty, from the easiest to the most difficult. Here we will list and explain 13 breathing techniques which are commonly used in Chinese Chi Kung.

1. Natural Breathing:
Frequently people who are just starting to practice Chi Kung will start right away to use advanced breathing methods. However, the

best way to grasp the key to the deeper breathing methods is to start by regulating the method of breathing you use every day.

You should understand that your natural breathing is constantly affected by your thoughts and emotions. For example, when you feel tense or excited, you breathe faster, and when you feel sad and depressed, you breathe slower. The lengths of inhalation and exhalation are also affected by your emotions. When you are happy, your exhalation is longer than your inhalation, but when you are sad, your inhalation is longer. So you can see that although you have always regulated your breathing, you have usually done it unconsciously.

People breathe in different ways. Little children and some adults still have the habit of abdominal breathing. Most middle-aged people breathe with their stomachs, and older people breathe with their chests. Regardless of how you breathe, the purpose is to bring oxygen into the lungs and expel carbon dioxide. Though we talk of abdominal breathing, in fact the air does not, or at least should not, go any lower. If air goes into your digestive system, it will cause pain, so it should be expelled immediately.

To regulate your natural breathing means to regulate your current pattern of breathing. You should not intentionally change your breathing habits while doing this training, because you would put your Yi on the new method and be distracted away from what you normally do and experience. Regulating the natural breath means concentrating your mind to understand your natural way of breathing, to feel the way you breathe, and finally to guide your breathing to a more relaxed and smoother stage.

In order to regulate your natural breathing, you must first be natural and comfortable, and your mind must get rid of emotional disturbances. Then, learn how to feel the muscles which are related to your breathing. Finally, you mind leads the muscles into a more relaxed stage, and you can feel or sense the Chi flow.

Choose any posture you like, as long as you feel comfortable and natural. Breathe through your nose. Do not actively control the breath, but simply pay attention to it and feel it. Breathe softly and gently. The final goal of the process involves training your natural breathing to be 1. Calm (Jing), 2. Slender (Shyi), 3. Deep (Shenn), 4. Continuous (Iou), and 5. Uniform (Yun). We will discuss these in more detail at the end of this chapter. After a while you will reach the stage of regulating your breathing without conscious effort, when your breathing will enter a new stage. Most important of all, however, is the experience you gain through practicing the technique of regulating your natural breathing. This experience becomes the seed which produces the deeper understanding you need to fathom the more difficult breathing techniques.

2. Chest Breathing:

Chest breathing, or breathing by expanding and contracting the rib cage, is one of the main methods of regulating the breath, especially in the external martial Chi Kung styles, as well as deep sea diving.

Chest breathing increases the capacity of your lungs, and therefore increases the amount of oxygen and carbon dioxide exchanged. It also allows you to hold your breath longer. External martial artists use this method to increase the amount of Air Chi they take in, which is used to support their muscular exercise. Weight lifters and people who do heavy labor also do this.

When you practice chest breathing, keep your mind and chest muscles relaxed. If they are tense, you will use more oxygen. In the training used by the external martial arts such as Tiger style, when you exhale you lead the Air Chi to your limbs. The more you practice, the more efficiently you will be able to do this. Although when you practice chest breathing your abdomen moves up and down slightly, you should understand that external martial artists generally do not pay attention to the abdomen until they get older. Once they pass 30, they will start to practice breathing lower and lower in the abdomen.

Practitioners of the internal martial arts do not consider increasing the lung capacity as important as the external stylists. Internal practitioners believe that the more you increase lung capacity, the more Fire Chi (air Chi) you will take in, which may scatter and confuse the mind and increase the Fire in the body. For an internal Chi Kung practitioner, regulating the breath means breathing lower down in the abdomen in the Dan Tien, instead of emphasizing the chest.

Before we finish discussing chest breathing, I would like to point out that your lungs behave like a rubber band: the more you stretch them the larger they will become. However, after you have practiced chest breathing for a long time, or even if you have done a good deal of heavy exercise, you should not stop exercising completely and suddenly. Once your lungs have expanded to a larger size, a sudden stop may cause part of your lungs to collapse, causing problems such as pneumonia. If you want to stop practice, you should cut down the exercises gradually and allow your lungs to adjust themselves. In external martial Chi Kung society, we often see that when a practitioner gets old and loses the ability to do the same exercises, he loses the ability to expand his lungs, and his lung capacity lessens. Consequently, the muscles which used to obtain a large amount of oxygen degenerate faster than normal. This is called "Sann Kung" (energy dispersion).

You can see that if you are not an external martial artist, you have no need to form the habit of chest breathing. Still, there are advantages to doing chest breathing from time to time. First, you will enliven the cells in the parts of the lungs which are not commonly used, and keep them from degenerating. Second, heavy chest breathing increases the supply of Air Chi, so that you can send a lot of Chi to the skin. This helps to open the tiny Chi channels in the skin and strengthens your Guardian Chi.

3. Normal Abdominal Breathing:

Abdominal Breath is the key to the Nei Dan (internal elixir) Chi Kung exercises. In abdominal, or Dan Tien breathing, there are two common ways of breathing: Normal Abdominal Breathing (Jeng Fuh Hu Shi) and Reverse Abdominal breathing (Faan Fuh Hu Shi). We will discuss Normal Abdominal Breathing first.

Normal abdominal breathing is the next step after chest breathing for the Chi Kung beginner. Abdominal breathing is a deep breathing exercises, but it is not like the breathing you do in the chest. Correct deep breathing involves slow, deep breaths that seem to go all the way down to your Dan Tien. It requires that your mind be relaxed and concentrated. This kind of breathing is called "Faan Torng" breath, or "Back to Childhood" breathing, because it is deep, soft, and natural like a child's. It is the first step in Nei Dan Chi Kung training.

In abdominal breathing the lungs are expanded and contracted by the muscles of the diaphragm and abdomen, rather than the chest muscles. There are several benefits to normal abdominal breathing:

A. Internal Organ Massage:

In abdominal breathing, the diaphragm and the muscles of the lower abdomen are constantly moving back and forth. This movement massages the internal organs, increasing the circulation of Chi and blood in and around them. This keeps them healthy and strong, avoiding the Chi stagnation which is one of the major causes of illness.

B. Invigorating the Abdominal Muscles:

Because babies naturally do deep abdominal breathing, their stomach muscles are constantly moving. Not only does this keep the Chi circulating around the organs, but it also loosens up the Chi channels which connect the front of the body to the legs and to the back. Usually, once you have given up your abdominal breathing, the Chi flow to the Governing vessel in your back becomes sluggish. This weakens the ability of the Governing vessel to regulate Chi throughout the body, and allows a number of problems to arise.

C. Increasing the efficiency of the Chi flow from the kidneys to the Lower Dan Tien:

One objective of Chi Kung practice is the strengthening of your Water Chi (Original Chi), which is converted from the Essence residing in your kidneys. As we have discussed, the Lower Dan Tien is the residence of this Chi. The muscular movement of the muscles in abdominal breathing help to lead Chi from the kidneys to your Lower Dan Tien and keep it there. The more abdominal breathing you do, the more Chi is led, and the more efficiently the Essence is converted. Abdominal breathing acts like an engine which is able to convert fuel into energy more efficiently than normal engines can, and thereby conserve more fuel.

D. To Increase the Water Chi:

Once you are able to increase the efficiency of the Essence-Chi conversion process, you will be able to create more Water Chi (Original Chi). Strong Water Chi is the key to successful Chi Kung practice. Water Chi is able to calm down your mind, strengthen your will, and firm your spirit. Since Water Chi is the major source of coolant for your Fire Chi, you are able to maintain your health and lengthen your life.

Normal abdominal breathing is an important part of Buddhist Chi Kung training, and so it is often called "Buddhist Breathing." To practice it, you must first use your Yi to control the muscles in your abdomen. When you inhale, intentionally expand your abdomen, and when you exhale, let it contract. If you practice for ten minutes three times a day, in a month you should be able to resume the abdominal breathing you did as a baby.

There is a very important rule when you practice: **DO NOT HOLD YOUR BREATH**. Your breath must be smooth, natural, continuous, and comfortable. Abdominal deep breathing is done in the lower abdomen, so you should not be expanding and contracting your chest. Instead, you should feel like you are drawing the air deep into your lower abdomen.

4. Reverse Abdominal Breathing:

The reverse abdominal breathing method is commonly used by Taoist Chi Kung practitioners, and so it is often called "Taoist Breathing." Since you are moving your abdomen, you gain the same health benefits that you do with the normal abdominal breathing.

However, in reverse abdominal breathing you move the abdomen in when you inhale and out when you exhale. There are many reasons for this. The major ones are:

A. Greater Efficiency in Leading Chi to the Extremities:

Whenever you exhale, you are expanding your Guardian Chi. When you inhale, you are conserving your Chi or even absorbing the surrounding Chi into your body. Experience teaches that when you intentionally try to expand your Chi during exhalation, it is easier to expand your abdominal muscles than to relax them. Try blowing up a balloon, and hold one hand on your abdomen. You will find that when you blow out, your abdomen expands rather than withdraws. Or imagine that you are pushing a car. In order to express your power, you have to exhale while you are pushing. If you pay attention to your abdomen while you are doing this, you will realize that your abdomen is expanding again. If you pull your stomach in when you are doing this, you will find that there is less power and that it feels unnatural.

Now imagine that you feel cold, and want to absorb energy from your surroundings. You will find that your inhalations are longer than your exhalations, and that your abdomen withdraws when you inhale, rather than expands.

Taoist Chi Kung practitioners have found that whenever you try to **INTENTIONALLY** expand or condense your Chi, your abdomen moves opposite to the way it moves during normal breathing. They realized that reverse breathing is a tool and a strategy that you may use to lead the Chi more efficiently. You can see that the foremost advantage to the Taoist reverse abdominal breathing is its ability to lead Chi to the extremities more naturally and easily than is possible with normal abdominal breathing. Once you have mastered the coordination of Yi, breath, and Chi, you will be able to lead Chi to any part of your body.

B. For Martial Arts:

The internal martial arts training of the Taoists is more advanced than that of the Buddhist or any other style. This is simply because the Taoists learned how to lead Chi to any part of the body more efficiently than any of the others. The key to this success is reverse abdominal breathing.

C. For more effectively raising the Chi in Marrow Washing Chi Kung:

In Marrow Washing Chi Kung, reverse abdominal breathing is able to raise Chi from legs to the brain more efficiently than the Buddhist methods.

Although there are many advantages to reverse abdominal breathing, there are also several disadvantages or problems which arise during training. Chi Kung practitioners who use Taoist breathing should be aware of these potential problems, especially during the early period of training. The major problems are:

A. Tensing the Chest:

In the reverse training, when you inhale the diaphragm moves down while the abdomen is withdrawing. The drawing in of the abdomen generates pressure upward, which makes it harder for the diaphragm to move down. This can cause pressure and tension below the solar plexus, which leads to Chi stagnation. This is especially common with people who have just started doing reverse breathing.

This pressure below the solar plexus may cause problems such as stomach ache, diarrhea, or even chest pain. The tension and pressure may cause the heart to beat faster. When this happens, the body becomes positive, the mind is scattered and confused, you become impatient, and your will is unsteady. Enduring this does not advance your Chi Kung -- it makes you sick and hinders your training.

Many Chi Kung masters will encourage their students to practice normal abdominal breathing until it feels natural and comfortable. Only then will they encourage reverse abdominal breathing. Reverse abdominal breathing starts with a small abdominal motion in coordination with the breathing. During practice you must always pay attention to the middle burner (from the solar plexus to the navel), keeping this area relaxed and comfortable. After a few months of practice, you will find that there is a point of compromise which allows your reverse breathing to be deep and which also keeps the chest area relaxed. When you reach this stage, you will have grasped the key to Taoist breathing. After you have practiced for a long time, you will realize that your mind does not have to be in conscious control of your breathing. It happens naturally whenever you are practicing Chi Kung.

The final stage of reverse abdominal breathing is moving your abdominal muscles like a rotating ball (Figure 9-1). Because the ball is round, your breathing no longer causes any tension in the middle burner area. If you train patiently, you will eventually be able to use reverse breathing naturally all the time.

Figure 9-1. Move your abdomen like a ball

B. Holding the Breath:

Because reverse breathing can cause tension and generate pressure in the chest area, people will sometimes unconsciously hold their breath. It is very important that the Chi Kung beginner understand that holding the breath while practicing is very harmful. There are some exercises in which you hold your breath, but unless you are doing these specific exercises, you should be careful to keep your breathing smooth and steady.

5. Holding the Breath Breathing:

Holding the breath breathing is a training technique for when a Chi Kung practitioner wishes to lead his Chi to a specific area and hold it there. For example, martial artists, especially in the external styles, will generate Chi in their limbs and then hold their breath. This causes the Chi to stay in the limbs so that they can use it for fighting. To use a more prosaic example, when pushing a car you will find sometimes that after you have exerted your power you hold your breath in order to make the power last longer. In internal Chi Kung practice, practitioners will often lead Chi to a specific spot and then gently hold their breath. This may be done to raise the potential in a cavity in order to dissolve a block. When an internal martial artist has an internal injury, he will often lead Chi to the injury and keep it there for a short time to energize the area and speed up the healing process. When he does this, he must hold his breath gently while keeping his body relaxed so that he can feel and lead the Chi.

You can see that holding the breath Chi Kung training is a higher level than those discussed above. Before you train this, you must have acquired mastery of the right breathing techniques and you must understand your body's Chi, otherwise you will make the situation worse. You should also understand that if you do not know the **Why** and **How** of the practice thoroughly, holding the breath is very dangerous -- especially in Nei Dan Chi Kung. When you hold your breath, the Chi will accumulate and stagnate. If this accumulated Chi stays in cavity or in the organs, it may affect the normal functioning of your body. It is very easy for a beginner to hold his Chi in his solar plexus and heart, which may cause damage to the heart or even death. **BEFORE STARTING HOLDING THE BREATH TRAINING, YOU MUST COMPLETE SMALL CIRCULATION AND GRAND CIRCULATION**.

In the external Chi Kung styles, holding the breath is not as dangerous as it is in the internal styles. Most of the external Chi Kung styles work with Chi in the limbs. Chi stagnation in the limbs is not as dangerous as stagnation in the body, where it can affect the internal organs.

In Nei Dan Chi Kung training there are three major purposes for holding the breath.

A. To lead Chi to the ends of or even beyond the body:

Remember that when you practice Nei Dan you must remain relaxed and calm, then you will be able to lead Chi to your skin. Normally, without special training it is very hard to move Chi to the hair or beyond the skin. Nei Dan Chi Kung practitioners found that, once they led Chi to their skin, if they gently held their breath they could use their mind to lead the Chi further. When Chi is held at the skin, the Chi potential is raised and the millions of tiny Chi channels are opened. This makes it easier for the Chi to reach past the skin. The more you train, the further beyond your body you will be able to expand it. It is said: "Transport Chi as though through a pearl with a hole with nine curves, not even the tiniest place won't be reached."(*2) You should be able to transport Chi to every part of your body, from deep inside the marrow to beyond the surface of the skin.

B. To move Chi without coordinating it with the breath:

You know that when you move the abdomen in and out the Chi is led out from the Dan Tien. Beginners usually have to coordinate this with their breathing in order to do it effectively. After several years of practice you may wish to lead the Chi (or as it is commonly said, generate the Chi) solely with your mind without coordinating it with your breathing. In order to do this, hold your breath for a short time, while keeping your body completely relaxed. Move your abdomen in and out, leading the Chi either upward or downward without coordinating it with your breathing. When you reach this stage, it is said that you have "picked up the little herb" (Tsae Sheau Yaw). This means both that the student is starting to be able to use his Chi Kung (as in picking up something to use it), and that he is bringing Chi (the herb) up his back. This exercise is done in the beginning stages of Chi Kung training, when most students still need to move the abdomen in order to coordinate the movement of Chi with the opening and closing of the Huiyin cavity and the anus.

C. Hibernation training:

One of the highest Chi Kung practices is training yourself to use oxygen more efficiently. Holding the breath is the most basic step of this training. You must train yourself to stay calm and relaxed even when your air supply is cut off. Your meditative mind should reach a level of sleeping meditation, like hibernating animals, in which your heart beat slows down. Once you have learned to use oxygen more efficiently, you will breathe less and less and be able to enter a deep sleep. We will discuss hibernation breathing later.

6. Full Inhale and Exhale Breathing:

In this type of abdominal breathing, you practice inhaling and exhaling to the maximum in coordination with the in and out motion of your abdomen. You also try to extend the length of each breath. When you practice this, you make a slight sound as you inhale and exhale. This training has several aspects.

A. Like the chest breathing discussed above, full inhale and exhale abdominal breathing increases the amount of oxygen you take in and the amount of carbon dioxide you put out. However, this exercise is one step ahead of chest breathing because the abdominal movement causes Chi to accumulate in the Dan Tien. This exercise also trains the abdominal muscles to expand and contract to their maximum.

B. When you make a slight sound while doing full inhale and exhale breathing, you raise your Yi and spirit to their maximum. This can help you in leading Chi to the surface of the skin and condensing it in the center of your body or into the marrow.

When you practice this type of breathing, keep your body as relaxed as possible. Your mind must be calm and clear, so that you can lead the Chi to the skin and condense it in the marrow. Do not make a habit

---

(*2). " 行氣如九曲珠，無微不到。"

of doing this full inhalation and exhalation all the time. Practice it only occasionally in order to enliven the lung cells which are not generally used. Full breathing is the key to skin breathing, which will be discussed next.

7. Body Breathing (Tii Shyi) or Skin Breathing (Fu Shyi):

Body breathing or skin breathing is one of the main goals of Chi Kung breathing. It means that when you breathe, your entire body is also breathing Chi through your skin. When you exhale you move Chi to your skin, and your pores open; and when you inhale you draw in Chi from outside, and your pores close. When you are able to lead Chi to your skin when you exhale, it feels like when you expose your skin to the hot sun on a winter day. In the hot sun, your pores open up to absorb and expel energy more easily. In Chi Kung training, however, you use your mind to lead the Chi to the skin to energize your pores from inside your body. Once the pores are energized they open wide, and when you inhale, the Chi is led inward and the pores close. After you have practiced Chi Kung for a while, you will want your Chi to reach every cell of your body -- especially the skin. Skin breathing allows you to open your pores so that the air can come in and remove the waste that accumulates in them. Leading Chi to the skin is a required step if you want your Chi to expand beyond your body. If you are able to reach this stage, your Chi will be able to reach anywhere your will leads it. You will have plenty of Chi, and your Chi circulation will be smooth everywhere. This is the key to maintaining health and lengthening your life.

When you train body breathing, center yourself in your Dan Tien and imagine that your body and Chi are like a big beach ball. Every time you inhale, your Yi brings all of the Chi to the center and the ball shrinks, and when you exhale, the imaginary ball expands. If you catch the trick, you will discover that this Chi ball gradually expands to cover your entire body. When you breathe, this Chi ball also breathes (Figure 9-2).

In the Taoist books, this body breathing or skin breathing method is considered one of the "Fwu Chi Faa" (Yield Chi Methods), and is included in the "Ling Bao Bih Faa" (Spiritual Treasure to Reach the End Method). In this training, start with a full inhalation and intentionally hold the air in your body. Then, slowly let the air out. When you practice this method, you are also beginning to do skin or body breathing. After you train for a long time, you will be able to extend the duration of the breaths and reach the goal of the "Guei Shyi" (Turtle Breath). It is believed that the turtle is able to live for several hundred years because it is able to exchange air directly through its skin.

8. Hands and Feet Breathing:

In Chinese meditation there are five places or centers (Wuu Hsin) which are considered to be the gates through which the Chi in the body communicates with the Chi which surrounds you. These centers are the face, the two Bubbling-Wells (Yongquan) on the bottom of your feet (Figure 9-3), and the two Labor Palaces (Laogong) in the center of your palms (Figure 9-4). Taoist Harn Shiu Tzuu said: "The feet breathe, continuously and unbroken, existing softly."(*3) Juang Tzyy said: "The normal person breathes in his throat, a real person (an immortal) breathes through his feet."(*4)

(*3). 涵虛祖曰：＂踵也者，相接不斷，緜緜若存也。＂

(*4). 莊子云：＂常人之息以喉，真人之息以踵。＂

Figure 9-2. Expanding the Chi
ball

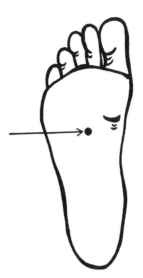

Figure 9-3. The Bubbling Well
cavity (Yongquan)

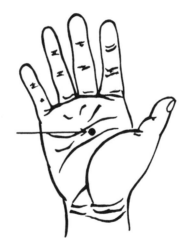

Figure 9-4. The Labor Palace cavity (Laogong)

The major purposes of these centers or gates are:

A. To regulate the body's Chi level:

For example, when the body is too positive because of fever, these five gates will release Chi to cool down the body. A very common treatment for fever in Chinese medicine is to place the feet in cold water, and to put alcohol in the center of the palms and blow on it. This speeds the lowering of the body's Chi level and, consequently, cools down the temperature of the body. You know that in the summertime when you are very hot, you can cool down by washing your face and hands in cold water. And remember how good it feels to immerse your feet in a nice cold stream?

B. To sense your surroundings:

Frequently you will first sense hot or cold on your face or the centers of your palms. This is because they are the centers or gates which allow you to communicate most directly with the environment. You have to be able to sense what is going on with the Chi around you before your body can adjust its Guardian Chi level to protect itself. Although the centers of the feet are also designed for this, these gates are not as sensitive as they used to be because of the use of shoes.

C. To absorb Chi from outside of your body:

When you feel cold, you use warm water to wash your face, hands, and feet. When you have a cold, placing your feet and hands in warm water will keep you warm because it allows you to absorb environmental Chi through the gates to nourish your body. In Chinese Chi Kung, it is very important to train yourself to absorb environmental Chi. When you are able to do this efficiently, you will be able to cut down on the amount of food and air that your body requires.

Generally speaking, the face center is the most important and sensitive gate among the five. The gates work in both directions: you are able to sense what is going on outside of you, but they also reveal what is going on inside you. Your face is the first part of you to sense whether the air is warm or cold, and four of your five senses are located in your face and head. On the other hand, your face clearly reflects your emotions, and often indicates what you are thinking. In the centers of your palms are the Laogong cavities. They are the gates which lead Chi to the skin of the entire palm and fingers. The more Chi you have flowing through your palms, the more Chi flows to the skin of the whole hand, and the greater your sensitivity of touch. Good Chi flow in the hands is also important for manual labor, which is why the cavities are called "Labor Palaces" (Laogong). The cavities in the bottom of the feet play a similar role. The are called "Bubbling Wells" (Yongquan) because the Chi is continually coming out of them.

Because these five gates are keys to adjusting the Chi in your body, Chi Kung meditators train until they are able to govern the Chi in these five areas efficiently. They are not only learning how to release excess Chi, but they are also learning how to absorb Chi from the environment. This practice will allow them to regulate their bodies' Chi by using the natural, environmental Chi which is considered more pure and clean than the Post-birth Chi converted from the food and air Essences. Medical Chi Kung practitioners train with the two gates in the palms so that they can increase their effectiveness in adjusting their patients' Chi. Martial artists train these two gates so that they can lead Chi to the hands more efficiently and energize the muscles. This also increases their ability to sense their opponent's energy, which is called "skin listening" in the internal martial styles. They also train the gates in the feet so that they can jump high, run fast, and kick powerfully. You can see from these examples that governing the Chi in the five gates is a serious concern in every style of Chinese Chi Kung.

In the previous section we discussed how the pores in the skin are millions of tiny Chi gates which allow you to sense the environment and exchange Chi with it. Unfortunately, since people have protected their bodies from the natural environment for so long by wearing clothes, we have lost a lot of the sensitivity that we used to have, and that animals still have. However, the hands and the face still have a lot of their sensitivity.

In order to govern the Chi in the gates, you must learn to breathe through the centers of your palms and feet. "Breathing" here means to exchange the Chi of the body for the Chi of the environment through special breathing techniques. Generally speaking, Taoist reverse abdominal breathing is the easiest way. In Taoist training, when you inhale you draw Chi from your limbs into the center of your body. While you are doing this, image that you are absorbing Chi from the environment through the gates. When you exhale, lead the Chi to the gates and release it into the air (Figure 9-5). After you train for a long time, you will be able to feel that, when you breathe, these five gates are also breathing. You must train until it becomes natural and you do not have to concentrate on it to do it. Remember: **REGULATE YOUR BREATHING UNTIL YOU NO LONGER NEED TO DO IT CONSCIOUSLY**. Naturally, before you can breathe through these gates, you must have mastered all of the basic breathing techniques which we have discussed before.

9. Thread Breathing (Guan Chi):

Thread breathing is a higher level breathing technique. Usually, before you reach this stage your energy or Chi body is already transparent. Thread breathing teaches you to lead the Chi anywhere in your body in coordination with your breathing. There are two major purposes to this training:

A. To adjust the Chi in the body:

Very often after you practice Chi Kung you will find that the Chi in one area is higher than in another. The thread breathing method, however, allows you to lead the Chi to other areas very effectively, whenever you want. This practice can also be used to adjust abnormal Chi levels caused by sickness.

B. To raise clean, pure Chi and to sink dirty, contaminated Chi:

In Chi Kung training, in order for you to reach the higher meditative stages, you must settle or sink your contaminated Fire Chi and raise up your pure Water Chi. The thread breathing method is also used to reverse the positions of the Water Chi and Fire Chi. This method is called "Kan Lii" (Fire-Water). When the

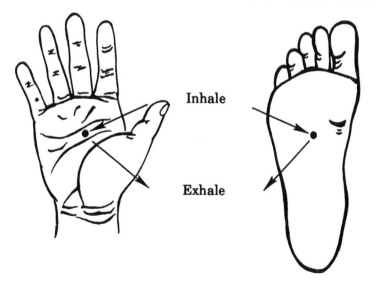

Inhale

Exhale

Figure 9-5. Exchanging Chi through the Chi gates

Fire Chi sinks to the Dan Tien, it will be controlled and settled. In Chi Kung training, it is also common to sink the Fire Chi to the bottom of the feet and to raise the Water Chi to the top of your head -- a process which threads your entire body together.

C. To open up the Chi channels and the blood vessels:

The thread breathing method can not only help you to complete Grand Chi Circulation, but it can also open up all of the other Chi branches in addition to the twelve major Chi channels.

You can see that thread breathing training involves leading the Chi to move within your body, a process which is different from the skin and gates breathing methods, in which Chi is exchanged with the natural environment. You should understand that the first requirement is that your body must be relaxed completely into the third level of relaxation, which will allow the Chi to move freely. The second requirement is that your mind must be within your body instead outside of your body. If your mind is not in your body, how will you be able to sense and lead the Chi? We will discuss regulating the mind later. Finally, you must learn how to coordinate your breathing with your mind and Chi. Naturally, it is impossible for a beginner to reach this stage. It normally takes at least 10 or more years of correct training.

We would like to remind you that many of the subjects discussed in this volume are presented as information, as a guide for understanding Chi Kung. It is almost impossible for anyone to grasp the keys simply by reading this book. As long as you remember: **DO NOT LOOK HIGH AND WALK LOW**, sooner or later you will reach your goal.

10. Hibernation Breathing (Don Main Far):

One of the highest levels of Chi Kung involves disciplining your spirit to leave your body and travel around. Often your spirit will leave your body for long periods of time, sometimes even for several months. In order to keep your physical body alive without food while your spirit is gone, your heartbeat must slow down, your body's use of energy must be kept to a minimum, and the energy must be used most efficiently. Hibernation breathing makes this possible, slowing your breathing rate down almost to a stop, and making it very shallow. Hibernation breathing is also trained in Indian Yoga.

In order to reach the stage of hibernation breathing, you must first have a deep level of experience with still meditation. You need to train your body, through fasting and other techniques, to slowly and efficiently convert stored food Essence into Chi. Your body must be completely relaxed and transparent to the flow of Chi. Naturally, before you are able to freely separate your spirit from your physical body, you usually need to complete the training for spiritual enlightenment. According to the Marrow Washing documents it usually takes twelve years of proper training as a hermit or priest.

11. Shen Breathing (Shen Shyi):

In religious Chi Kung, Shen breathing is one of the final practices in leading the Shen to separate from the body. Once the mind has been regulated into a deep, calm, and peaceful level, Shen breathing unites the Shen with the breathing so that they correspond to each other. Because breathing is your strategy in guiding and governing the Chi, your Shen can govern the Chi effectively only when your Shen and breathing are able to work together as one.

Naturally, you must first learn how to keep your Shen (Shoou Shen), and then how to firm it (Guh Shen). "Keep" here means to protect, to nourish, and to keep the Shen at its residence. "Firm" means to solidify, to strengthen, and to control it effectively in the Upper Dan Tien. After you have reached this level, you learn how to use your Yi to move your Shen away from its residence and finally separate from the physical body. In order to reach this final stage, you must first learn Shen breathing. When you start moving your Shen, first stays close to its residence, the way a small child stays near its home when it first starts to walk.

It is said in Taoist society: "Shen is the master of Chi, and it moves and stops with the Chi. Breathing is the secret key to the Chi's forward and backward. The secret key must have the master (Shen), and the master must have the Yi. Three things (Shen, breathing, and Yi) must be used at the same time. Then it will be the really marvelous and tricky Kung Fu of heavenly circulation. When one is missing, it is hard to reach the final goal."(*5) You can see that Shen is the headquarters of the Chi and moves together with it. The secret to controlling the movement of the Chi is the breathing. However, most important of all is what is behind the Shen. It is the Yi which ultimately controls the entire training. It is also said: "Shen and Chi move and stop together and not separately. The Yi stays at the center palace like a cart's axle. Wheels (Shen and Chi) and the axle (provide) mutual support. The axle does not move, but lets the wheels turn by themselves."(*6) Shen and Chi move together like the wheels. However, these wheels are directed and controlled by the axle. This axle is your mind (Yi). The mind keeps to the center so that it can direct what is happening, but it should not get involved in the turning of the wheels. The Taoist Tzyy Yang Tzuu said: "Slowly tend the herb furnace and watch the (cooking) timing, but keep peace in your Shen breathing and let nature be."(*7) This sentence means that when you are building your Chi at the Dan Tien, take it slow and easy. Pay attention to the timing to notice when the herb is done. However, you must keep your Shen breathing peacefully and let it happens naturally. The deep meaning of this sentence is that you must train until your Shen breathing becomes natural and you do not need your Yi to regulate your Shen any longer. It is also said in one of the Taoist classics: "Breathing is hidden in the Shen and Shen is hidden in the eyes. The large Tao (has) no shape and no appearance."(*8)

12. Real Breathing (Jen Shyi):

Real breathing, or Jen Shyi, comes from regulating normal

(*5). "神是與氣同行同住之主宰，息是進氣退氣之機關，機不可少主，主不可少意，三物並用，方為真正玄妙周天之功夫，缺一難成正果。"

(*6). "神氣同行同住而不離，其意主中宮如軸心，輪軸互用，軸不動而任輪之自轉也"。

(*7). 紫陽祖曰："謾守藥爐看火候，但安神息任天然。"

breathing. From real breathing is born embryonic breathing. Once you have regulated your normal breathing, you start abdominal breathing, whereby Chi is led from the kidneys to the Lower Dan Tien. This lays the foundation of real breathing. Then what is real breathing? It is said: "The inner scenery of 'real breathing' is (that) there is Chi moving up and down a few inches under the navel (Dan Tien)."(*9)

It is also said: "The 'real breathing,' one close one develop, on the top, it does not conflict with the heart; on the bottom, it does not conflict with the kidneys. The 'real person' (is able to) dive into the deep water, float swiftly (but) keep the regular center."(*10) "One close and one develop" means that the Chi is contracting and expanding. This saying explains that in real breathing, the Chi is generated in the Dan Tien and moves up and down. When it moves up it will not disturb the functioning of the heart, and when it moves down it will not affect the normal functioning of the kidneys. The heart and the kidneys are the most vital organs and must have normal Chi levels. It is therefore important when you do Chi Kung that you do not let the extra energy you develop interfere with the normal functioning of your body. A 'real person' is someone who has reached the stage of real breathing, and Chi is able to reach deep into every part of his body. Regardless of how this Chi moves, the mind (Yi) must remain at the Dan Tien, which is the "regular center."

It is also said: "The real breathing, like there like gone, soft and nonstop, one name 'internal breathing'. (Though) the external normal breathing is stopped, there is an up and down internal scenery at the Dan Tien."(*11) The Taoist song, Ling Yuan Ge (Spiritual Source Song) says: "Concentrate on the (training) of Chi until it reaches softness, and the Shen is able to stay long, to and fro of the 'real breathing' naturally leisurely."(*12) This sentence leads you to the key to real breathing. In order to reach the stage of real breathing, you must concentrate on training your Chi flow to be as soft as possible, and your spirit must concentrate and stay in one place, then someday you will sense the Chi's up and down movements and attain 'real breathing'.

(*8). 經曰："息隱神中神隱眸，大道無形固無相。"

(*9). "真息之內景為臍下約四五寸處，有氣上下往來。"

(*10). "真息者，一闢一闔，上不冲心，下不冲腎，`真人潛深淵，浮游守規中'也。"

(*11). "真息者，似有似無，綿綿不斷，一名內呼吸。外面之凡息雖斷，而丹田之中猶有一上一下之內景。"

(*12). 靈源歌曰："專氣致柔神久留，往來真息自悠悠。"

The Taoist San Feng Tzuu said: "Do not forget the Chi, regulate 'real breathing', but keep Shiu Wu (nothing), transport Kan (water) and Lii (fire)."(*13) This sentence means that in Chi Kung training you must always pay attention to the Chi and learn to regulate the 'real breathing'. Keep your mind at the Upper Dan Tien where your Shen resides. Shiu Wu means "nothing," and represents the place where the spirit resides because spirit was generated from nothing. If you are able to do this, you will be able to transport the Water Chi up to cool the Fire Chi.

13. Embryonic Breathing (Tai Shyi):

We mentioned in the first chapter that there are two major kinds of Chi: Pre-birth Chi or Original Chi (Yuan Chi), and Post-birth Chi. Original Chi is converted from the Original Essence you inherited from your parents, and Post-birth Chi is converted from the food and air Essence. Original Chi is generally considered to be Yin Chi or Water Chi, while Post-birth Chi is thought to be Yang Chi or Fire Chi.

It is said: "Producing the large herb is not different from growing things between heaven and earth. In all, it is only Yang and Yin, two Chi's. When the two Chi's provide each other and become one, the heaven and the earth will mutually interact."(*14) This means that in order to generate the herb (elixir), you must have both Yin Chi and Yang Chi. Both Chi's must mutually interact with each other, then a living thing or herb will be produced. The herb or living thing here means the embryo, which represents the beginning of a new life. Taoist Chang Tzyy-Chyong said: "Not assisting, not forgetting, the marvelous breathing. To cultivate human nature (the Tao), (you) must comprehend this Kung Fu. Regulate the two Chi's to originate the embryonic breathing. Then build your (herb or elixir) furnace in it."(*15) This sentence means that when you cultivate your Tao, you should not concentrate on (assist) nor ignore (forget) the marvelous strategy of breathing. In order to reach the embryonic breathing stage, you must learn to regulate the Yang and Yin Chi. After you can regulate your Yang and Yin Chi, you will be able to generate the elixir in it.

What then is embryonic breathing? It is said: "(When) the Shen is hidden at the Chi cavity, it is called the embryo. (When) the (Post-birth) Chi is able to reach to the cavity, it is called breathing."(*16)

(*13). 三丰祖曰："休忘氣，調真息，但守虛無運坎離。"

(*14). 圭旨曰："大藥之生，與天地生物不異，總只是陰陽二氣，二施一化，而玄黃相交矣！"

(*15). 張紫瓊曰："非助非忘妙呼吸，修行要解這功夫，調停二氣生胎息，而向中間設鼎爐。"

(*16). "藏神於氣穴曰胎，氣至氣穴為息，胎其神息其氣，功夫進至胎息，則不出不入，永無凡息矣！"

Before we continue, you should first understand what cavity is meant here. In Chi Kung, several places are called "Yuan Chiaw" which means "original cavity," or "original key point." One of these places is called "Hwang Tyng" or "Yellow Yard." Taoists used to wear yellow robes, so naturally this name is used frequently in Taoist society. The Hwang Tyng cavity is behind the navel and in front of the Mingmen (Figure 9-6). It is at the center of gravity of your body. This is the place where the baby's cells started to multiply. In embryonic breathing, your Shen is able to resides at the Hwang Tyng and the Post-birth Chi is able to reach it. Then the Yang Chi and Yin Chi interact, and a new "baby" is be born. The Taoist Li Ching-An said: "Shen and Chi combine to originate the super spiritual quality, Hsin and breath are mutually dependent to generate the holy embryo."(*17) Hsin here means mind and Shen.

The Taoist treatise Wuh Jen Pian (Treatise on Comprehending the Real) said: "There are three kinds of breathing. From coarse to fine, inhalation and exhalation through the nose is nose breathing. Keeping the center (Lower Dan Tien) and ascending and descending, is Chi breathing. (When) extremely calm and return to its root is called Shen

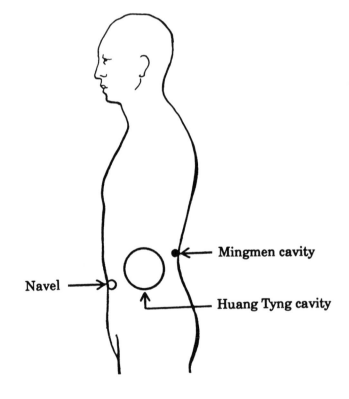

Navel

Mingmen cavity

Huang Tyng cavity

Figure 9-6. Huang Tyng Cavity

(*17). 李清菴詩云：" 神氣和合生靈質 ， 心息相依結聖胎 。"

breathing. Therefore, to number (means to evaluate), the breathing (meaning nose breathing) is not as high as regulating (abdominal real) breathing, and the regulating breathing is not as high as Shen breathing. When the Shen breathing becomes peaceful, then condense the Shen into the Chi cavity (Hwang Tyng), then the breathing is really deep."(*18) This saying explains the levels of breathing. First, you learn nose breathing from coarse to fine, until the breathing becomes relaxed, deep, smooth, and natural. Then you enter into abdominal breathing and eventually enter into real breathing. After you have reached the real breathing stage, you train Shen breathing until your Shen is able to reach the Hwang Tyng cavity and the Post-birth Chi is able to reach there also, so that the holy embryo will be generated and the elixir will be formed.

To conclude this section, it is important for a Chi Kung practitioner to learn the correct ways of regulating his breathing. There are many ways of regulating the breathing, which we have arranged from the most basic to the deepest and most difficult. To reach the final goal of embryonic breathing you must start with regulating the normal breathing. It is called "Byi Shyi," which means "nose breathing." From normal regular breathing, you will enter the abdominal breathing stage which enables you to build Chi at the Dan Tien. It is this Chi which will lead you to the door of real Chi Kung practice. This training is called "Chi Shyi," or "Chi breathing." When you have reached this level the Dan Tien Chi is able to move up and down following your breathing. You have now reached the target of "real breathing." Finally, you will lead the Post-birth Chi to the "Hwang Tyng Cavity" to interact with the Pre-birth Chi and generate the "holy embryo." When you have completed this stage, you will have formed the "Elixir." This stage of breathing is called "Tai Shyi," which means "embryonic breathing."

Reaching the final goal of embryonic breathing is very difficult. When you have reached this stage, you will have built the foundation of enlightenment. It is almost impossible to reach this stage without becoming a hermit. Very few Chi Kung practitioners have really done it. It is probable more feasible for the average person who is seeking good health and a long life to reach the stage of "real breathing."

9-4. General Keys to Regulating Normal Breathing

If you are a Chi Kung beginner, you should start with regulating your normal breathing, and not worry about any other Chi regulating breath training. This will gradually lead you into Chi breathing.

There are eight key words for air breathing which a beginning Chi Kung practitioner should remember during his normal breathing exercise. Once you understand them you will be able to shorten substantially the time needed to reach your Chi Kung goals. These eight key words are:

(*18). 悟真篇曰：＂息有三種：從粗入細，呼吸出入者鼻息也；規中升降者氣息也；靜極歸根者神息也。故數息不如調息，調息不如安息。神息既安，則凝神入氣穴，其息深矣。＂

1. Calm and Silent (Jing):
The mind is calm and the breathing is silent. When your mind is calm and peaceful, you will be able to judge what is going on correctly and will be able to regulate your breathing more efficiently. Unless you are engaged in special training for some specific purpose, keep your breathing silent so that it is relaxed and peaceful.

2. Slender (Shyi):
When you breathe, it is like a tiny stream -- it should be smooth, natural, and slender. This key will lead you into deeper levels of meditation and relaxation.

3. Deep (Shenn):
When you breathe deep, draw the air down into your abdomen. Draw the air in by moving your diaphragm down, rather than by expanding your chest. Only expand your chest if you are doing a chest expanding exercise. Deep breathing will lead you to abdominal breathing and build the foundation for your Chi Kung practice.

Deep and complete breathing does not mean that you inhale and exhale to the maximum. This would cause the lungs and the surrounding muscles to tense up, which in turn would keep the air from circulating freely, and hinder the absorption of oxygen. Without enough oxygen, your mind becomes scattered, and the rest of your body tenses up. In correct breathing, you inhale and exhale to about 70% or 80% of your maximum capacity, so that your lungs stay relaxed.

You can conduct an easy experiment. Inhale deeply so that your lungs are completely full, and time how long you can hold your breath. Then try inhaling to only about 70% of your capacity, and see how long you can hold your breath. You will find that with the latter method you can last much longer than with the first one. This is simply because the lungs and the surrounding muscles are relaxed. When they are relaxed, the rest of your body and your mind can also relax, which decreases significantly your need for oxygen. Therefore, when you regulate your breathing, the first priority is to keep your lungs relaxed and calm.

4. Long (Charng):
When you breathe, you should keep the breath as long as possible. However, you should remember that **BREATHING LONG DOES NOT MEAN HOLDING YOUR BREATH**. In order to breathe long, your lung must be very relaxed and your meditative mind must have reached a deep level. In this case, your heartbeat will slow down, and you will require less oxygen. Only under these conditions can your breathing be long.

5. Continuous (Iou):
Your breathing must be smooth, natural, and most important of all, continuous. Unless it is for a specialized training, your breath should be continuous and without stagnation. When you stop or hold your breath, your body will tense. Continuous breathing will help you relax and lead you to a deeper meditative mind.

6. Uniform (Yun):
Your breathing should be uniform. As we mentioned previously, your breathing is affected by your emotions. In order to attain uniformity in your breathing, you must regulate your emotional mind. Only this will allow you to keep your breath uniform and smooth.

7. Slow (Hoan):

Unless you are practicing a special training, your mind must be slowed down and you must take your time with your breathing. Take it easy and be natural. Do not rush your inhalation and exhalation.

8. Soft (Mian):

When you breathe, your breathing should be easy and soft. Soft breathing makes you relaxed and leads you to a deeper meditative mind.

9-5. Six Stages of Regulating the Breath

In Chi Kung society, there are six common words used in conjunction with regulating the breathing. They represent six stages in the practice. These words are:

1. Count (Su): Count the breaths (Su Shyi):

Counting is the first and most basic way to regulate the breathing. First, calm your mind and breath, following the eight keys to regulating explained above. Then, start to count your breaths slowly from one to ten and from ten to one. Alternatively, you may count only inhalations or exhalations. Paying attention to the counting keeps your mind from concentrating on your breathing and becoming tense. This helps you to lead your mind into a state of meditation. This is similar to the idea of counting sheep when you want to fall asleep.

2. Follow (Suei):

Follow means to follow the breathing (Suei Shyi). Once you can regulate your breathing with the counting method, you move on to this method. Be conscious of your breathing and follow the inhalation and exhalation. When you can do this without tensing up, your mind and breathing will unite and become one. The mind here means emotional mind, because it is the emotional mind which disturbs your calmness and peaceful thinking. It is said: "Hsin Shyi Shiang Yi" (*19) meaning "Heart (mind) and breathing (are) mutually dependent." When your mind is able to follow the breathing, the mind will enter a deeper meditative state and the breathing will slow down further. Following is an important technique in using the breathing and mind to help each other enter the deeper states of meditation.

3. Stop (Tzyy):

Stop means to stop thinking about your breathing (Tzyy Shyi). An ancient Taoist named Li Ching-An said: "Regulating breathing means to regulate the real breathing until (you) stop."(*20) This means that correct regulating means not having to consciously regulate. In other words, although you start by regulating your breath consciously, you must get to the point where the regulation happens naturally, and you no longer have to think about it. When you breathe, if you concentrate your mind on breathing, it is not true regulating, because the Chi in your lungs will become stagnant.

(*19). " 心息相依 "

(*20). " 調息要調無息息 "

When you reach the level of true regulating, no regulating is necessary, and you can use your mind efficiently to lead the Chi. Remember **WHEREVER THE YI IS, THERE IS CHI. IF THE YI STOPS IN ONE SPOT, THE CHI WILL BE STAGNANT. IT IS THE YI WHICH LEADS THE CHI AND MAKES IT MOVE.** Therefore, when you are in a state of correct breath regulation, your mind is free. There is no sound, stagnation, urgency, or hesitation, and you can be calm and peaceful. When you reach this stage, you have obtained the real key to meditation.

4. Look (Guan):

Look means to feel and to sense the breathing (Guan Shyi). It is also commonly called "Ting Shyi," or "listening to the breathing." The words looking and listening here do not mean actually looking with your eyes and listening with your ears. They refer to using your mind to feel and sense what is happening. In meditation this is called "Nei Shyi Fan Ting"(*21), meaning "To see internally and to listen inwardly." Therefore, in Chi Kung meditation you do not pay attention to anything outside of your body. You use your mind to feel and sense (look and listen) internally. When you have reached the stage of regulating the breathing without regulating, your mind will be free. Then you are able to concentrate your mind on the movement of the Chi, and you may lead the Chi wherever you wish. You will be able to lead the Chi to every cell of your body and feel that your body is transparent.

5. Return (Fan):

Fan Shyi (return breathing) means to return your breathing to its natural way. That also implies that in this stage you will have reached the level of regulating the breathing without regulating. That means when you have mastered this stage you will have not only returned your breathing to natural way, but have also reached the stage where your breathing combines with your mind and they become one. The breathing reflects the mind, and the mind reflects the breathing. Your breathing is now automatically regulated, and you no longer have to pay conscious attention to it, and your mind now regulates itself.

Regulating your mind requires that you understand the way (Tao) that Nature works. Your mind is now free and able to enter into a deep meditative state, and you can see beneath the surface of things and events and understand their real nature. The first step to this is understanding yourself. You need to comprehend the meaning of life. Breathing is the sign of life, and the dividing line of Yin and Yang. When you understand your breathing, you understand your life. This involves moving in your understanding from the poles of extreme Yin and extreme Yang to the middle, where all the fine gradations and shadings of existence are. When your mind is able to stay at the center, you are able to judge neutrally and see clearly. The two poles of Yin and Yang return back to their origin -- "Wu Chi" (No Extremities). Natural breathing lets your mind be clear, so you can look at yourself and search out the real you. Only after you understand yourself are you able to understand real nature or the real "Tao."

(*21). " 內視返聽 ."

Everything has its origin. In order to understand real nature, you must trace back to its origin. Fan Shyi is the process of returning yourself to your origin. This is a necessary step to becoming a "Buddha" or reaching "enlightenment." It is said: "Jiann Shing Leau Ran"(*22), which means "To see Nature and understand what it really is." When you have reached this stage, you have passed the stage of regulating your physical body and may concentrate on spiritual matters.

6. Clean (Jing):

"Clean" means "regulated," so in this method you use natural breathing to regulate your thoughts (Jing Shyi), although the term also refers to the stage when the breathing and the mind become one and the mind is regulated. Once you understand the real you and the real nature that lie beneath the surface appearances, you will use this breathing to regulate your mind into a state where you are free of emotions. Only then will you be able to reach the higher stages of spiritual cultivation. This cleaning process for the emotional mind is the final stage of religious Chi Kung. According to Buddhism, in order to become a Buddha, you must get rid of the seven emotions and six desires. Once you have reached this stage, your body is clean and your spirit is pure. When your mind and spirit has reached this stage, it is called "Jing" (clean).

To conclude this subject, and hopefully to stimulate you to further thought, I would like to introduce more poetry related to regulating the breath. You should always remember that breath training gives you techniques and strategies which enable you to regulate your body and mind in Chi Kung practice. By regulating the body, mind, and breathing, you will be able to regulate your Chi and lead it smoothly and naturally. Chi and breathing are mutually related and cannot be separated. This idea is explained frequently in Taoist literature. The Taoist Goang Cherng Tzyy said: "One exhale, the Earth Chi rises; one inhale, the Heaven Chi descends; real man's (meaning one who has attained the real Tao) repeated breathing at the navel, then my real Chi is naturally connected."(*23) This says that your abdomen should be the center of your breathing, almost as if you were breathing through your navel. The earth Chi is the negative (Yin) energy from your kidneys, and the sky Chi is the positive (Yang) energy which comes from the food you eat and the air you breathe. When you breathe from the navel, these two Chi's are able to connect and combine. Some people think that they know what Chi is, but they really don't. Once you connect the two Chi's, you will know what the "real" Chi is, and you may become a "real" man, which means one who has attained the Tao.

The Taoist book Chain Tao Jing Yen (Sing (of the) Tao (with) Real Words) says: "One exhale one inhale to communicate Chi's function, one movement one calmness is the same as (is the source of) creation

---

(*22). "見性了然."

(*23). 廣成子曰："一呼則地氣上升，一吸則天氣下降，人之反覆呼吸於蒂，則我之真氣自然相接。"

and variation."(*24) The first part of this statement implies again that the functioning of Chi is connected to breathing. The second part means that all creation and variation come from the interaction of movement (Yang) and calmness (Yin).

Hwang Tyng Ching (Yellow Yard Classic) says: "Breathe Original Chi to seek immortality."(*25) This means that in order to reach the goal of immortality, you must find and understand Original Chi, by means of correct breathing.

Moreover, the Taoist Wuu Jen Ren said: "Use post-birth breathing to look for the real person's (i.e. the immortal's) breathing place."(*26) In this sentence, it is clear that in order to locate the immortal breathing place (the Dan Tien), you must rely on and know how to regulate your post-birth, or natural, breathing. Through regulating your post-birth breathing, you will gradually be able to locate the residence of the Chi (the Dan Tien), and eventually you will be able to use your Dan Tien to breath like the immortal Taoists.

Finally, in the Taoist song Ling Yuan Dah Tao Ge (The Great Taoist Song of the Spirit's Origin) it is said: "The Originals (Original Jieng, Chi, and Shen) are internally transported peacefully, so that you can become real (immortal); (if you) depend (only) on external breathing (you) will not reach the end (goal)."(*27) From this song, you can see that internal breathing (breathing at the Dan Tien) is the key to training your three treasures and finally reaching immortality. However, you must first know how to regulate your external breathing correctly.

(*24). 唱道真言曰：＂一呼一吸通乎氣機，一動一靜同乎造化。＂

(*25). 黃庭經曰：＂呼吸元氣以求仙。＂

(*26). 伍真人曰：＂用後天之呼吸，尋真人呼吸處。＂

(*27). 靈源大道歌：＂元和內運即成真，呼吸外求終末了。＂

Chapter 10

Regulating the Emotional Mind (Tyau Hsin)

10-1. Introduction

The Taoists say: "(When) large Tao is taught, first stop thought; when thought is not stopped, (the lessons are) in vain."(*1) This means that when you first practice Chi Kung, the most difficult training is to stop your thinking. The final goal for your mind is the "thought of no thought."(*2) Your mind does not think of the past, the present, or the future, so you are independent of their influences. Your mind can be calm and steady, and you can gain peace. Only when you are in the state of "the thought of no thought" will you be relaxed and able to sense calmly and accurately.

You can see that regulating your mind is probably the second key to successful Chi Kung training. Regulating the mind is called "Tyau Hsin," which means "to regulate the (emotional) mind." In the third chapter we discussed the differences between the emotional mind (Hsin) and the wisdom mind (Yi). Before we discuss how to regulate your emotional mind, we would like to summarize the differences between Hsin and Yi.

1. Yi is the mind which is related to your wisdom and correct judgement. Yi is generated from clear thinking and is calm, peaceful, and clear. Hsin is the mind which expresses your feelings, emotions, and desires. Hsin can be excited, energized, and confused. When Hsin and Yi work together, your inner humanity and personality will be manifested.

2. Yi is considered the "Water Mind" and is nourished with the "Water Chi" (Original Chi) generated from Yuan Jieng (Original Essence),

---

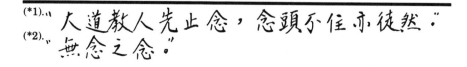

(*1).
(*2).

while the Hsin is considered the "Fire Mind" and is nourished with "Fire Chi" converted from the food and air Essences.

In Chi Kung training, regulating your mind means using your wisdom mind (Yi) to regulate your emotional mind (Hsin). After the emotional mind is under the control of wisdom mind, you will be calm and peaceful. Yi is the master of the Hsin. After your Yi has control of your Hsin, you will be able to regulate your Yi into a deeper meditative level and finally reach the stage of the "thought of no thought." This mind regulating practice is called "Chyn Yuan Juo Maa"(*3), which means "Seize the ape and catch the horse." The ape represents the Hsin and the horse represents the Yi. Hsin, the emotional mind, is like an ape which is always running around. You have to put it on a leash and train it so that, although it is still emotional and excitable, it is now under your control. The Yi is like a horse which is strong and very useful, but which still has to be trained and harnessed before it can be used. Once the horse is tamed and trained, it can be calm, steady, and peaceful.

The Taoist Chorng Yang Tzuu said: "Sleepy, then seize the ape and catch the horse, when you waken, again pluck 'Ling Jy', repeat the practice hundreds of days, only your heart (Hsin) knows. Conserve your real Chi, hide (it) at the Dan Tien, the human will not die."(*4) This saying means that if you feel sleepy while you are meditating, you should seize your Hsin (emotional mind) and catch the Yi (wisdom mind). The emotional mind makes you feel tired and sleepy. You should take control of your Yi and Hsin and wake yourself up by raising your spirit and keeping it at the center. Ling Jy (Fomes Japonica) is a hard, dark brownish fungus which is supposed to possess supernatural powers. Here, Ling Jy means the elixir which enables you to have a long life.

Once you have reached the stage of "no thought," your mind is clear enough to sense things accurately. You have to be able to sense things clearly inside your own body before you can direct the circulation of Chi and nourish your Shen. If your emotional mind (Hsin) is properly regulated, you can use it to sense what is going on inside you, and use your Yi to evaluate and correct the situation.

One of the most common processes of regulating the mind, which is especially popular with Scholars, was originated by Confucius. He said: "First you must be calm, then your mind can be steady. Once your mind is steady, then you are at peace. Only when you are at peace are you able to think and finally gain."(*5) This procedure can also be applied to non-scholar meditation or Chi Kung exercises: First **Calm**, then **Steady**, **Peace**, **Think**, and finally **Gain.** So, when you practice Chi Kung, you must first learn to be emotionally calm.

(*3). 〝擒猿捉馬〞

(*4). 重陽祖曰："睡則擒猿捉馬，醒來復採瓊芝，每依時百日，只許心知，惜真氣，藏丹田，其人不死。"

(*5). 孔子曰："先靜爾后有定，定爾后能安，安爾后能慮，慮爾后能得。"

Once calm, you will be able to see what you want and firm your mind (steady). This firm and steady mind is your intention or Yi (it is how your Yi is generated). Only after you know what you really want will your mind gain peace and be able to relax emotionally and physically. After you have reached this stage, you must concentrate or think in order to execute your intention. When your mind is thoughtful and concentrated, your Chi will flow and you will be able to gain what you wish.

In this chapter we will first discuss the concepts of Hsin (emotional mind) and Niann (thought). Once you understand these two concepts you will be able to learn how to control them and finally reach the goal of regulating the mind. One of the main purposes of regulating your mind is so that you can use it to lead or regulate the Chi. Therefore, we should review the relationship of Yi and Chi. Then we will discuss the concept of regulating the Chi in your organs. Finally, we will explain the relationship between Hsin, Yi, and Shen.

10-2. Hsin, Yi, and Niann

As discussed before, there are two concepts in Chinese which are both translated "mind." One is the emotional mind (Hsin), and the other is the wisdom mind (Yi). Both of these minds originate (generate) ideas. Most of these ideas last only a short time, and do not remain in your consciousness. However, many others remain, residing in your brain and affecting your thinking. When this happens, the idea generated from Hsin or Yi is matured, and become a "thought." A thought will continue to affect your thinking and decision-making, and oftentimes disturb your emotions. This matured thought is called "Niann" in Chinese. The Chinese frequently combine the two (idea and thought) and use the term "Hsin Niann" (emotional mind-thought) to distinguish the thoughts generated by Hsin from those generated by the wisdom mind, which would be called "Yi Niann" (wisdom mind-thought).

For example, when you hear something sad which upsets you, your emotional mind (Hsin) has grasped an idea which causes an emotional reaction in it. If this state of mind persists and continues to upset you emotionally, it has become a thought and is "Niann" instead of "Hsin." When you see a beautiful car and wish you owned it, this idea is called Hsin. If this idea continues to bother you, then it is "Niann." Hsin is the cause of thought, and thought is the product of Hsin.

The Yi is also able to generate thoughts. They are usually calm, wise thoughts which do not disturb you emotionally or mentally. However, what usually happens with most people is that the idea which the Yi has generated is taken over by the Hsin. For example, from your Yi, you know you should get up at six o'clock in the morning for Chi Kung practice. This idea is an Yi. However, when morning comes around, your emotional laziness has conquered the idea which was originally generated from Yi, and you decide to turn over and go back to sleep. In this case, the new idea (of laziness) is generated from Hsin. Once you finally get up, you feel guilty and sorry for yourself. If this emotional, conscious feeling persists, then it is a "thought" (Hsin Niann).

In Chi Kung, thoughts which originate with the emotional mind (Hsin) are classified as fire thoughts, because they are able to disturb or raise up your emotional feelings, while the thoughts which originated with the Yi are classified as water thoughts, because they can cool down your emotions. Generally speaking, in Chi Kung practice it is the emotional mind and thoughts which disturb and slow down your cultivation. Therefore, when regulating the mind is mentioned in Chi Kung society, they usually mean regulating the Hsin (emotional mind) and the thoughts it generates.

Regulating your Hsin means to cut down on the amount of ideas generated from your emotional feelings, and to disperse thoughts (Niann) which formed from Hsin concerning the past, present, and future. If you want to stop thoughts from being produced, you must find the source of the Hsin and the Niann. Only when you have traced them to their source will you be able to stop your thoughts at their root.

Buddhists believe that emotional feelings are generated by attachment to the seven emotions and the six sensory pleasures (Chii Ching Liow Yuh). The seven emotions are: happiness, anger, sorrow, joy, love, hate, and desire; and the six sensory pleasures are the pleasures derived from the eyes, ears, nose, tongue, body, and mind.

The Buddhists believe that all human suffering comes from these roots. In order to be emotionally neutral and become a Buddha, you must first cultivate your Hsin and become detached from all emotional roots. They are aiming for the state of the "Four Emptinesses" (Syh Dah Jie Kong)(*6), which means that the four elements (earth, water, fire, and air) are absent from the mind and one is indifferent to worldly temptations.

The first step toward reaching this goal of regulating the Hsin is "Guan Hsin," which means "inspect or look at (your) Hsin." In other words, you must first investigate yourself, and come to understand yourself. Therefore you must first withdraw all of your attention from the outside world, and concentrate it wholly on your inner world. This training is called "Nei Shyh Kung Fu,"(*7) which means "the Kung Fu of internal vision."

After you have found the roots of your emotional disturbance, you will start to regulate your Hsin. Regulating your Hsin involves using your Yi and conscious feeling to stop the activity in your Hsin, setting it free from the bondage of ideas, emotions, and conscious thoughts. When you reach this level, your mind will be calm, peaceful, empty, and light.

Naturally, most Chi Kung practitioners are not aiming at the goal of enlightenment or Buddhahood. Their major priorities are health, happiness, and longevity. Buddhist monks will generally retreat into the mountains and separate themselves from the normal human world to avoid emotional disturbance during their cultivation. As a general Chi Kung practitioner, you are aiming to regulate your Hsin with your Yi. You do not want to get rid of your emotional mind, but you want it to be controlled by your Yi. Through this training, you will be able to put your mind in neutral when necessary and attain your goal of a calm and peaceful life.

In Chi Kung practice, only if your mind has reached the stage of real calmness and peace will you be able to relax deep into your marrow and internal organs. Then your mind will be clear enough to see (feel) the internal Chi circulation, and communicate with your Chi and organs. Finally, your Yi will be able to regulate your Chi and lead it to a state of balance.

(*6). " 四大皆空 ."

(*7). " 內視功夫 ."

Although this theory is simple and easy to understand, in practice it is very difficult to regulate your mind. In the last several thousand years, meditators have developed several ways of doing it. In the next section we will list some of them for your reference.

10-3. Methods of Stopping Thought (Niann)

Before you start, you should understand that there are no techniques which are absolutely effective for everybody. It depends on the individual. It may also depend on the situation and timing. Remember that the final goal of regulating your thoughts is to reach **"THE THOUGHT OF NO THOUGHT."** In other words, to regulate your thoughts without thinking of regulating. Therefore, you must continue practicing until the regulating happens naturally and you do not need to consciously regulate your thoughts. Only when you reach this stage will your mind be free and neutral.

1. Stop and Look Method (Zyy Guan Faa):

Zyy means to stop and Guan means to look after, to investigate, and to take care of. This means that after your Yi has controlled your Hsin, you should concentrate on watching the thoughts as they appear. When one comes, you should stop it immediately, not allowing it to grow. You should keep your consciousness aware of what is happening and use your Yi to stop each new thought. This process is called "Zyy Niann Faa" (stopping thought method).

You will often find that, once you have stopped one thought, another one appears immediately. You stop that one, but another one pops up as if there is no end to the cycle. In order to stop this negative cycle, you must wait until your mind is clear, calm, and peaceful, and then put your Yi there before any more thoughts come up from the Hsin. If you can keep your mind in this neutral state, further thoughts will be stopped. The following are methods commonly used by meditators to stop the new thoughts from appearing.

Generally, there are three steps to stopping the Hsin and Niann:

A. Tie to the Origin and Stop Method (Shih Yuan Jyy):

Shih means to tie, to bind, Yuan means relationship, origin, and cause, and Jyy means to stop. In this training you bind your Hsin and Niann to one place in the same way that you would tie an ape to a post. If you can keep your Yi centered in a particular spot, you can control your Hsin and Niann, but if your Yi is weak, your Hsin and Niann will run wild.

There are two places which are commonly used to center your Yi. The first place is your nose. Place your Yi on your nose and pay attention to your breathing. Gradually, the generation of new Hsin and Niann will stop. The second common place is the Lower Dan Tien. Concentrate your Yi at the Dan Tien and feel and sense the generation and movement of Chi. Gradually your Hsin and Niann will become quiet.

B. Restrain the Hsin and Stop Method (Jyh Hsin Jyy):

Once you have tied up the ape, you still have to calm it down, or it will continue to run around the post. This is the taming process. Once you are able to bind your Hsin and Niann in one place, you must stop the thoughts from being generated by the Hsin. You need to understand the reason why the ape is still running wild, whether it is due to hunger or some disturbance, and you need to understand why your Hsin is still generating distracting thoughts. If you are taming an ape, in order to keep the ape in the cage without running wild, you must understand the feelings of the ape and try to solve the problem in order to calm it down. Once the ape realizes that he will not be able to escape and will not be harmed, and furthermore, that he will be taken good care of by the master, he will gradually get used to it and calm down.

C. To Comprehend the Real and Stop Method (Tii Jen Jyy):

This is the last step in stopping thought. In this step you analyze how Hsin and Niann are being continually generated. Like dealing with an ape, once you understand the cause of its wildness, you can determine how to calm it down. Only after you have calmed it down are you able to lead the Hsin to understand and comprehend the nature of reality. Finally, the new disturbances of your Hsin will be stopped. It is like educating the ape so that he understands that when he is staying with the master, he will have plenty of food and a nice place to stay. At this point you will not need to keep the ape tied up. Only when you are able to untie the ape (your mind) and have it stay calm and peaceful have you reached real regulation. Then the Hsin and Niann which are generated will not run wild, and the Yi will be able to direct them effortlessly.

There are also three ways of looking at or investigating your thoughts. They are called the Three Looks. When your mind is calm and peaceful, pay attention to your thoughts and learn how to analyze them.

A. The Empty Look (Kong Guan):

When you use the Empty Look you look at and investigate everything in this universe: how it is generated, and how it grows, changes, and finally dies. As you look at things, you discover why they happen and what their causes are, and you learn the effects they cause. Everything that happens is ultimately empty. Your experiences are vain, illusory, they gain you nothing but a feeling which is false and temporary in comparison with the existence of the universe. When your Hsin understands this principle, it will not continue to think. Buddhists believe that all motivations and desires generated from the emotional mind do not last long, and ultimately accomplish nothing. If you can see this, you will be able to stop the generation of new Hsin and Niann.

B. The False Look (Jea Guan):

Jea in Chinese means false, imaginary, not real. In this method, when you find yourself in a bad situation, perhaps stuck in traffic, you look into the past to see how the traffic jam may have come about, and you look into the future to see how it will surely clear up. You look into the past and future to help you control your Hsin in the present. However, since the past and future are not the **now**, they are false. In this method, you are looking at false things and using them to help yourself let go of unsettling feelings and control your Hsin.

C. The Centered Look (Jong Guan):

After you have used the other two Looks and your Hsin comprehends the nature of emotional disturbances, you will have seen through every emotional feeling and desire, and you will understand that they are all only temporary. Since your life is so short, you should not be bothered by empty emotional feelings. Once you have realized this, you will keep your attention on (look at) only the here and now. Your mind will now be centered and neutral. All of these Looks use your Yi to lead the Hsin to understand the truth about emotional feelings. Then Hsin will not bother the Yi again.

For example, if you are driving somewhere and suddenly get caught in a traffic jam, do you get upset? Most people would, but if you stop to think about it, what do you gain from getting upset? Will the jam disappear or will the cars start moving faster? What do you gain from getting upset, and what do you lose? If you understand all of this, you will see that there is no benefit derived from getting upset, and you will use the time more gainfully, perhaps by just enjoying the music on the radio. If you can do this, then your mind is centered and regulated.

2. The Behold and Think Method (Guan Sheang Faa):

Guan in Chinese means to admire, to look up to, or to view someone or something as an example. Sheang means to imagine, to think, or to meditate. In this method, when you meditate to regulate your Hsin you hold an image or idea in your mind of a person, such as Buddha, or something, such as moonlight, which occupies your attention. If you concentrate on this image, your Hsin will be steady and calm, and, consequently, your mind will be regulated. The person or thing upon which you concentrate is the source of the power which encourages and enables you to conquer your emotional mind.

The Guan Sheang method is widely used by Buddhists. When Christians meditate on the image of Christ to lead their minds into a steady, calm state and finally regulate their minds, they too are using the Guan Sheang method. In Taoist and Buddhist meditations, a Buddha is usually used as an image, and a poem or verse written by the Buddha will be read to help the Hsin be steady and peaceful. People use other things as images too. Sometimes people will use the moon, because it is peaceful, gentle, and calm, and can help you to lead your mind into a deep meditative state.

3. The One Point Spiritual Enlightenment Method (Yi Dien Ling Ming Faa):

Yi Dien means a point. Ling is the supernatural part of the Shen. Ming means enlightenment. In this technique you focus on the highest, most refined level of your Shen. You are looking to enlighten the supernatural Shen, or Ling, and focus it on a tiny point in your Upper Dan Tien. When you are doing this, your thought will have a target. This effort will regulate your Hsin and redirect it into a peaceful and calm state.

4. The Large Hand Stamp Method (Dah Shoou Yinn):

"Dah Shoou Yinn" literally means the "large hand stamp." Large Hand means the fingers, and stamp means pressing the fingers together. The Large Hand Stamp meditation method originated with the Indian Buddhists, and was later widely adopted by the Tibetan Buddhists. After a thousand years of study and practice, this method has become a major meditation technique in Tibetan Chi Kung practice.

In this practice, you press your fingers together in specific ways. The fingers of one hand may press fingers on the other hand, or on the same hand, or the fingers may be interlocked in certain ways.

Your mind concentrates on where you are pressing, and at the same time your concentrated mind leads your Shen to a higher state.

Leading your Shen to a higher state is the key to success in regulating. When your Shen is raised, your Yi is strong and the Hsin will be controlled. Frequently people will generate a sound or else shout to awaken and raise the Shen and stop the generation of distracting thoughts. For example, when you meditate you may discover that your emotional mind bothers you and you cannot stop it. If you open your eyes and look fiercely and utter the sound "Ha," you will stop the emotional thought and lead yourself to a new stage of meditation.

Religious meditators will often regulate their minds by raising their Shen. Another method is to concentrate the Shen, rather than raise it. When the Shen is focused, the Yi will naturally also be focused, and the Hsin will be controlled. Often a gong is used to help the meditator focus his Yi and Shen.

10-4. Yi and Chi

All of the above discussion focused on how to regulate your Hsin. Once your Hsin is regulated, your mind will be peaceful and calm, and your Yi will be able to direct and regulate the Chi.

However, in order to regulate your Chi effectively, you must train your Yi. The first step in this process involves understanding how the Yi communicates with your Chi. Communicate means to feel, to sense, and to correspond to. Your Yi must be able to sense and feel the Chi flow, and understand how strong and smooth it is. In Tai Chi Chi Kung it is said that your Yi must "listen" to your Chi and "understand" it. "Listen" means to pay careful attention to what you sense and feel. The more you pay attention, the better you will be able to understand. It is important to understand that paying attention to your Chi does not mean that your Yi is right with the Chi. It means that your Yi is aware of what is going on with the Chi, but it does not directly interfere with it. Only when you understand what is going on with the Chi can you set up an effective strategy which allows you to accomplish your goals. In Chi Kung, when you want your Chi to do a certain thing, your mind (Yi) must first generate an idea. In other words, you form a clear idea or visualize what you want your Chi to do. When a general wants his troops to do something, he must first know where they are, and then communicate to them where he wants them to go. In the same way, when you want your Chi to do something, you must understand how and where your Chi presently is, and form a clear idea or image of where you want it to go.

Next, you should know how to direct your soldiers. In Chi Kung training it is said: "Use your Yi (mind) to **LEAD** your Chi" (Yii Yi Yiin Chi)(*8). Notice the word **LEAD**. Chi behaves like water--it cannot be pushed, but it can be led or guided. When Chi is led, it will flow smoothly and without stagnation. When it is pushed, it will flood and enter the wrong paths. Since Chi follows wherever the Yi goes, you lead the Chi simply by placing your Yi wherever you want the Chi to go. For example, if you intend to lift an object, this intention is your Yi. Your Yi goes to the object, the Chi moves out into your arms, and

(*8). " 以意引氣 。"

the arms go to the object. The Yi moves upward and the Chi follows, and the arms lift the object. You should also remember: **WHEN THE YI IS STRONG, THE CHI IS STRONG, AND WHEN THE YI IS WEAK, THE CHI IS WEAK.**

You can see that in order to regulate your Chi, you must first train your Yi. You have to learn to concentrate it more than you normally do in your everyday life. It also means that you must train your Yi to understand and lead the Chi in your body. Your Yi is like a general on a battlefield, and the Chi is like the soldiers. As a general, you must be calm and know what you are doing. You must know the condition of your soldiers and how they can be arranged for battle.

It is said: "Your Yi cannot be on your Chi. Once your Yi is on your Chi, the Chi is stagnant."(*9) When you want to walk from one spot to another, you must first mobilize your intention and direct it toward the goal, then your body will follow. The mind must always be ahead of the body. If your mind stays on your body, you will not be able to move. It is as if you are a general conducting a battle. Although you should be aware of the situation of the soldiers, your mind cannot be on the soldiers. Your mind should be on strategy and where you should move your troops. If your mind is only on where the soldiers are now, you will not be able to lead your army to victory.

10-5. Yi and the Five Organs

One of the final goals in Chi Kung health training is to regulate the Chi in your five Yin organs. As mentioned several times, these five organs are the lungs, heart, kidneys, liver, and spleen. It is believed in Chinese Chi Kung society that these organs are the most vital organs and that they directly affect your health. If you want to have good health and slow down the degeneration of your body, you must regulate the Chi in these five organs so that it is neither too Yang nor too Yin. This process is called "Wuu Chi Chaur Yuan," or "The five Chi's toward their origins."

However, this is a very profound subject, and it is sometimes interpreted differently by Oriental physicians and by Chi Kung practitioners. In order to reach this target, your Yi must be able to sense the situation in these five organs. To do this, you must be able to relax deep into the organs, and then your Yi must be directed to a deep, sensitive level through meditation. If you are able to regulate your body and your Yi, you may be able to sense the different elements which make up your body: solid matter, liquids, gases, energy, and spirit. You may even be able to see or feel the different colors that are associated with the five organs -- green (liver), white (lungs), black (kidneys), yellow (spleen), and red (heart). When understood properly, it can give you a method of analyzing the interrelationship of your organs, and help you devise ways to correct imbalances.

Another method of regulating the five organs involves using the principle of the five elements (Wuu Shyng). Each of the five elements relates to one of the Yin organs: Metal to the the lungs, Fire to the heart, Water to the kidneys, Wood to the liver, and Earth to the spleen. The way the organs relate to one another is similar to how the elements relate to each other. You can use this concept to regulate your organs. For example, Metal (the lungs) can be used to adjust the heat

(*9). " 意在精神，不在氣，在氣則滯 ."

of the Fire (the heart), because metal can take a large quantity of heat away from fire, (and thus cool down the heart). When you feel uneasy or have heartburn (excess fire in the heart), you may use deep breathing to calm down the uneasy emotions or cool down the heartburn.

Naturally, it will take a lot of practice to reach this level. In the beginning, you should not have any ideas or intentions, because they will make it harder for your mind to relax and empty itself of thoughts. Once you are in a state of "no thought," place your Yi on your Dan Tien. It is said "Yi Shoou Dan Tien,"(*10) which means "The Yi is kept on the Dan Tien." The Dan Tien is the origin and residence of your Chi. Your mind can build up the Chi here (start the fire, Chii Huoo), then lead the Chi anywhere you wish, and, finally, lead the Chi back to its residence in the Dan Tien. When your Yi is on the Dan Tien, your Chi will always have a root. When you keep this root, your Chi will be strong and full, and it will go where you want it to. You can see that, when you practice Chi Kung, your mind cannot be completely empty and relaxed. You must find firmness within relaxation, then you can reach your goal.

10-6. Hsin, Yi, and Shen

In order to regulate your mind (Hsin and Yi) effectively, you must also know the relationship of your Hsin, Yi, and Shen. Hsin, Yi, and Shen are mutually related and cannot be separated. First, you should understand that in Chi Kung training your Yi is the origin of your being and the control tower, and Hsin is the energy source of your Shen. In order to raise up your Shen, your Yi must first generate an idea of raising your Shen. From this idea, under the control of your Yi, your Hsin will raise up the Shen to a higher energy state. For example, a common way of training Shen is to image that the Upper Dan Tien is on fire. This is the step of raising up the Shen to an energized state. Then you use your Yi to lead or to focus the fire spreading around the Upper Dan Tien to a tiny point. In this case, you have raised up your Shen with your Hsin, yet controlled it with your Yi.

Although the Hsin is able to raise up your Shen, it can also make you excited, which will lead your Shen away from its residence in the Upper Dan Tien. For example, if you receive surprising news, you may become excited and your Shen may be raised. Usually, when this happens your Yi loses its control of the Hsin, and you lose your calmness and clear judgement. In Chi Kung practice, **YOUR GOAL IS TO RAISE UP YOUR SHEN AS HIGH AS POSSIBLE AND STILL HAVE IT CONTROLLED AT ITS CENTER BY YOUR YI** (Figure 10-1). Many Chi Kung practitioners, especially monks, believe that once they have reached a high level of Chi Kung and can regulate their Hsin completely, they should be able to raise their Shen solely with their Yi, instead of with their Hsin.

You can see that when you regulate your Hsin and Yi you are regulating your Shen as well. There are many steps in using your Yi to regulate your Shen. They are: 1. Shoou Shen (to keep and protect the Shen), 2. Guh Shen (to firm and solidify the Shen), 3. Ding Shen (to stabilize and to calm the Shen), 4. Ning Shen (to condense or to focus

_____

(*10). "意守丹田．"

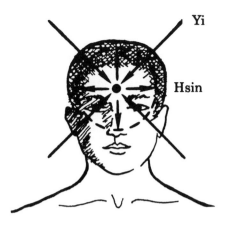

Figure 10-1. Use Yi to control Hsin at the Upper Dan Tien

the Shen), 5. Yeang Shen (to nourish, to raise, or to nurse the Shen), and 6. Liann Shen (to refine, to train, or to discipline the Shen). We have discussed these briefly in the third chapter, and we will cover them again when we discuss regulating the Shen.

Chapter 11

Regulating the Essence (Tyau Jieng)

11-1. Introduction

Of the three roots, Jieng, Chi, and Shen, Essence (Jieng) is probably the most important element in successful Chi Kung practice. To regulate your Essence means to conserve it and convert it into Chi without any waste. You must learn how to keep your Original Essence in the kidneys, its residence, by strengthening the kidneys. You must also learn how to conserve the Essence by not abusing it, and by learning how to convert it into Chi efficiently.

As mentioned, the Essences which are converted into Chi can be classified as Fire Essence, which is obtained from food and air, and Water Essence, which you inherit from your parents. In order to reduce the Fire Chi, you must reduce the Fire Essence by taking in high quality food and air. There are many texts available which discuss this idea.

When Chi Kung practitioners refer to Essence, they are usually referring to Original Essence, which is also called Water Essence. It is usually of more importance in Chi Kung training than the Fire Essence. It is easy to regulate Fire Essence, but you need a lot of understanding and training to regulate the Water Essence.

As mentioned in the third chapter, Chinese medical society calls two pairs of your body's organs kidneys: your real kidneys (also called the internal kidneys; "Nei Shenn"), and the testicles or ovaries. The testicles are also referred to as the "external kidneys" (Wai Shenn). It is believed that after your birth, your Original Essence stays in your internal kidneys. The internal kidneys are closely related to the external kidneys. When the Original Essence in the kidneys is converted into Original Chi, part of it is used to nourish the external kidneys and enliven the production of sexual Essence or hormones. Clearly, if your internal kidneys are weak and the Original Chi cannot be converted efficiently from the Original Essence, the production of hormones or Essence by the testicles will also be reduced. Therefore, if you wish to regulate your Essence, you must first learn how to regulate the Original Essence in the internal kidneys.

In Marrow Washing Chi Kung, the sexual Essence is the main source which is converted into Chi to fill up the four Chi vessels (reservoirs) in your legs. It is also believed that part of this Chi is led through the Thrusting vessel (Chong Mei) through the spine marrow to the brain to nourish it. When people get old and start to lose their sexual vitality, they often lose their memory and their legs become weak. This is simply because there is an insufficient amount of sexual Essence to supply Chi to the brain and the four vessels in the legs. For this reason, the main task in Marrow Washing Chi Kung is to increase the production of sexual Essence and convert it efficiently into Chi. This will be discussed in the YMAA book "Muscle/Tendon Changing and Marrow Washing Chi Kung." Here we will discuss regulating the Essence in the internal kidneys.

11-2. Strengthening Your Kidneys

In order to regulate your Original Essence, you must first take care of its residence, the kidneys, so that the Essence will be protected. The first step to strengthening the kidneys is to keep them healthy. This is called "Guh Shenn," which means "to firm and to solidify the kidneys." To strengthen the kidneys is called "Chyang Shenn."

Guh Shenn and Chyang Shenn (to Firm and to Strengthen the Kidneys):

Several thousand years of study and experimentation have yielded many ways to maintain the health of and strengthen the kidneys. All of them work by maintaining the Chi in the kidneys at the proper level. In order to do this you need to know how the kidneys are affected by weather, food, and emotions (Table 11-1).

	WOOD 木	FIRE 火	EARTH 土	METAL 金	WATER 水
Direction	East	South	Center	West	North
Season	Spring	Summer	Long Summer	Autumn	Winter
Climatic Condition	Wind	Summer Heat	Dampness	Dryness	Cold
Process	Birth	Growth	Transformation	Harvest	Storage
Color	Green	Red	Yellow	White	Black
Taste	Sour	Bitter	Sweet	Pungent	Salty
Smell	Goatish	Burning	Fragrant	Rank	Rotten
Yin Organ	Liver	Heart	Spleen	Lungs	Kidneys
Yang Organ	Gall Bladder	Small Intestine	Stomach	Large Intestine	Bladder
Opening	Eyes	Tongue	Mouth	Nose	Ears
Tissue	Sinews	Blood Vessels	Flesh	Skin/Hair	Bones
Emotion	Anger	Happiness	Pensiveness	Sadness	Fear
Human Sound	Shout	Laughter	Song	Weeping	Groan

Table 11-1. Table of Correspondences associated with the Five Phases

1. Kidneys and the Weather:

Your kidneys are Yin organs. When the weather is cold, especially during the winter, the surrounding air is also Yin, and the Chi level of the kidneys is diminished. When this happens, the Chi flow will be sluggish and the back will become sore and ache, especially the lower back. It is therefore important that the kidney area be protected so that Chi will not be lost out of your body. The best method is to wear warm clothes, especially around your waist. In addition, you should learn a few massage techniques to improve Chi circulation in the kidney area and to use the Chi in your hands to nourish the kidneys. We will now discuss a few massage techniques which are commonly used in Chi Kung.

A. Massaging the Kidneys Directly:

This is the most common technique. Use the center of your palms to rub the back over the kidneys with a circular motion. The tops of both circles should move inward toward each other. There is a Chi gate or cavity called Laogong in the center of your palm (Figure 11-1). This cavity belongs to the Pericardium. The Pericardium includes the blood vessel which enters into the heart and the membranous sac which encloses the heart. In the Chinese medical theory of the five elements, the heart is classified as fire and the kidneys are classified as water.

Therefore, when you use the center of your palms to massage the kidneys, you are using fire to warm up the water, and are therefore nourishing the kidneys. When you massage the kidneys with a circular motion, the top of the motion should be inward (Figure 11-2) in order to nourish the kidneys. If you rub in the opposite direction, you are spreading the Chi away. When you rub the kidneys, you do not have to press heavily. Place your hands on the skin firmly and circle. In just a minutes or so, you will feel the Chi inside near the kidneys circulating in the same direction. This means that you have improved the Chi circulation there. Naturally, you will be more relaxed and the massage will be more

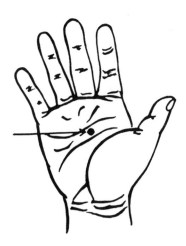

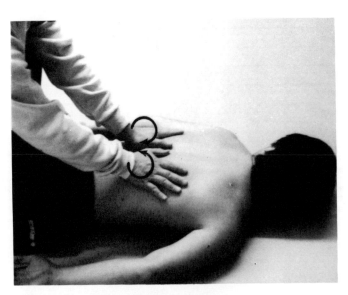

Figure 11-1. The Laogong cavity   Figure 11-2. Massaging the kidneys

effective if someone else can massage you. This direct massage is very effective and useful in winter time. Please remember that you should warm up your hands first, cold hands will drain Chi from the kidneys.

B. Massaging the Bubbling Wells:

Massaging the Bubbling Well cavities (Yongquan)(Figure 11-3) is probably the second best techniques in nourishing the Chi and improving the Chi circulation around the kidneys. The Bubbling Well cavities belong to the Kidney Chi channel. Usually the thumb is used to massage these two cavities with a circular motion (Figure 11-4). You may also use the center of your palm to rub the bottom of your feet (Figure 11-5). Alternatively, you may rub your palms against each other first until they are very warm, then place the centers of your palms (Laogong cavities) on the top of the Bubbling Well cavities. In this case, you are using the heart fire to nourish the kidney water.

C. Massaging with Movement:

Massaging the kidneys with movement is a common Wai Dan Chi Kung practice, and is used in such exercises as "The Eight Pieces of Brocade." The method is simple and very effective. Generally, there are two major movements which are able to massage the kidneys and improve the kidneys' Chi circulation. The first movement is bending forward (Figure 11-6). This stretches and tenses the two major sets of muscles on the sides of the spine, and presses down on the kidneys which are beneath them. You should stay there for about five seconds and then straighten your body. This releases the pressure on the kidneys and lets them return to their original state. Doing these movements repeatedly massages the kidneys.

The second movement is twisting your upper body to the sides (Figure 11-7). Though the muscles are stretched differently than in the preceding exercise, the principle and effect are the same.

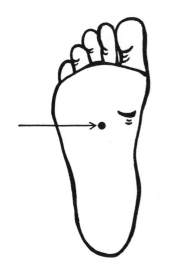

Figure 11-3. The Yongquan cavity

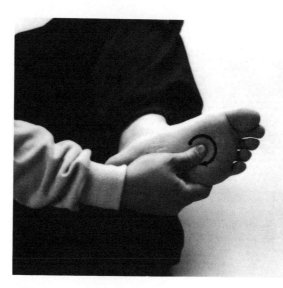

Figure 11-4.Massaging the Yongquan cavity with a
thumb

Figure 11-5. Massaging the Yong-quan cavity with a hand

Figure 11-6. Bend forward to
massage the kidney

Figure 11-7. Twisting sideways to
massage the kidneys

This movement, in addition to massaging the kidneys, also loosens the entire spine and the back muscles, and increases Chi circulation in the Governing Chi vessel (Du Mei) in the back. You may also combine the last two movements to massage your kidneys (Figure 11-8).

2. The Kidneys and Food:

In order to maintain your health and lengthen your life, you must always be concerned with what you eat. Everything you eat will be converted into Chi and nourish your body. According to Chinese medicine, too much acidic food can make your body too Yang, and too much alkaline food can make it too Yin. For example, eating too much acidic food will increase heartburn, and soft drinks will cool down the fire and body heat. Different kinds of food will place stress on different organs. For example, too much alcohol will increase the working load and stress on your liver.

There are also several foods which, when eaten to excess, will affect the condition of your kidneys. For example, too much salt will weaken your kidneys, so you should moderate the amount of salt you eat, especially as you get older. Experience has also shown that eating too much eggplant will weaken your kidneys. Ginseng is good for the kidneys in the wintertime, but it is not as good in the summer since you always have enough Chi to nourish the kidneys then. Many Chinese herbalists have studied and experimented with different prescriptions of herbs for different organs. We will leave this subject to a more qualified author.

Figure 11-8. Twist and bend to massage the kidneys

3. The Kidneys and Emotions:

From Table 11-1 you can also see that your emotions are closely related to the condition of your organs. In order to protect your kidneys, you should avoid fear. Fear originates in your mind. You should understand that fear will not solve any problems. You must face your problems and find the solutions. Once your mind is clear, you will know how to avoid situations which cause you fear. This is the process of regulating your mind, and is the way to maintain your kidneys in good condition.

11-3. Regulating the Essence (Tyau Jieng)

The above discussion concentrated on how to protect the residence of your Essence. Now we must discuss how to regulate the Essence itself. To regulate the Essence is to convert it into Chi in the most efficient way, and to conserve the use of the Essence. This is a very broad subject, and it is difficult to say which is the best way to conserve your Essence, since it depends on individual lifestyles and habits. However, we will discuss some of the most common methods which might give you a deeper understanding of regulating your Essence.

1. Increasing the Efficiency of the Conversion of Essence into Chi:

a. Abdominal exercises:

It is very important in Chi Kung training to know how to lead the Chi which was converted from Original Essence to its residence, the Lower Dan Tien. The trick to this is abdominal exercises. When you move your lower abdomen in and out in coordination with your breathing, the muscles need more Chi than they normally do. The muscles therefore draw in both the Post-birth Chi which was converted from the Essence of food and air, and the Pre-birth Chi which was converted from your Original Essence in the kidneys. The Chi which the muscles don't need is stored in the Dan Tien for future use.

According to Chinese acupuncture, there are two cavities called Shenshu (Kidney Doors) or Jiengmen (Essence Doors) located on your back (Figure 11-9). They are the gates used to regulate the Chi level of the kidneys. Whenever the Chi level is too Yang in the kidneys, Chi will leak out of your body through these two doors. Normally, when you are young, your Essence is strong, fresh, and vigorous, and you have an abundant supply of Chi. Some of this Chi will leak out through these two gates and be wasted. One way to reduce this Chi leakage is to lead it to the front with abdominal exercises and store it in the Dan Tien.

After you have practiced a lot of Chi Kung you will develop the ability to lead the Chi from the kidneys to the Lower Dan Tien simply by thinking or meditating about it. At this time, the physical abdominal exercises will no longer be necessary.

b. Protecting the Essence Doors:

Not only should you know how to lead Chi to the Dan Tien, you should also know how to protect the Essence Doors, especially during the winter. As mentioned earlier, Chinese medicine classifies the kidneys as Yin. In the winter the surrounding air is also Yin, in fact it is more Yin than the kidneys. Because of this, the Chi in the kidneys will leak out into the air. If you want to prevent this, you must dress warmly, and be especially careful to keep the kidney area warm. Often Chi Kung practitioners will massage the kidney doors to warm the kidneys and increase the

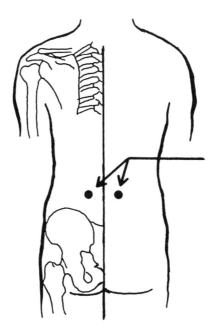

Figure 11-9. The Shenshu cavities

conversion of Chi, and at the same time use abdominal exercises or concentration to lead the Chi forward to be stored in the Dan Tien. You should remember that you will be strong and healthy only when your Dan Tien and Chi reservoirs are full.

c. Massaging the kidneys and the Bubbling Well cavities:

Massaging the kidneys and the Bubbling Well cavities improves and smoothes the Chi circulation in the kidneys, and keeps them functioning at high efficiency. It also improves the efficiency of the Jieng and Chi conversion. This has been covered in the previous section.

d. Marrow Washing training:

In Marrow Washing Chi Kung, the Essence of the testicles or ovaries is converted into Chi. Although the testicles or ovaries are not the internal kidneys themselves, they are closely related to them. Normally, you may increase the Jieng to Chi conversion of the internal kidneys through Marrow Washing practices which work with the testicles and ovaries. Many techniques are used to stimulate the sexual organs and increase the production of Essence. Once the Essence is full, it is converted into Chi and used to fill up the Chi reservoirs in the legs. This Chi is then led up through the marrow of the spine to nourish the brain. This will be discussed in more detail in the second volume of the YMAA Chi Kung book series: "Muscle/Tendon Changing and Marrow Washing Chi Kung."

2. Conserving Your Essence (or Chi):

Conserving your Essence means abusing neither it nor the Chi which was converted from it. If you waste an excessive amount of Chi, the Chi in your body will be deficient because the conversion process of Essence into Chi is very slow. One of the most serious ways that a man can abuse his Chi and Essence is through too much sexual activity. Too much sex drains Chi out of your Chi reservoirs and lowers the level of Chi in the whole body. Since Essence must be converted into Chi to replace the loss, you also decrease your supply of Essence.

In Chinese medical science, it is believed that sperm is a product of the Essence which is stored in the testicles (sperm is called Jieng Tzyy, which means "the sons of Essence"). Chi is required to produce sperm and hormones from your Essence. After you have sex, it takes at least three days for the Chi nourishment of the groin to reach its normal level. This is why, in traditional training, it is urged that the practitioners not practice Chi Kung (especially Nei Dan, which involves the lower abdominal area) for at least three to four days after sexual activity. After the Chi has recovered its normal level, conservatively speaking, it will take about one week for the normal male to replenish his supply of sperm Essence. In ejaculation, Chi is drained out of the man's reservoirs, especially in the legs, and is passed into the woman's body. Roughly estimated, a man might lose about 40% of his Chi with one ejaculation, and if he has another ejaculation soon after, he will lose 40% of the remaining Chi. Naturally, this figure varies from person to person.

Women do not have to worry about losing Chi. As a matter of fact, they receive the man's Chi and use it to nourish their body. However, there are some Chi Kung techniques whereby the man retains his Chi and makes his body's Chi level lower than the woman's . In this case, the man is the one who benefits. There are a number of books available on Taoist sexual practices which can be consulted for further information.

Chapter 12

Regulating the Chi
(Tyau Chi)

12-1. Introduction

If you take a look at your whole being, you will see how your body is made up of a number of parts: 1. Physical body (including water), 2. Air (mainly Oxygen), 3. Mind (Hsin and Yi), 4. Chi, and 5. Shen. All of these five elements are closely related and cannot be separated. Among these five, Chi is the energy which makes the other four function. Whenever the Chi flow is stagnant or stops, you will sicken and die. For this reason, one of the major goals of Chi Kung training is to regulate the Chi in your body. When Chi flows normally and smoothly, all the other elements will be well-nourished and will retain their normal, healthy condition, and you can expect to live a long time.

In Chi Kung practice, before you can regulate your Chi you must first regulate your body, breath, and mind. If you compare your body to a battlefield, then your mind is like the general who generates ideas and controls the situation, and your breathing is his strategy. Your Chi is like the soldiers who are led to various places on the battlefield. Your Essence is like the qualitative background of your soldiers. For example, if your soldiers are well educated, highly disciplined, and strong of body, you will have a strong army. In addition to this, in order to win a battle, you and your soldiers must also have high morale. This morale is your Shen. All of these elements are necessary, and all must be coordinated with each other if you are to win the war against sickness and aging.

If you want to arrange your soldiers most effectively for battle, you must know which area of the battlefield is most important, and the points at which you are vulnerable (where your Chi is deficient) and need to send reinforcements. If you have more soldiers than you need in one area (excessive Chi), then you can send them somewhere else where the ranks are thin. As a general, you must also know how many soldiers are available for the battle, and how many you will need for protecting yourself and your headquarters. To be successful, not only do you need good strategy (breathing), but you also need to communicate effectively with your troops, or all of your strategy will be in vain. When your Yi (the general) knows how to regulate the body (knows the battlefield), how to regulate the breathing (set up the strategy), and how to effectively regulate the Chi (direct your soldiers), you will be able to reach the final goal of Chi Kung training.

12-2. What Chi Should be Regulated?

As discussed in the third chapter, Chi can be classified into many different categories according to their origins or according to the roles they play in the body. According to the origin of the Chi, the Chi can be identified as Pre-birth (or Original) Chi, or Post-birth Chi. Pre-birth Chi was converted from the Original Essence you inherited from your parents, while the Post-birth Chi was converted from the food and air you take in. The first step in regulating the quality of your Chi is regulating your Essence, which was discussed in a previous chapter. The next step is regulating the Chi according to its function. From this point of view, you have both "Managing Chi" and "Guardian Chi."

1. Managing Chi:

A. Regulating the Chi in the eight vessels and twelve Chi channels:

The first task in regulating the Managing Chi is to regulate the Chi supply to the twelve internal organs through the 12 Chi channels. In order to reach this goal, you must also learn to regulate the Chi in your eight Chi vessels. To continue with the battlefield analogy, the twelve internal organs are like a line of twelve forts, and your eight vessels are like the eight training camps behind the lines which supply soldiers to the front line. In the front line, if any one of the forts is lost, the others are placed in jeopardy, and the whole line may be lost. It is therefore important to keep the right number of troops in each fort so that the whole arrangement can function efficiently. Both quality and quantity are important in this.

Among these twelve forts are six which are considered positive (Yang). These are the nourishing and absorbing systems, and handle the digestive and absorptive functions. These six Yang organs are the Stomach, Large Intestine, Small Intestine, Urinary Bladder, Gall Bladder, and Triple Burner. The other six organs are considered negative (Yin), and are responsible for storing the body's Essence and maintaining life. These organs are the Lungs, Heart, Kidneys, Liver, Spleen, and Pericardium (although the Lungs absorb oxygen, Chinese medicine considers them to be one of the life managing organs).

Normally, the Yang organs have more Chi than the Yin organs. Five of the Yin organs (excluding the Pericardium) are considered the most important organs, and determine whether you win or lose the battle for your health. They decide your life and death. You must regulate their Chi first. In Chi Kung it is said "Wuu Chi Chaur Yuan," which means to lead the "Five Chi's to their Origins." This means that in order to reach the goal of health, you must regulate the Chi in these five organs to its original levels. Only then will they function properly, and degeneration be kept to a minimum.

B. Nourishing the Brain and Shen with Chi:

The second task in regulating the Managing Chi is regulating the Chi supply to the top of your head to nourish your brain and Shen. In Chi Kung practice, your brain and the Shen are considered to be the headquarters of your thinking and Chi. If you do not have the best personnel and facilities in your headquarters, it will not function well, and the whole body will be unhealthy. Your brain generates the Yi, which is like a general, and your Shen is like the morale which is able to raise up the soldiers' fighting spirit. It is this Shen which enables the entire fighting unit to work and communicate in the most efficient way.

In Marrow Washing Chi Kung, it is believed that the brain and the Shen are the most important factors in maintaining health and lengthening life. If you are able to nourish your brain and Shen with Chi constantly, you will be able to direct your Chi to regulate the entire body, and will have won most of the battle.

2. Guardian Chi:

Regulating the Guardian Chi is different from regulating the Chi which circulates in the twelve channels and the Chi which nourishes the brain. When you regulate your Guardian Chi, you are regulating the Chi out from the Chi channels to the surface of the skin. This means you lead the Chi outward to the surface of your skin and inward to the bones.

The function of your Guardian Chi is to generate a Chi shield around you to prevent any negative influences from invading your body. The size of your Chi shield is adjusted according to the weather and the environment around you. If you are able to keep this Chi shield strong, the Chi will smoothly reach out to your hair and beyond, and your hair and skin will stay healthy.

The Chi should also be led inside so that it penetrates even the bone marrow. The marrow manufactures blood cells. When your marrow has plenty of Chi, it will produce fresh and healthy blood cells which will keep your whole body functioning optimally and protect it internally.

12-3. Regulating the Chi (Tyau Chi)

Regulating the Chi is one of the main goals of Chi Kung training. Regulating includes adjusting, protecting, keeping, and raising. You can see that the definition of regulating the Chi is very wide and the purposes are varied. Many Chi Kung styles have been created and developed to reach the different goals of Chi cultivation. To scholars, regulating means keeping and protecting the Chi circulation in the body. To medical doctors, regulating means adjusting and correcting the Chi level. To martial artists, regulating means concentrating, and leading the Chi to energize the muscles more efficiently. To Buddhists, regulating means protecting, nourishing, and cultivating. To Taoists, regulating means building up, raising, training, and disciplining.

Although when you practice one category of Chi Kung you also cover some of the training done by other categories, the emphasis is different. For example, if you learn to regulate the Chi from a medical Chi Kung style, although you also reach the goal of maintaining health and training to build up your Chi, you will be using methods designed mainly for curing illnesses. Therefore, in order to learn how to regulate Chi, you should know what your goal is, and how deeply you would like to enter. Then, you will be able to decide which category you want to learn.

Nobody knows your body and its inner workings better than you do. After all, you live in it, and you are the only one who is able to feel it directly. Therefore, you are the one who is best qualified to judge which Chi Kung style is the most beneficial for you. If you are a Chi Kung beginner, I suggest that you start with one of the easier systems developed by scholars and medical doctors, such as "The Eight Pieces of Brocade" or "Five Animal Sports." They are easier to understand, learn, and experience without incurring any potential of serious danger. Training in these systems will teach you the "why," "what," and "how." For example, by studying scholarly Chi Kung you may grasp the idea of regulating the mind, and from practicing medical Chi Kung you may come to understand more clearly how to regulate your body. It does not matter which Chi Kung style you have decided to train deeply. Before you regulate your Chi, you must always regulate your body, breathing, and mind. Once you have gained the experience and understood the theory, you will be able to understand the deeper martial or religious Chi Kung such as "Small Circulation," "Large Circulation," or "Marrow Washing Chi Kung" more easily.

In this section, I believe that we should first discuss two major subjects before going on to the general concepts of regulating the Chi. These two subjects are: A. the communication between your Yi and Chi and, B. Two general attitudes toward regulating the Chi.

A. Communication Between Yi and Chi:

Learning how to open communications between your Yi and Chi is probably the most crucial factor in successful Chi Kung training. There are two ways that Chi flows in your body. One of them is the natural, automatic circulation which is responsible for the internal functioning of the body. This circulation does not need your conscious attention. For example, you do not need your Yi to lead the Chi to the organs to keep them functioning. This happens naturally and automatically. However, if you desire to lift an object, first your Yi must generate the idea of lifting, and this idea or intention will lead Chi to the arms to energize the muscles. You understand already that the muscles do not function without Chi, any more than an electric fan will run without electric current.

Regardless of which purpose a Chi Kung practitioner is training for, first he must learn how to increase the communication between his Yi and Chi. Communication means not only that your Yi is leading the Chi -- your Yi must also feel or sense what is going on with the Chi. This mutual interaction allows you to understand the Chi situation. It is commonly said in internal arts society that: "First, you must listen carefully, then you will be able to understand." "Listen" here means to "feel" or to "sense." Only if your Yi is able to communicate and understand the situation, will you be able to regulate the Chi. It is just like in a battle, the general in his headquarters must be able to communicate efficiently with his soldiers, otherwise he will not be able to apply his strategy.

In Chi Kung, in order for your Yi to communicate with your Chi, you must first regulate your body, your breathing, and your mind. These three prerequisites are the major paths to regulating your Chi. After you have regulated of these three elements, the communication between your mind and Chi will happen automatically and naturally. At first, your mind is able to feel or even sense the Chi flow. After you have been doing this for a while, you start to understand the Chi. It is as if you are learning a new language. The more you practice and experience it, the more you will be familiar with it and understand it. Only then is your mind able to direct and lead it.

B. Two Attitudes toward Regulating the Chi:

In order to regulate your Chi so that it moves smoothly and in the correct paths, you need more than just efficient Yi-Chi communication. You also need to know how to generate Chi. If you do not have enough Chi in your body, how can you regulate it? In a battle, if you do not have enough soldiers to carry out your strategy, you have already lost.

In Chinese Chi Kung society, there are two major attitudes in regulating the Chi. Both of them have their own theories, disadvantages, and advantages. From these two different viewpoints were developed two major approaches to regulating the Chi. One is called "Yeang Chi" and the other is called "Liann Chi." Yeang means to gradually raise, nourish, keep, and protect; while Liann means to refine, train, build, and strengthen. According to analysis of the available documents, it seems that the Scholars and the Buddhists favor Yeang Chi, with the Buddhists becoming the authorities in both theory and training, while the Taoists and martial artists train more Liann Chi which, in regard to health, is considered more advanced. It is not surprising that medical Chi Kung exercises include both, and vary according to training purposes.

In practicing regulating the Chi, it is crucial to increase the quantity of Chi while maintaining a neutral state in the body. As you know, excess (Yang) or deficient (Yin) Chi will cause health problems and speed up aging. It is important, therefore, to learn how to fill up the Chi reservoirs (8 Chi vessels) without letting this abundant Chi overflow into the 12 Chi channels. In the Yeang Chi training, the scholars and Buddhists practice the ways of nursing and protecting the Chi first. Then they learn to gradually raise up or cultivate the Chi to a healthier level. This gentle and conservative method is meant to maintain a healthy Chi flow without significantly affecting the Chi level and the natural circulation. This training is especially important when the practitioners are getting old and the Chi level in the reservoirs is lower.

In Liann Chi training, the Taoists work on training and refining their Chi, and also on strengthening or increasing the Chi level in the Chi reservoirs. Taoists Chi Kung practitioners believe that in order to obtain the goal of longevity, not only must you maintain smooth Chi flow, but you must also increase the Chi level to strengthen the physical organs. They believe that the quality and strength of your physical body can be improved by nourishing the Chi correctly.

Your body is like an electrically powered machine in that it needs current to run, and if you continually run an inadequate current through it, it will deteriorate quickly. However, your body is different from a machine in that if you gradually increase the amount of current, your body will adjust to the current, and will become stronger and start to function better. It is just like if you are able to run five miles a day and do so on a regular basis, you will maintain your health and a certain amount of strength. This is the scholarly and Buddhist way. However, if you gradually increase the distance as time goes on, your body will readjust itself to fit the new requirement, and your conditioning will improve. This is the Taoist way.

You can see that the scholarly and Buddhist way is gentle and more conservative, while the Taoist way is more active. Sometimes the Taoist training methods are more difficult and dangerous than those of the Buddhists. They always need to keep track of what is happening in their physical bodies as they train, and be careful that the Chi they have built up is not mishandled and does not move the wrong way.

Beginners in Chi Kung should first learn how to keep their Chi flowing smoothly. Only after you understand yourself and Chi Kung theory should you start training gradually to refine and train your Chi to a higher level. This normally takes at least ten years of correct practice under the instruction of a qualified master.

How to Regulate the Chi:

Every Chi Kung style has its own unique methods for regulating the Chi. Because regulating the Chi is one of the final goals of Chi Kung, methodology will be the major subject when we introduce the different Chi Kung styles in the future. In order to help you grasp the general theory of how to regulate Chi, we will introduce the general concepts of regulating your Managing Chi, Guardian Chi, and the five organs' Chi.

A. Regulating the Managing Chi:

a. Chi vessels and channels:

One of the goals of regulating the Managing Chi involves regulating the Chi in the eight vessels and twelve Chi channels. The key targets of the regulating are keeping the Chi vessels full, and keeping the Chi circulating in the twelve channels smoothly with the right Chi level.

Though many scholarly and medical Chi Kung styles studied this subject, it was probably not until about 500 A.D. that specific and deep training was introduced. This was done by Da Mo in his Yi Gin Ching (Muscle/Tendon Changing Classic). He was most concerned with two of the eight vessels, the Conception and Governing vessels. It is believed that these two vessels govern the twelve Chi channels, and so the "small circulation," was developed to train them. Once you have completed the training of the small circulation, you will then train the "grand circulation" which will help you to open up all of the blockages along the twelve channels. This will improve the smooth circulation of the Chi significantly and, therefore, help you to reach the goal of strengthening your physical body.

Although after Da Mo numerous styles were created to achieve the same purpose, they still follow the same training theory and principles.

b. Brain and Shen:

The brain is the headquarters and the Shen (spirit) is the Chi control center of your whole being. Therefore, keeping them functioning normally is the key to health and the door to increasing your longevity. In order to regulate your Managing Chi, you must first regulate its headquarters. For this reason, Da Mo passed down a training methods in "Shii Soei Ching" (Marrow Washing Classic).

In Marrow Washing Chi Kung training, you learn how to fill up the Chi in the other six vessels. It also teaches you how to lead Chi to your head to nourish your brain and Shen. We discussed Marrow Washing training briefly in Chapter 6. For a detailed discussion, see the book: "Muscle/Tendon Changing and Marrow Washing Chi Kung."

B. Regulating the Guardian Chi:

Though regulating the Guardian Chi is not considered as critical as regulating the Managing Chi, it still plays an important role in Chi Kung training. The target of regulating the Guardian Chi is to strengthen the Chi circulation to your skin to generate a Chi shield against negative influences and to maintain healthy growth of your hair and nails.

Guardian Chi training is found in both Wai Dan and Nei Dan. There are several common methods:

a. Massage:

Massage is the easiest way. It increases Chi circulation near the skin and therefore leads Chi to the skin.

b. Slapping:

Though slapping is part of massage, there are several exercises which particularly emphasize the effectiveness of slapping or lightly beating the skin, which stimulates and leads Chi to the skin.

c. Physical exercise:

Physical exercise is probably the most common method. When you move or exercise, an abundance of Chi is led to the extremities to energize the muscles. Afterwards, the excess Chi moves out through the skin, increasing the Chi circulation there, and finally dissipates into the surrounding air. When you do this, you normally exercise until you start sweating, which indicates that Chi has been led to the skin and is energizing the pores.

d. Internal Chi expansion:

Internal Chi expansion is the hardest, but probably the most effective way to lead Chi to the skin to generate a Chi shield. This is the method which Chi Kung practitioners use. There are many ways to do it. For example, when you have achieved a certain degree of mental concentration, you may imagine that your body is on fire. You will begin to feel warm, and this feeling and the idea of strengthening your Chi shield will lead Chi to the skin. Another way is to imagine that you are a beach ball. As you inhale and exhale, imagine that the ball is shrinking and expanding. After training for a while, you will feel that when you exhale your body expands and all of the pores open. This training will be discussed more thoroughly in a later volume.

C. Regulating the Chi of the Five Organs:

Regardless of which style of Chi Kung you use to reach the goal of health and longevity, they all teach how to regulate the organ Chi, especially of the five Yin organs (Lungs, Heart, Liver, Kidneys, and Spleen).

When you regulate your organ Chi, your mind must be able to understand the condition of each organ. In order to do this, your body must be able to relax deep into the organs so that the Chi can flow smoothly there. Also, your meditative mind must be able to sense and communicate with the organs.

There are many ways to regulate the organ Chi. Wai Dan uses certain movements to affect specific organs. For example, you can bend forward so that the back muscles press down on the kidneys, and then straighten up so that the pressure is released. This massages the kidneys and increases the Chi circulation.

In Nei Dan, you use your mind to lead Chi to the organs. You need to be able to feel and sense the condition of the organs, and you also have to understand the relationships between the five organs, the five elements, and the emotions. For example, the liver belongs to the element wood and is related to the emotion anger. Whenever you are angry, the liver becomes tense and the normal Chi circulation is upset. Your heart belongs to the element fire and is related to the emotion happiness. When you are too happy you become very excited. This brings an excess of Chi to the heart and may cause problems. You can see that you have to regulate your emotional mind before you can use your Yi to regulate the Chi in your organs. For example, if you are very excited and your heart is beating too rapidly, put your mind on your lungs and breathe deeply. This will draw the excess Chi from the heart and cool it down. You can see that Nei Dan is much harder than Wai Dan.

Diet is also useful in regulating the organ Chi. For example, too much alcohol will make your liver, heart, and lungs too Yang. Tobacco and drugs will make the Chi circulation in your lungs stagnant. Table 11-1 explains the relationship between the properties of food and your organs. The easiest way to regulate your Chi is by controlling your diet.

Chapter 13

Regulating the Spirit (Tyau Shen)

13-1. Introduction

There is one thing which is supremely important in battle, and that is fighting spirit. You may have the best general who knows the battlefield well and is also an expert strategist, but if his soldiers do not have high fighting spirit (morale), he may still lose. Remember, **SPIRIT IS THE CENTER AND ROOT OF A FIGHT.** When you keep this center, one soldier can be equal to ten soldiers. When his spirit is high, a soldier will obey his orders accurately and willingly, and his general will be able to control the situation efficiently. In a battle, in order for a soldier to have this kind of morale, he must know how to fight, why he is fighting, and what he can expect after the fight. Knowing what he is doing and why will raise up his spirit, strengthen his will, and increase his patience and endurance.

It is the same with Chi Kung training. In order to reach the final goal, you must have three basic moral virtues: will, patience, and endurance. You must also know what, why, and how. Only then will you be able to be sure of your target and know what you are doing.

Shen, which is the Chinese term for spirit, originates from Yi (the wisdom mind). When the Yi is firm, Shen will be steady and calm. When Shen is strong, the Yi is firm. **SHEN IS THE MENTAL PART OF A SOLDIER. WHEN SHEN IS HIGH, THE CHI IS STRONG AND EASILY DIRECTED. WHEN THE CHI IS STRONG, SHEN IS ALSO STRONG.**

In Chi Kung training, it is said: "Yii Shen Yuh Chi"(*1) which means to use your Shen to govern the Chi. Shen is thought of as the headquarters which controls the movement of Chi, and it is able to

(*1). " 以神馭氣 "

raise or calm the Chi and move it wherever you desire. You may have noticed that when your spirit is high, you can somehow find enough energy to do just about anything. If your Yi is also concentrated and is able to control your Shen at its residence, your judgement will be clear and calm. It is believed in Chi Kung training that when your Shen is properly trained it can lead your mind to supernatural states.

It is also believed that when your Shen is high it is able to lead the Chi smoothly and fluidly to an injured place to speed healing. We have all heard of cases where the doctor felt that a patient was so sick that he would not be able to last for a month. The patient, however, felt differently, and was determined to survive. His spirit was so high that, through sheer force of will, he was able to far outlast the doctor's prognosis. In such cases, some patients even experience miraculous cures. According to Chi Kung theory, this patient's spirit led Chi to the damaged place and overcame the physical damage.

Many people have experienced another phenomenon. A man's boss tells him that if he completes a big project in a very limited time, he will get a week's vacation. The man concentrates totally on the project, working day and night with very little sleep. He is very enthusiastic about the job, finding it challenging and exciting, and is surprised at how healthy and energetic he feels. Finally the job is done. When the man finally gets to relax on his vacation, suddenly he becomes sick. According to Chi Kung theory, this is easy to explain. When you are deeply involved in something for which you are responsible, your spirit is high. This high spirit energizes the Chi in your body so that it flows strongly and smoothly and your Guardian Chi is strong. This keeps you from getting sick. Once you relax, your spirit is lowered and your Chi is not energized any more. Sickness will then be able to break through the shield of your Guardian Chi. Most often you catch a cold.

These two examples should give you an idea of how the Shen is able to affect your health and longevity. Because it plays such an important role, Shen training is considered one of the final stages of Chi Kung. Training and refining your Shen into a supernatural state is a necessary step in achieving Taoist enlightenment and Buddhahood.

13-2. Regulating the Spirit (Tyau Shen)

In general, there are four major tasks in regulating your Shen: learning how to raise your Shen, how to keep it at its residence and strengthen it, how to coordinate it with your breathing, and finally how to use your Shen to direct your Chi effectively. All of these are called "Liann Shen" by Taoists Chi Kung practitioners. Liann means to refine, to train, or to discipline. In religious Chi Kung, there is another ultimate goal in regulating the Shen, and that is to train it to be independent enough to leave the physical body. This final goal will be discussed in books discussing religious Chi Kung.

1. Raising up the Shen (Yeang Shen):

Yeang means to nourish, to raise, or to nurse. Yeang Shen has been the main task for Scholars and Buddhists in their training to regulate the Shen. Shen needs to be nourished by Chi. Normally, the Fire Chi which comes from food and air is able to raise up the Shen easily, however, this Fire Chi also increases emotional disturbance and therefore leads the Shen away from its residence. Using your Yi, which is nourished by the Water Chi, to raise up your Shen is harder. However, if you are able to do it, this Shen can be stronger and more concentrated than when you use the Fire Chi. In

Chi Kung practice, you are learning how to adjust your Hsin and Yi to raise up your Shen. If you are able to use your Hsin and Yi properly, your Shen will be raised but not excited, and it will be able to remain at its residence.

Learning how to raise up the Shen the right way is almost like raising a child. You need a great amount of patience and perseverance. One way to raise a child is to help him restrain his attraction to the seven emotions and six desires. Another way is to let him keep this contact with his human nature, yet educate him and help him to develop his wisdom so that he can make clear judgements. It is a long process, and demands a lot of understanding and patience. In Chi Kung, raising the Shen is not a question of increasing your emotional excitement. This would scatter the Yi, and your Shen would become confused and lose its center. Yeang Shen training builds a strong center for your spirit, and helps the spirit take control over a larger part of your life.

2. Keeping Shen in its residence and training it:

After raising your Shen, you must learn how to keep it at its residence and train it. As with a child of a certain age, you must be able to keep his mind in the family instead of straying outside and running wild. Then you will be able to educate him. In Chi Kung training, to keep and train the Shen includes four major steps:

A. Shoou Shen:

Shoou means to keep and to protect. The very beginning of the training involves learning how to keep your Shen at its residence. While it is relatively easy to raise your spirit, it is much harder to keep it in its residence. In Shoou Shen training, in order to keep the Shen in its residence you must use your regulated mind to direct, to nurse, to watch, and to keep the Shen there. It is just like keeping your child at home instead of letting him leave home and run wild. You must be patient and control your temper (regulate your mind). You can see, therefore, that the first step in regulating your Shen is to regulate your Hsin and Yi. If you lose your patience and temper, you will only make the child want to leave home again. Only when you have regulated your Hsin and Yi will you be able to watch and to keep your Shen effectively.

B. Guh Shen:

Guh means to solidify and to firm. After you can keep your Shen in its residence, you then learn how to firm and solidify it (Guh Shen). Guh Shen means to train your Shen to stay at its residence willingly. After you are able to control your child in the house, you must make him want from his heart to stay. Only then will his mind be steady and calm. Naturally, in order to reach this stage, you will need a lot of love and patience to educate him until he understands how important it is for him to stay home him and grow up normally and healthily. Chi Kung training operates on the same principle. The second step of Shen training is to make the Shen willing to stay in its residence. In order to do this, your mind must be able to regulate all emotional thoughts. Only then will your Shen be able to stay in its residence in peace.

C. Ding Shen:

Ding Shen means to stabilize and to calm the Shen. When you have brought your child into the stage of peace, he will not be as excited by and attracted to outside emotional distractions. In regulating your Shen you must learn to calm down the Shen so that it is energized but not excited. Then the mind will be peaceful and steady.

D.Ning Shen:

Ning means to concentrate, to refine, to focus, and to strengthen. You can see from the above three processes that keeping, firming, and stabilizing are the foundation of the cultivation of your Shen. It is like a child who is able to stay at home willingly with a calm and steady mind. Only then will you be able to teach and train him. In Chi Kung, once you have passed these three initial steps, you will learn to condense and to focus your Shen in a tiny spot. The Condensing the Shen stage is where you can train the Shen to a higher spiritual state. When the Shen is focused in a tiny point, it is like a sunbeam which is focused through a lens. The smaller the point, the stronger its beam.

3. Combining Shen with the breathing:

After the Shen has been trained to a high degree, you can put it to work. The first assignment for your Shen is coordination with your breathing. Remember, in Chi Kung training your breathing carries out your strategy. When this strategy is directed by your Shen, it will be able to obtain maximum results. This is called "Shen Shyi Shiang Yi,"(*2) which means "the Shen and the breathing are mutually dependent." In Chi Kung training, this is called "Shen Shyi" which means "Shen breathing." At this stage, your Shen and breathing have united into one. When you have accomplished this, your Chi will be led most efficiently. Naturally, this is not an easy task. In order to reach this stage, you must have regulated your body, breathing, and mind.

4. Combining Shen with Chi:

The last stage of regulating Shen for health involves learning to use the Shen to direct the circulation and distribution of Chi in the most efficient way. In Chi Kung society, this stage is called "Shen Chi Shiang Her,"(*3) which means "the Shen and Chi combine together." In a battle, if the spirit of the soldiers is kept high, their fighting ability and efficiency will be increased, and the strategy will be carried out more thoroughly.

Obviously, cultivating your Shen is a long and painstaking process. There is no limit to Shen cultivation. The more you refine it, the higher it is able to go. In religious Chi Kung training, the final stage of regulating the Shen is to train the Shen to separate from the physical body. In order to reach this goal, you must first accomplish the preceding four phases of training. Only when your Shen and Chi are combined will the Chi nourish the Shen so that it grows and matures. We will discuss this subject in a later volume.

(*2). " 神息相依 "

(*3). " 神氣相合 "

Chapter 14

Important Points in Chi Kung Practice

14-1. Introduction

Chi Kung is the science of working with the body's energy field. This is something completely new for most people, and so you will encounter many new experiences, have many questions, and even experience difficulties or unusual phenomena which may lead you away from correct practice. If you are a beginner and have not built up a strong Chi field in your body, straying from correct practice may not significantly harm your health. However, if you have reached a level where you have built up strong Chi circulation, incorrect practice may be harmful and dangerous. You will not just stop making progress in your training, but you will probably also disturb your normal Chi circulation. Therefore, before you start training you should study the common phenomena and deviations (which means entering the wrong path) which many Chi Kung practitioners have experienced before. You should also study the cause of deviation and understand how to correct the mistakes. However, it is important for you to remember that you shouldn't **expect** these things to happen. **EXPECTATION IS THE WORST EMOTIONAL DISTURBANCE.** What will happen will happen, what won't happen, won't.

In this chapter, we will first discuss the common phenomena which may be experienced by the Chi Kung beginner. This section will help the beginner to avoid confusion and to stop his mind from wandering. As you advance in the training, you will have many different sensations. Usually this is a sign that you are progressing. We will discuss some of the common sensations in the third section. Then we will discuss the most important subject in Chi Kung practice: the causes of the deviations and how to correct them. Finally, in the last section we will list 24 rules for Chi Kung practice.

14-2. Common Experiences for Chi Kung Beginners

In this section we will discuss many of the phenomena which Chi Kung beginners often experience in practice. Some of these phenomena are common, and normally caused by improper posture, timing, training methods, or other reasons. Since most beginners cannot generate a significant amount of Chi, these phenomena are usually harmless. However, if you ignore these clues and continue to train incorrectly, you will build bad habits which may eventually bring you harm. It is therefore important that you pay attention to them, understand them, and study their causes.

1. The Mind is Scattered and Sleepy:

The Taoist Ni Wan Tzuu said: "For one hundred days (of Chi Kung practice), prohibit sleepiness. Sleepiness and confusion (make the mind) scattered and disordered, and (you will finally) lose the real."(*1) This sentence says that when the beginner practices Chi Kung, he will frequently be sleepy and his mind will be scattered. If you do not keep this from happening, you will have lost the real way (Tao) of training. Having a scattered and disordered mind is one of the most common experiences of beginners. This happens because your Yi is not able to control your emotional Hsin. Though your Yi is strong, your Hsin is even stronger. In this case, you must first regulate your Hsin and analyze the causes and the possible results of this disturbance. After you completely comprehend the nature and cause of your emotional disturbance, you will know the why, how, and what, and it will be easier for your Yi to control your Hsin and bring you peace. Only when you do this will you be able to keep your mind from being confused and scattered.

It is also common for beginners to fall asleep, especially in still meditation. One reason this happens is because of physical and mental fatigue. When you are tired, your spirit is low and your mind is disordered. If you find this happening, the best thing is to stop trying to practice, and either relax or take a nap. If you try to force yourself to continue, you will only do more harm than good. A good way to relax is to lie down comfortably and pay attention to your breathing. Every time you exhale, bring your relaxation to a deeper level. Pretty soon your breathing and heart beat will slow down, and you will feel nicely rested. After the rest, your mind will be clear and your spirit will be fresh. Now you will be able to raise your Shen and keep it at its residence. When you have reached this stage, you will find your spirit and mind centered and balanced.

2. Feeling Cold:

This usually happens during still meditation. In moving Chi Kung exercises you are usually energizing your body, so you tend to feel warm and your body is more Yang. However, in still meditation you are calming down your mind, slowing down your breathing, and reducing your pulse rate. This causes your body to be more Yin. Especially in winter, when you are in a relaxed meditative state your body releases energy into the surrounding air and becomes even more Yin. It is therefore advisable, when you meditate in the early morning or in the winter, to wear warm clothes and to cover your legs, especially your knees, with a blanket.

(*1). 泥丸祖曰：" 百日之中功忌昏 · 昏迷散亂
失却真 ˮ

However, sometimes you will feel cold even when you are dressed warmly and the room is a comfortable temperature. This is most likely caused by your mind. Your mind has a very significant influence on the circulation and distribution of Chi in your body. Sometimes you can feel cold because of nervous tension, emotional upset, or fear. Have you ever had the experience, during a hot summer day, of something happening which makes you suddenly afraid, and you feel a chill run through your body? Since your mind has such an effect on you, it is important to regulate your mind before you meditate, so that you are calm and steady.

3. Numbness:

Numbness is very common in Chi Kung training. For example, when you sit for a long time in meditation, your blood and Chi circulation slow down, reducing the supply of oxygen and nutrition to your legs. This is very common with beginners. When this happens, you should not continue your meditation, because your concentration and relaxation will be affected. Stretch your legs and massage the bottoms of your feet, especially the Bubbling Well cavities. This will speed up the recovery of the circulation. If you meditate regularly and consistently, you will find that you can sit longer and longer without your legs becoming numb. This is because your body has a natural instinct to readjust the oxygen and nutrition supply system to fit the new situation. Normally, after six months of regular practice, you will be able to sit at least 30 minutes without any problem.

Numbness will sometimes also happen in moving Chi Kung training while you are standing. This is most common when you are standing stationary for a long period of time, such as when you are doing the Da Mo's Yi Gin Ching. The numbness occurs most frequently in the ankles and heels, because your body's weight presses down on them and cuts down the circulation. In this case, after you have finished your practice, simply walk for a few minutes or rock back and forth on your heels and toes a few times. This will restore the circulation in a few seconds.

There are certain Chi Kung styles which use stationary postures to build up Chi in specific areas, and later let this accumulated Chi circulate in the body. In this case, numbness and soreness are expected and normal.

4. Soreness and Pain:

Soreness and pain are frequently caused by incorrect posture. If you do not understand the theory of the exercise, you may cause yourself serious injury. The joints are particularly susceptible. For example, the wrong posture in sitting meditation can cause backpain. If you do not correct it, you may even injure your spine. Another common example is the horse stance. When done incorrectly, the knees can be injured seriously. Therefore, before you practice you must first accurately understand the theory and the training methods.

In martial Chi Kung training, certain parts of the body or the joints will be trained in order to increase their strength. In this case, soreness and pain are expected. In this type of training you must build your strength gradually. Normally, it will take at least six months for your muscles to grow and adapt to the new situation. If you are impatient and speed up the training, the weak muscles will lose their capacity to function normally and the ligaments around the joints will be injured.

5. Half of the Body Feels Hot:

Sometimes in Chi Kung practice, half of your body will feel hot. It may be the left, right, upper, or lower half, or just one portion of your body will feel cold while the rest feels hot. This usually happens when you are emotionally upset, when you are sick, or when you are just recovering from illness. At such times your Chi is unbalanced, and if you practice Chi Kung then, you may interfere with the body's natural efforts to achieve a new Chi balance. It is therefore very important to be aware of what is going on with your body and emotions when you practice Chi Kung.

This imbalance will sometimes happen when your Chi Kung training emphasizes one side more than the other. It is always best to develop the Chi evenly. When Chi is developed in a balanced way, your Yi will also be balanced and strong. This will increase the efficiency of your training significantly.

6. Headache and Eye Ache:

For a beginner, the most common cause of headache during Chi Kung practice is failure to keep your breathing smooth. For example, you may hold your breath without even noticing it. This causes your body to be tense, which stagnates the Chi and blood flow and reduces the oxygen supply to the head, causing a headache. There are times when you will want to hold your breath in Chi Kung practice, for example during certain martial practices like iron shirt training. However, as a Chi Kung beginner, you should not practice holding your breath.

Eye ache is a common phenomenon during still meditation. There are two main reasons for eye ache. Sometimes, to help a student keep his mind within his body, a Chi Kung master will ask him to focus his eyes on the tip of his nose. It is said in Chi Kung society that "Yean Guan Bih, Bih Guan Hsin,"(*2) which means "The eyes watch the nose, and the nose watches the heart." In order to keep your mind within your body and to avoid being distracted by what is going on around you, you should first restrain your vision. Once you have done this, you are able to move your mind to your heart and regulate your emotional mind. However, you should understand that you do this with your mind, not with your physical body. It is a common problem that a beginner will actually use his eyes to stare at his nose. This is the major cause of eye ache. When you practice, your eyes may be open or closed, but your mind is focused on your nose. It is important to always be relaxed and comfortable. Any time the eye muscles are not kept relaxed, they will tense up and cause pain.

Another time when the eyes may ache during Chi Kung practice is when you are training to focus the Shen at its residence. You should remember that when you do this you must not use force. Use your mind to lead the Shen to its center constantly but gently. If you use mental force to reach the goal, you will cause not only eye ache but also headache.

7. Trembling Body:

Body trembling is a very common phenomenon in Chi Kung practice. While this occurs most commonly in the limbs, sometimes you may also experience trembling in part of your torso. This is a

---

(*2). "眼觀鼻，鼻觀心．"

11. Coughing:

Beginners sometimes have trouble with coughing during practice. There are several possible reasons. The most common reason is that the breathing is not being regulated smoothly. You may be breathing too fast or holding your breath. If this is the case, use your Yi to regulate the breathing until you do not have to regulate it anymore.

The second possible reason is that your body is not regulated correctly. For example, if you press your head backward too much, the front of the throat will be tense, and will cause you to cough.

The third possible reason is that the air is too dry. When you practice, you often increase the flow of air through your throat. Dry air will cause you to cough. However, if you keep the tip of your tongue touching the roof of your mouth, you will generate enough saliva to keep your mouth moist.

12. Sexual Excitation:

It is normal to have sexual feelings and even to become sexually excited during Chi Kung, especially when practicing Nei Dan. This is because you are starting to do abdominal breathing again, and this increases Chi circulation in your lower body and stimulates the production of hormones in the testicles and ovaries. While this increases sexual desire, you should remember that you are practicing Chi Kung to increase the production of hormones and use these hormones to raise your Shen. If you cannot regulate your mind, and waste this extra supply of hormones in excessive sexual activity, you are harming your health and perhaps even shortening your life.

Sexual excitation is especially a problem in Marrow Washing Chi Kung. This training teaches many methods of stimulating hormone production so that the hormones or Essence can be converted into Chi to nourish the Shen and brain. People who do not understand the training or who have a weak will may end up wasting what they have gained through their practice.

14-3. Sensations Commonly Experienced in Still Meditation

In the beginning stage of Chi Kung practice you learn how to regulate your body, breathing, and mind. Then when you start to practice Chi Kung, especially sitting meditation, you can enter into a deep level of meditation where the Chi readjusts and balances itself, reaching every little place in your body. When this happens, you may experience many kinds of feelings or even have visions in your mind. Many of these feelings cannot be experienced when you are not in meditation. The Chinese call these sensations "Jiing Chi," which means "Chi scenery" or "Chi view," because they are generated by the Chi. We will now discuss some of the common sensations you might experience. Do not expect that you will experience all of these sensations, or that everyone will experience them. It all depends on the individual, the time of day, and even the environment in which you are sitting.

1. The "Eight Touches" (Physical and Sensory Phenomena):

The "Ba Chuh" (eight touches) are sensations which are often felt during Chi Kung practice, such as sensations of heat, someone touching you, or heaviness. In Chinese they are called "Chuh Gaan" (touch and feel) or "Dong Chuh" (moving touch). Some practitioners list these eight phenomena as: A. Moving (Dong), B. Itching (Yeang),

C. Cool (Liang), D. Warm (Noan), E. Light (Ching), F. Heavy (Jong), G. Harsh (Seh), and H. Slippery (Hwa). Other practitioners list a different eight: A. Shake (Diaw), B. Ripple (Yi), C. Cold (Leeng), D. Hot (Reh), E. Float (Fwu), F. Sink (Chern), G. Hard (Jian), and H. Soft (Roan).

You should understand that all of these sensations are common and normal in Chi Kung practice. Even Chi Kung beginners will sometimes feel them. If you experience something, analyze it to determine the source or cause. If it is a natural phenomenon and the result of the redistribution of Chi, let it happen and don't worry about it. Conversely, if any of the above phenomena occur for other reasons, correct the circumstances that are causing them. For example, if you feel cold because the room temperature is too low, either put on more clothing or turn up the thermostat.

Do not expect these phenomena, do not look for them, and do not be worried about them. Simply follow nature and let it happen. Take it easy and continue your practice. Keep your mind clear and calm, and do not be disturbed or distracted by anything that happens.

2. Sensations of Movement or Vibration:

This is a different sensation from what we mentioned above where one part of the body spontaneously starts to move or tremble. This sensation happens in still meditation in the Dan Tien area. When you train your sitting meditation for a while, you might first experience a feeling of warmth in your lower abdomen. After a couple of weeks you may find that the area around your Dan Tien starts to vibrate by itself. This means that the Chi is full at the Dan Tien and it is time for you to use your Yi to lead the Chi through the small circulation. Normally, this is the first sensation which people beginning sitting meditation experience. It gives you the confidence that you are practicing correctly and that you are making progress.

3. Sensations Inside the Abdomen:

Once you feel the warmth and vibration in your Dan Tien, the abundant Chi will spread out through your abdomen. The motion of your abdomen as you breathe increases this Chi circulation in your intestines. Sometimes this causes sounds in the intestines, and the release of gas. After this happens for a while, you will feel warmth and other sensations in your abdomen, and you will feel the Chi flowing smoothly and strongly. Sometimes this may make you sweat. After you have practiced for a while, these sensations will disappear as all the channels in the abdomen open up and the Chi is able to move without any stagnation.

4. The Sensation of Lightness:

After you have completed your small circulation, and the Chi is circulating smoothly inside your body, you may experience that when you enter into a deep state of meditation, your physical body seems to disappear, or your body feels light and airy. This is a very comfortable sensation. However, if you let your mind be distracted by this sensation, it will disappear. You should be aware of what is happening, but don't pay attention to it. Usually, in order to reach this stage, you must have regulated your body into a very deep state of relaxation, where your breathing and heartbeat slow down to the minimum, and your mind is extremely calm and peaceful.

5. White Scenery (Clouds) in the Empty Room:

Sometimes, when you have entered a deep meditative state, you will suddenly feel your physical body disappear and your Chi mix with the surrounding Chi. When this happens, it seems that the entire room is empty, and filled with a white cloud or fog. If you pay attention to this scenery, it will disappear immediately because your mind is not familiar with emptiness, and generates an image of familiar, physical scenery to fill the void.

If you find yourself experiencing this white emptiness, just sense or feel it, do not put your attention on it. This scenery will happen only when your mind is completely regulated into a highly concentrated and relaxed state. The Taoist Wuh Yi Tzyy said: "(If you) desire to fill the abdomen (with Chi), must first empty the Hsin (regulate the Hsin). (If you) desire to generate the White, (you) must first empty the room."(*3) This sentence tells you that in order to train yourself to make the Chi full in your abdomen, you must first have an empty Hsin. That means you must regulate your Hsin until there is no Hsin. Only then will your mind be able to concentrate your Yi in your Lower Dan Tien to Start the Fire (build up the Chi). White here means simple, pure, clean, light, like fog, like clouds, and represents the disappearance of the physical body. In order to make your Chi unite with the surrounding Chi, you must first let go of and ignore all of the objects in your mind's "room," including your physical body.

6. Six Other Sensations:

When you reach a higher level of Chi Kung meditation, there are six other common sensations which you may experience. These are A. Dan Tien is hot as if it were on fire. B. The (internal) kidneys feel like they are boiling in water. C. The eyes are emitting a beam of light. D. Winds are being generated behind the ears. E. An eagle is shouting behind your head. F. Your body is energized and your nose trembles. These six phenomena are called the "Six Verifications" by Taoist Yu Tzuu, because they verify that you are following the correct approach in your meditation.

7. Six Transportations:

When you have reached the level of regulating your Shen, your Shen will be high and its Ling's supernatural power will be able to reach farther than any ordinary person's. Your mind will then be able to communicate with the six natural powers:

A. Seeing the Present:

Your mind is so clear that it can analyze and understand events or incidents clearly and thoroughly. This happens because, when you have learned to regulate your mind, you are able to see things or events from a neutral point of view, without being confused by your Hsin. Since most people cannot do this, you can see more clearly than most people.

B. Understanding the Past and Seeing the Future:

Your mind is able to understand the past and predict the future. Since your mind is clear, you will be able to analyze what

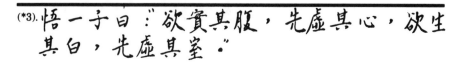

(*3). 悟一子曰："欲實其腹，先虛其心，欲生其白，先虛其室。"

has happened, understand its causes and see the results. As your experience with objectively analyzing the past accumulates, you will be able to see what will happen in the future, since people remain the same and history always repeats itself.

C. Viewing the Entire Universe:

When your meditation has reached the highest stage, your spirit is able to feel or sense the entire universe. You will (spiritually) see the mountains, the sky, rivers, oceans, etc. At this stage your Chi and the universe's Chi have united into one and you are able to freely exchange information.

D. Hearing the Sounds of the Universe:

Through your spirit you are able to listen to and understand all of the sounds generated by the variations of natural Chi, including the wind, rain, waves, and many other things. You will also be able to hear spirits and communicate with them.

E. Seeing a Person's Destiny:

After you have experienced all of the changes of the natural Chi field, and accumulated all of the past information related to human beings, you will be able to see a person's mind, personality, and true nature, and this will let you see his destiny. You will even be able to see his spiritual future, whether it involves enjoyment (heaven) or suffering (hell).

F. Knowing a Person's Thoughts:

Since you have energized your spirit and brain to a highly sensitive state, your brain will be open to a much wider band of wavelengths. You will be able to match wavelengths with other people's minds, and see their thoughts.

Taoist Wuu Jen Ren said: "Return to emptiness to combine with the Tao; after you have reached steadiness and (your spirit is) able to leave (your body), (your spirit is) able to suddenly enter, suddenly leave (your body). Then you are able to communicate with the six or ten (nature powers), and are able to transform into thousands of changes and ten thousand variations; nothing cannot be done."(*4) This is the stage of Buddhahood and Enlightenment, where you are able to separate your spirit from your body and unite with nature.

14-4. Deviations and Corrections

Once you are able to build up the Chi in your body, especially at the Dan Tien, if you are not cautious your Chi might deviate from the correct path and bring you into a dangerous situation. This is caused by lack of knowledge, misunderstandings, or wrong training methods. In Chi Kung practice, deviations are called "Tzoou Huoo Ruh Mo,"(*5) which means "Mislead the Fire and enter the Devil." "Mislead the fire" means to lead the Chi into the wrong path, and "Enter the Devil" means that the mind enters the domain of evil. When this happens during Chi Kung practice, serious problems or injury usually result. In

---

(*4). 伍真人云：" 還虛合道，出定以後，倏出倏定也可，六通十通皆能，千變萬化，無所不能。"

(*5). " 走火入魔 "

this section, we will discuss the causes of common Chi Kung deviations. Then we will discuss the deviations and how to correct them.

Causes of Deviations:

1. **The Chi Kung style trained does not fit the individual or the circumstances:**

   Many practitioners do not understand that every style of Chi Kung has its own special training methods and objectives. Each Chi Kung set was created by a knowledgeable Chi Kung master to train a specific group of people. For example, iron shirt Chi Kung is used to train people whose bodies are already stronger than the average person's. If you are weak and force yourself to train iron shirt, you will encounter difficulties and deviations. Therefore, when you choose a Chi Kung style for your training, you must first know your body's condition, the purpose of your training, and if the Chi Kung style chosen will help you to improve your health. Naturally, you must first have a good knowledge of each style. Normally, for a beginner, a knowledgeable master must help you to decide the style to practice. However, with Chi Kung styles which are used to improve one's general health, such as "The Eight Pieces of Brocade" and "Five Animal Sports," you do not have to worry too much about deviations caused by choosing the wrong style. Such styles were created for the average person, so you are safe as long as you follow the instructions.

2. **Lack of a firm mind or a knowledgeable teacher:**

   The most important thing in Chi Kung training is to find a knowledgeable teacher and stay with him. Without a qualified teacher, there is a good chance you may be taught incorrect practices. Once you have found a good teacher, do not lose your patience or confidence and change to another teacher. If you do that, you may change from one training theory to another, which will only increase your confusion. If you train Chi Kung without patience, perseverance, confidence, and a strong will, sooner or later you will find yourself in a situation which is confusing, where deviations can occur.

3. **Anticipating phenomena:**

   One of the most common causes of deviation in Chi Kung is expectation of phenomena that you have heard or read about. Just because someone else has experienced something doesn't mean that you will experience it also. If you expect something to happen, and especially if you try to make it happen, you are very likely to fall into wrong practices. In no time at all you will be mislead by the wrong sensations or by experiences created solely by your mind.

4. **The body and mind are not regulated:**

   Many Chi Kung practitioners have encountered serious deviations caused by body tension. For example, after a long day at work, your body is tired and the muscles are still tense. Before practicing Chi Kung, you should calm down your mind, regulate your breathing, and help your body to relax and recover from its fatigue. Any attempt to circulate Chi when you are tired is dangerous.

   Deviations are also common when people circulate Chi before their minds are regulated. For example, if you are excited or mad, your Yi is unsteady, and it is dangerous to use it to lead your Chi. If you cannot regulate your mind, you should not practice.

   If you practice under either of these circumstances, your Chi can become stagnant or enter the wrong paths. It is very common to experience a headache or various pains in the body. You should remember that regulating your body, breathing, and mind are the basic requirements before you regulate your Chi.

5. Losing Patience:

It is very common for some practitioners to lose their patience during practice and use their Yi aggressively to lead the Chi. This is very dangerous, especially for beginners. When you practice Chi Kung, you must take your time, and be patient and confident. Your understanding and experience will grow with practice. When the time is right, what will happen will happen. For example, many Chi Kung beginners practice circulating Chi in the small circulation before they really know what Chi is, and before they can move their abdomens in a relaxed and easy way. This will only cause problems. It is like a child playing with fire before he knows what it is or what it can do.

6. Mixing Imagination with the Chi Kung exercises:

Chi Kung is a science. It is not a religion or a superstitious belief. Imagination will lead you to the wrong path, and it is a major cause of fear. Imagination is the major cause of "entering the domain of the devil." Most people who have imagination are lacking in scientific knowledge and understanding. The are still confused and wondering what they are doing.

7. External Interference:

Some of the worst deviations are caused by external disturbances during Chi Kung meditation. For example, you are meditating when suddenly you are shocked by the telephone ringing, a loud noise, or a friend talking to you. Such things can cause serious injury, especially when you are circulating Chi in the small circulation or are practicing other higher levels of Chi Kung practice where great concentration is necessary. Therefore, before you practice you should prevent all possible disturbances.

8. Believing Non-professional Opinions:

A common human failing that most of us share is that we tend to believe and trust other people's judgement more than our own. We are especially open to advice from our friends. When you encounter a problem during practice, do not discuss it with anyone who is not experienced with Chi Kung. You can discuss it with your teacher or your fellow students, but it is best not to talk about it with friends who are not practicing Chi Kung. You are likely to be much better qualified to evaluate things than they are.

9. Not following the advice and rules of the masters:

The last part of this section will discuss 24 rules which you should observe while practicing Chi Kung. You must believe in and obey these rules to avoid the most common causes of serious problems in practice.

Though we have pointed out many possible causes of deviation and danger, you should not let this scare you away from practicing Chi Kung. Every scientific study or practice always has some level of risk. For example, you would not ban swimming simple because some people drown, and you shouldn't refuse to drive a car even though many people are killed or injured by them. The proper approach to any of these things is to understand what you are doing, know the source of potential problems, define the training rules, and proceed cautiously

Most of the deviations we will discuss happen to Chi Kung practitioners who are able to generate a strong Chi flow, yet still do not understand and master the regulation of the body, breathing, and mind. You should understand that once you generate strong Chi in your body, if you do not know how to lead it, it may move into the wrong paths and affect your body's normal Chi circulation. This is harmful and even dangerous. That is why they are called "deviations" rather than "phenomena," which is the term we used earlier in the chapter to refer to experiences which beginners have.

Deviations and Corrections:

1. Headache:

Earlier in the chapter we discussed the headaches which beginners have. Here we will discuss the potentially very serious headaches which happen to people who have developed more Chi.

This headache is generally caused by an excess of Chi and blood, or a lack of oxygen in the brain. The excess of Chi and blood is usually caused by forced concentration, which means the mind is not regulated properly. Even when you are concentrating, both your Yi and body should be relaxed. If you force yourself to concentrate, your mind will lead Chi and blood to your head, you will become even more tense, and you will get a headache. It is just like when you can't sleep, it's no good trying to force yourself to sleep. You have to want to fall asleep, but you have to relax and let it happen.

The headache caused by lack of oxygen usually occurs when your breathing is not regulated properly. For example, beginners will frequently try so hard to concentrate their Yi that they unconsciously hold their breath. Holding the breath reduces the oxygen supply to the brain and causes headaches. It is therefore very important for the beginner to regulate his breath until it is smooth and natural. That means regulating the breath without regulating. Only then should he learn to concentrate his mind on leading the Chi.

If you get a headache while practicing Chi Kung, stop training immediately. Regulate your breathing until it is smooth, and lead your body into a state of deep relaxation. This will help all of the Chi channels in the neck to open, and the Chi and blood which has accumulated in your head will be able to move down to your body. Externally, you may massage both temples (Figure 14-2) and lead the Chi and blood down. You should also massage the Fengtzu (Wind Pond) cavity (Figure 14-3) on the back of your neck, as well as the muscles there, pushing downward to lead the blood and Chi out of your head. Finally, put the center of your palm on the Baihui (Hundred Meetings) cavity on the crown of your head and lightly circle around for a few times, and then follow the muscles on the back of the neck downward (Figure 14-4).

2. Stagnant Chi in the Upper Dan Tien:

When you have stagnant Chi in your Upper Dan Tien, it feels like you have a piece of fly paper stuck on your third eye. This usually happens when you have been concentrating there very intensely. Normally, when you concentrate your Shen, your Upper Dan Tien area feels comfortably warm. However, if you feel uncomfortable, the Chi is stagnant. When this happens, massage your Upper Dan Tien and lead the Chi towards the temples and down the sides of the neck (Figure 14-5). Another way is to massage your Upper Dan Tien with your middle finger a few

Figure 14-2. Massaging the temples

Figure 14-3. Massaging the Fengtzu cavities

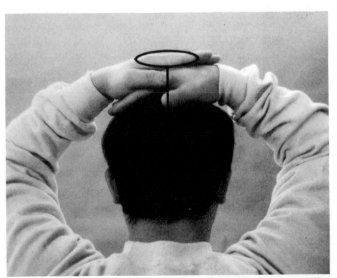

Figure 14-4. Massage the Baihui cavity down the back

Figure 14-5. Massage from the Upper Dan Tien to the temples and downward

times, then lead the Chi down to the eye bridge, finally spreading the Chi down over your face (Figure 14-6).

3. Dan Tien Feels Expanded and Uncomfortable:

Although this is a phenomenon which is more common with beginners, people with some experience may also encounter it. It usually happens when you use too much force to move your abdominal muscles in and out. If you train for a long time, the muscles will be tired and you will not be able to control them. When you train your abdomen to move in and out, it must remain soft and relaxed. If the muscles are tense, the Chi will stagnate there. If you find that your abdomen feels uncomfortable and the Chi is stagnant there, overlap your hands and massage your abdomen in a circular manner a few times (Figure 14-7), then open your hands and brush the Chi down to the thighs (Figure 14-8).

4. Pressure and Discomfort at the Diaphragm:

This uncomfortable feeling usually happens when you use reverse abdominal breathing. It can also happens during normal breathing if you are not regulating your breathing correctly. In reverse abdominal breathing, as you inhale you push the diaphragm down while pulling your abdominal muscles in. This can cause a feeling of pressure and discomfort. Therefore, when you practice, you should start your reverse breathing on a smaller scale, with smaller movements of the abdomen. After you have practiced for a while, you will realize that there is a limit to how far you can move your abdomen without feeling pressure on your diaphragm. However, if you already feel uncomfortable, that means that the Chi is stagnant because of pressure and tension around the diaphragm. You should stop training immediately. Overlap your hands and gently press in on the solar plexus a few times (Figure 14-9), then brush downward and to the sides (Figure 14-10).

5. Back Pain:

Back pain in Chi Kung is usually caused by incorrect posture. This happens especially during sitting meditation. Incorrect posture can cause your Chi circulation to stagnate. It can also increase pressure and tension on the muscles. If you have back pain, stop practice immediately. If you force yourself to continue, you will only disturb your mind and make everything worse. If possible, have someone massage the painful area (Figure 14-11), following the spine downward

Figure 14-6. Massage from the Upper Dan Tien down to the eye bridge and spread over the face

Figure 14-7. Massage from the Lower Dan Tien

Figure 14-8. From the lower Dan Tien down the thighs

Figure 14-9. Massage the solar plexus
(Middle Dan Tien)

Figure 14-10. From the solar plexus to
the sides

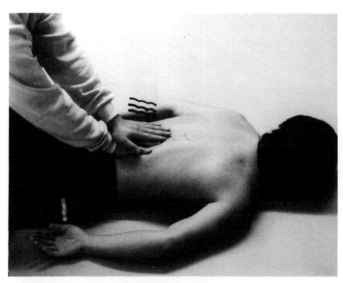

Figure 14-11. Massaging the back

to the hips (Figure 14-12), and spread the Chi to the sides of the body and downward to the legs.

6. Nocturnal Emissions:

This happens when you have built up your Chi and do not know how to keep it and circulate it. If you do a lot of Dan Tien exercises the Chi will be full there, your sexual organs will be energized, and your body will produce more hormones. This will increase your sexual desire, and cause frequent erections, often without apparent causes such as physical or mental stimulation. If you do not have any sexual activity, internal sexual pressure builds up, and your body will automatically release the pressure through nocturnal emissions about once a month. If you practice Chi Kung and the semen is released automatically more than twice a month, then it is not normal. That means you are not converting the Essence into Chi and circulating it properly. In order to convert the Essence into Chi and circulate it, when your Chi is full you should coordinate the movement of your Huiyin cavity and anus with your breathing. This training will be discussed in more detail when we discuss the small and grand circulation and the Marrow Washing Chi Kung in the next volume.

This problem can also occur when the Chi level in your lower body is lower than normal. When the lower part of your body is deficient due to sickness or excessive walking, there is not enough Chi to keep the muscles functioning normally, and you will occasionally experience nocturnal emissions. This can also happen if you train Chi Kung incorrectly, or if you get involved in Chi Kung before you have completely recovered from an illness. In this case, massage your Lower Dan Tien and abdominal area until they are warm after each Chi Kung practice.

7. The Chi Circulates Strongly by Itself:

Sometimes people will build up Chi faster than their Yi can control it. This can be extremely dangerous. It is like starting to drive a car when you don't know how to steer. If you cannot control your Chi, it may go the wrong way and cause serious injury. Many beginning Chi Kung students are enthusiastic and impatient, and try to regulate their Chi

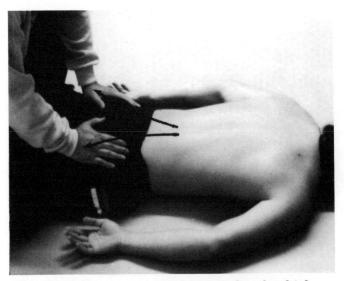

Figure 14-12 .Spread the Chi downward to the thighs

before they are able to regulate their body, breathing, and mind. When they feel the Chi move around by itself, especially while training the small circulation, they are elated because they think it is a sign that they are making progress. When you find that your Chi is building up and you cannot control it, you should stop practice completely for a period of time. Practice regulating your body, breathing, and mind until you are confident and understand what you are doing. Only then should you start regulating your Chi. The wisest course is to consult with an experienced master. However, many times you will find the Chi moving or distributing by itself on a small scale. This usually does not last too long and stops by itself. This is nothing to worry about, and you should simply continue your practice with a calm and peaceful mind.

Do not confuse this experience with what happens when you train certain Chi Kung exercises which build up Chi in a particular area so that it will later circulate strongly by itself. These exercises were designed for that purpose, and the automatic, strong Chi flow is expected.

8. Chi Entering the Wrong Path:
The main reason that Chi enters the wrong path is that your mind is scattered and not regulated. If your Chi is strong and your mind is not regulated, the Chi may go anywhere. It might make your internal organs too Yang or too Yin, and you could become ill. Chi Kung without a regulated mind is like a car with a drunken driver -- it is extremely dangerous. Always remember: **REGULATE YOUR BODY, BREATHING, AND MIND FIRST BEFORE YOU REGULATE YOUR CHI.** If you are already ill because of Chi Kung practice, stop practice immediately! Relax and get enough rest, and wait until the Chi regains its balance. You usually do not need to see a doctors; if you keep calm and relaxed the Chi will balance itself. When you start again, begin with the most basic regulating exercises first, so that you do not fall into the same problem again.

9. Stiff Tongue:
When the tongue is stiff in Chi Kung practice, it can stagnant the Chi in the small circulation. Practice relaxing your tongue as the tip lightly touches the roof of your mouth. Only when you can do this naturally and comfortably should you start practicing the small circulation.

14-5. The Twenty-Four Rules for Chi Kung Practice
In this section we will list the twenty-four rules which have been passed down by generations of Chi Kung masters. These rules are based on much study and experience, and you should observe them carefully.

1. Don't be Stubborn about Plans and Ideas
(Yuh Jyr Wang Niann): 頂執妄念
This is one of the easiest mistakes for beginners to make. When we take up Chi Kung we are enthusiastic and eager. However, sometimes we don't learn as fast as we would like to, and we become impatient and try to force things. Sometimes we set up a schedule for ourselves: today I want to make my Dan Tien warm, tomorrow I want to get through the tailbone cavity, by such and such a day I want to complete the small circulation. This is the wrong way to go about it. Chi Kung is not like any ordinary job or task you set for yourself -- **YOU CANNOT MAKE A PROGRESS SCHEDULE FOR CHI KUNG.** This will only make your thinking rigid and stagnate your progress. **EVERYTHING HAPPENS WHEN IT IS TIME FOR IT TO HAPPEN. IF YOU FORCE IT, IT WILL NOT HAPPEN NATURALLY.**

2. Don't Place your Attention in Discrimination (Jwo Yi Fen Bye): 着意分別

When you practice, do not place your attention on the various phenomena or sensations which are occurring. Be aware of what is happening, but keep your mind centered on wherever it is supposed to be for the exercise you are doing. If you let your mind go to wherever you feel something "interesting" happening, the Chi will follow your mind and interfere with your body's natural tendency to rebalance itself. Do not expect anything to happen, and don't let your mind wander around looking for the various phenomena. Furthermore, don't start evaluating or judging the phenomena, such as asking "Is my Dan Tien warmer today than it was yesterday?" Don't ask yourself "Just where is my Chi now?" When your mind is on your Chi, your Yi is there also, and this stagnant Yi will not lead the Chi. **BE AWARE OF WHAT IS HAPPENING, BUT DON'T PAY ATTENTION TO IT**. When you drive a car, you don't watch yourself steer and work the pedals and shift gears. If you did, you'd drive off the road. You simply put your mind on where you want to go and let your body automatically drive the car. This is called regulating without regulating.

3. Avoid Miscellaneous Thought Remaining on Origins (Tzar Niann Pan Yuan): 雜念攀緣

This is a problem of regulating the mind. The emotional mind is strong, and every idea is still strongly connected to its origin. If you cannot cut the ideas off at their source, your mind is not regulated, and your should not try to regulate your Chi. You will also often find that even though you have stopped the flow of random thoughts going through your mind, new ideas are generated during practice. For example, when you discover your Dan Tien is warm, your mind immediately recalls where this is mentioned in a book, or how the master described it, and you start to compare your experience with this. Or you may start wondering what the next step is. All of these thoughts will lead you away from peace and calm, and your mind will end up in the "Domain of the Devil." Then your mind will be confused, scattered, and very often scared, and you will tire quickly.

4. Hsin Should not Follows the External Scenery (Hsin Swei Wai Jiing): 心隨外景

This is also a problem of regulating the mind (Hsin). When your emotional mind is not controlled, any external distraction will lead it away from your body and to the distraction. You must train yourself so that noises, smells, conversations and such will not disturb your concentration. It is all right to be aware of what is happening, but your mind must remain calmly, peacefully, and steadily on your cultivation.

5. Regulate your Sexual Activity (Ruh Farng Shy Jieng): 入房施精

You should not have sexual relations at least 24 hours before or after practicing Chi Kung, especially martial or religious Chi Kung. The Essence-Chi conversion training is a very critical part of these practices, and if you practice Chi Kung soon after sex, you will harm your body significantly. Sex depletes your Chi and sperm, and the Chi level in the lower portion of your body is lower than normal. When you practice Chi Kung under these conditions, it is like doing heavy exercise right after sex. Furthermore, when your Chi level is abnormal, your feeling and sensing are also not accurate. Under these conditions, your Yi can be misled and its accuracy affected. You should wait until the Chi level regains it normal balance before your resume Chi Kung. Only then will the Essence-Chi conversion proceed normally and efficiently.

One of the major purposes of Chi Kung is to increase the Essence-Chi conversion and use this Chi to nourish your body. Once a man has built up a supply of Chi, having sex will only pass this Chi on to his partner. As a matter of fact, many Chi Kung masters insist that you should not have sex three days before and four days after practice.

During sexual relations the female usually gains Chi while the male loses Chi during ejaculation. The woman should not practice Chi Kung after sex until her body has digested the Chi she has obtained from the man. There are certain Taoist Chi Kung techniques which teach men how not to lose Chi during sexual activity, and teach women how to receive Chi from the man and digest it. We will leave the discussion of this subject to Chi Kung masters who are qualified and experienced in it.

6. Don't be Too Warm or Too Cold (Dah Uen Dah Harn): 大溫大寒

The temperature of the room in which you are training should not be too hot or too cold. You should practice in the most comfortable environment which will not disturb your mind and cultivation.

7. Be Careful of the Five Weaknesses and Internal Injuries (Wuu Lau Ann Shang): 五癆暗傷

Five weaknesses means the weaknesses of five Yin organs: the heart, liver, lungs, kidneys, and spleen. When you realize that any of these five organs is weak, you should proceed very gradually and gently with your Chi Kung practice. Chi Kung practice is an internal exercise which is directly related to these five organs. If you do not move gradually and gently, it is like forcing a weak person to run 10 miles right away. This will not build up his strength, instead it will injure him more seriously.

For the same reason, when you have an internal injury your internal Chi distribution and circulation is already disturbed. If you practice Chi Kung your feelings may be misled, and your practice may worsen your problem and interfere with the natural healing process. There are certain Chi Kung exercises which are designed to cure internal injuries, but to use them properly you need to have a very good understanding of the Chi situation of your body.

8. Avoid Facing the Wind when Sweating (Tzuoh Hann Dang Feng): 坐汗當風

Don't practice in the wind, especially facing the wind. When you practice Chi Kung you are exercising either internally, or both internally and externally. It is normal to sweat, and since you are relaxed, your pores are wide open. If you expose your body to cold wind, you will catch cold.

9. Don't Wear Tight Clothes and Belt (Jiin Yi Shuh Dai): 緊衣束帶

Always wear loose clothes during practice because this will help you to feel comfortable. Keep your belt loose, too. The abdomen is the key area in Chi Kung practice, and you must be careful not to limit the movement of this area because it will interfere with your practice.

10. Don't Eat too Much Greasy and Sweet Food (Tau Tieh Fair Gan): 饕餮肥甘

You should regulate your eating habit while you are practicing Chi Kung. Greasy or sweet food will increase your Fire Chi, making your mind scattered, and your Shen will stray away from its residence. You should eat more fruit and vegetables, and keep away from alcohol and tobacco.

跋床懸腳

11. Don't Hang your Feet off the Bed (Bar Chwang Shyuan Jywe):

In ancient times the most common place in Chi Kung practice was sitting on your bed. Since most beds were high, if you sat on the edge of the bed your feet would hang off the side of the bed above the floor. When you practice Chi Kung your feet should touch the floor. If they do not, all of the weight of your body will press down on the lower part of your thighs and reduce the Chi and blood circulation. Furthermore, when you practice you should nor put your feet up on the table, because this position will also stagnate the Chi and blood circulation.

12. Don't Practice with a Full Bladder (Jeou Zen Sheau Biann): 久忍小便

You should go to the toilet before you start your practice. If you need to go during practice, stop your practice and do so. Holding it in disturbs your concentration.

13. Don't Scratch an Itch (Sau Jua Yeang Chuh): 搔抓癢觸

If you itch because of some external reason, such as an insect walking on you or biting you, do not be alarmed and keep your mind calm. Use your Yi to lead the Chi back to its residence, the Dan Tien. Breathe a couple of times and gradually bring your consciousness back to your surroundings. Then you may scratch or think of how to stop the itching. However, if the itching is caused by Chi redistribution in the Chi Kung practice, remain calm and do not move your mind there. Simply ignore it and let it happen. Once it has reached a new balance, the itching will stop. If you scratch this kind of itch it means that your mind has been disturbed, and also that you are using your hands to interfere with the natural rebalancing of your body's Chi.

猝呼驚悸

14. Avoid Being Suddenly Disturbed or Startled (Tsuh Hu Jing Jih):

You should avoid being suddenly disturbed or startled. However, if it does happen, calm down your mind. You must absolutely prevent yourself from losing your temper. What has happened has happened, and getting mad cannot change anything. What you should do is prevent it from happening again. Most important of all, though, is learning how to regulate your mind when you are disturbed.

15. Don't Take Delight in the Scenery (Twe Jiing Huan Shii): 對景歡喜

It is very common during practice to suddenly notice something that is going on inside of you. Perhaps you feel Chi moving more clearly than ever before, or you start to sense your bone marrow, and you feel elated and excited. You have just fallen into a very common trap. Your concentration is broken, and your mind is divided. This is dangerous and harmful. You have to learn how to be aware of what is going on inside you without getting excited.

16. Don't Wear Sweaty Clothes (Jeou Jwo Hann Yi): 久著汗衣

This happens mostly in moving Chi Kung practice, especially in martial Chi Kung training. When your clothes are wet from sweat you will feel uncomfortable, and your concentration will be affected. It is better to change into dry clothes and then resume practice.

17. Don't Sit When Hungry or Full (Ji Bao Shang Tzuoh): 飢飽上生

You should not practice Chi Kung when you are hungry or when your stomach is full. When you are hungry it is hard to concentrate, and when you are full your practice will affect your digestion.

18. Heaven and Earth Strange Disaster (Tian Dih Tzai Guay): 天地災怪

It is believed that your body's Chi is directly affected by changes in the weather. It is therefore not advisable to practice Chi Kung when there is a sudden weather change, because your practice will interfere with your body's natural readjustment to the new environment. You will also be unable to feel and sense your Chi flow as you do normally. You must always try to remain emotionally neutral whenever you do Chi Kung; even if you are disturbed by a natural disaster like an earthquake, you must remain calm so that your Chi stays under control.

19. Listen Sometimes to True Words (Jen Yan Oou Ting): 真言偶聽

You need to have confidence when you practice Chi Kung. You should not listen to advice from people who do not have experience in Chi Kung and who are not familiar with the condition of your body. Some people listen to their classmates explain how they reached a certain level or how they cured a certain problem, and then blindly try to use the same method themselves. You need to understand that everyone has a different body, everyone's health is slightly different, and everyone learns differently. When the time comes for you to learn something new, you will understand what you need. Play it cool and easy, and always have confidence in your training.

20. Don't Lean and Fall Asleep (Huen Chern Ching Yii): 昏沉傾欹

You should not continue your Chi Kung training when you are sleepy. Using an unclear mind to lead Chi is dangerous. Also, when you are sleepy your body will not be regulated and will tend to lean or droop, and your bad posture may interfere with the proper Chi circulation. When you are sleepy it is best to take a rest until you are able to regain your spirit.

21. Don't Meditate When You Have Lost Your Temper or are Too Excited (Dah Nuh or Dah Leh Ruh Tzuoh): 大怒大樂入坐

You should not meditate when you are too excited due to anger or happiness. Since your mind is scattered, meditation will bring you more harm than peace.

22. Don't Keep Spitting (Tuu Tarn Wu Duh): 吐痰無度

It is normal to generate a lot of saliva while practicing Chi Kung. The saliva should be swallowed to moisten your throat. Don't spit out the saliva because this is a waste, and it will also disturb your concentration.

23. Don't Doubt and Become Lazy (Sheng Yi Shieh Dai): 生疑懈怠

When you first start Chi Kung, you must have confidence in what you are doing, and not start doubting its validity, or questioning whether you are doing it right. If you start doubting right at the beginning you will become lazy, and you will start questioning whether you really want to continue. In this case, you will not have any success and your practice will never last.

24. Do not Ask for the Speedy Success (Buh Chyow Suh Shiaw): 不求速効

This is to remind you that Chi Kung practice is time consuming and progress is slow. You must have patience, a strong will, and confidence to reach your goal. Taking it easy and being natural are the most important rules.

PART THREE

THE CHI CHANNELS
AND VESSELS

Chapter 15

General Concepts

In this chapter we will explain a number of concepts and terms which are used in discussing Chi. You will find that many of the terms have already been discussed in previous chapters. We believe however, that it will be helpful to refresh your memory, as well as introduce new terms, to help you understand later discussions. Chapter 16 will review the twelve Chi channels and their relationship to health and Chi Kung, and Chapter 17 will discuss the eight extraordinary vessels.

Chi:

Chi is the energy which circulates within the body. As we noted in Chapter 3, your entire body is like a factory and your organs are like many machines operating inside this factory. Your brain is like management, directing the entire operation. In order to keep the factory functioning properly, you need a power supply. The power supply is connected to each machine with many wires and cables. Each machine must receive the appropriate level of power; too much power will damage the machine and shorten its life, and too little power will not enable the machine to function properly. You can see that without a proper power supply in the factory, production will be off, and if the power supply stops, the entire factory is dead. It is the same with your body. When your body does not have a normal energy (Chi) supply, the organs will not function properly, and you will become sick; and if the Chi circulation stops, you will die.

You should realize that your entire body is alive, including every blood cell, every nerve tissue, and every muscles fiber. All of these physical, fundamental structures of the body need Chi to maintain their existence and their ability to function. The system which distributes Chi throughout your body is much like the wiring system in a factory, connecting the power source to the machines.

From the viewpoint of function, Chinese medical science classifies Chi in the following ways:

A. Organ Chi:

This Chi is responsible for the functioning of the organs.

B. Channel Chi:
This Chi is responsible for the transportive and moving functions of the channels.

C. Nourishing Chi:
The main responsibilities of this Chi are transforming and creating blood. Nourishing Chi also moves with the blood and helps the blood to nourish the tissues of the body.

D. Guardian Chi: (Also commonly translated as Protective Chi).
This Chi circulates outside the channels and the Organs. Guardian Chi's responsibilities are to warm the organs, to travel between the skin and the flesh to regulate the opening and closing of the pores, and to protect and moisten the skin, hair, and nails. This Chi is able to provide the body with a defense capability against external negative influences such as cold weather.

E. Ancestral Chi:
This Chi gathers (resides) in the chest with its center at the Shanzhong cavity (Co-17). Ancestral Chi is able to travel up to the throat and down to the abdomen. It is responsible for breathing and speaking, regulating heart beat, and, when cultivated through meditation, Ancestral Chi can strengthen the body.

Blood:
The Western concept of blood is only part of the Chinese conception of blood. Although blood is seen as a red fluid, in Chinese medical science it is also regarded as a force which is involved with the sensitivity of the sense organs and the inner vitality of the body. Since the main responsibility of blood is to carry nourishment to every part of the body, it clearly is closely related to Nourishing Chi.

Chi and Blood:
In Chinese medicine, Chi is considered Yang and blood is considered Yin. Chi is said to be the "commander" of blood because blood relies on Chi for its generation out of food and air, and for its power to move through and remain in the blood vessels. It is also said that blood is the "mother" of Chi because the strength of Chi depends upon the nutrition and moisture carried in blood. Therefore, Chi and blood are believed to complement each other.

Organs (Viscera):
The concept of the Organs in Chinese medicine differs significantly from that of Western medicine. In Chinese medicine the Organs are systems of functions, and not mere physical objects. Generally, this means that within the description of the Organs, almost all of the body's functions can be defined and explained.

In Chinese medical science, the Organs are divided into two main groups: the Yin (Inner) and Yang (Outer) Organs. There are six Yin organs and six Yang organs. Five of the Yin organs (excluding the Pericardium) are called "Tzang," which means viscera. These five (Liver, Heart, Spleen, Lungs, and Kidneys) are considered the core of the entire system. Usually, when a discussion involves the channels and all the Organs, the Pericardium is added; otherwise it is treated as an adjunct of the Heart. According to Chinese medicine, the Yin Organs "store and do not drain." That means that their functions are directed toward sustaining homeostasis, both physically and mentally..

The Six Yang Organs are called "Fuu," which means 'bowels,' and include the Gall Bladder, Small Intestine, Large Intestine, Stomach,

Bladder, and Triple Burner. According to Chinese medicine, these Yang Organs "drain and do not store." This refers to their responsibility in the transformation and the disposal of food and waste. All the Yang Organs receive food or a by-product of food, and then pass it along.

In Table 15-1, you will notice that each Yang Organ is associated with a Yin Organ by a special Yin/Yang relationship (or Inner/Outer relationship). Pairs of related Yin and Yang Organs belong to the same Phase, and their Chi channels are sequential to each other in Chi circulation. They are so closely linked that a disease in one will usually affect the other.

Yin and Yang:

We have discussed the concept of Yin and Yang in Chapter 7. Yin and Yang are not contradictory. Nor is one considered "good," and the other "bad." To obtain health, a harmony is sought between them and any imbalance is avoided. Remember, Yin and Yang are relative, not absolute.

Five Phases (Five Elements)(Wuu Shyng):

The five phases are Wood, Fire, Earth, Metal, and Water. They are also commonly translated as the "Five Elements." In Chinese, Shyng means to walk or to move; probably more pertinent, it means a process. The Five Phases are thought of as the five properties inherent in all things. Each phase symbolizes a category of related functions and qualities. For example, Wood is linked with active functions that are in phase with growth or with increasing. Fire expresses that the functions have reached a maximum state and are ready to decline. Metal represents that the functions are declining. Water symbolizes that the functions have declined and are ready to grow. And finally, Earth is associated with balance or neutrality. Therefore, Earth is the center point of the five phases.

	WOOD 木	FIRE 火	EARTH 土	METAL 金	WATER 水
Direction	East	South	Center	West	North
Season	Spring	Summer	Long Summer	Autumn	Winter
Climatic Condition	Wind	Summer Heat	Dampness	Dryness	Cold
Process	Birth	Growth	Transformation	Harvest	Storage
Color	Green	Red	Yellow	White	Black
Taste	Sour	Bitter	Sweet	Pungent	Salty
Smell	Goatish	Burning	Fragrant	Rank	Rotten
Yin Organ	Liver	Heart	Spleen	Lungs	Kidneys
Yang Organ	Gall Bladder	Small Intestine	Stomach	Large Intestine	Bladder
Opening	Eyes	Tongue	Mouth	Nose	Ears
Tissue	Sinews	Blood Vessels	Flesh	Skin/Hair	Bones
Emotion	Anger	Happiness	Pensiveness	Sadness	Fear
Human Sound	Shout	Laughter	Song	Weeping	Groan

Table 15-1. Table of Correspondences associated with the Five Phases

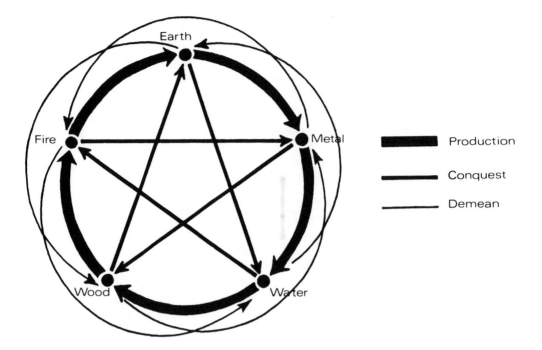

Figure 15-1. The relationships between the five phases

The relationships between the five phases are shown in Figure 15-1.

Chi Channels and Vessels:

"Ching" is commonly translated "meridians" or "primary Chi channels." Your body has twelve channels, which Chinese medicine considers to be like rivers of Chi. Each channel, although referred to in the singular, is actually a pair of mirror-image channels, one on either side of the body. One end of each of these twelve channels is associated with one of the twelve organs, while the other end is connected to a toe or finger (six channels are connected to the fingers and the other six are connected to the toes).

There are eight "Chi Mei" or "Chi vessels" in your body. They are often compared to reservoirs because they store Chi for your system. They can also be compared to batteries and capacitors in an electrical system. Batteries store and then release electrical current, and capacitors regulate the electrical current in the same way that the vessels regulate the Chi in your channels and organs.

There are other Chi channels called "Lou" or "Chi branches." There are millions of Lou spreading out from the channels to distribute Chi to every cell in the body. The Lou carry Chi from the channels outward to nourish the skin, hair, eyes, nails, etc., and also inward to the bone marrow to maintain the production of blood cells. Lou also connect the organs, enabling them to communicate and cooperate with each other.

The next term you must know is "Shiuh," which is translated as "cavity." Your body has more than seven hundred of these cavities, through which acupuncturists access the Chi channels with needles or other methods.

In order for you to be healthy, the Chi must flow smoothly and continuously in the channels. However, sometimes there are blockages, and the flow becomes stagnant. Blockages can be caused by eating poor quality food, by injuries, or by the physical degeneration that occurs as you age. Another problem is when the Chi is not flowing at the proper level. Acupuncturists have several ways of treating these problems, including the insertion of needles in certain cavities to adjust the flow of Chi.

Chapter 16

The Twelve Primary Chi Channels

16-1. Introduction

In this chapter we will briefly review the twelve primary Chi channels. As a Chi kung practitioner you need to know how the Chi in each channel and related organ can be affected by the seasons, the weather, emotions, and food. Table 15-1 offers you a guideline to these relationships.

You should also know the Organ's Yin and Yang. As seen in the last chapter, there are six Yang organs and six Yin organs. Each Yang organ is associated with a Yin organ by a special Yin/Yang relationship. Pairs of Yin and Yang organs belong to the same phase in the Five Phases, their channels are sequential to each other in the circulation of Chi, their functions are closely related, and disease in one usually affects the other. In Chinese medicine, the channel corresponding to the Yang organ is often used to treat disorders of its related Yin organ.

In the limbs, the Yang channels are on the external side of the limbs while the Yin channels are on the internal side. Generally speaking, the outsides of the limbs are more Yang and are more resistant and prepared for an attack, while the internal sides are more Yin and weaker.

The organs are further subdivided in order to distinguish the different levels of the Yin/Yang characteristics. The Yang organs are divided into Greater Yang (Taiyang), Lesser Yang (Shaoyang), and Yang Brightness (Yangming). The Yin organs are divided into Greater Yin (Taiyin), Lesser Yin (Shaoyin), and Absolute Yin (Jueyin). In the following discussion, all of the classifications will be shown in the title, for example: the Lung Channel of Hand -- Greater Yin.

16-2. The Twelve Primary Channels

The Lung Channel of Hand -- Greater Yin (Figure 16-1)

1. Course:

Course #1:

   (1). Stomach (Jong Jiao, Middle Triple Burner) -- (2). Large Intestine -- (3). Diaphragm -- (4). Lung -- (5). Throat -- (6). Upper Arm -- (7). Mid-Elbow -- (8). Forearm -- (9). Wrist -- (10). Thenar -- (11). Pollex (Shaoshang, L-11).

Course #2:

   (12). Above the styloid process at the wrist -- (13). Index Finger (Shangyang, LI-1).

2. Related Viscera:

   Lung (Pertaining Organ), Large Intestine, Stomach, and Kidney.

3. Cavities:

   Zhongfu (L-1), Yunmen (L-2), Tianfu (L-3), Xiabai (L-4), Chize (L-5),Kongzui (L-6), Lieque (L-7), Jingqu (L-8), Taiyuan (L-9), Yuji (L-10), and Shaoshang (L-11).

4. Discussion:

   The Lungs (Yin) and the Large Intestine (Yang) are considered paired Organs. From Table 15-1 you can see that they belong to Metal in the Five Phases, the westerly direction, the season of autumn, the dry climatic condition, the color white, the pungent taste, the rank odor, the emotion of sadness, and the sound of weeping. Their opening is the nose, and they govern skin and hair.

   In Chi Kung practice, since the Lungs belong to Metal, they are able to regulate heartburn. The Heart belongs to Fire. Whenever the Heart has excess Chi, deep breathing is able to lead the Heart's fire to the Lungs, and therefore cool the heartburn. When the weather is changing from damp, hot summer into drier and chilly autumn, Lungs are the first organ to sense the change. If your Lungs are not able to readjust themselves to fit the new situation smoothly, you will catch a cold. The Lung access the outside world through your nose. The Lungs are responsible for taking Chi from the air, and for the energy (Chi) state of the body.

   Breathing is considered a strategy for leading Chi to the extremities such as skin and hair. When your breathing is regulated properly, you are able to strengthen your body's Guardian Chi and generate an expansive Chi shield to protect your body. You are also able to raise or lower your Chi state through your breathing. For example, when you are angry, deep breathing is able to calm your excited Chi state.

   The Lungs are sensitive to emotional changes, especially when you are sad or angry. They also control that part of the liquid metabolism which distributes liquid to the skin.

   Because the Lungs are usually the first to be attacked by exogenous diseases, they are called the Delicate Organ. These diseases can also cause what is called the Non-Spreading of the Lung Chi. The main symptom of a problem with the Lungs is coughing, which is a form of Rebellious Chi (since the Lung Chi normally flows downward). If coughing is also accompanied by lassitude, shortness of breath, light foamy phlegm, and weakness in the voice, it is called Deficient Lung Chi. However, if the cough is a dry one, with little phlegm, a parched throat and mouth, and Deficient Yin symptoms (such as night sweating, low grade fever, red cheeks, etc.), the condition is referred as Deficient Lung Yin.

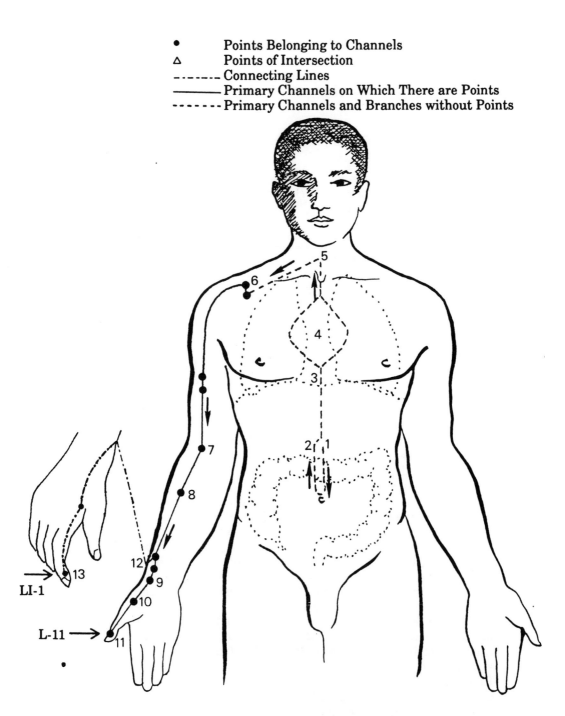

- Points Belonging to Channels
△ Points of Intersection
------- Connecting Lines
——— Primary Channels on Which There are Points
------- Primary Channels and Branches without Points

LI-1

L-11

Figure 16-1. The Lung Channel of Hand-Greater Yin

The Large Intestine Channel of Hand -- Yang Brightness (Figure 16-2)

1. Course:

Course #1:

(1). Index finger (Shangyang, LI-1) -- (2). Wrist -- (3). Elbow -- (4). Shoulder Joint -- (5). Governing vessel at Dazhui (Gv-14) -- (6). Supraclavicular Fossa (Quepen, S-12) -- (7). Lung -- (8). Diaphragm -- (9). Large Intestine.

Course #2:

(6). Supraclavicular fossa -- (10). Neck -- (11). Cheek -- (12). Lower Gum -- (13). Renzhong (Gv-26) -- (14). Side of the nose (Yingxiang, LI-20).

2. Related Viscera:

Large Intestine (Pertaining Organ), Lung, and Stomach.

3. Cavities:

Shangyang (LI-1), Erjian (LI-2), Sanjian (LI-3), Hegu (LI-4), Yangxi (LI-5), Pianli (LI-6), Wenliu (LI-7), Xianlian (LI-8), Shanglian (LI-9), Shousanli (LI-10), Quchi (LI-11), Zhouliao (LI-12), Hand-Wuli (LI-13), Binao (LI-14), Jianyu (LI-15), Jugu (LI-16), Tianding (LI-17), Futu (LI-18), Heliao (LI-19), and Yingxiang (LI-20).

4. Discussion:

The Lungs (Yin) and the Large Intestine (Yang) are considered paired Organs. From Table 15-1 you can see that they belong to Metal in the Five Phases, the westerly direction, the season of autumn, the dry climatic condition, the color white, the pungent taste, the rank odor, the emotion of sadness, and the sound of weeping. Their opening is the nose, and they govern skin and hair.

The main function of the Large Intestine is the metabolism of water and the passing of water. It extracts water from the waste material received from the Small Intestine, sends it on to the Urinary Bladder, and excretes the solid material as stool. Many disorders affecting this Organ are categorized as Spleen and Stomach patterns. Certain abdominal pains are considered manifestations of a blockage of Chi or blood in the Large Intestine.

In Chi Kung, the Dan Tien in the lower abdomen is considered the residence of Original Chi. In order to keep this Chi at its residence, this area must be strong and healthy. The Chi circulating around the Intestines must not be stagnant. When you practice Chi Kung you must learn how to regulate your breathing to smooth the Chi flow in the Large Intestine and the Lungs. This will allow you to relax the front of your body and regulate the Chi flow in the other organs.

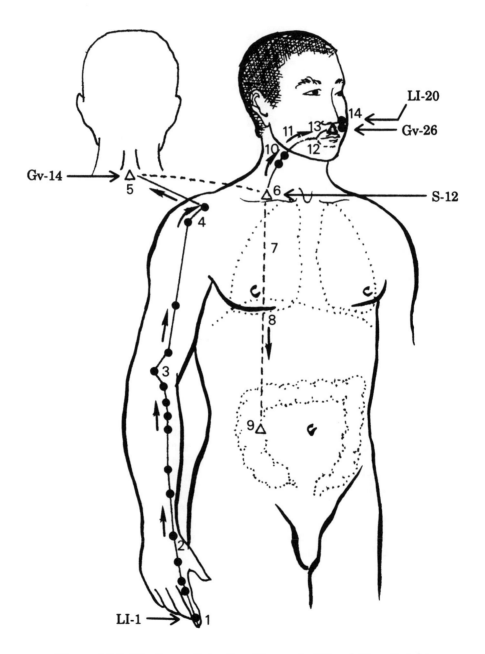

Figure 16-2. The Large Intestine Channel of Hand-Yang Brightness

The Stomach Channel of Foot -- Yang Brightness (Figure 16-3)

1. Course:

Course #1:

(1). Sides of the nose (Yingxiang, LI-20) -- (2). Root of the nose -- (3). Lateral side of the nose -- (4). Upper gum -- (5). Renzhong (Gv-26) -- (6). Chengjiang (Co-24) -- (7). Daying (S-5) -- (8). Jiache (S-6) -- (9). Ear -- (10). Hair line -- (11). Shenting (Gv-24).

Course #2:

(7). Daying (S-5) -- (12). Renying (S-9) -- (13). Throat -- (14). Into the chest -- (15). Through the diaphragm to Zhongwan (Co-12).

Course #3:

(16). Infraclavicular fossa -- (17). Along the sides of the umbilicus -- (18). Qichong (S-30). -- (19). Biguan (S-31) -- (20). Futu (S-32) -- (21). Dubi (S-35) -- (22). Lateral side of tibia -- (23). Dorsal aspect of the foot -- (24). Lateral side of the tip of the second toe (Lidui, S-45).

Course #4:

(25). Below the knee -- (26). Lateral side of the middle toe.

Course #5:

(27). Dorsum of the foot (Chongyang, S-42) -- (28). Along the medial margin of the hallus and emerges out at its tip (Yinbai, Sp-1).

2. Related Viscera:

Stomach (Pertaining Organ), Spleen, Heart, Small Intestine, and Large Intestine.

3. Cavities:

Chengqi (S-1), Sibai (S-2), Juliao (S-3), Dicang (S-4), Daying (S-5), Jiache (S-6), Xiaguan (S-7), Touwei (S-8), Renying (S-9), Shuitu (S-10), Qishe (S-11), Quepen (S-12), Qihu (S-13), Kufang (S-14), Wuyi (S-15), Yingchuang (S-16), Ruzhong (S-17), Rugen (S-18), Burong (S-19), Chengman (S-21), Liangmen (S-21), Guanmen (S-22), Taiyi (S-23), Huaroumen (S-24), Tianshu (S-25), Wailing (S-26), Daju (S-27), Shuidao (S-28), Guilai (S-29), Qichong (S-30), Biguan (S-31), Femur-Futu (S-32), Yinshi (S-33), Liangqiu (S-34), Dubi (S-35), Zusanli (S-36), Shangjuxu (S-37), Tiaokou (S-38), Xiajuxu (S-39), Fenglong (S-40), Jiexi (S-41), Chongyang (S-42), Xiangu (S-43), Neiting (S-44), Lidui (S-45).

4. Discussion:

The Spleen (Yin) and the Stomach (Yang) are paired Organs. They belong to Earth in the Five Phases, the central direction, the season of long summer (the end of summer), the climatic condition of dampness, the color yellow, the emotion of pensiveness, the taste of sweetness, fragrant odor and the sound of singing. Their opening is the mouth and they control the flesh and the limbs.

The Yin/Yang relationship between the Spleen and the Stomach is a particularly strong example of the relationship between organs. The Stomach receives food while the Spleen transports nutrients. The Stomach moves things downward while the Spleen moves things upward. The Stomach likes dampness while the Spleen likes dryness.

Though there are some patterns relating to Deficiency of the Stomach (many of these originate in the Spleen), most Stomach disorders are caused from Excess. Stomach Fire gives a painful, burning sensation in the Stomach, unusual hunger, bleeding of the gums, constipation, and halitosis.

The Stomach, which is located in the middle Sanjiao (Middle Triple Burner) area, is the first step in converting food into Chi. Food is dissolved in the Stomach before being sent to the Intestines for absorbing. The absorbed Essence is then converted into Chi and circulated through the entire body.

The Stomach is related to the emotion of pensiveness. When you are upset, the Stomach will not function normally. In Chi Kung, regulating the mind is the first step to maintaining the Stomach in a healthy condition. What food you eat is the second consideration. The proper amount and the proper quality of food will help you to obtain high quality Chi to circulate in your body.

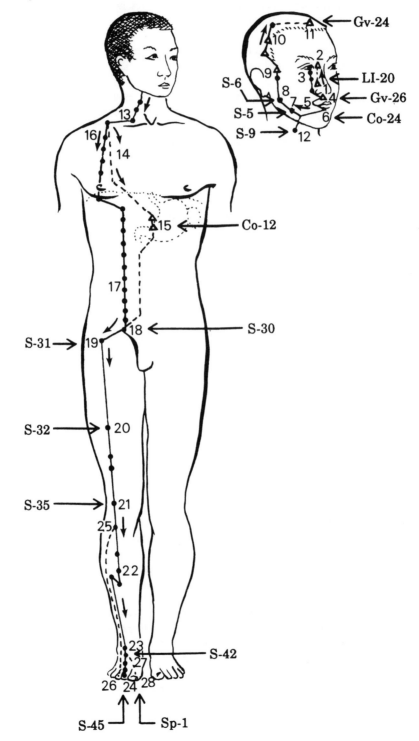

Figure 16-3. The Stomach Channel of Foot-Yang Brightness

The Spleen Channel of Foot -- Greater Yin (Figure 16-4)

1. Course:
Course #1:

(1). Medial tip of the big toe (Yinbai, Sp-1) -- (2). Anterior border of the medial malleolus -- (3). Along the posterior border of the tibia -- (4). Medial aspect of the leg -- (5). Medial aspect of the art. genus -- (6). Anterior medial aspect of the thigh -- (7). Enter the abdomen -- (8). Zhongji (Co-3) and Guanyuan (Co-4)-- (9). Pertains to the Spleen and communicates with the Stomach -- (10). Riyue (GB-24) and Qimen (Li-14) -- (11). Penetrates the diaphragm through Zhongfu (L-1) -- (12). Throat -- (13). Root of the tongue.

Course #2:

(9). Stomach -- (14). Through the diaphragm and disperses into the Heart.

2. Related Viscera:
Spleen (Pertaining Organ), Stomach, Heart, Lung, and Intestines.

3. Cavities:
Yinbai (Sp-1), Dadu (Sp-2), Taibai (Sp-3), Gongsun (Sp-4), Shangqiu (Sp-5), Sanyinjiao (Sp-6), Lougu (Sp-7), Diji (Sp-8), Yinlingquan (Sp-9), Xuehai (Sp-10), Jimen (Sp-11), Chongmen (Sp-12), Fushe (Sp-13), Fujie (Sp-14), Daheng (Sp-15), Fuai (Sp-16), Shidou (Sp-17), Tianxi (Sp-18), Xiongxiang (Sp-19), Zhourong (Sp-20), Dabao (Sp-21).

4. Discussion:
The Spleen (Yin) and the Stomach (Yang) are paired Organs. They belong to Earth in the Five Phases, the central direction, the season of long summer (the end of summer), the climatic condition of dampness, the color yellow, the emotion of pensiveness, the taste of sweetness, fragrant odor, and the sound of singing. Their opening is the mouth and they control the flesh and the limbs.

The Spleen is the main Organ of digestion. Its function is to transport nutrients and regulate the blood (regulate means to keep it within the channels). It is responsible for the transformation of food into nourishment.

When the Spleen is weak, the body will not be able to use the nourishment available in food. This will cause general lassitude and fatigue, and a pasty complexion. The upper abdomen is considered the province of the Spleen. Deficient Spleen Chi is shown by a sense of malaise or fullness in that area. Because it is required that the transportive function of the Spleen distribute its Chi upward, weakness in the Spleen will usually cause diarrhea. Spleen Chi is also regarded as the Middle Chi, and it is responsible for holding the Viscera in place. Insufficiency of the Middle Chi will presage prolapsed Stomach, Kidneys, etc. In more serious cases, the Spleen Yang Chi will be Deficient, which is manifested in diarrhea, cold limbs, and abdominal pain that can be soothed by the warmth of frequent hot drinks.

If many of the above symptoms are accompanied by bleeding, especially from the digestive tract or uterus, it is called Spleen Not Controlling the blood.

Cold and Dampness Harassing the Spleen is a manifestation type characterized by a pent-up feeling in the chest and a bloated sensation in the abdomen, lassitude, lack of appetite and taste, a feeling of cold in the limbs, a dark yellowish hue to the skin, some edema and diarrhea or watery stool. The Cold and Dampness prevent the Spleen from performing its transforming and transporting functions. This leads to a great disturbance in water metabolism and is one of the origins of Phlegm.

In Chi Kung training, one of the final goals is to regulate the Chi flow to its original (normal) level in the five Yin Organs. Among them, the Spleen is the last and the hardest organ to regulate. It is believed that if you are able to regulate the Chi in your Spleen to a normal and healthy condition, you will have grasped the key to health and longevity.

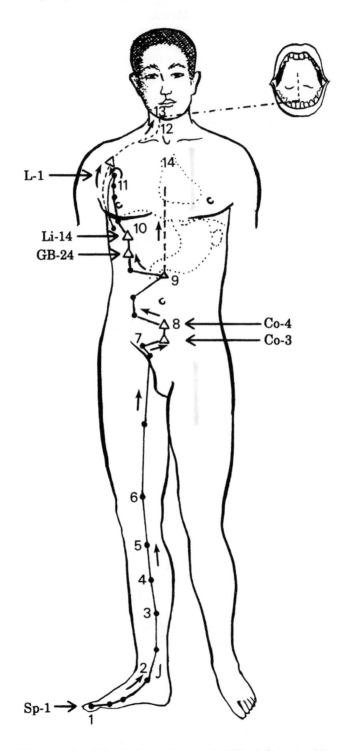

Figure 16-4. The Spleen Channel of Foot-Greater Yin

The Heart Channel of Hand -- Lesser Yin (Figure 16-5)

1. Course:
Course #1:
    (1). Heart -- (2). Lung -- (3). Below the axilla -- (4). Upper arm -- (5). Antecubital fossa -- (6). Between ossa metacarpal IV and V -- (7). Tip of the little finger (Shaochong, H-9).

Course #2:
    (1). Heart -- (8). Diaphragm -- (9). Small Intestine.

Course #3:
    (1). Heart -- (10). Throat -- (11). Tissues surrounding the eye.

2. Related Viscera:
    Heart (Pertaining Organ), Small Intestine, Lung, and Kidney.

3. Cavities:
    Jiquan (H-1), Qingling (H-2), Shaohai (H-3), Lingdao (H-4), Tongli (H-5), Yinxi (H-6), Shenmen (H-7), Shaofu (H-8), Shaochong (H-9).

4. Discussion:
The Heart and the Small Intestine are paired Organs. The Heart is considered Yin, and the Small Intestine is considered Yang, balancing this paired channel. These two organs correspond to Fire in the Five Phases, the southerly direction, the summer season, the climatic condition of heat, the color red, the emotion of happiness, the sound of laughter, the taste of bitterness, the odor of burning. Their point of entry is the tongue, they control the blood vessels and are reflected in the face.

Almost all of the problems and disorders of the Heart are associated with weakness. The four major types of Heart weakness are Deficient Heart Chi, Deficient Heart Yang, Deficient Heart Blood, and Deficient Heart Yin.

The main functions of the Heart are associated with the spirit and the blood vessels. The Heart governs the blood vessels and is responsible for moving blood through them. It also stores the spirit, and is the Organ usually associated with mental processes. Therefore, some forms of emotional distress, dizziness, palpitations, shortness of breath, and lack of vitality are common to the Heart's diseases. Deficient Heart Chi is symbolized by general lassitude, panting and shallow breathing, and frequent sweating. If the face is swollen to an ashen gray or bluish-green and the limbs are cold, it is called Deficient Heart Yang. The symptoms of restlessness, irritability, dizziness, absentmindedness, and insomnia are typical signs of Deficient Heart Blood. In Deficient Heart Yin cases, developments with a flushed feeling in the palms and face, low grade fever, and night sweating will occur.

The symptom of Heart Excess arises from an excess of Heart Fire. This is manifested by fever, occasionally accompanied by delirium, a racking pulse, intense restlessness, insomnia or frequent nightmares, a bright red face, a red or blistered and painful tongue, and often a burning sensation during urination. The latter symptom is the result of Heat being transferred from the Heart to the Small Intestine, which interferes with the Small Intestine's role in metabolism and the body's management of water.

In Chi Kung society, it is believed that the mind is associated with the Heart, and that it is also directly related to the spirit. As discussed in the third chapter, the term Heart (Hsin) is usually used to represent the emotional mind or idea. The Middle Dan Tien at the solar plexus is considered the residence of the Fire Chi. This Fire is used to nourish the brain and the spirit (Shen) at its residence, the Upper Dan Tien or third eye. In Chinese medicine it is said that the Heart is the temple of the spirit because it supplies Fire Chi and can nourish the spirit without limit.

Generally speaking, the Heart is very sensitive during the summertime. The Heart is a Yin channel, and when the summer Yang comes it can increase the Heart's Chi level and cause problems. Emotional disturbances, such as excitement from happiness, is considered harmful to the Heart as well, especially during the summertime. Chi Kung emphasizes regulating the Heart in the summer.

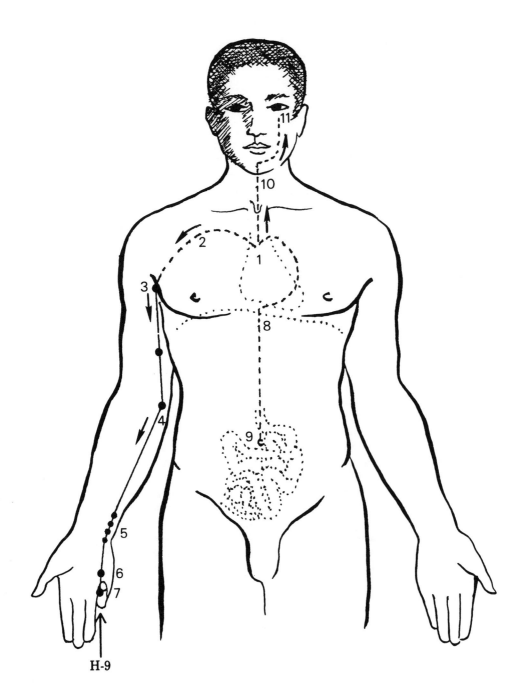

Figure 16-5. The Heart Channel of Hand-Lesser Yin

The Small Intestine Channel of Hand -- Greater Yang (Figure 16-6)

1. Course:
Course #1:
  (1). Tip of the digitus minimus (Shaoze, SI-1) -- (2). Wrist -- (3).
  top of elbow -- (4). Dorsal surface of the upper arm -- (5).
  Shoulder -- (6). Circle around the superior and inferior fossa of
  the scapula -- (7). Meets Dazhui (Gv-14) -- (8). Enters the
  supraclavicular fossa -- (9). Heart -- (10). Passes along the
  esophagus -- (11). Diaphragm -- (12). Stomach -- (13). Small
  Intestine.
Course #2:
  (8). Supraclavicular fossa -- (14). Neck -- (15). Cheek -- (16).
  Tongziliao (GB-1) -- (17). Into the ear.
Course #3:
  (18). Cheek -- (19). Jingming (B-1) -- (20). Distributes over
  zygoma obliquely.

2. Related Viscera:
  Small Intestine (Pertaining Organ), Heart, and Stomach.

3. Cavities:
  Shaoze (SI-1), Qiangu (SI-2), Houxi (SI-3), Hand-Wangu (SI-4),
  Yanggu (SI-5), Yanglao (SI-6), Zhizheng (SI-7), Xiaohai (SI-8),
  Jianzhen (SI-9), Naoshu (SI-10), Tianzong (SI-11), Bingfeng (SI-
  12), Quyuan (SI-13), Jianwaishu (SI-14), Jianzhongshu (SI-15),
  Tianchuang (SI-16), Tianrong (SI-17), Quanliao (SI-18),
  Tinggong (SI-19).

4. Discussion:
The Heart and the Small Intestine are paired Organs. The
Heart is considered Yin, and the Small Intestine is considered
Yang, balancing this paired channel. These two organs correspond
to Fire in the Five Phases, the southerly direction, the summer
season, the climatic condition of heat, the color red, the emotion of
happiness, the sound of laughter, the taste bitterness, the odor of
burning. Their point of entry is the tongue. They control the
blood vessels and are reflected in the face.

The major function of the Small Intestine is to separate waste
material from the nutritious elements in food. The nutritious
elements are then distributed throughout the body and the waste
is sent on to the Large Intestine.

The Small and Large Intestines are located in the Lower Dan
Tien. In order to store the Original Chi converted from Original
Essence, the abdomen must be healthy and the Chi circulation in
the area of the Intestines must be smooth and natural. The best
way to reach this goal is through abdominal breathing exercises.
One such exercise is to lead the Original Chi upward following the
Heart and Small Intestine Chi channels to cool down the Heart
Fire.

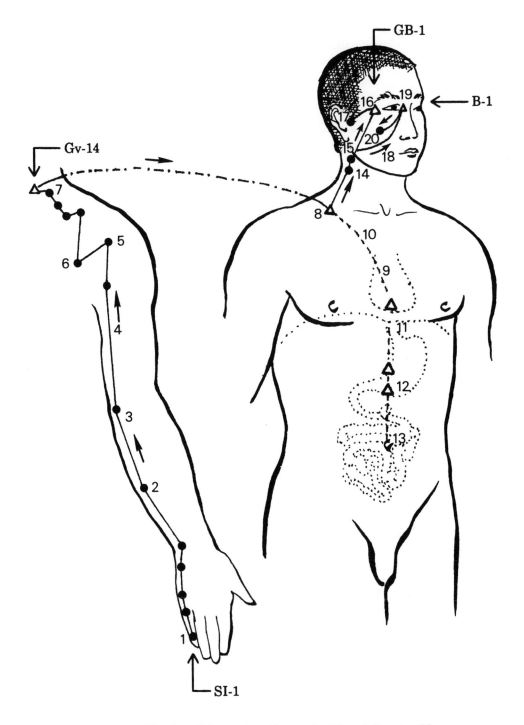

Figure 16-6. The Small Intestine Channel of Hand-Greater Yang

The Urinary Bladder Channel of Foot -- Greater Yang (Figure 16-7)

1. Course:
Course #1:

(1). Canthus medial -- (2). Shenting (Gv-24) -- (3). Baihui (Gv-20).

Course #2:

(3). Baihui (Gv-20) -- (4). Fubai (GB-10), Head-Qiaoyin (GB-11), and Wangu (Head-Wangu, GB-12), etc.

Course #3:

(3). Baihui (Gv-20) -- (5). Naohu (Gv-17) -- (6). Neck -- (7). Dazhui (Gv-14) and Taodao (Gv-13) -- (8). Lumber region -- (9). Kidney -- (10). Urinary Bladder.

Course #4:

(8). Lumbar region -- (11). Crosses the buttock -- (12). Popliteal fossa.

Course #5:

(6). Neck -- (13). Medial side of the scapula -- (14). Lumber region -- (15). Lateral side of the thigh -- (16). Popliteal fossa -- (17). M. gastrocnemius -- (18). Pushen (B-61)-- (19). The lateral side of the tip of the small toe (Zhiyin, B-67).

2. Related Viscera:
Urinary Bladder (Pertaining Organ), Kidney, Brain, and Heart.

3. Cavities:
Jingming (B-1), Zanzhu (B-2), Meichong (B-3), Quchai (B-4), Wuchu (B-5), Chengguang (B-6), Tongtian (B-7), Luogue (B-8), Yuzhen (B-9), Tianzhu (B-10), Dashu (B-11), Fengmen (B-12), Feishu (B-13), Jueyinshu (B-14), Xinshu (B-15), Dushu (B-16), Geshu (B-17), Ganshu (B-18), Danshu (B-19), Pishu (B-20), Weishu (B-21), Sanjiaoshu (B-22), Shenshu (B-23), Qihaishu (B-24), Dachangshu (B-25), Guanyuanshu (B-26), Xiaochangshu (B-27), Pangguanshu (B-28), Zhonglushu (B-29), Baihuanshu (B-30), Shangliao (B-31), Ciliao (B-32), Zhongliao (B-33), Xialiao (B-34), Huiyang (B-35), Fufen (B-36), Pohu (B-37), Gaohuangshu (B-38), Shentang (B-39), Yixi (B-40), Geguan (B-41), Hunmen (B-42), Yanggang (B-43), Yishe (B-44), Weicang (B-45), Huangmen (B-46), Zhishi (B-47), Baohuang (B-48), Zhibian (B-49), Chengfu (B-50), Yinmen (B-51), Fuxi (B-52), Weiyang (B-53), Weizhong (B-54), Heyang (B-55), Chengjin (B-56), Chengshan (B-57), Feiyang (B-58), Fuyang (B-59), Kunlun (B-60), Pushen (B-61), Shenmai (B-62), Jinmen (B-63), Jinggu (B-64), Shugu (B-65), Foot-Tonggu (B-66), and Zhiyin (B-67).

4. Discussion:
The Kidneys (Yin) and the Urinary Bladder (Yang) are paired Organs. They correspond to Water in the Five Phases, the winter season, the cold climatic condition, the southerly direction, the color black, the emotion of fear, the taste of salt, a rotten smell, and the sound of groaning. Their sensory organ is the ear. Their opening is the urethra. They control the bones, marrow, and brain, and their health is reflected in the hair of the head.

The main function of the Urinary Bladder is to transform fluids into urine and excrete it from the body.

In Chi Kung, the Urinary Bladder has never enjoyed serious attention. However, its pairing partner the Kidney is one of the most important organs -- one with which all Chi Kung practitioners are concerned and train most often. The reason for this is simply that the Kidneys are the residence of the Original Essence.

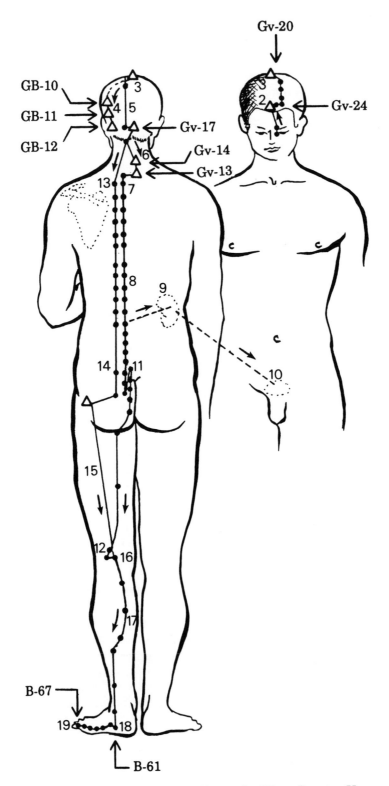

Figure 16-7. The Urinary Bladder Channel of Foot-Greater Yang

The Kidney Channel of Foot -- Lesser Yin (Figure 16-8)

1. Course:
Course #1:
> (1). Small toe -- (2). Inferior aspect of the navicular tuberosity (Rangu, K-2) -- (3). Behind the malleolus medialis -- (4). Spreads to the heel -- (5). M. gastrocnemius -- (6). Medial side of the popliteal fossa -- (7). Posterior aspect of the thigh -- (8). Enters Kidney -- (9). Communicates with the Urinary Bladder -- (10). Guanyuan (Co-4) and Zhongji (Co-3).

Course #2:
> (9). Kidney -- (11). Liver and diaphragm -- (12). Enters the Lung -- (13). Along the throat -- (14). Root of the tongue.

Course #3:
> (12). Lung -- (15). Heart and spreads to the chest.

2. Related Viscera:
> Kidney (Pertaining Organ), Urinary Bladder, Liver, Lung, Heart, and other organs.

3. Cavities:
> Yongquan (K-1), Rangu (K-2), Taixi (K-3), Dazhong (K-4), Shuiquan (K-5), Zhaohai (K-6), Fuliu (K-7), Jiaoxin (K-8), Zhubin (K-9), Yingu (K-10), Henggu (K-11), Dahe (K-12), Qixue (K-13), Siman (K-14), Abdomen-Zhongzhu (K-15), Huangshu (K-16), Shangqu (K-17), Shiguan (K-18), Yindu (K-19), Abdomen-Tonggu (K-20), Youmen (K-21), Bulang (K-22), Shenfeng (K-23), Lingxu (K-24), Shencang (K-25), Yuzhong (K-26), and Shufu (K-27).

4. Discussion:

The Kidneys (Yin) and the Urinary Bladder (Yang) are paired Organs. They correspond to Water in the Five Phases, the winter season, the cold climatic condition, the southerly direction, the color black, the emotion of fear, the taste of salt, a rotten smell, and the sound of groaning. Their sensory organ is the ear. Their opening is the urethra. They control the bones, marrow, and brain, and their health is reflected in the hair of the head.

The Kidneys store Original Essence (Yuan Jieng) and are therefore responsible for growth, development, and reproductive functions. They play the primary role in water metabolism and control the body's liquids, and also hold the body's most fundamental Yin and Yang.

Because the Kidneys are the repositories of the basal Yin and Yang of the body, any disorder, if sufficiently chronic, will involve the Kidneys. More significantly, a disease of the Kidneys will usually lead to problems in other Organs. Methods of strengthening the Kidneys are therefore used by both medical and Chi Kung societies to increase or maintain vitality and health. The symptoms of Deficient Kidney Yang or Yin are typical symptoms of the disorder, and will appear to a certain extent as Deficient Yang or Yin patterns in any Organ.

It is easy to understand and memorize the symptoms of Deficient Kidney Yin if one learns the correspondences of the Kidneys and remembers that Yin represents the constructive, nourishing, and fluid aspects of the body. Usually, the lower back is weak and sore, there is ringing in the ears and loss of hearing acuity, the face is ashen or dark, especially under the eyes. It is common to feel dizziness and thirst, and to experience night sweats and low grade fevers. In addition, men have little semen and tend toward premature ejaculation, while women have little or no menstruation.

Deficient Kidney Yang symptoms are significantly associated with loss of energy or warmth. Similar to Deficient Kidney Yin, there is commonly ringing in the ears, dizziness, and soreness in the lower back. However, the soreness is characterized by a feeling of coldness, lassitude, and fatigue. Weakness in the legs can be noticed. In men, there is a tendency toward impotence, and in both sexes, clear and voluminous urine or incontinence.

Usually, Deficient Kidney Yin generates similar disorders in the Heart and Liver, while Deficient Kidney Yang disturbs the functions of the Spleen and Lungs. The progression could be in the opposite direction. When this pattern is associated with the Lungs, it is called "Kidney Not Receiving Chi," a type of wheezing characterized by difficult breathing, mainly during inhalation. In addition to the Deficient Kidney Yang symptoms, this condition is also manifested by a faint voice, coughing, puffiness in the face, and spontaneous sweating.

The Kidneys perform an important role in the metabolism of water. If these functions are disrupted, the condition of Deficient Kidneys will lead to Spreading Water.

In Chi Kung practice, Essence (Jieng) is considered the most original source of human vitality. Chi is converted from Essence, and this Chi supplies the entire body and nourishes the brain and spirit. It is believed by both Chinese medical and Chi Kung societies that the Kidneys are the residence of Original Essence. In order to protect your inherent Essence, you must strengthen your Kidneys. Only when your Kidneys are strong will you be able to keep your Essence at its residence. Therefore, keeping the Kidneys healthy has become one of the most important subjects in Chi Kung.

Maintaining the Kidneys in a healthy state includes protecting the physical kidneys from degeneration, and maintaining a smooth and correct level of Chi flow. In order to reach this goal, the diet must be considered. For example, too much salt is harmful to the Kidneys. Eating too much eggplant will weaken the Kidneys. In addition, the condition of the body is also important. Such things as over-working without proper rest will increase tension on the Kidneys and make the Chi flow stagnant. In winter, the Kidneys will have more tension than in summer. Due to this, the Chi flow is more stagnant in the wintertime than in the summertime. Therefore, back pain problems increase in the winter.

In order to protect the Kidneys, Chi Kung practitioners have studied the relationship of the Kidneys to nature, food, and even to emotional states. They have developed massage techniques and specific exercises to increase Chi circulation in the Kidneys during the winter. Since the health of the Kidneys is related to the emotions as well, learning how to regulate the mind in order to regulate the Chi has become one of the major training methods in Chi Kung.

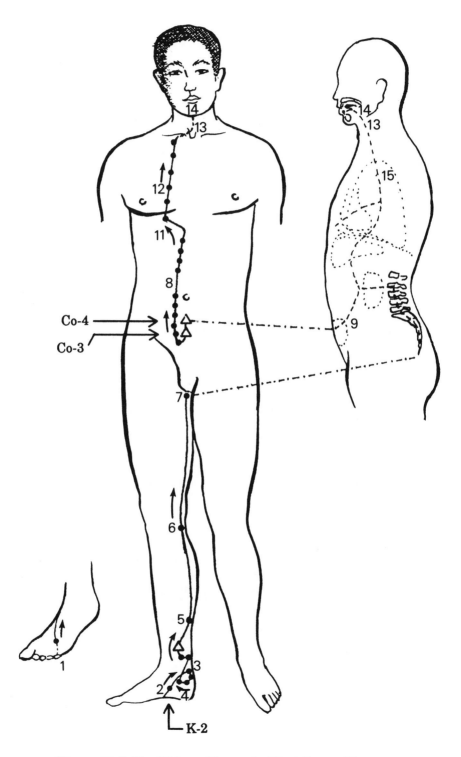

Figure 16-8. The Kidney Channel of Foot-Lesser Yang

The Pericardium Channel of Hand -- Absolute Yin (Figure 16-9)

1. Course:

Course #1:

(1). Pericardium -- (2). Below the armpit -- (3). Axilla -- (4). Forearm -- (5). Wrist -- (6). Palm -- (7). Tip of middle finger (Zhongchong, P-9).

Course #2:

(1). Pericardium -- (8). Diaphragm -- (9). Connects Triple Burner (Sanjiao).

Course #3:

(6). Palm (Laogong, P-8) -- (10). Tip of ring finger (Guanchong, TB-1).

2. Related Viscera:

Pericardium (Pertaining Organ) and Triple Burner (Sanjiao).

3. Cavities:

Tianchi (P-1), Tianquan (P-2), Quze (P-3), Ximen (P-4), Jianshi (P-5), Neiguan (P-6), Daling (P-7), Laogong (P-8), and Zhongchong (P-9).

4. Discussion:

The Pericardium (Yin) and the Triple Burner (Yang) are paired Organs. They are said to correspond to the "Ministerial Fire," as opposed to the "Sovereign Fire" of the Heart and Small Intestine. Though the Pericardium has no separate physiological functions, it is generally mentioned with regard to the delirium induced by high fevers.

The regulation of Chi in the Pericardium is considered a very important subject in Chi Kung. It is believed that the Heart, the most vital organ in your body, must have a proper level of Chi circulation in order to function normally. The Chi level of the Heart can be raised easily to an abnormal state by illness, emotional disturbance, exercise, or injury. The function of the Pericardium is to dissipate the excess Chi from the Heart and direct it to the Laogong cavity (P-8), located in the center of the palm. From Laogong, the excess Chi will be released naturally and hence, regulate the Heart's Chi level. The Laogong cavity is used in Chi Kung massage to reduce the body's temperature during a fever. You can see that the purpose of the Pericardium is to regulate the Chi in the Heart through the Laogong cavity.

You should understand that in Chi Kung it is believed that there are five centers (called gates) where the Chi of the body is able to communicate with the surrounding environment, and, consequently, regulate the Chi level in your body. Two of these five centers are the Laogong cavities, and two others are Yongquan (K-1), used to regulate the Chi in the Kidneys. The fifth one is your face. The face is connected and related to many of your organs. Whenever any of your organ Chi is not normal, it shows on your face.

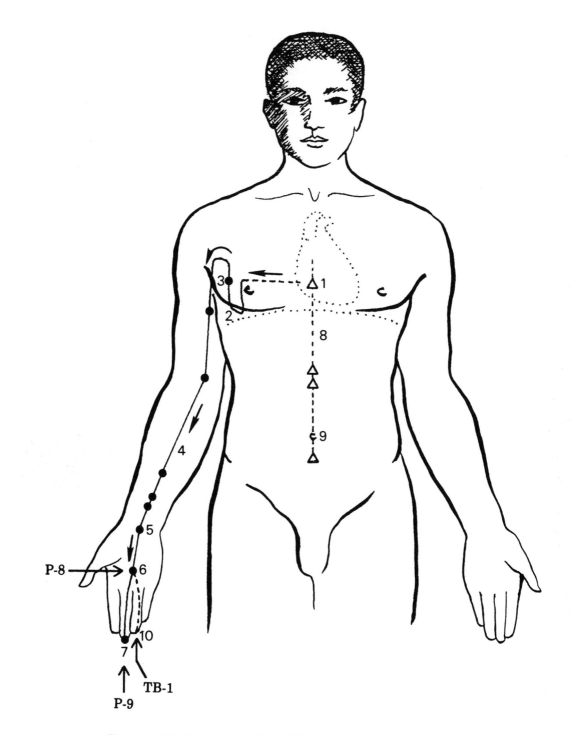

Figure 16-9. The Pericardium Channel of Hand-Absolute Yin

The Triple Burner Channel of Hand -- Lesser Yang (Figure 16-10)

1. Course:
Course #1:
   (1). Tip of the ring finger (Guanchong, TB-1) -- (2). Between the ossa metacarpal IV and V -- (3). Wrist -- (4). Dorsal side of the forearm -- (5). Passing the olecranon -- (6). Lateral aspect of the upper arm -- (7). Shoulder -- (8). Jianjing (GB-21) -- (9). Enters the supraclavicular fossa -- (10). Branches out in the chest, communicating with the pericardium -- (11). Diaphragm -- (12). Links successively the upper, middle, and lower portions of the body cavity.
Course #2:
   (10). Shanzhong (Co-17) -- (13). Supraclavicular fossa -- (14). Neck -- (15). Dazhui (Gv-14) -- (16). Posterior border of the ear -- (17). Xuanli (GB-6) and Hanyan (GB-4) -- (18). Quanliao (SI-18).
Course #3:
   (19). Retro-auricular region where it enters the ear -- (20). Emerges in front of the ear -- (21). Lateral canthus.

2. Related Viscera:
   It pertains to the upper, middle and lower portions of the body cavity (Sanjiao) and communicates with the Pericardium.

3. Cavities:
   Guanchong (TB-1), Yemen (TB-2), Hand-Zhongzhu (TB-3), Yangchi (TB-4), Waiguan (TB-5), Zhigou (TB-6), Huizong (TB-7), Sanyangluo (TB-8), Sidu (TB-9), Tianjing (TB-10), Qinglengyuan (TB-11), Xiaoluo (TB-12), Naohui (TB-13), Jianliao (TB-14), Tianliao (TB-15), Tianyou (TB-16), Yifeng (TB-17), Qimai (TB-18), Luxi (TB-19), Jiaosun (TB-20), Ermen (TB-21), Ear-Heliao (TB-22), and Sizhukong (TB-23).

4. Discussion:
   At least as far back as the 3rd century A.D., in the "Classic of Difficulties" (Nan Ching) the Triple Burner was regarded as "having a name but no form." In the "Inner Classic" (Nei Ching), the Triple Burner was considered an Organ that coordinated all the functions of water metabolism. In other traditional documents, the Burners were considered three regions of the body that were used to group the Organs. The Upper Burner includes the chest, neck, and head as well as the functions of the Heart and Lungs. The Middle Burner is the region between the chest and the navel, and includes the functions of the Stomach, Liver, and Spleen. The Lower Burner spans the lower abdomen, and the functions of the Kidneys and Urinary Bladder. Therefore, the Upper Burner has been compared to a mist which spreads the blood and Chi, the Middle Burner is like a foam which churns up food in the process of digestion, and the Lower Burner resembles a swamp where all the impure substances are excreted.
   Regulating the Chi to a normally "smooth-flow" state is one of the main Chi Kung training methods for maintaining health. It is normally done through Wai Dan exercises, and it is believed that the Chi must flow around internal organs smoothly in order for them to maintain their normal functions. This means that in order to keep Chi flow smooth and the organs healthy, you must first learn how to regulate and relax muscles that are holding and related to a given organ. External movements also exercise internal muscles. One of the most common external exercises is regulating the Triple Burner by

lifting your hands up above your head and then moving them down slowly. These up and down arm movements extend and relax the internal muscles and therefore increase Chi flow.

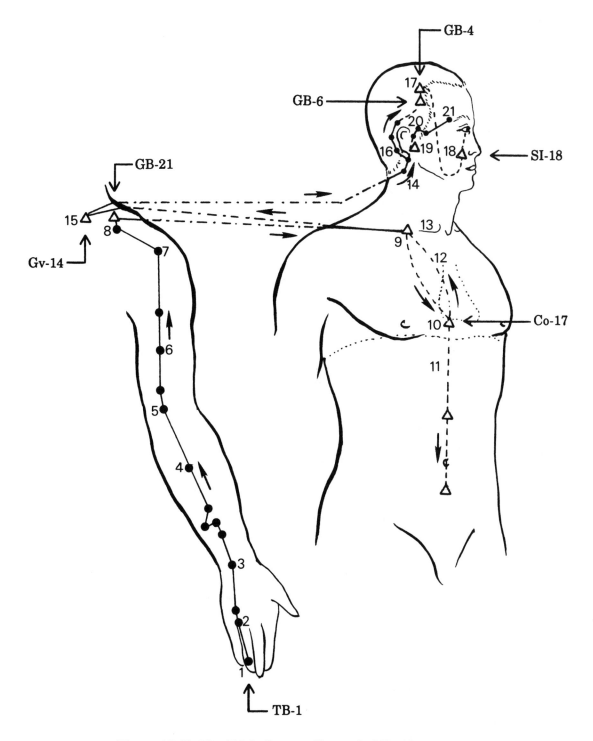

Figure 16-10. The Triple Burner Channel of Hand-Lesser Yang

The Gall Bladder Channel of Foot -- Lesser Yang (Figure 16-11)

1. Course:

Course #1:

    (1). Outer canthus of the eye (Tongziliao, GB-1) -- (2). Nose-Heliao (TB-22) -- (3). Jiaosun (TB-20) -- (4). Dazhui (Gv-14) -- (5). Enters the supraclavicular fossa.

Course #2:

    (6). Retro-auricular region, passes through Yifeng (TB-17) -- (7). Tinggong (SI-19) and Xiaguan (S-7).

Course #3:

    (1). Outer canthus of the eye -- (8). Daying (S-5) -- (9). Infraorbital region -- (10). Jiache (S-6) -- (11). Supraclavicular fossa -- (12). Into the chest -- (13). Tianchi (P-1) -- (14). Communicates with the Liver -- (15). Pertains to the Gall Bladder -- (16). Inside of the hypochondrium -- (17). Around the pubes -- (18). Hip (Huantiao, GB-30).

Course #4:

    (19). Supraclavicular fossa -- (20). Axilla -- (21). Lateral aspect of the chest -- (22). Through the hypochondrium -- (23). Zhangmen (Li-13) -- (24). Along the lateral aspect of thigh -- (25). Knee -- (26). Anterior aspect of the fibula -- (27). Anterior aspect of the malleolus -- (28). Lateral side of the tip of the 4th toe or Zuqiaoyin (GB-44).

Course #5:

    (29). Dorsum of the foot (Linqi, GB-41) -- (30). Big toe (Dadun, Li-1).

2. Related Viscera:

Gall Bladder (Pertaining Organ), Liver, and Heart.

3. Cavities:

Tongziliao (GB-1), Tinghui (GB-2), Shangguan (GB-3), Hanyan (GB-4), Xuanlu (GB-5), Xuanli (GB-6), Qubin (GB-7), Shuaigu (GB-8), Tianchong (GB-9), Fubai (GB-10), Head-Qiaoyin (GB-11), Head-Wangu (GB-12), Benshen (GB-13), Yangbai (GB-14), Head-Linqi (GB-15), Muchuang (GB-16), Zhengying (GB-17), Chengling (GB-18), Naokong (GB-19), Fengchi (GB-20), Jianjing (GB-21), Yuanye (GB-22), Zhejin (GB-23), Riyue (GB-24), Jingmen (GB-25), Daimai (GB-26), Wushu (GB-27), Weidao (GB-28), Femur-Juliao (GB-29), Huantiao (GB-30), Fengshi (GB-31), Femur-Zhongdu (GB-32), Xiyangguan (GB-33), Yanglingquan (GB-34), Yangjiao (GB-35), Waiqiu (GB-36), Guangming (GB-37), Yangfu (GB-38), Xuanzhong (GB-39), Qiuxu (GB-40), Foot-Linqi (GB-41), Diwuhui (GB-42), Xiaxi (GB-43), Foot-Qiaoyin (GB-44).

4. Discussion:

    The Liver (Yin) and the Gall Bladder (Yang) are paired Organs. They correspond to Wood in the Five Phases, the direction east, the spring season, the climatic wind, the color green, the emotion of anger, the taste of sour, the odor goatish, and the sound of shouting. Their point of entry is the eyes. They control the sinews (muscles and joints), and their health is reflected in the finger and toe nails.

    The main function of the Gall Bladder is storing and excreting the gall produced by the Liver. Together with the Heart, the Gall Bladder is responsible for decision-making.

    The main disease related to the Gall Bladder is a disorder affecting the flow of gall, usually caused by Dampness and Heat. This is commonly manifested by pain in the region of the Liver, an oppressive sensation of fullness in the abdomen, and yellowish eyes, skin, urine, and tongue.

The Gall Bladder has never enjoyed serious attention during Chi Kung training. Its paired partner the Liver however, has received much more attention.

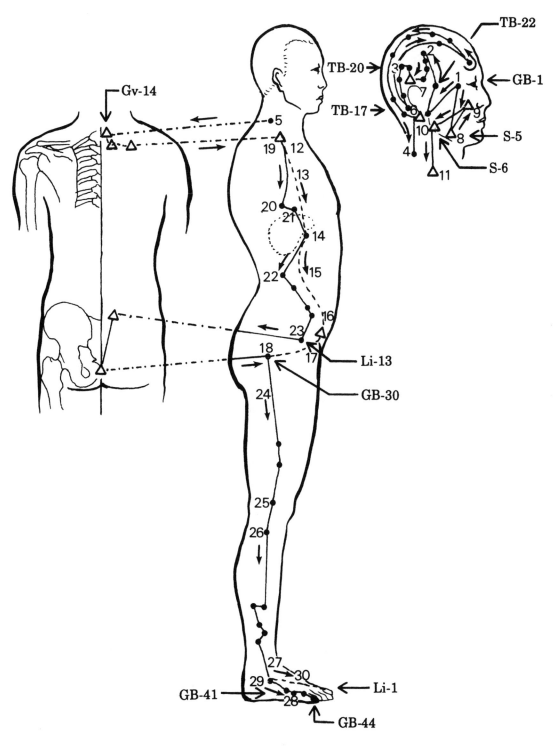

Figure 16-11. The Gall Bladder Channel of Foot-Lesser Yang

The Liver Channel of Foot -- Absolute Yin (Figure 16-12)

1. Course:
Course #1:
 (1). Behind the nail of the big toe -- (2). Malleolus medialis --
 (3). Sanyinjiao (Sp-6) -- (4). Side of shin -- (5). Side of knee --
 (6). Medial aspect of the thigh -- (7). Chongmen (Sp-12) and
 Fushe (Sp-13) -- (8). Pubic region -- (9). Lower abdomen --
 (10). Qugu (Co-2), Zhongli (Co-3), and Guanyuan (Co-4) -- (11).
 Liver -- (12). Lower chest -- (13). Neck posterior -- (14). Upper
 palate -- (15). Tissues of the eye -- (16). Forehead -- (17).
 Vertex.
Course #2:
 (15). Eye -- (18). Cheek -- (19). Curves around the inner surface
 of the lips.
Course #3:
 (20). Liver -- (21). Through diaphragm -- (22). Lung.

2. Related Viscera:
 Liver (Pertaining Organ), Gall Bladder, Lung, Stomach, and
 brain.

3. Cavities:
 Dadun (L-1), Xingjian (L-2), Taichong (L-3), Zhongfeng (L-4),
 Ligou (L-5), Tibia-Zhongdu (L-6), Xiguan (L-7), Ququan (L-8),
 Yinbao (L-9), Femur-Wuli (L-10), Yinlian (L-11), Jimai (L-12),
 Zhangmen (L-13), and Qimen (L-14).

4. Discussion:
 The Liver (Yin) and the Gall Bladder (Yang) are considered
paired Organs. They correspond to Wood in the Five Phases, the
direction east, the spring season, the climatic of wind, the color
of green, the emotion of anger, the taste of sour, the odor goatish,
and the sound of shouting. Their point of entry is the eyes. They
control the sinews (muscles and joints), and their health is
reflected in the finger and toe nails.

 The main task of the Liver is spreading and regulating Chi
throughout the entire body. Its unique character is flowing and
free. Therefore, depression or frustration can disturb the
functioning of the Liver. In addition, the Liver is also
responsible for storing blood when the body is at rest. This
characteristic, together with its control over the lower abdomen,
makes it the most critical Organ in regards to women's
menstrual cycle and sexuality.

 Depression or long-term frustration can stagnate the Liver's
spreading function and result in continuing depression, a bad
temper, and a painful, swollen feeling in the chest and sides. If
this condition worsens, it may cause disharmony between the
Liver and the Stomach and/or Spleen. This disorder is
symbolized by the "rebellion" of Chi in the latter Organs,
whereby Chi moves in the opposite direction than is normal. For
example, the Stomach Chi normally descends, so rebellious Chi
means hiccoughing, vomiting, etc. In the case of the Spleen, the
Chi ordinarily moves upward, so rebellious Chi in this Organ
means diarrhea.

 Depression of the Liver Chi is the main cause of many women's
disorders, including menstrual irregularities, swollen and
painful breasts, etc.

One of the most important responsibilities of the Liver is the storage of blood with intended emphasis upon nourishing and moistening. Whenever the Liver blood is deficient, the Liver will not be able to handle the function of moistening. This is generally shown as dry and painful eyes with blurred or weak vision, lack of suppleness or pain in moving the joints, dry skin, dizziness, and infrequent or spotty menstruation. If the Deficient Liver Yin has become serious, the conditions Rising Liver Fire or Hyper Liver Yang Ascending occur. These occurrences are evidenced in ill-temper, restlessness, headache, vertigo, red face and eyes, and a parched mouth. If the Liver Yin is so deficient that it is incapable of securing the Liver Yang, many of the symptoms appear as disorders of the head. Weakness in the lower joints may also be manifested.

The Liver is one of the five Yin Organs whose Chi level the Chi Kung practitioner wants to regulate. Since the Liver and the Gall Bladder are directly connected, when the Liver's Chi is regulated, the Chi circulating in the Gall Bladder will also be regulated. Many methods have been developed for regulating the Liver Chi. Wai Dan Chi Kung works through the limbs. For example, when the arms are moved up and down, the internal muscles surrounding the Liver will be moved and the Chi around the Liver will be circulated smoothly. In Nei Dan Chi Kung, it is believed that the Liver is closely related to your mind. It is also believed that when your mind is regulated, the Chi circulation in the Liver will be normal and therefore the Liver will function properly.

16-3. Important Points

1. The Spleen, Liver, and Heart are the Organs with the most direct relationship with the blood. The Spleen filters the blood (modifying the blood's structure), the Liver stores the blood, and the Heart moves it. Any problem associated with the blood will involve at least one of these Organs.

2. The Liver and the Kidney are closely related. Their channels cross in many places. The Liver stores blood; the Kidney stores Essence. These substances, both of which are Yin, have a considerable influence on the reproductive functions.

3. The Heart (Upper Burner, Fire) and the Kidney (Lower Burner, Water) keep each other in check and are dependent upon one another. The spirit of the Heart and the Essence of the Kidneys cooperate in establishing and maintaining human consciousness.

4. The Spleen's digestive function is associated with the distributive functions of the Liver. Disharmony between these two results in various digestive troubles. The transportive and digestive functions of the Spleen (also called the Middle Chi) depend upon the strength of the Kidney Yang.

5. Although the Lungs govern Chi, Chi from the Lung must mix with Essence from the Kidneys before Original Chi can be produced. The Lungs govern Chi, the Liver spreads Chi, and the Kidneys provide its basis.

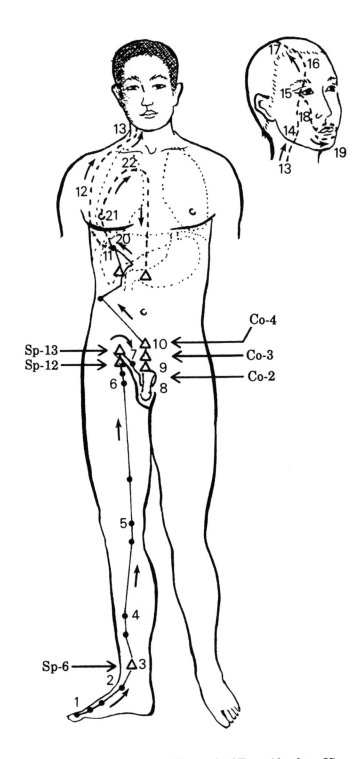

Figure 16-12. The Liver Channel of Foot-Absolute Yin

Chapter 17

The Eight Extraordinary Chi Vessels

17-1. Introduction

The eight extraordinary Chi vessels and the twelve primary Chi channels (meridians) comprise the main part of the channel system. Most of the eight vessels branch out from the twelve primary channels and share the function of circulating Chi throughout the body. These vessels form a web of complex interconnections with the channels. At the same time, each has its own functional characteristics and clinic utility independent of the channels.

Traditional Chinese medicine emphasizes the twelve primary organ-related channels and only two of the eight vessels (the Governing and the Conception vessels). The other six vessels are not used very often simply because they are not understood as well as the other channels, and there is still a lot of research being conducted on them. Although they were discovered two thousand years ago, little has been written about them. There is a lot of research on the extraordinary vessels being conducted today, especially in Japan, but the results of one researcher often contradict the results that another has achieved.

In this section we would like to compile and summarize the important points from the limited number of available documents. Since references from original Chinese sources are very scarce, and references from Western textbooks are tentative, esoteric, or in disagreement with one another, I have used my own judgement in selecting ideas and details.

What are the Eight Vessels?

The eight vessels are called "Chyi Ching Ba Mei." Chi means odd, strange, or mysterious. Ching means meridian or channels. Ba means eight and Mei means vessels. Chyi Ching Ba Mei is then translated as "Odd Meridians and Eight Vessels" or "extraordinary meridian (EM)." Odd has a meaning of strange in Chinese. It is used simply because these eight vessels are not well understood yet. Many Chinese doctors explain that they are called "Odd" simply because there are four vessels that are not paired. Since these eight vessels also serve the function of homeostasis, sometimes they are called "Homeostatic Meridians." French acupuncturists call them "Miraculous Meridians" because they were able to create therapeutic effects when all other techniques had failed. In addition, because each of these channels exerts a strong effect upon psychic functioning and individuality, the command points are among the most important psychological points in the body. For this reason, they are occasionally called "The Eight Psychic Channels."

These vessels are: 1. Governing Vessel (Du Mei); 2. Conception Vessel (Ren Mei); 3. Thrusting Vessel (Chong Mei); 4. Girdle Vessel (Dai Mei); 5. Yang Heel Vessel (Yangchiao Mei); 6. Yin Heel Vessel (Yinchiao Mei); 7. Yang Linking Vessel (Yangwei Mei); and 8. Yin Linking Vessel (Yinwei Mei).

History:

The first brief mention of some of these eight vessels is found in the second part of the Nei Ching chapter of the book "Hwang Dih Nei Ching Suh Wenn" (The Yellow Emperor's Classic)(Han dynasty, circa 100-300 B.C.) by Ling Shu. Also, some of the vessels were mentioned in Bian Chiueh's classic "Nan Ching" (Classic of Difficulties) (Chin and Han dynasty, 221 B.C. to 220 A.D.). It was not until the 16th century that all eight vessels were deeply studied by Li Shyr-Jen (1518-1593 A.D.) and revealed in his book "Chyi Ching Ba Mei Kao" (Deep Study of the Extraordinary Eight Vessels). From then until only recently, very few documents have been published on this subject. Although there is more research being published in the last few years, there is still no single document which is able to define this subject systematically and in-depth.

General Functions of the Eight Vessels:
A. Serve as Chi Reservoirs:

Because the eight vessels are so different from each other, it is difficult to generalize their characteristics and functions. However, one of the most common characteristics of the eight vessels was specified by Bian Chiueh in his "Nan Ching." He reported that **THE TWELVE ORGAN-RELATED CHI CHANNELS CONSTITUTE RIVERS, AND THE EIGHT EXTRAORDINARY VESSELS CONSTITUTE RESERVOIRS.** The reservoirs, especially the Conception and Governing vessels, absorb excess Chi from the main channels, and then return it when they are deficient.

You should understand however, that because of the limited number of traditional documents, as well as the lack of modern, scientific methods of Chi research, it is difficult to determine the precise behavior and characteristics of these eight vessels. The main difficulty probably lies in the fact that they can be taken at different levels, because they perform different functions and contain every kind of Chi such as Ying Chi, Wey Chi, Jieng Chi, and even blood.

When the twelve primary channels are deficient in Chi, the eight vessels will supply it. This store of Chi can easily be tapped with acupuncture needles through those cavities which connect the eight vessels with the twelve channels. The connection cavities behave like the gate of a reservoir, which can be used to adjust the strength of the Chi flow in the rivers and the level of Chi in the reservoir. Sometimes, when it is necessary, the reservoir will release Chi by itself. For example, when a person has had a shock, either physically or mentally, the Chi in some of the main channels will be deficient. This will cause particular organs to be stressed, and Chi will accumulate rapidly around these organs. When this happens, the reservoir must release Chi to increase the deficient circulation and prevent further damage.

B. Guarding Specific Areas Against 'Evil Chi':

The Chi which protects the body from outside intruders is called "Wey Chi" (Guardian Chi). Among the eight vessels, the Thrusting vessel, the Governing vessel, and the Conception vessel play major roles in guarding the abdomen, thorax, and the back.

C. Regulating the Changes of Life Cycles:

According to Chapter 1 of "Su Wen," the Thrusting vessel and the Conception vessel also regulate the changes of the life cycles which occur at 7 year intervals for women and 8 year intervals for men.

D. Circulating Jieng Chi to the Entire Body, Particularly the Five 'Ancestral Organs':

One of the most important functions of the eight vessels is to deliver Jieng Chi (Essence Chi, which has been converted from Original Essence and sexual Essence) to the entire body, including the skin and hair. They must also deliver Jieng Chi to the five ancestral organs: the brain and spinal cord, the liver and gall bladder system, the bone marrow, the uterus, and the blood system.

17-2. The Eight Extraordinary Vessels

The Governing Vessel (Du Mei)(Figure 17-1)

1. Course:

Course #1:

(1). Perineum -- (2). Along the middle of the spine -- (3). Fengfu (Gv-16) -- (4). Enters the brain -- (5). Vertex -- (6). Midline of the forehead across the bridge of the nose -- (7). Upper lip.

Course #2:

(8). Pelvic region -- (9). Descends to the genitals and perineum -- (10). Tip of the coccyx -- (11). Gluteal region (intersects the Kidney and Urinary Bladder channels) -- (12). Returns to the spinal column and then joins with the Kidneys.

Course #3:

(13). Inner canthus of the eye -- (14). Two (bilateral) branches, ascend across the forehead -- (15). Converge at the vertex (enters the brain) -- (16). Emerges at the lower end of the nape of the neck -- (17). Divides into two branches which descend along opposite sides of the spine to the waist -- (18). Kidneys.

Course #4.

(19). Lower abdomen -- (20). Across the navel -- (21). Passes through the Heart -- (22). Enters the trachea -- (23). Crosses the cheek and encircles the mouth -- (24). Terminates at a point below the middle of the eye.

***This vessel intersects Fengmen (B-12) and Huiyin (Co-1).

2. Cavities:

Changqiang (Gv-1), Yaoshu (Gv-2), Yaoyangguan (Gv-3), Mingmen (Gv-4), Xuanshu (Gv-5), Jizhong (Gv-6), Zhongshu (Gv-7), Jinsuo (Gv-8), Zhiyang (Gv-9), Lingtai (Gv-10), Shendao (Gv-11), Shenzhu (Gv-12), Taodao (Gv-13), Dazhui (Gv-14), Yamen (Gv-15), Fengfu (Gv-16), Naohu (Gv-17), Qiangjian (Gv-18), Houding (Gv-19), Baihui (Gv-20), Qianding (Gv-21), Xinhui (Gv-22), Shangxing (Gv-23), Shenting (Gv-24), Suliao (Gv-25), Renzhong (Gv-26), Duiduan (Gv-27), and Yinjiao (Gv-28).

3. Discussion:

The Governing Vessel is the confluence of all the Yang channels, over which it is said to "govern." Because it controls all the Yang channels, it is called the "Sea of Yang Meridians." This is apparent from its pathway because it flows on the midline of the back, a Yang area, and in the center of all Yang channels (except the Stomach channel which flows in the front). The Governing Vessel governs all the Yang channels, which means that it can be used to increase the Yang energy of the body.

Since the Governing Vessel is the "Sea of Yang Meridians" and it controls or governs the back, the area richest in Guardian Chi (Wey Chi), it is also responsible for the circulation of the body's Guardian Chi to guard against external evil intruders. The circulation of Guardian Chi starts from Fengfu (Gv-16), and moves down the Governing Vessel to Huiyin (Co-1). It is said that it takes 21 days for the Guardian Chi to flow from Fengfu to Huiyin, and 9 days from Huiyin to the throat, making it a monthly cycle.

According to Chinese medical science, Guardian Chi is Yang Chi and therefore represents the "Fire" of the body. Its quick and ubiquitous circulation keeps the fire going in the body and controls the loss of body heat. Guardian Chi is also inextricably linked with the fluids that flow outside the channels, in the skin and flesh. Consequently, through the breathing (under control of the Lungs), Guardian Chi is responsible for the opening and the closing of the pores, and also controls the sweat.

The Governing vessel is also responsible for nourishing the five ancestral organs, which include the brain and spinal cord. This is one of the ways in which the Kidneys "control" the brain, as is said in Chinese medicine.

Because of their importance to health, the Governing vessel and the Conception vessel are considered the two most important Chi channels to be trained in Chi Kung, especially in Nei Dan. Training related to these two vessels includes: 1. How to fill them with Chi so that you have enough to regulate the twelve channels, 2. How to open up stagnant areas in these two vessels so that the Chi flows smoothly and strongly, 3. How to effectively direct the Chi to nourish the brain and raise up the Shen, 4. How to effectively govern the Chi in the twelve channels, and nourish the organs, 5. How to use your raised Shen to lead the Guardian Chi to the skin and strengthen the Guardian Chi shield covering your body.

In Nei Dan Chi Kung training, when you have filled up the Chi in these two vessels and can effectively circulate the Chi in them, you have achieved the "Small Circulation." In order to do this, you must know how to convert the Essence stored in the Kidneys into Chi, circulate this Chi in the Governing and Conception vessels, and finally lead this Chi to the head to nourish the brain and Shen (spirit).

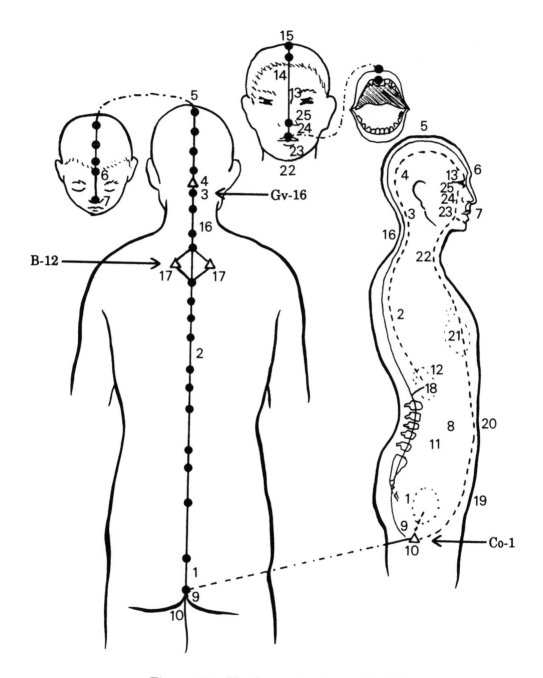

Figure 17-1. The Governing Vessel (Du Mei)

The Conception Vessel (Ren Mei)(Figure 17-2)

1. Course:

Course #1:

(1). Lower abdomen below Qugu (Co-2) -- (2). Ascends along the Midline of the abdomen and chest -- (3). Crosses the throat and jaw -- (4). winds around the mouth -- (5). Terminates in the region of the eye.

Course #2:

(6). Pelvic cavity -- (7). Enters the spine and ascends along the back.

***This vessel intersects Chengqi (S-1) and Yinjiao (Gv-28).

2. Cavities:

Huiyin (Co-1), Qugu (Co-2), Zhongli (Co-3), Guanyuan (Co-4), Shimen (Co-5), Qihai (Co-6), Abdomen-Yinjiao (Co-7), Shenjue (Co-8), Shuifen (Co-9), Xiawan (Co-10), Jianli (Co-11), Zhongwan (Co-12), Shangwan (Co-13), Juque (Co-14), Jiuwei (Co-15), Zhongting (Co-16), Shanzhong (Co-17), Yutang (Co-18), Chest-Zigong (Co-19), Huagai (Co-20), Xuanji (Co-21), Tiantu (Co-22), Lianquan (Co-23), and Chengjiang (Co-24).

3. Discussion:

Ren in Chinese means "direction, responsibility." Ren Mei, the "Conception Vessel," has a major role in Chi circulation, directing and being responsible for all of the Yin channels (plus the Stomach channel). The Conception Vessel is connected to the Thrusting and Yin Linking vessels, and is able to increase the Yin energy of the body.

This vessel nourishes the uterus (one of the five ancestral organs) and the whole genital system. It is said in the Nei Ching that the Conception and Thrusting vessels contain both blood and Essence (Jieng), and both flow up to the face and around the mouth. They contain more blood than Essence in men, and thus promote the growth of the beard and body hair. Because women lose blood with their menstruation, they contain proportionately less blood and hence, no beard or body hair.

It was described in the Su Wen that both the Conception and Thrusting vessels control the life cycles every 7 years for women and every 8 years for men. It is the changes taking place in these vessels at those intervals that promote the major alterations in our lives.

In addition, the Conception vessel also controls the distribution and "dispersion" of Guardian Chi all over the abdomen and thorax via numerous small Chi branches (Lou). This vessel also plays an important role in the distribution of body fluids in the abdomen.

In Chi Kung society, this vessel and the Governing vessel are considered the most important among the Chi channels and vessels, and must be trained first. It is believed that there is usually no significant Chi stagnation in the Conception vessel. However, it is important to increase the amount of Chi you are able to store, which also increases your ability to regulate the Yin channels.

The Thrusting Vessel (Chong Mei)(Figure 17-3)

1. Course:

Course #1:

(1). Lower abdomen -- (2). Emerges along the Path of Chi -- (3). Tracks the course of the Kidney channel -- (4). Ascends through the abdomen -- (5). Skirts the navel -- (6). Disperses in the chest.

Course #2:

(6). Chest -- (7). Ascends across the throat -- (8). Face -- (9). Nasal cavity.

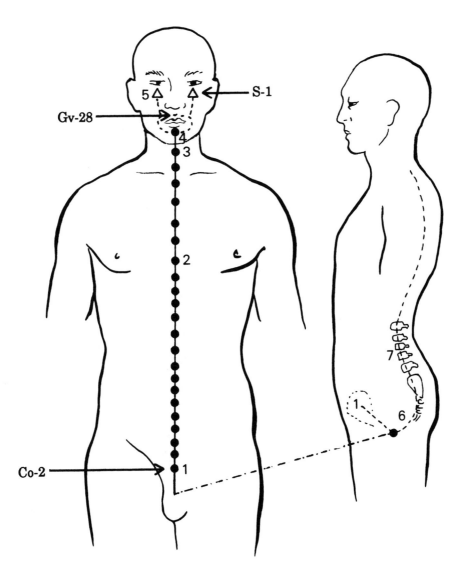

Figure 17-2. The Conception Vessel (Ren Mei)

Course #3:

(1). Lower abdomen -- (10). Below the Kidney -- (11). Emerges along the Path of Chi -- (12). Descends along the medial aspect of the thigh -- (13). Popliteal fossa -- (14). Medial margin of the tibia and the posterior aspect of the medial malleolus -- (15). Bottom of the foot.

Course #4:

(16). Tibia -- (17). Toward the lateral margin of the bone -- (18). enters the heel -- (19). Crosses the tarsal bones of the foot -- (20). Big toe.

Course #5:

(21). Pelvic cavity -- (22). Enter the spine and circulates through the back.

***This vessel intersects Huiyin (Co-1), Yinjiao (Co-7), Qichong (S-30), Henggu (K-11), Dahe (K-12), Qixue (K-13), Siman (K-14), Zhongzhu (K-15), Huangshu (K-16), Shangqu (K-17), Shiguan (K-18), Yindu (K-19), Tonggu (K-20), and Youmen (K-21).

2. Discussion:

One of the major purpose for the Thrusting vessel is to connect, to communicate, and to mutually support the Conception vessel. Because of this mutual Chi support, both can effectively regulate the Chi in the Kidney channel. The Kidneys are the residence of Original Chi and are considered one of the most vital Yin organs.

The Thrusting vessel is considered one of the most important and decisive vessels in successful Chi Kung training, especially in Marrow Washing. There are many reason for this. The first reason is that this vessel intersects two cavities on the Conception vessel: Huiyin (Co-1) and Yinjiao (Co-7). Huiyin means "meeting with Yin" and is the cavity where the Yang and Yin Chi is transferred. Yinjiao means "Yin Junction" and is the cavity where the Original Chi (Water Chi, or Yin Chi) interfaces with the Fire Chi created from food and air. The Thrusting Vessel also connects with eleven cavities on the Kidney channel. The Kidney is considered the residence of Original Essence (Yuan Jieng), which is converted into Original Chi (Yuan Chi).

The second reason for the importance of the Thrusting Vessel in Chi Kung training is that this vessel is connected directly to the marrow of the spinal cord and reaches up to the brain. The major goal of Marrow Washing Chi Kung is to lead the Chi into the marrow and then further on to the head, nourishing the brain and spirit (Shen).

And finally, the third reason is found in actual Chi Kung practice. There are three common training paths: Fire, Wind, and Water. In Fire path Chi Kung, the emphasis is on the Fire or Yang Chi circulating in the Governing vessel and therefore strengthening the muscles and organs. The Fire path is the main Chi training in Muscle/Tendon Changing (Yi Gin Ching) Chi Kung. However, the Fire path can also cause the body to become too Yang, and therefore speed up the process of degeneration. In order to adjust the Fire to a proper level, Marrow Washing Chi Kung is also trained. This uses the Water path, in which Chi separates from the route of the Fire path at the Huiyin cavity (Co-1), enters the spinal cord, and finally reaches up to the head. The Water path teaches how to use Original Chi to cool down the body, and then to use this Chi to nourish the brain and train the spirit. Learning to adjust the Fire and Water Chi circulation in the body is called Kan-Lii, which means Water-Fire. You can see from this that the Thrusting vessel plays a very important role in Chi Kung training.

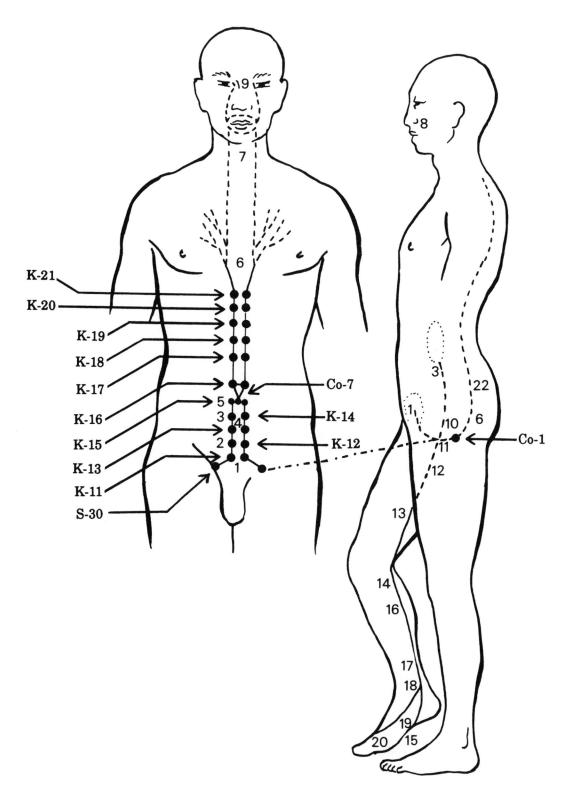

Figure 17-3. The Thrusting Vessel (Chong Mei)

The Girdle Vessel (Dai Mei)(Figure 17-4)

1. Course:

(1). Below the hypochondrium at the level of the 2nd lumbar vertebra -- (2). Turns downward and encircles the body at the waist like a girdle.

***This vessel intersects Daimai (GB-26), Wushu (GB-27), and Weidao (GB-28).

2. Discussion:

The major purpose of the Girdle vessel is to regulate the Chi of the Gall Bladder. It is also responsible for the Chi's horizontal balance. If you have lost this balance, you will have lost your center and balance both mentally and physically.

From the point of view of Chi Kung, the Girdle vessel is also responsible for the strength of the waist area. When Chi is full and circulating smoothly, back pain will be avoided. In addition, because the Kidneys are located nearby, this vessel is also responsible for Chi circulation around the Kidneys, maintaining the Kidneys' health. Most important of all for the Girdle vessel is the fact that the Lower Dan Tien is located in its area. In order to lead Original Chi from the Kidneys to the Lower Dan Tien, the waist area must be healthy and relaxed. This means that the Chi flow in the waist area must be smooth. The training of the Girdle vessel has been highly developed, and will be discussed in a later YMAA Book.

The Yang Heel Vessel (Yangchiao Mei)(Figure 17-5)

1. Course:

(1). Below the lateral malleolus at Shenmai (B-62) -- (2). Ascends along the lateral aspect of the leg -- (3). Posterior aspect of the hypochondrium -- (3). Lateral side of the shoulder -- (4). Traverses the neck -- (5). Passes beside the mouth -- (6). Inner canthus (joins the Yin Heel vessel and the Urinary Bladder channel) -- (7). Ascends across the forehead -- (8). Winds behind the ear to Fengchi (GB-20) -- (9). Enters the brain at Fengfu (Gv-16).

***This vessel intersects Shenmai (B-62), Pushen (B-61), Fuyang (B-59), Jingming (B-1), Juliao (GB-29), Fengchi (GB-20), Naoshu (SI-10), Jugu (LI-16), Jianyu (LI-15), Dicang (S-4), Juliao (S-3), Chengqi (S-1), and Fengfu (Gv-16).

2. Discussion:

While the preceding four vessels (Governing, Conception, Thrusting, and Girdle) are located in the trunk, this and the next three are located in the trunk and legs. (In addition, each of these four vessels is paired.) For millions of years, man has been walking on his rear legs, which do much more strenuous work than the arms do. I believe that it was because of this that, as evolution proceeded, the legs gradually developed these vessels to supply Chi support and regulate the channels. If this is true, it may be that, as time goes on and man uses his legs less and less, in a few million years these vessels will gradually disappear.

You can see from the way that the Yang Heel vessel intersect with other Chi channels that it regulates the Yang channels, such as the Urinary Bladder, the Gall Bladder, the Small Intestine, and the Large Intestine. The Yang Heel vessel is also connected with the Governing vessel. The Chi filling this vessel is supplied mainly through exercising the legs, which converts the food Essence or fat stored in the legs. This Chi is then led upward to nourish the Yang channels. It is believed in Chi

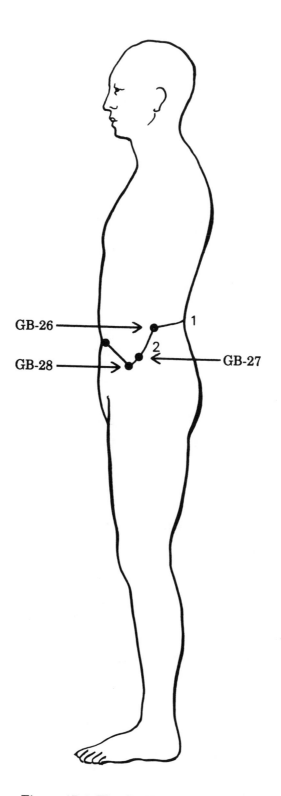

GB-26

GB-28

1

2

GB-27

Figure 17-4. The Girdle Vessel (Dai Mei)

Kung that, since this vessel is also connected with your brain, certain leg exercises can be used to cure headaches. Since a headache is caused by excess Chi in the head, exercising the legs will draw this Chi downward to the leg muscles and relieve the pressure in the head.

Most of the training that relates to this vessel is Wai Dan. Wai Dan Chi Kung is considered Yang, and specializes in training the Yang channels, while Nei Dan Chi Kung is considered relatively Yin and emphasizes the Yin channel more.

The Yin Heel Vessel (Yinchiao Mei)(Figure 17-5)

1. Course:

(1). Zhaohai (K-6) below the medial malleolus -- (2). Extends upward along the medial aspect of the leg -- (3). Crossing the perineum and chest entering the supraclavicular fossa -- (4). Ascends through the throat and emerges in front of Renying (S-9) -- (5). Traverses the medial aspect of the cheek -- (6). Inner canthus (joins the Urinary Bladder channel and Yang Heel vessels) -- (7). Ascends over the head and into the brain.

***This vessel intersects Zhaohai (K-6), Jiaoxin (K-8), and Jingming (B-1).

2. Discussion:

The Yin Heel vessel is connected with two cavities of the Kidney channel. Therefore, one of the major sources of Chi for this vessel is the conversion of the Kidney Essence into Chi. It is believed in Chi Kung society that the other major Chi source is the Essence of the external Kidneys (testicles). In Marrow Washing Chi Kung, one of the training processes is to stimulate the testicles in order to increase the hormone production and increase the conversion of the Essence into Chi. At the same time, you would learn how to lead the Chi in this vessel up to the head to nourish the brain and spirit (Shen). With this nourishment, you would be able to reach Buddhahood or enlightenment. From a health and longevity point of view, the raised spirit will be able to efficiently direct the Chi of the entire body and maintain your health.

The Yang Linking Vessel (Yangwei Mei)(Figure 17-6)

1. Course:

(1). Jinmen (B-63) on the heel -- (2). Ascends along the lateral aspect of the leg -- (3). Lower abdomen -- (4). Slants upward across the posterior aspect of the hypochondrium -- (5). Across the posterior axillary fold to the shoulder -- (6). Ascends the neck and crosses behind the ear -- (7). Proceeds to the forehead -- (8). Doubles back over the head -- (9). Fengfu (Gv-16).

***This vessel intersects Jinmen (B-63), Yangjiao (GB-35), Jianjing (GB-21), Fengchi (GB-20), Naokong (GB-19), Chengling (GB-18), Zhengying (GB-17), Muchuang (GB-16), Head-Linqi (GB-15), Yangbai (GB-14), Benshen (GB-13), Tianliao (TB-15), Naoshu (SI-10), Yamen (Gv-15), Fengfu (Gv-16), and Touwei (S-8).

2. Discussion:

The Yang Linking vessel regulates the Chi mainly in the Yang channels: the Urinary Bladder, Gall Bladder, Triple Burner, Small Intestine, and Stomach channels. It is also connected with the Governing vessel at Yamen (Gv-15) and Fengfu (Gv-16). This vessel and the Yang Heel vessel have not been emphasized much in Chi Kung, except in Iron Shirt training where these two and the Governing vessel are trained.

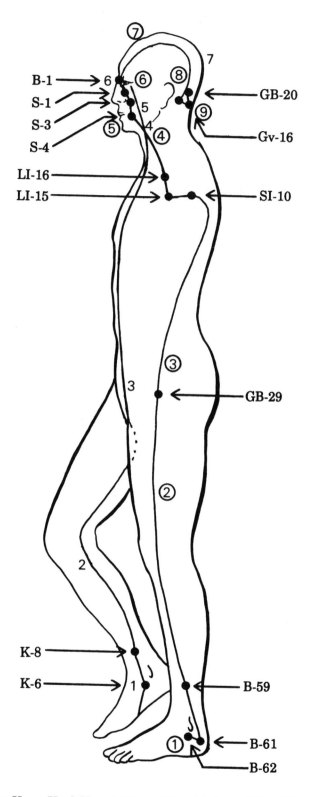

Figure 17-5. The Yang Heel Vessel (Yangchiao Mei) and The Yin Heel Vessel(Yinchiao Mei)

The Yin Linking Vessel (Yinwei Mei)(Figure 17-6)

1. Course:

(1). Lower leg at Zhubin (K-9) -- (2). Ascending along the medial aspect of the leg -- (3). Enters the lower abdomen -- (4). Upward across the chest -- (5). Throat (meets Tiantu (Co-22) and Lianquan (Co-23)).

***This vessel intersects Zhubin (K-9), Chongmen (Sp-12), Fushe (Sp-13), Daheng (Sp-15), Fuai (Sp-16), Qimen (Li-14), Tiantu (Co-22), and Lianquan (Co-23).

2. Discussion:

The Yin Linking vessel has connections with the Kidney, Spleen, and Liver Yin channels. The Yin Linking vessel also communicates with the Conception vessel at two cavities. This vessel is not trained much in Chi Kung.

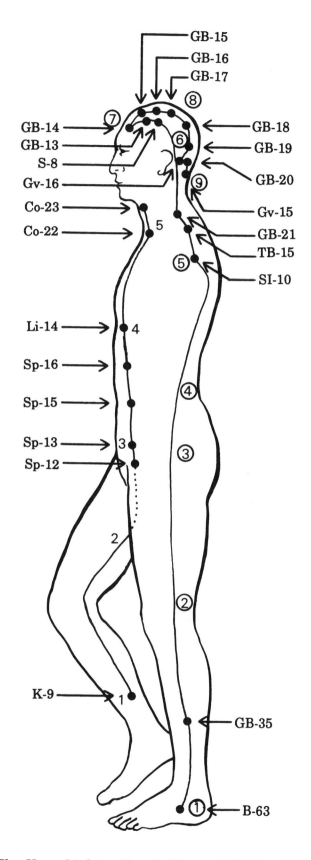

Figure 17-6. The Yang Linking Vessel (Yangwei Mei) and The Yin
LinkingVessel (Yinwei Mei)

PART FOUR

CONCLUSION

4. When Chi is transferred from one person to another, what, other than heat and bioelectricity, is transferred? I have often wondered how one person can be more effective in transferring his Chi than another person. There must be some extra power which is transferred to the patient emotionally to help the patient himself build up an EMF and cure himself internally. What is this power -- brainwave, emotional touch, or self-confidence buildup?

5. Why was the character for the Chinese word Chi changed? Was this change caused by confusion due to similar pronunciation? Many times it is found that ancient words are confused with other words because their pronunciation is similar. Since most Chinese people could neither write nor read, this idea seems plausible. If it was so, how could those Chi Kung experts or medical doctors let it happen? Or was it changed purposely in order to distinguish Human Chi (Chinese word meaning "no fire") from other natural energies? I cannot find any document which explains this difference satisfactorily.

6. Why has the character for "air" supplanted the ancient word for Chi (which meant "no fire")? The character meaning "air" is commonly used by the Chinese as a general term for different kinds of energy. This has confused me from the beginning of my Chi Kung practice. One of the most plausible explanations is the following: Air or oxygen (called Kong Chi) does not change its form when it is taken into the body and delivered to the cells to be converted through biochemical reaction into carbon dioxide. On the other hand, the food Essence must be converted into a form of bioenergy before it can be absorbed by the body. Is it why the "air" Chi is used to represent energy?

7. What is the scientific explanation for the halo around the head, or the glow around the body, of a meditator? Though I try to explain these phenomena as air de-ionization generated by the body's electrical charge, an experiment needs to be conducted to determine whether this is true.

8. How can Chi be used to bounce someone away with only a touch? We have heard in the Chinese martial arts that a very good Chi Kung master is able to bounce (or shock) an enemy away with a simple touch. When someone touches a high voltage wire, his body reacts instinctively to protect him, and bounces him away. The wire does not exert any physical power. Is this what happens with the Chi Kung master? Does he pass electricity into the other person's heart so that his body bounces him away instinctively?

9. How exactly does Chi nourish the blood, nerves, and cells?

10. If Chi is bioelectricity, how can we use modern technology to increase bioelectric circulation in the body and reach the same goals as the Chi Kung practices which allow us to obtain health, longevity and spiritual enlightenment? It was not possible to generate electrical and magnetic fields in ancient times; however, it is very easy to create them today. We should be able to find a way to use external electrical or magnetic fields to increase the circulation, correct the level of Chi, and keep the marrow clean. Naturally, caution is always the first consideration. We do not know yet how this modern technology will affect us. It may produce adverse reactions. How can a field which is created through external processes duplicate the mental calm necessary for enlightenment? Even if the circulation can be opened, will not attachment to the world inhibit clarity of focus? Won't there then be the danger of people who are exceptionally powerful physically who do not have the discipline to control their power? It will be necessary to do research on a very wide scale.

11. How do clouds and fog affect the Chi circulation in the body? We know that low clouds are able to generate an electric field which affects the

human energy field. Does fog do this as well? When you are in fog, do the charges surround you uniformly? Can this affect your Chi circulation?

About Spirit (Shen):

1. When does the spirit start in a baby? How do we know if a baby has spirit or not, and how do we determine when it first has spirit? Does it have spirit before birth, or only after it is separated from its mother?

2. How is spirit generated in a newly born baby? Where does spirit originate? Does it start when a baby starts to think? Does it exist only in humans?

3. What are the differences between the spirit and the soul? Since there is no exact translation from Chinese into English, I will need the exact difference and definition of these words.

4. Can the spirit and soul exist even if there is no physical life form? It is believed in the Chinese religions that the spirit and soul can exist even after death. Are spirit and soul an energy form? Are they part of the non-human natural energy, or are they the residues of human energy?

5. How do we define spirit (Shen) and mind? The relationship between the Shen and the mind is very confusing. Is Shen generated from mind? If Shen must be generated from mind, then can Shen exist after physical death? If Shen can exist after death, does this Shen have a mind and can it think independently? How do they relate to brainwaves? Can Shen be measured?

6. How do we generate a "spiritual baby Shen" in Chi Kung training? In Chi Kung, in order to reach the final goal of enlightenment you must train yourself until you have given birth to a baby Shen. Only when this baby has grown to be independent will your spirit not die, but live forever. Is this true? Scientifically, how can this happen? Can we use modern science to explain this, or is it still beyond what today's science can grasp? If we believe that a highly cultivated mind is able to speed up the process of evolution, then this mind may be able to reach many other things which are still beyond human understanding. The science we understand is still in the infant stage. Remember, we cannot use today's science to gauge the potential of science.

7. Does a newborn child need an already-existing spirit? Some religions say that a newborn baby does in order to form a complete human. If so, where does this spirit come from? From the people who died before? If a newborn baby needs this pre-existing spirit, then how does the population keep increasing? Where do the new spirits originate? Do they come from the sun, or universal energy? Could spirits from other planets immigrate to the earth and be born into human bodies?

8. Is there another dimension which we cannot usually see, but, when the time is right, we are able to touch? There are many accounts of very sick or dying people being able to see or sense the same kind of new world. Is this a spirit world? Is this a new dimension which we cannot see until the time is right? How do we reach this dimension from the scientific standpoint?

9. Does spirit make its own decisions or is it affected by natural Chi? Can a spirit think? How can it help a person who is alive? Through brainwave communication? Or is a spirit only some human energy residue roaming around in the energy world and being affected by surrounding energy forces?

10. Do the spirits of enlightened people who have died continue to exist? If so, can these spirits help the living? Remember if your answer is yes, you have agreed that the spirit and soul can exist even after your death.

When you pray, do you actually receive help from God or the spirits of the dead, or are you helping yourself by building your self-confidence?

11. Can a highly concentrated mind make an object move without touching it? What is the theory behind this phenomenon? We have heard of people who are able to move things through thinking. If this is true, then how can brainwave energy become so strong that it can do this? Are miracles done with brainwaves?

12. Can the spirit really leave a living body and travel, or is it only that the brainwaves sense something and match its frequency so that you can be aware of it? Also, we have heard that when someone is hypnotized, he is able to sense many things which are beyond his capability while he is in a normal state of consciousness. Is this similar to what happens when a person seems to leave his body during meditation?

13. When someone is able to communicate with animals, is this brainwave correspondence? I once saw a woman on a live TV show who seemed to be able to communicate with all kinds of dogs. The information she learned was verified by the owners. If this was real, was it brainwave communication? Do the brains of animals and man function on the same frequency band, or do the bands just partially overlap?

14. Can one person affect another person's thinking through brainwave correspondence?

15. Can modern technology create an electromagnetic wave whose wavelength is close to or equivalent to the human brainwave? Our technology seems to have already progressed that far. If this is so, will a brainwave machine be able to generate a wave which will affect your thinking and judgement? This would truly be "brainwashing." Will the wars of the future be wars of brainwave machines?

16. If it is possible to make a brainwave machine, can we determine what frequencies are associated with crime and then somehow block those frequencies? Is it possible to really brainwash criminals? Of course, if such a machine fell into the hands of criminals, they would have a powerful tool for evil. Can we accept the moral responsibility for changing an individual's brainwave?

17. Can a good Chi Kung meditator avoid being controlled and affected by a brainwave machine? Personally, I believe that a Chi Kung practitioner who has reached the stage of regulating his mind effectively would be able to avoid the effects of a brainwave machine. However, how long would he be able to do this?

18. What is the width of the brainwave band? What existing materials can shield them out? Metal is usually a good insulator against radiowaves, but can it also keep out brainwaves? If not, is there any material which can be used to shield against brainwaves?

19. What is the relationship between spirit (Shen) and brainwaves? I personally believe that when your Shen is high, your brainwaves will be stronger and, probably, more focused. Is this true?

About Channels, Vessels, and Cavities:

1. In ancient times, how did they find out about and locate Chi channels, vessels, and cavities? There is no record of how those ancient Chinese doctors discovered this. How did they find them with such accuracy? How did they learn how to use them to cure illness?

2. How do plugged up channels interfere with the Chi flow? This is a simple question, but the answer is not easy. It will take the most advanced technology to find out exactly how the Chi channels are plugged up. Is it caused by an accumulation of fat which significantly

reduces the tissue's electric conductivity, or simply by some defect in the body's electrically conductive tissues?

3. How do the channels conduct Chi? How many stimuli can make the Chi move? If Chi is a bioelectric energy, then the question is: how many EMF are there which can make the energy move, and where are they?

4. How do the vessels store Chi? If Chi is bioelectric energy, then is a Chi vessel like a battery or a capacitor which is able to store and release energy when necessary?

5. What do the Chi channels and vessels actually look like? So far, no one has been able to show an accurate drawing. However, if they are areas where the electrical conductivity is different than elsewhere, then we should be able to conduct experiments to find out just how the Chi channels and vessels are shaped.

6. How can we design a highly sensitive machine to accurately locate all of these Chi channels and cavities? This would be very helpful for acupuncture practice.

7. Why are there four vessels on the legs and none on the arms? Is it because people use their legs more than their arms? I believe that the vessels in the legs evolved to supply extra Chi to the legs and regulate it more efficiently.

8. Are there any other vessels which have not been discovered? It is possible that there are other, smaller vessels in the body which have not been discovered yet. For example, I believe that there should be vessels in the arms, since people use their arms a lot.

9. What is the actual meaning of opening a channel (commonly called opening the gate) in Chi Kung practice? What actually happens? Is it that the channel recovers its electrical conductivity? What is the best way to do this?

10. Can we use modern bioelectric technologies to open the channels and increase the smoothness of the Chi circulation?

11. Can we use modern bioelectric technology to fill up the Chi reservoirs? If the vessels are bioelectric capacitors, then we might be able to use external electrical or magnetic methods to refill them. We would then have enough Chi to nourish the whole body, and slow down the aging process significantly.

12. What actually happens when an experienced Chi Kung master helps a student open his channels? Does the master really use his Chi (electricity) and transport it into the student's body to do the job, or does the master only offer some stimulation and confidence to the student, and in fact, does a student open them by himself? Both are possible.

13. Exactly what are cavities? Do all of the cavities have higher electric conductivity or do they differ in capacity? Is increased electrical conductivity the only criteria for locating cavities, or did the ancients have other criteria in addition to this?

14. Why are there cavities? Is the purpose of cavities to circulate Chi to the surface of the skin to nourish it, and to regulate the Chi channels? Are there any other purposes other than these?

15. What does acupuncture actually do to correct the Chi? We need a more complete explanation through modern experimentation and scientific study.

About Mutual Chi Nourishment:

1. According to Chi Kung documents, two people can practice together to balance their Chi through mutual Chi nourishment. The person with the stronger Chi lowers his Chi volume while the weaker one gains Chi. Two people with weak Chi can help each other build up their Chi. In this kind of mutual Chi nourishment, both persons must be able to coordinate with

each other in every aspect -- especially in breathing. Emotionally, they must be willing to share with each other. In this kind of practice, must love get involved? If not, how are you able to touch and share Chi with each other? If the answer is "Yes," isn't it against the principle of meditation that the mind should be simple, calm, and peaceful, with no emotional disturbance?

2. When two people practice mutual Chi nourishment, do they actually share Chi, or do they stimulate each other's minds to enhance the brain's EMF and thereby increase their own Chi circulation, or both?

3. From the Chi Kung point of view, love is a natural way of causing mutual Chi nourishment. A person who loves someone can help him recover from illness. Can this be considered a form of Chi Kung?

4. Is sexual activity the ultimate natural way of mutual Chi nourishment? Sex is a natural human desire. Through regular sexual activity, a person is able to obtain mental calmness and peace, and release the pressure generated by emotional disturbance. Can this be considered a form of Chi Kung practice?

5. When the male ejaculates during sex, he loses Chi to the female. How does this happen? Is this why women live longer? If the female has reached a higher level of Chi Kung, can the male receive the Chi instead of losing it?

6. Exactly how is Essence and Chi lost during ejaculation? In certain Chi Kung practices, men are taught how to avoid ejaculation. How is Chi transmitted under such circumstances?

7. If sex is considered beneficial for Chi Kung practice, why did all of the Buddhist monks and many of the Taoists hide in the mountains and avoid sexual contact? Is this because they were afraid that sex and love would destroy the calm and peaceful mind they were cultivating?

8. Why did the Taoists develop so many techniques which used sexual activity for Chi nourishment? Could these techniques have been studied by those Taoists whose minds could not be calm? Or did they want, on the one hand to reach enlightenment, and the other hand to enjoy a natural, normal human life.

9. There are no documents that discuss exchanging Chi with animals, such as dogs and cats. Can a person obtain Chi from animals? Theoretically, it should be possible. It has been found that cats have high Chi levels, which enable them to help older men and women maintain their Chi level. Can ways be developed to help older people through this?

About Health and Longevity:

1. Can we use external electric or magnetic stimulation to cure sicknesses in the same way that Chi Kung and acupuncture do? Perhaps the process can be duplicated by using external electric or magnetic stimulation to increase or reinstate the normal bioelectric circulation. Chi Kung has cured many kinds of cancer. Can the equivalent be achieved with modern electric and magnetic technologies?

2. Can the immune system be strengthened through electric and magnetic stimulation to cure AIDS and cancer? It is believed that the immune system is related closely to the body's bioenergy system. Can we increase the EMF of the brain and strengthen the bioenergy circulation in the body?

3. Is it dangerous to use electricity and magnetics in acupuncture when we do not understand Chi science completely? So far, there is no conclusive or theoretical report about the use of electricity and magnetics in acupuncture, even though they are being widely used. Is it safe for general practice, or do we need more research?

4. Is practicing Chi Kung to obtain a longer life the correct goal? I believe that if someone really wants to have a much longer life, he must separate

himself from human society to avoid emotional disturbance. However, when he does this he loses the meaning of human life. I believe that the correct purpose of the Chi Kung practice is to obtain a healthy physical and mental body while you are still able to experience life. You will extend your life span somewhat because you are healthy, and you will still be able to experience human life.

5. What is the meaning of life? Can Chi Kung help you understand it? Does a long life mean more to you than a happy life? If you want to have both, what should you do? Chi Kung practice has helped me understand myself, nature, and what I was, am, and will be. It has stopped my wondering and confusion. How about you? Are you expecting the same thing?

6. Can we use modern technology to reach the same goal as marrow washing training and obtain a longer life without giving up our emotional feelings? I feel certain that once we understand exactly how marrow washing Chi Kung training works, we will be able to use modern technology to quickly reach the same goal.

About Chi and Modern Living:

1. Can we use ice to maintain the body's Chi balance during the summer? It was not possible to research this before refrigerators were invented. In the summertime, when the Heart is on fire, can we place a piece of ice on the center of the palm to cool the Heart, or will the ice quench the Heart fire too quickly and cause problems? How about if we use alcohol instead of ice?

2. How does being on the night shift affect a person's Chi circulation? In ancient times, few people worked at night, so there are no documents available today which discuss this. Since the time of day has to be taken into account when giving acupuncture treatments, will being on the night shift affect the treatment?

3. How is Chi circulation affected when you travel several time zones in a short period of time? Does jet lag indicate that the body's Chi is disturbed?

About the Human Magnetic Field:

1. Theoretically, there are two magnetic poles formed in the human body by the Earth's magnetic field. Do these two poles reverse when you move from the Northern Hemisphere to the Southern Hemisphere?

2. The Earth's magnetic field starts at the South Magnetic Pole and goes to the North Magnetic Pole. Since the human south magnetic pole seems to be on the head, does this mean that the brains of people in the Northern Hemisphere constantly receive energy nourishment? If the human magnetic poles are reversed in the Southern Hemisphere, does this mean that the brains of people there constantly lose nourishment?

3. Does this explain why the most highly developed technology has been created in the Northern Hemisphere?

4. If people in the Southern Hemisphere have their south magnetic poles in the abdomen, do they have more Lower Dan Tien energy, and does this help them live longer?

5. When people are sick, can they speed their recovery by flying to the equator, where the effect of the Earth's magnetic field is minimized? I believe that many human sicknesses are caused, or worsened, by disturbances in the body's electromagnetic field. The energy of the earth can worsen the situation, since your body has lost its natural balance. Can you remove this hindrance to your recovery by moving to the Equator?

6. We are surrounded by energy fields, both natural and man-made. Can we insulate a room against them to help people convalesce? Would this also be a good place to meditate?

Others:

1. Are there specific spots on the earth where the natural energy is especially beneficial for Chi Kung? Many Chi Kung practitioners believe that there are places where Heaven or Earth Chi is able to nourish your Chi and speed up your training. Is this true? Would these areas be good for hospitals?

2. What happens when we are exposed to a strong electric or magnetic field for a long time? How does this affect the body? Can it possibly energize our vital force and improve our health?

3. Since ancient times, Chi Kung practitioners have claimed that there is a Chi Kung practice which can make their bodies light. Is this true? Is this beyond a modern, scientific explanation?

4. Some people can hold a piece of burning charcoal in their hands, or walk barefoot on a bed of glowing coals. How is this done?

5. The Chinese people have been using jade to regulate Chi in their bodies or absorb excess Chi for generations. Has this ever been investigated scientifically?

6. Can we use electrical technology to increase the Chi on the head to prevent hair loss or increase hair growth?

7. Meditators talk about absorbing energy from the earth through the feet. Is this different from magnetic energy?

8. Can a highly trained Chi Kung practitioner predict the future, or is this simply a matter of judgement, combined with experience and wisdom? It is often said that some Chi Kung masters are able to read your mind and even predict your future. I believe that it is possible to read minds through brainwave correspondence. However, predicting the future requires more than this. Intelligence and wisdom are needed, and a lot of experience. A person's personality is the main cause of success, and it can be read in his face and even in his palms. Is this how the future is read, or is there another way?

9. How does the material your clothing is made of affect your health? Natural materials such as cotton and wool dissipate some of your energy to the surrounding environment. Most man-made materials generate a Chi (or electric) shield which does not allow your Chi to communicate with nature. This affects your body's electromagnetic field and perhaps even disturbs your Chi circulation. This needs to be investigated.

10. How does the weather affect our moods? Moods may be caused by the electric fields generated between low clouds and the ground. These strong, natural, electric fields will affect your body's electromagnetic field, and may cause sickness or emotional disturbance.

11. Is there a way to energize the muscles to a higher level via external electric or magnetic stimulation, or must we rely on traditional practices? If it is possible, would it be fair in competitive sports such as boxing or football? Is the way in which body builders use electrical stimulation of the muscles safe?

12. Is there any danger involved in these experiments? We don't understand the human body very well, and we are such delicate and complicated animals. Naturally, many of the experiments can be performed on other animals first. However, since the inner energy field is closely related to emotions, it is probable that most of the experiments need to be conducted directly on humans.

13. Why do many Taoist Chi Kung practitioners hide themselves in caves for their cultivation? Is it because a cave is able to isolate the individual from external energy disturbances (magnetic fields or ions in the clouds)?

Chapter 19

Conclusion

You can see that in order to maintain your health and slow down the aging process, you must keep your twelve Chi rivers running smoothly at the proper Chi level without stagnation. In addition, you must also keep the Chi reservoirs full so that they can properly regulate the Chi flow in the Chi rivers.

Chi Kung was designed to focus on these two targets. It keeps Chi running smoothly in the channels by opening up areas which can cause the flow to stagnate. The first step in this is learning how to regulate your body into a deep, relaxed state. The next step is regulating your breathing and your mind to lead your mind and spirit into a deep, peaceful, and calm state. Now your organs will not be stressed by emotional disturbances, and can function most efficiently. Only when you have reached the stage at which you can regulate your body, breathing, and mind, will you be able to feel and sense the Chi flow in your body. Only then will you be able to regulate your Chi effectively.

Wai Dan (external elixir) Chi Kung is based on this principle. It relies on limb exercises in coordination with mind concentration to build Chi in the limbs, and then lets this Chi flow back into the organs. Wai Dan Chi Kung is aimed at the Chi channels.

However, in order to fill up the Chi in the vessels, another method must be used. Nei Dan Chi Kung builds up Chi in the Dan Tien, which is located in the Chi vessels. First the Conception and Governing vessels are filled, and then the other six.

These achievements did not satisfy the Chi Kung practitioners. In order to reach a deeper level of Chi Kung training and approach the goals of longevity and enlightenment, two more things are required. One of these is keeping the blood healthy. Blood cells carry nutrition and oxygen to every cell of your body. When the blood is healthy, it will significantly slow the aging process. Since the blood cells are manufactured in the bone marrow, it is essential to keep the marrow clean.

The higher Chi Kung practitioners also seek spiritual independence. In order to attain this goal, the Chi must be led to the head to nourish the brain and spirit, making it possible for the practitioner to reach the stage of enlightenment or Buddhahood.

Hundreds of Chi Kung styles were created based on these requirements. However, the most important ones are the Muscle/Tendon Changing Classic and the Marrow Washing Classic. The Muscle/Tendon Changing Classic was designed to change the physical body (including the organs) from weak to strong, and to keep the twelve Chi channels running smoothly while filling up the Chi in the two major vessels (Conception and Governing vessels). When you train Muscle/Tendon Changing Chi Kung, you build the foundation of physical health.

After you have reached an advanced stage of Muscle/Tendon Changing Chi Kung training, for example completing the Small and Grand Circulation, you should start Marrow Washing Chi Kung. Marrow Washing Chi Kung fills up the other six vessels, keeps the marrow clean and fresh, and uses the Chi to nourish the brain and spirit. When you have completed this, you will have reached the highest level of Chi Kung training. However, it is not easy to reach this stage. It usually requires that you separate yourself from normal human society, and perhaps live in the mountains like a priest or hermit. It will also require more than 30 years of accurate training.

This volume is meant to serve as a map directing you to the Chi Kung treasure. It will give you the directions and knowledge necessary to start your trek to health and longevity. Beyond showing you the What and How of practice, this book is designed to explain the Why, based on my current understanding. It is my wish that this book stimulate the general Western public to open its collective mind to this new concept. Although I have tried my best, it is not surprising that many questions remain. The science of Chi Kung is so wide and deep in knowledge, and so long in history, that it is not possible for one individual to cover every aspect. I hope that other knowledgeable Chi Kung practitioners and researchers will also share their experience and understanding with the general public.

Although I believe that this book has not covered all aspects of the discussion, I do have confidence that it has given you the key to opening the gate to the mystery. With this book as a directory, you should come to understand the general concepts of Chinese Chi Kung. Once you understand this book, you should start walking. Without walking, the target will never be reached. It is a long and challenging job. You will need a lot of enthusiasm, patience, and strong will to accomplish it. The process will help you to understand yourself and nature much better and more clearly and, therefore, help you live your life in a more meaningful way.

Although this book has discussed the general theory and categories of Chi Kung, it has not discussed any style specifically. Therefore, YMAA plans to publish another seven books to discuss the details of training in different styles. These books will be:

1. *MUSCLE / TENDON CHANGING AND MARROW WASHING CHI KUNG* -- The Secret of Youth (Yi Gin Ching and Shii Soei Ching)
2. *CHI KUNG MASSAGE* -- Chi Kung Tuei Na and Cavity Press for Healing (Chi Kung Ann Mo and Chi Kung Dien Shiuh)
3. *CHI KUNG AND HEALTH* -- For Healing and Maintaining Health
4. *CHI KUNG AND THE MARTIAL ARTS* -- The Key to Advanced Martial Arts Skill (Shaolin, Wuudang, Ermei, and others)
5. *BUDDHIST CHI KUNG* -- Charn, The Root of Zen
6. *TAOIST CHI KUNG* (Dan Diing Tao Kung)
7. *TIBETAN CHI KUNG* (Mih Tzong Shen Kung)

On your way to study and research, I would like to remind you that your thoughts should not be restricted and limited by traditional culture and conventional, conservative morality. Accepting a new culture is not a betrayal of tradition. Daring to remove the masks which everybody has put on since they started to be affected by tradition and the world of conventional reality is not shameful but brave. During this new era in which human beings have enjoyed incredible material progress in a mere 100 years, you must dare to face and accept different cultures. Tradition must be examined. In this new era, different cultures have a chance to interface with each other. It is the responsibility of our generation to create and refine this new mixed culture and pass it to the next generation. This is a difficult challenge for all of us. However, you must understand that the future is in our hands, and we must accept the challenge, becoming the pioneers of this era.

In order to accomplish this job, I would like to give you a few things to keep in mind in the course of your study and research. These are:

1. Avoid Prejudice:

All culture and tradition which has survived must have its benefits. Perhaps some of them do not fit in our world, however, they deserve our respect. Remember, if you get rid of your past, you have pulled out your root. Naturally, you should not be stubborn and claim that the traditional culture is absolutely right, or claim that an alien culture must be better than the traditional culture. What you should do is keep the good of the traditional and absorb the best of the alien.

2. Be Objective in Your Judgement:

You should consider every new statement you read from both sides so that you can analyze it objectively. When you evaluate, emotional opinions should be considered, but they should not dominate your judgement.

3. Be Scientific:

Although there are many occurrences which still cannot be explained by modern science, you should always remember to judge scientifically. New sciences will be developed. Phenomena which could not be tested in ancient times should be examined with modern equipment.

4. Be Logical and Make Sense:

When you read or study, in your mind you should always ask "Is it logical and does it make sense?" When you keep these questions in mind, you will think and understand instead of believe blindly.

5. Do not Ignore Prior Experience:

Prior experience which has been passed down is the root of research. You should always be sincere and respectful when you study the past. From the past, you will come to understand the present. By understanding the present, you will be able to create the future. The accumulation of experience is the best teacher. You should respect the past, be cautious about the present, and challenge the future.

China has more than 7000 thousand years of culture. There have been many brilliant accomplishments, and Chi Kung is only one of them. There has never been such open communication between different cultures as we have today. It is our responsibility to encourage the general public to accept, study, and research other cultures. In this way, the human race will be able to adopt the good parts of each culture and live in a more peaceful and meaningful way.

Chinese Chi Kung is part of traditional Chinese medical science. It has brought the Chinese thousands of years of calm, peaceful, and happy lives. I believe that this brilliant part of Chinese culture will help Westerners, especially in the spiritual part of training. Further publications must be encouraged. Wide scale scholastic and scientific study, research, and tests must be conducted, especially by universities and medical organizations.

In this way, we will be able to introduce this new culture to the Western world in a short time.

I predict that the study of Chinese medical science and internal, meditative Chi Kung will attain great results in the next decade. I invite you to join me and become a pioneer in this new field in the western world.

Appendix A

Glossary

Ann Mo: 按摩
Literally: press rub. Together they mean massage.

Ba Duann Gin: 八投錦
Eight Pieces of Brocade. A Wai Dan Chi Kung practice which is said to have been created by Marshal Yeuh Fei during the Song dynasty (1127-1279 A.D.).

Ba Kua: 八卦
Literally: Eight Divinations. Also called the Eight Trigrams. In Chinese philosophy, the eight basic variations; shown in the I Ching as groups of single and broken lines.

Ba Kua Chang: 八卦掌
Eight Trigrams Palm. One of the internal Chi Kung martial styles, believed to have been created by Doong Hae-Chuan between 1866 and 1880 A.D.

Charn (Zen): 禪 (忍)
A Chinese school of Mahayana Buddhism which asserts that enlightenment can be attained through meditation, self-contemplation, and intuition, rather than through study of scripture. Charn is called Zen in Japan.

Chang Chuan: 長拳
Chang means long, and Chuan means fist, style, or sequence. A style of Northern Chinese Kung Fu which specializes in kicking and long range fighting. Chang Chuan has also been used to refer to Tai Chi Chuan.

Chi: 氣
The general definition of Chi is: universal energy, including heat, light, and electromagnetic energy. A narrower definition of Chi refers to the energy circulating in human or animal bodies.

Chi Kung: 氣功
Kung means Kung Fu (lit. energy-time). Therefore, Chi Kung means study, research, and/or practices related to Chi.

Chi Mei: 氣脈
Chi vessels. The eight vessels involved with transporting, storing, and regulating Chi.

Chi Shyh: 氣勢

Shyh means the way something looks or feels. Therefore: the feeling of Chi as it expresses itself.

Chii Ching Liow Yuh: 七情六慾.

Seven emotions and six desires. The seven emotions are happiness, anger, sorrow, joy, love, hate, and desire. The six desires are the six sensory pleasures associated with the eyes, ears, nose, tongue, body, and mind.

Chii Huoo: 起火

To start the fire. In Chi Kung practice: when you start to build up Chi at the Dan Tien.

Chin Na: 擒拿

Literally, grab control. A type of Chinese Kung Fu which emphasizes grabbing techniques to control the opponent's joints in conjunction with attacking certain acupuncture cavities.

Ching: 經

Channel. Sometimes translated meridian. Refers to the twelve organ-related "rivers" which circulate Chi throughout the body.

Chuh Gaan: 觸感

Literally: touch feel. Chuh Gaan refers to the unusual feelings or phenomena experienced during Chi Kung practice.

Chyi Ching Ba Mei: 奇經八脈

Literally: strange channels odd vessels. Usually referred to as the eight extraordinary vessels, or simply as the vessels. Called odd or strange because they are not well understood and do not exist in pairs.

Chyn Yuan Jou Maa: 擒猿捉馬

To seize the ape and catch the horse. A common name for the practice of regulating the mind in Chinese Chi Kung society. The ape represents the emotional mind and the horse represents the calm and wise mind. In regulating the mind training, you must be able to control your emotional mind and make your wisdom mind steady.

Dah Shoou Yinn: 大手印

Large hand stamp. A common Tibetan meditation technique in which some of the meditator's fingers press against each other.

Dan Diing Tao Kung: 丹鼎道功

The elixir cauldron way of Chi Kung. The Taoists' Chi Kung training.

Dan Tien: 丹田

Literally: Field of Elixir. Locations in the body which are able to store and generate Chi (elixir) in the body. The Upper, Middle, and Lower Dan Tien are located respectively between the eyebrows, at the solar plexus, and a few inches below the navel.

Dan Tien Chi: 丹田氣

Usually, the Chi which is converted from Original Essence and is stored in the Lower Dan Tien. This Chi is considered "water Chi" and is able to calm down the body. Also called Shian Tian Chi (pre-birth Chi).

Dien Shiuh: 點穴

Dien means "to point and exert pressure" and Shiuh means "the cavities." Dien Shiuh refers to those Chin Na techniques which specialize in attacking acupuncture cavities to immobilize or kill an opponent.

Dih: 地

The Earth. Earth, Heaven (Tian), and Man (Ren) are the "Three Natural Powers" (San Tsair).

Dih Lii Shy: 地理師

Dih Lii means geomancy and Shy means teacher. Therefore Dih Lii Shy means a teacher or master who analyzes geographic locations according to formulas in the I Ching (Book of Change) and the energy distributions in the Earth.

Ding Shen: 定神

To stabilize the spirit. To keep the spirit at one place (usually the Shang Dan Tien located at the third eye). One of the exercises for regulating the Shen in Chi Kung.

Dong Chuh: 動觸

Literally: moving touch. Refers to the unusual, automatic movements or feelings sometimes experienced during Chi Kung practice. Also called Chuh Gaan.

Ermei Dah Perng Kung: 峨嵋大鵬功

Dah Perng is a kind of large bird which existed in ancient China. Dah Perng Kung is a style of Chi Kung which imitates the movements of this bird. This style was developed at Ermei mountain in China.

Ermei Mountain: 峨嵋山

A mountain located in Szechuan province in China. Many martial Chi Kung styles originated there.

Feng Shoei Shy: 風水師

Literally: wind water teacher. Teacher or master of geomancy. Geomancy is the art or science of analyzing the natural energy relationships in a location, especially the interrelationships between "wind" and "water," hence the name. Also called Dih Lii Shy.

For Jia (For Jiaw): 佛家 (佛教)

Literally: Buddhism family. Jiaw means religion. Therefore: the Buddhist Religion.

Fuu: 腑

The bowels. The Yang organs: the Gall Bladder, Small Intestine, Large Intestine, Stomach, Bladder, and Triple Burner.

Gaan Jywe: 感覺

Literally: to touch and feel. In the second stage of relaxation, you are able to physically feel what is going on inside your body. This occurs before the stage of sensing.

Goe: 鬼

Ghost. When you die, if your spirit is strong, your soul's energy will not decompose and return to nature. This soul energy is a ghost.

Goe Chi: 鬼氣

The Chi residue of a dead person. It is believed by the Chinese Buddhists and Taoists that this Chi residue is a so called ghost.

Guan Chi: 貫氣

Guan means to thread together. Guan Chi is one of the Chi Kung trainings in which a practitioner leads Chi from one place to another.

Guei Shyi: 龜息

Turtle breathing. In Chinese Chi Kung society, it is believed that a turtle is able to live for a long time because it knows how to breath through its skin. Therefore, skin breathing in Chi Kung is called turtle breathing.

Guh Jieng: 固精

To solidify the Essence. A Chi Kung exercise for keeping and firming the Essence.

Guh Shen: 固神

Guh means to firm and solidify. An exercise for regulating the Shen in which you firm and strengthen the spirit at its residence.

Hou Tian Chi: 後天氣

Post-birth Chi. This Chi is converted from the Essence of food and air, and is classified as "fire Chi" since it can make your body too Yang.

Hsin: 心

Literally: Heart. Refers to the emotional mind.

Hsing Yi Chuan: 形意拳

Literally: Shape-mind Fist. An internal style of Kung Fu in which the mind or thinking determines the shape or movement of the body. Creation of the style attributed to Marshal Yeuh Fei.

Huoo Chi: 火氣

Fire Chi. Chi which tends to make the body positive or Yang.

Hwang Tyng: 黃庭

Yellow yard. 1. A yard or hall in which Taoists, who often wore yellow robes, meditate together. 2. In Chi Kung training, a spot in the abdomen where it is believed that you are able to generate an "embryo."

Hwen: 魂

The soul. Commonly used with the word Ling, which means spirit. Taoists believe that a human being's Hwen and Poh originate with his Original Chi (Yuan Chi), and separate from the physical body at death.

Hwo Chi: 活氣

Hwo means alive. Hwo Chi is the Chi of a living person or animal.

I Ching: 易經

Book of Changes. A book of divination written during the Jou dynasty (1122-255 B.C.).

Jea Guu Wen: 甲骨文

Oracle-Bone Scripture. Earliest evidence of the Chinese use of the written word. Found on pieces of turtle shell and animal bone from the Shang dynasty (1766-1154 B.C.). Most of the information recorded was of a religious nature.

Jeng Chi: 正氣

Righteous Chi. When a person is righteous, it is said that he has righteous Chi, which evil Chi cannot overcome.

Jieng: 精

Essence. The most refined part of anything.

Jieng Chi: 精氣

Essence Chi. The Chi which has been converted from Original Essence.

Jing: 勁

A power in Chinese martial arts which is derived from muscles which have been energized by Chi to their maximum potential.

Jong Dan Tien: 中丹田

Middle Dan Tien. Located in the area of the solar plexus, it is the residence of fire Chi.

Kan: 坎

A phase of the eight trigrams representing water.

Kung Fu: 功夫

Literally: energy-time. Any study, learning, or practice which requires a lot of patience, energy, and time to complete. Since practicing Chinese martial arts requires a great deal of time and energy, Chinese martial arts are commonly called Kung Fu.

Kuoshu: 國術

Literally: national techniques. Another name for Chinese martial arts. First used by President Chiang Kai-Shek in 1926 at the founding of the Nanking Central Kuoshu Institute.

Liann Chi Huah Shen: 練氣化神

To refine the Chi to nourish the spirit. Part of the Chi Kung training process in which you learn how to lead Chi to the head to nourish the brain and Shen (spirit).

Liann Jieng Huah Chi: 練精化氣

To refine the Essence and convert it into Chi. One of the Chi Kung training processes through which you convert Essence into Chi.

Liann Shen: 練神

To train the spirit. To refine and strengthen the Shen and make it more focused.

Liann Shen Leau Shing: 練神了性

To refine the spirit and end human nature. This is the final stage of spiritual Chi Kung training for enlightenment. In this process you learn to keep your emotions neutral and try to be undisturbed by human nature.

Lii: 離

A phase of the Ba Kua, Lii represents fire.

Ling: 靈

The spirit of being, which acts upon others. Ling only exists in high spiritual animals such as humans and monkeys. It represents an emotional comprehension and understanding. When you are alive, it implies your intelligence and wisdom. When you die, it implies the spirit of the ghost. Ling also means divine or supernatural. Ling is often used together with Shen (Ling Shen) to mean "supernatural spirit." It is believed that Chi is the source which nourishes the Ling and is called "Ling Chi," meaning "supernatural energy, power, or force."

Ling Jy: 靈芝

Ling Jy (Fomes Japonica) is a hard, dark brownish fungus which is supposed to posses supernatural powers. In Chi Kung society, sometimes Ling Jy means the elixir which enables you to have a long life.

Liu Ho Ba Fa: 六合八法

Literally: six combinations eight methods. A style of Chinese internal martial art reportedly created by Chen Bor during the Song dynasty (960-1279 A.D.).

Lou: 絡

The small Chi channels which branch out from the primary Chi channels and are connected to the skin and to the bone marrow.

Mih Tzong Shen Kung: 密宗神功

Literally: Secret Style of Spiritual Kung Fu. Tibetan Chi Kung and martial arts, originally passed down secretly.

Ming Tian Guu: 鳴天鼓

To beat the heavenly drum. A Chi Kung practice for waking up and clearing the mind in which the back of the head is tapped with the fingers.

Nei Dan: 內丹

Literally: internal elixir. A form of Chi Kung in which Chi (the elixir) is built up in the body and spread out to the limbs.

Nei Kung: 內功

Literally: internal Kung Fu. Chinese martial arts which start with internal training and the cultivation of Chi.

Nei Shenn: 内腎

Literally: internal Kidneys. In Chinese medicine and Chi Kung, the real Kidneys; while Wai Shenn (external Kidneys) refers to the testicles.

Nei Shyh Kung Fu: 内視功夫

Nei Shyh means to look internally, so Nei Shyh Kung Fu refers to the art of looking inside yourself to read the state of your health and the condition of your Chi.

Ning Shen: 凝神

To condense or focus the spirit. In Chi Kung training, after you are able to keep your spirit in one place, you learn how to condense it into a tiny spot and make it stronger.

Poh: 魄

Vigorous life force. The Poh is considered to be the inferior or animal soul. It is the animal or sentient life which is an innate part of the body which, at death, returns to the earth with the rest of the body. When someone is in high spirits and gets vigorously involved in some activity it is said he has Poh Li, which means he has "vigorous strength or power."

Reh Chi: 熱氣

Reh means warmth or heat. Generally, Reh Chi is used to represent heat. It is used sometimes to imply that a person or animal is still alive since the body is warm.

Ren: 人

Man or mankind.

Ren Chi: 人氣

Human Chi.

Ren Shyh: 人事

Literally: human relations. Human events, activities, and relationships.

Ru Jia: 儒家

Literally: Confucian family. Scholars following Confucian thoughts; Confucianists.

San Bao: 三寶

Three treasures. Essence (Jieng), energy (Chi), and spirit (Shen). Also called San Yuan (three origins).

San Huea Jiuh Diing: 三花聚頂

Three flowers reach the top. One of the final goals of Chi Kung whereby the three treasures (Essence, Chi, and Shen) are led to the top of the body to nourish the brain and spirit center (Upper Dan Tien).

San Guang: 三關

Three lights. In Chinese Chi Kung it is said that the Liver has the Hwen (soul) light, which shows in the eyes; the Lungs have Poh (vigorous life force) light, which shows in the nose; and the Kidneys have the Jieng (Essence) light, which show in the ears.

Sanjiao: 三焦

Triple burner. In Chinese medicine, the body is divided into three sections: the upper burner (chest), the middle burner (stomach area), and the lower burner (lower abdomen).

Sann Kung: 散功

Literally: energy dispersion. A state of premature degeneration of the muscles where the Chi cannot effectively energize them. Caused by earlier overtraining.

San Tsair: 三才

Three powers. Heaven, Earth, and Man.

San Yuan: 三元

Three origins. Also called "San Bao" (three treasures). Human Essence (Jieng), energy (Chi), and spirit (Shen).

Shang Dan Tien: 上丹田

Upper Dan Tien. Located at the third eye, it is the residence of the Shen (spirit).

Sheau Jou Tian: 小周天

Literally: small heavenly cycle. Also called small circulation. In Chi Kung, when you can use your mind to lead Chi through the Conception and Governing vessels, you have completed "Sheau Jou Tian."

Shen: 神

Spirit. According to Chinese Chi Kung, the Shen resides at the Upper Dan Tien (the third eye).

Shen Chi Shiang Her: 神氣相合

The Shen and the Chi are combined together. The final stage of regulating the Shen.

Shen Shyi: 神息

Spirit breathing. The stage of Chi Kung training where the spirit is coordinated with the breathing.

Shen Shyi Shiang Yi: 神息相依

The Shen and breathing mutually rely on each other. A stage in Chi Kung practice.

Shiah Dan Tien: 下丹田

Lower Dan Tien. Located in the lower abdomen, it is believed to be the residence of water Chi (Original Chi).

Shian: 仙

An immortal. A person who has attained enlightenment or Buddhahood, whose spirit can separate from and returned to his physical body at will.

Shian Tian Chi: 先天氣

Pre-birth Chi. Also called Dan Tien Chi. The Chi which was converted from Original Essence and is stored in the Lower Dan Tien. Considered to be "water Chi," it is able to calm the body.

Shii Soei Ching: 洗髓經

Literally: Washing Marrow Classic, usually translated Marrow Washing Classic. A Chi Kung training which specializes in leading Chi to the marrow to cleanse it. It is believed that Shii Soei Ching training is the key to longevity and reaching spiritual enlightenment.

Shing Ming Shuang Shiou: 性命双修

Human nature life double cultivation. Originally Buddhist, though now predominantly Taoist approach to Chi Kung emphasizing the cultivation of both spirituality (human nature) and the physical body.

Shiuh: 穴

Literally: cave or hole. An acupuncture cavity.

Shoei Chi: 水氣

Water Chi. Chi created from Original Essence, which is able to calm your body.

Shuang Shiou: 双修

Double cultivation. A Chi Kung training method in which Chi is exchanged with a partner in order to balance the Chi in both people.

Shyh Jia: 釋家

Literally: Sakyamuni family. Since Buddhism was created by Sakyamuni, it means Buddhism.

Suann Ming Shy: 算命師

Literally: calculate life teacher. A fortune teller who is able to calculate your future and destiny.

Syh Dah Jie Kong: 四大皆空

Four large are empty. A stage of Buddhism where all of the four elements (earth, water, fire, and air) are absent from the mind so that one is completely indifferent to worldly temptations.

Syy Chi: 死氣

Dead Chi. The Chi remaining in a dead body. Sometimes called ghost Chi (Goe Chi).

Tai Shyi: 胎息

Embryo breathing. One of the final goals in regulating the breath, embryo breathing enables you to generate a "baby Shen" at the Hwang Tyng (yellow yard).

Tao: 道

The way. The "natural" way of everything.

Tao Jia (Tao Jiaw): 道家 (道教)

The Tao family. Taoism. Created by Lao Tzyy during the Jou dynasty (1122-934 B.C.). In the Han dynasty (c. 58 A.D.), it was mixed with Buddhism to become the Taoist religion (Tao Jiaw).

Tian: 天

Heaven or sky. In ancient China, people believed that heaven was the most powerful natural energy in this universe.

Tian Chi: 天氣

Heaven Chi. It is now commonly used to mean the weather, since weather is governed by heaven Chi.

Tian Shyr: 天時

Heavenly timing. The repeated natural cycles generated by the heavens such as: seasons, months, days, and hours.

Tii Shyi: 體息

Body breathing or skin breathing. In Chi Kung, the exchanging of Chi with the surrounding environment through the skin.

Ting Shyi: 聽息

To listen to the breathing. A technique for regulating the mind. If you are able to pay attention to your breathing, your mind will not be distracted by surrounding activities.

Tong Guan: 通關

To pass through the gates. In Chi Kung training, the opening of blockages (gates) which hinder the free flow of Chi through the channels.

Tuei Na: 推拿

Literally: push grab. Tuei Na is one of the traditional Chinese massage styles which specializes in using pushing and grabbing to adjust abnormal Chi circulation and cure sicknesses.

Tzang: 臟

Viscera. The six Yin organs. Five of these are considered the core of the entire human system: the Liver, Heart, Spleen, Lungs, and Kidneys. Usually, when a discussion involves the channels and all the Organs, the Pericardium is added, otherwise it is treated as an adjunct of the Heart.

Tzoou Huoo Ruh Mo: 走火入魔

Walk into the fire and enter into the devil. In Chi Kung training, if you have led your Chi into the wrong path it is called "walking into the fire," and if your mind has been led into a confused state, it is called "entering into the devil."

Tzyy Wuu Liou Juh: 子午流注

Tzyy refers to the period around midnight (11:00 PM - 1:00 AM), and Wuu refers to midday (11:00 AM - 1:00 PM). Liou Juh means the flowing tendency. Therefore: a schedule of the Chi circulation showing which channel has the predominant Chi flow at any particular time, and where the predominant Chi flow is in the Conception and Governing vessels.

Wai Dan: 外丹

External elixir. External Chi Kung exercises in which a practitioner will build up his Chi in his limbs and then lead it into the center of the body for nourishment.

Wai Shenn: 外腎

External Kidneys. The testicles.

Wey Chi: 衛氣

Protective Chi or Guardian Chi. The Chi at the surface of the body which generates a shield to protect the body from negative external influences such as colds.

Wuu Chi Chaur Yuan: 五氣朝元

Five Chi's toward origins. A goal of Chi Kung wherein the Chi of the five Yin organs (Heart, Lungs, Liver, Kidneys, and Spleen) is kept at the right (original) level. This will keep the organs from being either too Yang or too Yin, and will slow the degeneration process.

Wuudang Mountain: 武當山

Located in Fubei province in China.

Wuu Hsin: 五心

Five centers. The face, the Laogong cavities in both palms, and the Yongquan cavities on the bottoms of both feet.

Wuu Hsing: 五行

Five phases. Also called the five elements. Metal, wood, water, fire, and earth, representing the five phases of any process.

Wushu: 武術

Literally: martial techniques. A common name for the Chinese martial arts. Many other terms are used, including: Wuyi (martial arts), Wukung (martial Kung Fu), Kuoshu (national techniques), and Kung Fu (energy-time). Because Wushu has been modified in mainland China over the past forty years into gymnastic martial performance, many traditional Chinese martial artist have given up this name in order to avoid confusing modern Wushu with traditional Wushu. Recently, mainland China has attempted to bring modern Wushu back toward its traditional training and practice.

Yang: 陽

In Chinese philosophy, the active, positive, masculine polarity. In Chinese medicine, Yang means excessive, overactive, overheated. The Yang (or outer) organs are the Gall Bladder, Small Intestine, Large Intestine, Stomach, Bladder, and Triple Burner.

Yeang Shen: 養神

Yeang means to raise, nourish, and maintain. Shen means spirit. Yeang Shen is the main Buddhist approach to regulating the Shen.

Yi: 意

Mind. Specifically, the mind which is generated by clear thinking and judgement, and which is able to make you calm, peaceful, and wise.

Yi Gin Ching: 易筋經

Literally: changing muscle/tendon classic, usually called The Muscle/Tendon Changing Classic. Credited to Da Mo around 550 A.D., this work discusses Wai Dan Chi Kung training for strengthening the physical body.

Yii Shen Yuh Chi: 以神馭氣

Use the Shen (spirit) to govern the Chi. A Chi Kung technique. Since the Shen is the headquarters for the Chi, it is the most effective way to control it.

Yii Yi Yiin Chi: 以意引氣

Use your Yi (wisdom mind) to lead your Chi. A Chi Kung technique. Chi cannot be pushed, but it can be led. This is best done with the Yi.

Yin: 陰

In Chinese philosophy, the passive, negative, feminine polarity. In Chinese medicine, Yin means deficient. The Yin (internal) organs are the Heart, Lungs, Liver, Kidneys, Spleen, and Pericardium.

Yi Shyh: 意識

Literally: Yi recognize. To use the Yi (wisdom mind) to sense and understand a situation. In order to do this, your Yi must search for information, evaluate it, and then reach a final decision. Yi Shyh is similar to "sense" in English, however, Yi Shyh is more active and aggressive.

Yi Shoou Dan Tien: 意守丹田

Keep your Yi on your Dan Tien. In Chi Kung training, you keep your mind at the Dan Tien in order to build up Chi. When you are circulating your Chi, you always lead your Chi back to your Dan Tien before you stop.

Ying Chi: 營氣

Managing Chi. The Chi which manages the functioning of the organs and the body.

Yuan Chi: 元氣

Original Chi. The Chi created from the Original Essence inherited from your parents.

Yuan Chiaw: 元竅

Original key point. Key points to the training.

Yuan Jieng: 元精

Original Essence. The fundamental, original substance inherited from your parents, it is converted into Original Chi.

Appendix B

Translation of Chinese Terms

揚俊杰 Tim Chun-Chieh Yang
楊俊敏 Yang Jwing-Ming
武術 Wushu
功夫 Kung Fu
白鶴 Pai Huo
曾金灶 Cheng Gin-Gsao
擒拿 Chin Na
太極拳 Tai Chi Chuan
高濤 Kao Tao
淡江學院 Tamkang College
台北縣 Taipei Hsien
長拳 Chang Chuan
李茂清 Li Mao-Ching
國術 Kuoshu
勁 Jing
連步拳 Lien Bu Chuan
功力拳 Gung Li Chuan
外丹氣功 Wai Dan Chi Kung
易筋經 Yi Gin Ching
洗髓經 Shii Soei Ching
推拿 Tuei Na
按摩 Ann Mo
點穴 Dien Shiuh
武當 Wuudang
峨嵋 Ermei
禪 Charn
忍 Zen
丹鼎道功 Dan Diing Tao Kung
宓宗神功 Mih Tzong Shen Kung
漢 Han
梁 Liang

清 Ching
精 Jieng
氣 Chi
神 Shen
意 Yi
心 Hsin
丹田 Dan Tien
三花聚頂 San Huea Jiuh Diing
五氣朝元 Wuu Chi Chaur Yuan
外丹 Wai Dan
內丹 Nei Dan
坎 Kan
離 Lii
調身 Tyau Shenn
調息 Tyau Shyi
調心 Tyau Hsin
念 Niann
調精 Tyau Jieng
調氣 Tyau Chi
調神 Tyau Shen

Chapter 1

從外建功 Tsorng Wai Jiann Kung
遠心之外功運動 Yeuan Hsin Jy Wai Kung Yunn Dong
陽 Yang
陰 Yin
散功 Sann Kung
從內築基 Tsorng Nei Jwu Ji
向心之內功運動 Shiang Hsin Jy Nei Kung Yunn Dong
性命双修 Shing Ming Shuang Shiou
天氣 Tian Chi
電氣 Diann Chi

熱氣 Reh Chi
人氣 Ren Chi
活氣 Hwo Chi
死氣 Syy Chi
危氣 Goe Chi
正氣 Jeng Chi
氣勢 Chi Shyh
功 Kung
易經 I Ching
天 Tian
地 Dih
人 Ren
三才 San Tsair
八卦 Ba Kua
氣化論 Chi Huah Luenn
天時 Tian Shyr
地理師 Dih Lii Shy
風水師 Feng Shoei Shy
人事 Ren Shyh
算命師 Suann Ming Shy
道 Tao
內功 Nei Kung
六合八法 Liu Ho Ba Fa
形意 Hsing Yi

Chapter 2

商 Shang
安陽 An Yang
河南 Henan
殷墟 Yin Shiu
甲骨文 Jea Guu Wen
內經 Nei Ching
砭石 Bian Shyr
周 Jou
老子 Lao Tzyy
李耳 Li Erh
道德經 Tao Te Ching
專氣致柔 Juan Chi Jyh Rou
史記 Shyy Gi
莊子 Juang Tzyy
南華經 Nan Hwa Ching
秦 Chin
難經 Nan Ching
扁鵲 Bian Chiueh
金匱要略 Gin Guey Yao Liueh
張仲景 Chang Jong-Jiing
周易參同契 Jou I Tsan Torng Chih
魏伯陽 Wey Bor-Yang
東漢 East Han
張道陵 Chang Tao-Ling
道教 Tao Jiaw
晉 Gin
華陀 Hwa Tor
君倩 Jiun Chiam
五禽戲 Wuu Chyn Shih
葛洪 Ger Horng
抱朴子 Baw Poh Tzyy

陶弘景 Taur Horng-Jiing
養身延命錄 Yeang Shenn Yan Ming Luh
達磨 Da Mo
隋 Swei
唐 Tarng
巢元方 Chaur Yuan-Fang
諸病源候論 Ju Bing Yuan Hou Luenn
千金方 Chian Gin Fang
孫思邈 Suen Sy-Meau
外台秘要 Wai Tai Mih Yao
王燾 Wang Taur
宋 Song
金 Gin
元 Yuan
養身訣 Yeang Sheng Juue
張安道 Chang An-Tao
儒門視事 Ru Men Shyh Shyh
張子和 Chang Tzyy-Her
蘭室秘藏 Lan Shyh Mih Tsarng
李果 Li Guoo
格致餘論 Ger Jyh Yu Luenn
朱丹溪 Ju Dan-Shi
張三丰 Chang San-Feng
王唯一 Wang Wei-Yi
銅人俞穴尺針灸圖 Torng Ren Yu Shiuh Jen Jeou Twu
仁宗 Ren Tzong
南宋 Southern Song
岳飛 Yeuh Fei
虎步功 Hwu Buh Kung
十二庄 Shyr Er Juang
叫化功 Jiaw Huah Kung
保身秘要 Bao Shenn Mih Yao
曹元白 Tsaur Yuan-Bair
養身膚語 Yeang Sheng Fu Yeu
陳繼儒 Chen Jih-Ru
醫方集介 Yi Fang Jyi Jieh
汪汛庵 Uang Fann-An
內功圖說 Nei Kung Twu Shwo
王祖源 Wang Tzuu-Yuan
明 Ming
火龍功 Huoo Long Kung
太陽 Taiyang
八卦掌 Ba Kua Chang
董海川 Doong Hae-Chuan

Chapter 3

三寶 San Bao
三元 San Yuan
固精 Guh Jieng
練精化氣 Liann Jieng Huah Chi
練氣化神 Liann Chi Huah Shen
練神了性 Liann Shen Leau Shing
精煉 Jieng Liann
精細 Jieng Shih
精良 Jieng Liang
精明 Jieng Ming
精子 Jieng Tzyy

元精 Yuan Jieng
腎俞 Shenshu
精門 Jieng Men
氣血 Chi Shiee
元氣 Yuan Chi
先天氣 Shian Tian Chi
後天氣 Hou Tian Chi
丹田氣 Dan Tien Chi
水氣 Shoei Chi
火氣 Huoo Chi
衝脈 Chong Mei
營氣 Ying Chi
衛氣 Wey Chi
心神不寧 Hsin Shen Buh Ning
神志不清 Shen Jyh Buh Ching
魂 Hwen
神魂 Shen Hwen
靈 Ling
鬼 Goe
靈鬼 Ling Goe
靈魂 Ling Hwen
神明 Shen Ming
養神 Yeang Shen
靈神 Ling Shen
仙 Shian
神仙 Shen Shian
神不守舍 Shen Bu Shoou Sheh
精神 Jieng Shen
聚精會神 Jiuh Jieng Huey Shen
仙胎 Shian Tai
神志 Shen Jyh
返精補腦 Faan Jieng Buu Nao
心意 Hsin Yi
以心會意 Yii Hsin Huey Yi
以意會身 Yii Yi Hyey Shenn
心神 Hsin Shen
意志 Yi Jyh
食氣 Shyr Chi
下丹田 Shiah Dan Tien
氣海 Qihai
子午流注 Tzyy Wuu Liou Juh
返童 Faan Torng
起火 Chii Huoo
中丹田 Jong Dan Tien
上焦 Shang Jiao
中焦 Jong Jiao
下焦 Shiah Jiao
三焦 Sanjiao
上火 Shang Huoo
火氣 Huoo Chi
以精化氣 Yii Jieng Huah Chi
以氣化神 Yii Chi Huah Shen
練神返虛 Liann Shen Huan Shiu
粉碎虛空 Feen Suory Shiu Kong

Chapter 4
通關 Tong Guan
小周天 Sheau Jou Tian
通三關 Tong San Guan
大周天 Dah Jou Tian

Chapter 5
孟子 Mencius
儒家 Ru Jia
道家 Tao Jia
莊周 Juang Jou
修氣 Shiou Chi
練氣 Liann Chi
安天樂命 An Tian Leh Ming
修身俟命 Shiou Shenn Ai Ming
葉明 Yeh Ming
點脈 Dim Mak
鐵布衫 Tiee Buh Shan
金鐘罩 Gin Jong Jaw
外功 Wai Kung
硬功 Ying Kung
散功 Sann Kung
無極氣功 Wu Chi Chi Kung
七情六慾 Chii Ching Liow Yuh
禪宗 Charn Tzong
慧可 Huoy Kee
繼光 Jih Guang
僧璨 Seng Tsann
道信 Tao Shinn
弘忍 Horng Zen
慧能 Huoy Neng
禪宗六祖 Charn Tzong Liow Tzuu
神會 Shen Huey
開元 Kai Yuan
禪宗七祖 Charn Tzong Chii Tzuu
喇嘛 Laa Ma
元始天尊 Yuan Shyy Tian Tzuen
玉皇大帝 Yuh Hwang Dah Dih
太上老君 Tai Shang Lao Jiun
閻羅王 Yan Luo Wang
以精化氣 Yii Jieng Huah Chi
以氣化神 Yii Chi Huah Shen
金丹大道 Gin Dan Dah Tao
双修 Shuang Shiou
道外採藥 Tao Wai Tsae Yaw
清修派 Ching Shiou Pay
栽接派 Tzai Jie Pay

Chapter 6
絡 Lou
會陰 Huiyin
任脈 Ren Mei
督脈 Du Mei
骨髓 Guu Soei
腦髓 Nao Soei
陰蹻脈 Yinchaio Mei

Chapter 7
拱手 Goong Shoou
陽明 Yangming

峨嵋大鵬功 Ermei Dah Perng Kung
认意引氣 Yii Yi Yiin Chi
意守丹田 Yi Shoou Dan Tien

Chapter 8
身心平衡 Shenn Hsin Pyng Herng
感覺 Gaan Jywe
意識 Yi Shyh
馬步 Maa Bu
眼高手低 Yean Kau Shoou Di

Chapter 9
空氣 Kong Chi
心息相依 Hsin Shyi Shiang Yi
吐納 Tuu Na
靜 Jing
細 Shyi
深 Shenn
悠 Iou
勻 Yun
正腹呼吸 Jeng Fuh Hu Shi
反腹呼吸 Faan Fuh Hu Shi
返童 Faan Torng
採小藥 Tsae Sheau Yaw
體息 Tii Shyi
膚息 Fu Shyi
靈寶畢法 Ling Bao Bih Faa
伏氣法 Fwu Chi Faa
龜息 Guei Shyi
五心 Wuu Hsin
湧泉 Yongquan
勞宮 Laogong
涵虛祖 Harn Shiu Tzuu
貫氣 Guan Chi
神息 Shen Shyi
守神 Shoou Shen
固神 Guh Shen
紫陽祖 Tzyy Yang Tzuu
真息 Jen Shyi
靈源歌 Ling Yuan Ge
三丰祖 San Feng Tzuu
虛無 Shiu Wu
張紫瓊 Chang Tzyy-Chyong
元竅 Yuan Chiaw
黃庭 Hwang Tyng
命門 Mingmen
李涆菴 Li Ching-An
悟真篇 Wuh Jen-Pian
鼻息 Byi Shyi
胎息 Tai Shyi
長 Charng
緩 Hoan
綿 Mian
數 Su
隨 Suei
聽息 Ting Shyi
見性了然 Jiann Shing Leau Ran
淨 Jing

廣成子 Goang Cherng Tzyy
黃庭經 Hwang Tyng Ching
伍真人 Wuu Jen Ren
靈源大道歌 Ling Yuan Dah Tao Ge

Chapter 10
摘猿捉馬 Chyn Yuan Juo Maa
重陽祖 Chorng Yang Tzuu
靈芝 Ling Jy
四大皆空 Syh Dah Jie Kong
觀心 Guan Hsin
內視功夫 Nei Shyh Kung Fu
止觀法 Jyy Guan Faa
繫緣止 Shih Yuan Jyy
制心止 Jyh Hsin Jyy
體真止 Tii Jen Jyy
假觀 Jea Guan
中觀 Jong Guan
觀想法 Guan Sheang Faa
一點靈明法 Yi Dien Ling Ming Faa
大手印 Dah Shoou Yinn
五行 Wuu Shyng
意守丹田 Yi Shoou Dan Tien
練神 Liann Shen

Chapter 11
內腎 Nei Shenn
外腎 Wai Shenn
固腎 Guh Shenn
強腎 Chyang Shenn

Chapter 12

Chapter 13
認神馭意 Yii Shen Yuh Chi
神息相依 Shen Shyi Shiang Yi
神氣相合 Shen Chi Shiang Her

Chapter 14
泥丸祖 Ni Wan Tzuu
眼觀鼻，鼻觀心 Yean Guan Byi, Byi Guan Hsin
鳴天鼓 Ming Tian Guu
景氣 Jiing Chi
八觸 Ba Chuh
觸感 Chuh Gaan
動觸 Dong Chuh
動 Dong
癢 Yeang
涼 Liang
暖 Noan
輕 Ching
重 Jong
澀 Seh
滑 Hwa
掉 Diaw
猗 Yi
冷 Leeng
熱 Reh
浮 Fwu
沉 Chern

堅 Jian
軟 Roan
悟一子 Wuh Yi Tzyy
兪袓 Yu Tzuu
走火入魔 Tzoou Huoo Ruh Mo
風池 Fengtzu
百會 Baihui
頑執妄念 Yuh Jyr Wang Niann
著意分別 Jwo Yi Fen Bye
雜念攀緣 Tzar Niann Pan Yuan
心隨外景 Hsin Swei Wai Jiing
入房施精 Ruh Farng Shy Jieng
大溫大寒 Dah Uen Dah Hann
五癆暗傷 Wuu Lau Ann Shang
坐汗當風 Tzuoh Hann Dang Feng
茶衣來韌 Jiin Yi Shuh Dai
偷鐵肥甘 Tau Tieh Fair Gan
破床懸腳 Bar Chwang Shyuan Jywe
久忍小便 Jeou Zen Sheau Biann
搔抓癢胭 Sau Jua Yeang Chuh
猝呼驚悸 Tsuh Hu Jing Jih
對景歡喜 Twe Jiing Huan Shii
久眉汗衣 Jeou Jwo Hann Yi
飢飽上坐 Ji Bao Shang Tzuoh
天地災怪 Tian Dih Tzai Guay
美言偶聽 Jen Yan Oou Ting
昏況傾欹 Huen Chern Ching Yii
大怒大樂入坐 Dah Nuh, Dah Leh Ruh Tzuoh
吐痰無度 Tuu Tarn Wu Duh
生疑懈怠 Sheng Yi Shieh Dai
不求速効 Buh Chyow Suh Shiaw

Chapter 16
太陽 Taiyang
少陽 Shaoyang
陽明 Yangming
太陰 Taiyin
少陰 Shaoyin
厥陰 Jueyin

Chapter 17
奇經八脈 Chyi Ching Ba Mei
帶脈 Dai Mei
陽蹻脈 Yangchiao Mei
陽維脈 Yangwei Mei
陰維脈 Yinwei Mei
黃帝內經素問 Hwang Dih Nei Ching Suh Wenn
靈樞 Ling Shu
李時珍 Li Shyr-Jen
奇經八脈考 Chii Ching Ba Mei Kao
精氣 Jieng Chi

Chapter 18

Chapter 19

Appendix A
四川 Szechuan
蔣介石 Chiang Kai-Shek

南京 Nanking
沈博 Chen Bor
飽力 Poh Li
湖北 Fubei
武藝 Wuyi
武功 Wukung